A

PROFILE HISTORY

OF THE

UNITED STATES

SECOND EDITION

GILMAN M. OSTRANDER

A PROFILE HISTORY OF THE UNITED STATES

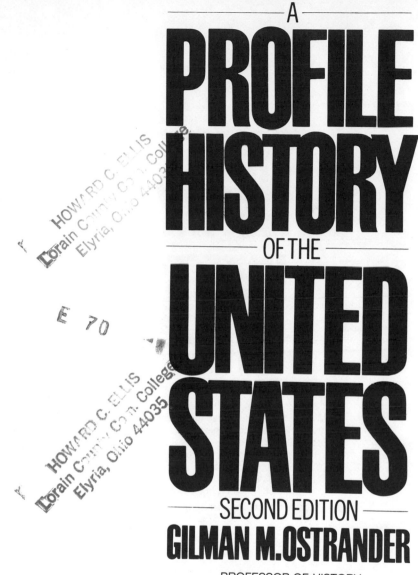

SECOND EDITION

GILMAN M. OSTRANDER

PROFESSOR OF HISTORY
UNIVERSITY OF WATERLOO

McGraw-Hill Book Company

New York   St. Louis   San Francisco   Düsseldorf   Johannesburg   Kuala Lumpur
London   Mexico   Montreal   New Delhi   Panama   Rio de Janeiro   Singapore
Sydney   Toronto

A
PROFILE HISTORY OF THE UNITED STATES

*Library of Congress Catalog Card Number
79–38735*

1 2 3 4 5 6 7 8 9 0 MAMM 7 9 8 7 6 5 4 3 2

This book was set in Helvetica Light
by Rocappi, Inc., and printed and bound
by The Maple Press Company, Inc.
The designer was Alan Peckolick; the
drawings were done by Vantage Art, Inc.
The editors were Robert P. Rainier,
Robert Weber, and James R. Belser.
Sally Ellyson supervised production.

PREFACE

This textbook is particularly written for that student who in the course of his precollege education has been taken back to 1492 and led from there to the present in at least one and perhaps two or three required courses in American history. Upon arriving at college, such a student will despair to find himself being put back once again on Watling's Island with Christopher Columbus, this time confronting a bigger textbook than ever, through which he must march once more past the old familiar milestones—1607, 1776, 1861, and so on—down to the present and the end of the course.

Fortunately for that student, there is much in American history that is not comprehended in the philosophy of a course taught according to a single textbook, with its four causes of this and its three consequences of that. Big generalizations in textbooks inevitably conceal vast amounts of ignorance on the part of textbook writers, except in those special areas where the writers happen to have concentrated their attentions during their careers as historians. The textbook writer must rely heavily on the findings of many specialists, who tend to be busily disagreeing among themselves. Even when dealing with that very subject upon which he happens to be the world's leading authority, he must painfully foreshorten the truth, as he has perceived it, in order to fit the material into its allotted space.

Consequently, the intelligent student of any textbook is in a position to bring many of its broad generalizations into question through reading the relevant authorities cited by the author (in this text in bibliographies at the end of chapters). And in any major library there will be ample primary sources to enable the student to test conclusions of those very authorities who enabled him to refute the very vulnerable text. This *Profile History* is designed, by virtue of its brevity, to detain the student as little as possible from embarking upon his own historical investigations. It has been written in the spirit of Carl Becker's admonition that Everyman should be his own historian, examining main points of controversy on the basis of his own experience with life, supported by the inexhaustibly rich vicarious experience of history.

As the student becomes involved in an area of history, he will be struck by the amount of disagreement in interpretations, and perhaps even the factual inaccuracy, that he can charge against leading specialists in the field. It may be—and often has been—objected that a field of knowledge cannot be worth much if its authorities continue endlessly in their pursuit of truth without ever reaching it except in picayune matters of detail such as the date 1492. But people always appeal to the past to guide them in the present; it is therefore enormously important for people to use all their knowledge of the past in such a way as to misread and misapply it as little as possible. The American who is confronted throughout his life with newspaper editorials and politicians' speeches will find his way among them much more satisfactorily if he has his own informed opinion about what Washington or Jefferson or Lincoln really meant or what the First or Fifth or Fourteenth Amendment really means.

American history will always have a special appeal for Americans, because it is the story of themselves. When Aeneas, in the court of Dido, observed works of art depicting events from the Trojan War, he was enlivened—despite the disastrous conclusion of those events—by the thought that he was a part of what he saw. History tends to appeal to people more strongly when they gain the sense of having taken part in it themselves. The college student is accordingly advised to start this book with the last chapter, to put himself self-consciously into history, before going on to Chapter 1 and Marco Polo and Christopher Columbus.

Gilman M. Ostrander

CONTENTS

EUROPE AND AMERICA

THE VIKINGS

> They steered a westerly course past the cape and found great shallows at ebb tide, so that their ship was beached and lay some distance from the sea. But they were so eager to go ashore that they could not bear to wait till the tide rose under their ship. They ran up on the shore to a place where a stream flowed out of a lake. . . . When spring came, they made the ship ready and sailed away. Leif gave this country a name to suit its resources: he called it Vinland.

The Vinland of this Norse saga was probably Nova Scotia, and the year was probably 1002. When Leif Ericson returned with tales of his discoveries, other Vikings sailed to America from Greenland. They may have made the trip intermittently during the next three centuries. Or perhaps none of them, including Leif, ever came at all; no conclusive evidence has been uncovered to confirm those fourteenth-century sagas. Claims made for early Irish and Portuguese landings in America have nearly nothing to go on but speculation. Not until half a millennium after Leif's reputed discovery was Europe made aware of the existence of two huge continents hidden beneath its western horizons.

Until the close of the fifteenth century awareness of the New World would have served a European little better than knowledge of Europe would have served an American Indian. For one thing, it was not until the fifteenth century that ships were evolved in Europe fit to make the voyage. The Vikings of Leif Ericson's day, Europe's foremost sailors, possessed single-masted open vessels capable of sailing into the wind, and other Europeans soon copied them. In the thirteenth century the modern rudder came into being, and in the fourteenth and fifteenth centuries the three-masted sailing ship was developed, that remained the basic type for the next five hundred years.

NORTH AMERICA

ATLANTIC OCEAN

PACIFIC OCEAN

SOUTH AMERICA

Hudson 1610

Frobisher 1576

Hudson, 1609

Cartier 1536

Caboto 1497

Verrazano 1524

Columbus 1492

Columbus 1493

Drake 1577

Coronado 1540

Cortes 1519

Pineda 1519

De Soto 1541

Balboa 1513

VOYAGES OF DISCOVERY

EUROPEAN SOCIETY

In any event, Europe until the fifteenth and sixteenth centuries was altogether too disorganized to engage in such large-scale undertakings as the establishment of permanent settlements in America. In theory and in spirit, fifteenth-century Europe was united in its allegiance to one God and in its obedience to one Universal Church. Europe was Christendom, shining forth in a pagan world, united against Mongol and Moslem and certain of its own final triumph. But the Catholic Church was itself rent with discord, divided for a time between rival popes and hopelessly incapable of maintaining peaceful order within its diocese. Underlying the jumble of empires, kingdoms, principalities, dukedoms, and knights' castles, the basic unit of organization remained the great estate, with its thousands of scattered acres, its hundreds of serfs and semiserfs, and its primitive barter economy. The manorial system was a sprawling, sluggish resistance to political change and economic improvement.

It was in the coastal city-states, especially those in the Mediterranean, that men were moved by the enterprise and change of the commercial revolution. Efforts during the late Middle Ages to win the Holy Land from the Muslim had brought Europeans in closer contact with the commercial civilization of the Middle East and with the spices, silks, porcelains, carpets, and metalwork of the Orient. Europe was dependent for its luxuries upon this Eastern trade, and the city-states of Italy—Venice, Pisa, Florence, Genoa—were enriched and civilized by it.

The gold florin was first minted in Florence in 1252; Venice began coining ducats in 1280. Joint-stock companies operated in Italy in the fourteenth century, permitting risks to be shared and larger accumulations of capital to be amassed. Renaissance Italy in large measure evolved the methods necessary for the discovery and exploitation of the New World. The perpetually quarreling city-states themselves failed to provide the political basis for such colonial undertakings, but to a remarkable extent Italy provided the bankers, map makers, ship builders, mathematicians, captains, and sailors who opened the New World to the national states that emerged in Western Europe during the fifteenth and sixteenth centuries.

The new national monarchies owed much to the commercial revolution. It tore at the web of feudal restrictions and created middle-class support for the kings in opposition to the feudal barons. Kings drew upon the middle class for the lawyers and administrators and the money their growing governments needed. Gunpowder was introduced from China, and new inventions made money more readily convertible into power, including firearms, blast furnaces to build heavy armaments, and artillery to break down the walls of castles. The Crusades had brought Western monarchs in contact with Oriental despotism, and they applied this experience, notably in the areas of taxation and military arts, to the creation of absolute monarchies in the West. At the same time, the Crusades appear to have aroused in Western soldiers a sense of national loyalty that strengthened the state and the crown against the Universal Church and against provincial lords.

The European national state was a new development in human history, creating an order of power not shared by the world's dynasties and empires. Geographically, Western Europe was but a peninsula on the great Eurasian continent, and one that was divided and distracted by incessant national wars, but now it went forth in confidence to dominate the world.

First of the new monarchies was Portugal. Securely bounded by mountains and ocean, Portugal achieved a sense of national unity in the victorious twelfth- and thirteenth-century struggles against the Moors, and it went on to strengthen its nationality under a long line of capable kings and to extend its empire to Africa, Asia, and America. Spain emerged in the fifteenth century victorious against the Moors and achieved political unity with the marriage of Ferdinand of Aragon and Isabella of Castile. In France, meanwhile, Louis XI was moving energetically against the nobles, and in England Henry Tudor survived the Wars of the Roses to bring that nation under strong central government.

Spain, supreme among the nations for a century, entered upon a centuries-long decline late in the 1500s. The Spanish Armada met defeat in 1588, and the Netherlands rose in revolt to win independence from Spain a generation later. With its decline, a new era of colonization began. The Dutch, the French, and the English set forth almost simultaneously at the opening of the seventeenth century to compete in exploiting the New World. By then Spain and Portugal had enjoyed more than a century's start on them, and Spain was entrenched in an empire that extended from Santa Fe to Buenos Aires.

EXPLORATION

In a prison in Genoa at the close of the thirteenth century Marco Polo, the traveler, dictated his *Book of Various Experiences* from which Europe learned for the first time of the vast Asian empire of Kublai Khan. Polo told of the power and wealth of the court at Peking and of such unknown lands as Tibet, Burma, Japan, Java, Madagascar, and Zanzibar. His work fired the imaginations of Europeans who in the course of the Crusades had acquired their first intimations of distant realms, rich and fine beyond their own understandings. Trade with Arab merchants of the Middle East sifted into Europe manufactured goods and spices which brought great wealth to the merchant princes of the Italian city-states. To find a direct route to the Spice Islands became the burning wish of European monarchs and merchants in the fifteenth, sixteenth, and seventeenth centuries. In the course of them European explorers ranged the globe seeking other avenues to this wealth than the one that Europe was unable to win eastward from Alexandria in its struggle with Islam.

Beginning early in the fifteenth century, Portugal, under the direction of Prince Henry the Navigator, almost annually sent out expeditions which explored the Azores and made their way down the coast of Africa. In 1488 Bartholomeu Diaz emerged from a storm to find that he had rounded the Cape of Good Hope and was on the eastern coast of Africa. A decade later Vasco da Gama set forth beyond the cape to win the Eastern trade for Portugal. On the Malabar Coast of India, amid bloody struggles with the established, marvelously polyglot Eastern traders, the Portuguese captured the colony of Goa, which they retained until 1961. From there they proceeded around the subcontinent of India to China and the East Indies winning the trade.

Meanwhile, the theoretical possibility of an alternative route to China, westward across the Atlantic, suggested itself on the basis of both the knowledge and the misinformation of late fifteenth-century Europe in world geography. That the world was round was widely known and taught in the European universities. As to its size there were differences of opinion, and errors in calculation, as in the case of Behaim's globe of 1492, sometimes made it so small that a China trade appeared practicable. Christopher Columbus of Genoa was apparently more optimistically misled than most investigators in his calculations. He estimated the distance from the Canary Islands to Cathay to be about 2,500 miles, and it was he who first seriously conceived the idea of the Western route.

Portugal was the logical nation to advance such a project, but the Portuguese knew too much to accept the global miscalculations of Columbus and therefore turned him down. But after eight years of campaigning Columbus won the support of Queen Isabella of Spain, and in 1492, on a smooth sea, under pleasant skies, the *Niña,* the *Pinta,* and the *Santa Maria* sailed, in a month and three days, from the Canary Islands to the Bahamas. Then and on three subsequent trips to the Caribbean Columbus, as he himself boasted, "placed under their Highnesses' sovereignty more land than there is in Africa and Europe." He furthermore established the colony of Hispaniola that became the starting point for the incredible conquests of the next two generations.

In 1513 Vasco Nuñez de Balboa moved in twenty-five days through 45 miles of jungle in Darien to discover the Pacific. In 1519 Ferdinand Magellan set forth from Seville on the greatest voyage of discovery in history to find the route to the Spice Islands. Moving down the coast of South America, he discovered the treacherous straits that bear his name; their navigation alone took longer than had the entire first voyage of Columbus. Outriding storms and mutiny, he sailed his fleet off into the Pacific, where he was three months out of sight of land before his ships arrived at Guam. From there they sailed to the Philippine Islands, where Magellan was killed in the course of native warfare but not before he heard his Malayan servant converse with natives in the Malayan tongue and so knew he had achieved the exploring feat of the ages. Three years after setting sail, one of the five ships and 18 of the original 239 men rounded the world and returned to Spain.

In the twenties and thirties the Spanish conquistadores, soldiers of fortune directing their own private enterprises, swiftly subdued the great empires of

Latin America with small companies of men. In America, as in India and the Orient, such incredible conquests were made possible in part by internal rivalries, which brought tribes to the side of the European conqueror. In part they were achieved by virtue of a spirit of absolute self-assurance in what surely must have appeared ludicrously impossible situations. Hernando Cortes, invading Mexico in 1519 with a force of 550 men, seventeen horses, and ten cannons, marched to Mexico City and overthrew Montezuma II and his Aztec empire (aided by the Aztec conviction that he was Quetzalcoatl, the conquering king of a former century, so it was believed, who had been expected to return one day to reassert his authority). So it was also with Pizarro against the Incas in Peru, with Montejo in Yucatan, with Alvarado in Guatemala, and with Jiménez de Quesada in New Granada. Within two decades by slender means the main conquest of Latin America was complete, and the Spanish Crown in company with the Catholic Church moved rapidly to assert centralized authority over the territory which private adventurers had brought within its power.

If Portugal lost the main opportunity by refusing the offers of Columbus and also Magellan, it nevertheless gained from the Pope, following the first voyage of Columbus, sovereignty over all American lands within somewhat more than 1,000 miles of the Cape Verde Islands, a decision that gave Portugal title to Brazil. Then in 1500, whether accidentally or by design, Pedrálverez Cabral landed on the coast of Brazil and claimed it for Portugal. As with the Spanish, private initiative conquered the territory before the Crown moved in to assert centralized authority. In 1580 Philip II united Spain and Portugal under one rule and so was the sovereign of America. However, northern America was rejected by the Spanish because of its seeming lack of gold and silver mines and fountains of youth, and it lay open to the nations of northern Europe.

Though Spanish explorers ranged through much of what became the United States, the uninviting nature of the plains regions as well as the lack of precious metals had discouraged their settlement north of Santa Fe. The first Europeans after the Norsemen to penetrate the North Atlantic seaboard apparently were nameless French, English, and Portuguese fishermen interested in cod rather than conquest. The great French explorer Jacques Cartier seemed not surprised to come upon a group of Breton fishermen in the course of his discovery of the St. Lawrence River in the 1530s. These fishermen were among the many sailors who went among new lands and returned without leaving a mark on history. Ambitious kings were not moved to found empires by a desire for fish, even if perhaps they should have been. On the other hand, tall tales were told by the Indians of gold and silver and also of a nearby western ocean which held out promise of a Northwest Passage to the Orient. While searching for all these, Cartier discovered Quebec. He found no gold and silver, however, nor any ocean and Northwest Passage, and France left the region to the fishermen until the settlement of Quebec in 1608 by Samuel de Champlain.

England, with earlier claims in North America than France, was similarly slow to capitalize on them. In 1497, a year after the second American voyage of Columbus, another sailor from Genoa, Giovanni Caboto, was commissioned by Henry VII of England and sailed to Cape Breton, where he claimed the land for the English King. The delighted Tudor monarch presented a gift of £10 "to hym that founde the new Isle." During the following century English fishermen came increasingly to dry their catch on the banks of Newfoundland, and English sea dogs familiarized themselves with the Americas while making wide-ranging raids upon Spanish and Portuguese colonial ports.

In the 1560s John Hawkins entered the slave trade between Africa and South America in the face of the Spanish monopoly of it. In 1577 his flag captain Francis Drake sailed on his three-year freebooting voyage around the world, while Martin Frobisher discovered Hudson Strait. Sir Walter Raleigh and Sir Humphrey Gilbert tried vainly to establish permanent American colonies by their own private efforts and fortunes, to find to their sorrow that "private purses are cold comforts to adventurers." Spain remained a fearsome hazard to any English colonizing venture. Then the defeat of the Spanish Armada opened new possibilities, the accession of James I to the English throne in 1603 brought peace with Spain and with Scotland, the joint-stock company was being successfully applied to various areas of English trade, and England was at last in a position to profit from tightfisted Henry VII's £10 investment.

AMERICAN INDIANS

Awaiting the European adventurers were an estimated 15 to 20 million native Americans, including about 7 million in Mexico and perhaps 850,000 in what became the United States. Their initial contact with the Europeans was sometimes friendly and mutually beneficial and sometimes fierce, treacherous, and bloody; in the long run the fierce and bloody tendency prevailed almost everywhere. The opening of America entailed one of the greatest slaughterings of people in human history. In Mexico the native population declined to about 2 million following the conquest and stands at about 2.5 million today. In the United States, the Indian population was down to 220,000 in 1910, though it has since increased to three times that number.

Although Columbus named them Indians, thinking he had reached East Indies, the native Americans were evidently of north Asian origin. At some time during the previous forty-five thousand years they had made their way to Alaska by way of the Bering Strait and gradually occupied the entire Western Hemisphere. These Americans, who spoke an estimated twenty-two hundred distinct dialects and languages, represented wide variations in physical appearance as well as in culture, and they did not think of themselves as a single people. Only within recent years has the idea of "Indian" as a meaningful term for these native Americans begun to have any significance to them, together with the idea of an ethnic quality of "Indianness."

Despite the diversity of American Indian cultures and the utter lack of any sense of common Indian purpose, the Indians of North and South America did tend to share common social as well as physical characteristics. They held religious beliefs involving many spirits and shamans, or medicine men, but centering upon one supreme being or divine force. Indian society tended everywhere to be organized along family-clan lines, and the idea of communal rather than private ownership of property was a typical native American point of view.

Advanced civilizations emerged in America at least as early as three thousand years ago or so with the Olmec culture in the area of Veracruz and Tabasco. Olmec culture, which flourished down to about 400 B.C., manifested itself in urban religious centers with temple mounds, monumental stone carvings, and huge sacrificial altars. The glyph writing and the calendar system that was part of Olmec culture probably originated with it.

Between 300 B.C. and A.D. 300, Zapotec culture thrived in the region of Oaxaca in Mexico. A highly stratified society, the Zapotecs distinguished themselves in their architectural and ornamental skills, catering to a metropolitan aristocratic class. A major Zapotec deity was Quetzalcoatl, the Plumed Serpent, bringer of civilization, for whom elaborate rituals involving animal and human sacrifices were carried out. To the north, in central Mexico, Toltec society flowered in the ninth and tenth centuries A.D., marked by brilliant palaces and pyramids and metalwork in copper and gold. Mayan civilization flourished at the same time in Central America and produced scholarship in mathematics and astronomy that in important respects was farther advanced than in any other known civilization of the world at that time. Mayan civilization grew out of the forbidding environment of the tropical rain forest; Incan civilization in Peru thrived on the steep sides of the Cordillera Mountains that descended down to desert beaches in a region where but 2 percent of the land was arable.

The Aztecs emerged as a warrior tribe and established their capital, which became Mexico City, around the beginning of the fourteenth century. The city was ruled by twenty clans, each represented in a council of state that elected a Chief of Men. When Cortes arrived in 1519, the city had a population of 60,000 and ruled an empire of perhaps 5 million, under the Chief of Men Montezuma II. It was in the field of administration that the Aztecs advanced most conspicuously over their predecessors, although Cortes was able to demonstrate that the system suffered from fatal flaws. The Aztecs inherited gods and ranked them in hierarchies. Quetzalcoatl was one. The war god Huitzilopochtli was their highest god, however, requiring bloody religious rituals that entailed tortures and self-tortures and human sacrifices by the thousands. Cortes eradicated this cruel culture, together with a generous majority of the population that had lived by this culture.

In the region that became the United States, the Pueblo culture of the South-west is distinguished by a historical past that can be dated as early as the third century B.C. The multistory apartment dwellings of the Pueblo Indians remained impregnable during many centuries of attacks by enemy tribes, and Pueblo Indians remained secure in their farming pursuits and the development of their crafts: basket weaving, pottery making, and the fashioning of jewelry. Pueblo culture reached its period of greatest vitality by A.D. 1100 and then, three centuries later, for reasons that are only to be guessed at, entered a period of major disruption. Thereafter new groups were formed out of various tribes, and new pueblos were constructed in new locations. The Zuñi and Hopi (meaning "peaceful ones") are the leading nations today that resulted from this resettle-ment nearly five centuries ago.

The Pueblo Indians have guarded their traditional ways more successfully than any other Indian tribes in the United States. Occupied and christianized by the Spanish in the late fifteenth century, these Indians organized the Pueblo Revolt of 1680 to drive the Spanish out. They were obliged to submit to reoccu-pation twelve years later, but under circumstances that left them a large amount of autonomy, which they continued to retain. Today the largest pueblo is the Zuñi pueblo in New Mexico, which houses 2,500 persons in a five-story dwelling.

Pueblo communities were virtually priestly orders, the men spending almost half of their days in religious observances, for which underground rooms—ki-vas—were constructed. Religion in the pueblos involved the worship of many deities and beneficent spirits, or kachinas, who were believed to visit the pueb-los six months out of the year as messengers of the gods. Masked impersonators of kachinas circulated in the community, passing out painted dolls to the children and maintaining a high level of religious consciousness. The children were raised very permissively but also were inculcated with fear of evil spirits as a consequence of wrongdoing, resulting in a gently but firmly conformist social system.

No historically continuous culture comparable to Pueblo culture exists else-where in the United States, but the Hopwellian culture of the Ohio Valley, which reached its height around the tenth or eleventh century A.D., did exert influence over much of what became the United States. This was a mound-building culture which was skilled in agriculture, probably corn, squash, and beans for the most part, and in craftsmanship, including incised pottery, cloth, copper work, pearl beads, and engraved tablets. For centuries the region was a trading center reaching markets from the Great Plains to the Atlantic. The Hopwellian culture was followed in the Southeast by the temple-mound Mississippi culture, a generally peaceful society that valued leisure and good times and supported itself by agriculture, supplemented by hunting and fishing.

Until the coming of the Europeans, all the Indians south of the subarctic region depended more or less on agriculture for their livings, including the

Plains Indians, who also depended on the buffalo hunt. Beginning in the mid-sixteenth century, however, the Plains Indians acquired horses and guns and were able to roam the plains wildly and at will. The heyday of these Indian horsemen of the plains was from the mid-eighteenth century to the times of Sitting Bull and Geronimo in the 1870s and 1880s. During this period, the Plains culture exhibited the colorful ferocity that made it world-famous: the feathered war bonnets, the embroidery and beadwork, the moccasins and leggings, and the sun dance around the sacred painted pole, from which Indian braves suspended themselves by skewers hooked into their chests. In 1876, Col. George A. Custer allowed them one final tremendous triumph, and then, facing the slaughter of the buffalo herds and increased military force against themselves, they were obliged to surrender to life on reservations.

The war-bonneted Plains Indians and the Pueblo pottery makers have contributed most to the popular image of the American Indian, but it was the Indian of the Eastern forest region who chiefly affected the lives of Anglo-American settlers during the first two centuries after Jamestown and Plymouth. These belonged mainly to three general language groups: the Algonquins in New England south to the middle colonies, the Muskhogean in the Southeast, and the Iroquois Five Nations (Mohawk, Cayuga, Oneida, Onondaga, and Seneca) maintaining an aggressively independent position centering in upstate New York throughout the colonial period.

The Algonquins characteristically distinguished themselves at fishing, the Muskhogean at agriculture, and the Iroquois at fighting. However, there were numerous tribes within these groupings, and only the Iroquois had much sense of identity beyond their individual tribal villages. And even within the villages, authority of the headmen tended to be limited and the options of the individual brave open.

Among these Eastern Indians, the Iroquois were the most successful in organizing an effective confederation, chiefly through the auspices of the women. The basic unit in the League of Iroquois was the "fireside," consisting of the mother and her children. Above this, women representing groups of families held authority and appointed men to official positions in the league. Thus loosely but durably organized, the Iroquois were distinguished for their diplomatic ability as well as for their cruelty and their effectiveness in warfare, whether fighting for glory, revenge, or property or to settle disputes over hunting grounds. In religion, they worshipped the Master of Life, or supreme being, and held an idealistic view of the individual as belonging to a society which, in turn, was united with the whole of nature.

The Iroquois remained on friendly terms with the white settlers throughout most of the colonial period, and initially at least, the Eastern Indians in general gave the white man a friendly greeting upon his arrival. From the Indian point of view, the white man represented a superior power in a material and military sense and perhaps in a religious sense. And since the Indians shared no sense of Indianness to unite them against the whites, their first concern tended to be to win white support against rival tribes. And in the effort to win this support, the Indians instructed the whites on how to raise maize, which was the essential requirement for white survival, and how to hunt and dress and smoke and in other ways protect and enjoy themselves in this strange environment.

Initial benefits to the Indians, or at least to certain tribes of Indians, from the adoption of European methods and tools and weapons was inevitably followed by the destruction of Indian society. Tribal warfare that had gone on indefinitely in the era of bows and arrows and spears and shields resulted in the swift destruction or evacuation of tribes in the era of gunpowder. The Iroquois survived and extended their power down to the Revolutionary and early national period through diplomatic means, and the Creeks survived in Georgia and Alabama down through the War of 1812 by the same means, but eventually they too fell victims to white land hunger.

It was among the Indians of the Southeast—Choctaws, Chickasaws, Cherokees, and Seminoles as well as Creeks—that white ways were most widely adopted. These peoples were more advanced agriculturally than other American Indians to begin with, and they accustomed themselves to Anglo-American concepts of property rights, including slave property rights. But white race consciousness and land hunger destroyed them anyway, and in the 1830s and 1840s they were forcibly removed from their lands and marched down the Trail of Tears to dusty reservations in Oklahoma.

At the time Columbus arrived in America, the Pacific Coast region was probably the most densely settled part of what was to become the United States, and particularly California, which had an estimated population of 350,000. There were more than one hundred major tribes in California, divided into six parent language stocks. The dominant pattern of life was a sedentary and comparatively peaceful one that depended on a diet of acorns, prepared by a rather complicated process, plus fish and game and roots and berries. Society was organized on the basis of extended family groups under headmen who enjoyed little authority. Prominent in the culture of these California Indians were songs and dances and stories that were social rather than ceremonial for the most part and were accompanied by musical instruments, including flutes, whistles, mouth bows, and a variety of drums.

When the Spanish priests and soldiers arrived on the scene, these Indians were rounded up into villages, where they were regimented and harshly disciplined and in the process decimated. Then came the gold rush, and an estimated 70,000 Indians were destroyed during the 1850s. Only 15,000 remained in 1900, but the number has been steadily increasing since then. In the Pacific Northwest, where life depended basically on salmon fishing and where the remarkable institution of the potlatch celebrated the worship of opulence, Indians proved somewhat more successful in resisting the incursions of the whites. In recent years, however, their fishing rights, guaranteed in perpetuity, have been gradually abrogated and the basis for their traditional way of life ended.

SCIENCE AND
THE NEW WORLD

The Indians were assumed to be descended from Adam and Eve, but it was difficult to understand how. In this and in many other ways, the spectacle of the New World radically altered basic conceptions which educated Europeans had held since Aristotle's time and earlier. Aristotelian climatology, with its idea of parallel climate zones, was early repudiated by the American experience. The Aristotelian system described a torrid zone where human habitation was impossible, yet in America the most advanced civilizations had flourished for centuries in this zone. And climate in America did not compare to that of Europe along the same parallels of latitude, as Englishmen who wintered in Newfoundland learned.

Once a southerly correction had been made below the latitude of England, the land from lower New England to the Carolinas was indeed found to be similar in many respects to old England, but attempts to transplant English crops to the new soil resulted in failures that were often surprising and sometimes disastrous. It became evident that the New World supported varieties of plant and animal life that were different from those of the Old World. This represented a serious problem of survival and, after that, from a religious point of view. Seventeenth-century Englishmen accepted the biblical account of the creation of heaven and earth, including the account of Adam and Eve and of Noah and the flood. Presumably Noah had stocked the ark with elk and bison and corn and potatoes and other plant and animal life indigenous to America. But where had he found the room, and how had these varieties become separated from those that remained in the Old World?

But it was the fact of the American Indian that most seriously challenged old assumptions. Black Africans had been known to Europeans since ancient times, and various theories had worked them into the family of Adam and Eve. Now additional theories were necessary to relate this new man, the American Indian, to the facts of the Book of Genesis. A favorite theory was that the Indians were descended from the Ten Lost Tribes of Israel, a theory supported by similarities between Indian tribal laws and the laws of the Pentateuch. The facts of America somewhat strained the credulity of Europeans in areas of religion, tradition, history, and ancient science. And vaguely and generally, the discovery of America and its subsequent exploitation and settlement tended to lessen the sense of their own all-importance that Europeans had heretofore possessed.

ECONOMIC GEOGRAPHY
OF NORTH AMERICA

As for the English, if on closer examination the American scene proved stranger than it had first appeared, it was still true that the North American lands they possessed were the most congenial to Europeans that North America offered. The winters were somewhat colder and the summers somewhat hotter than in England, and American corn and potatoes had to take the place of English wheat and Scotch oats and barley, but from Georgia to Maine America provided an inviting setting for the transplantation of English society.

Conditions were the more favorable for settlement in that the much-indented Atlantic coastline provided numerous serviceable harbor facilities and not a few truly excellent harbors, and they were joined to navigable waterways. This was notably true where settlers founded the towns of Boston, Newport, New York, and Philadelphia, as well as Charleston, where, it was said, the Ashley and Cooper Rivers joined to form the Atlantic Ocean. To the end of the colonial period, Philadelphia was probably the American city with the best access to the hinterland by navigable waterways. It was rivaled by New York, servicing the Hudson River Valley and much of New Jersey, but not until the Erie Canal connected the port of New York with the Great Lakes in the 1820s did New York achieve its unrivaled position as the national metropolis.

Southward from Philadelphia, the succession of parallel rivers and streams flowing eastward to the Atlantic continued down to Florida. On the one hand, this system suited the purposes of the large plantations, each with its own wharf along its own waterway. On the other hand, it rendered north-south wagon transportation virtually impossible. It was apt to be safer and simpler to travel between the Chesapeake region and Charleston by way of London than to attempt the trip directly.

English settlements clung to these waterways throughout the seventeenth century, and few settlers ventured inland beyond the fall line, the point beyond which the river ceased to be navigable. The second major obstacle to the westward advance was the Appalachian mountain range from New England to Georgia, which provided a series of parallel ridges to serve as Indian fortifications against the encroachments of the whites. It was the advance of the English and the French together into this area in the 1750s that started the French and Indian War in 1754. Then during the Revolutionary era the Appalachians ceased to serve as a barrier to the westward movement, which thereafter swiftly preempted the areas of Kentucky and Tennessee and the Ohio Valley.

Once across the Appalachians, settlers oriented themselves to the streams and rivers that were tributary to the Mississippi or, in the South, to parallel rivers flowing into the Gulf of Mexico. During the early years of the trans-Appalachian settlement, various Western schemes to form a separate nation were readily suggested by geographic circumstances. They ceased to seem so promising when the Louisiana Purchase placed the port of New Orleans in federal American hands and when canals and toll roads opened up east-west avenues of transportation.

Until the 1830s the idea of one single continental federal republic appeared too vast and unwieldy to contemplate. Even so ardent an expansionist as Sen. Thomas Hart Benton of Missouri declared the Rocky Mountains to be the terminating line beyond which the republic could not expand. At the same time, however, the idea of all North America as a great Anglo-Saxon realm was widely entertained, and with the coming of the railroad the practical idea of one united transcontinental nation took form and then swiftly became fact.

Whatever differences with the seventeenth-century British church and state may have impelled Englishmen to begin their lives again in the American wilderness, their initial intention had been to recreate England in America as faithfully as possible, except for the evils in the English system that had driven them to America in the first place. Once settled in America, however, the attention of these English colonists tended to be drawn increasingly to the West—to what Frederick Jackson Turner called "the hither edge of free land." Even for those on seaboard plantations or in Boston and Philadelphia countinghouses, the West was always attractively full of economic opportunities.

But if the frontier tended to orient Eastern society away from the Old World, it much more thoroughly westernized those who themselves entered the westward movement. "The wilderness masters the colonist," Turner wrote. ". . . It strips off the garments of civilization and arrays him in the hunting shirt and the moccasin. . . . The fact is that here is a new product that is American." Writing on the eve of the American Revolution, the French-American philosopher Crèvecœur spoke of the peaceful American farmer who followed in the wake of the frontiersman as "a new man, who acts upon new principles; he must therefore entertain new ideas and form new opinions." By the close of the colonial period, the composite Anglo-Scotch-Irish-German-Swiss-Dutch-French American about whom Crèvecœur was writing had become a new and significant subject of natural history for enlightened Europeans, just as the American Indian had been a new subject of natural history a century before and earlier.

BIBLIOGRAPHY FOR CHAPTER 1

Wallace Notestein, The English People on the Eve of Colonization, 1603-1630 (1954)
E. P. Cheyney, The European Background of American History, 1300-1600 (1904)
W. H. McNeill, The Rise of the West (1963)
J. H. Parry, The Age of Reconnaissance (1963)
J. B. Brebner, The Explorers of North America, 1492-1806 (1933)
Bernard De Voto, Course of Empire (1950)
Garrett Mattingly, The Armada (1959)
A. L. Rowse, The Expansion of Elizabethan England (1955)
W. P. Webb, The Great Frontier (1952)
Alvin Josephy, Jr., The Indian Heritage of America (1968)
W. T. Hagan, American Indians (1961)

CHAPTER 2

COLONIAL SETTLEMENT

SETTLEMENT OF VIRGINIA

In 1606 James I issued two business charters: one to the Virginia Company of London, authorizing settlement of what later became southern Pennsylvania, North Carolina, Virginia, and Maryland, and the other to the Virginia Company of Plymouth, covering what later became New England and the middle colonies. The patents overlapped each other, probably to provide altercations which would place the Crown in the role of mediator. Both were joint-stock companies, financed by private subscription, and both, hopeful of rich returns in gold and silver, immediately organized expeditions and sent out colonizing parties.

Inexperienced and ill-provided, the New England settlement of the Virginia Company of Plymouth foundered, and the survivors were returned to London. The Jamestown settlement of the London Company, as the Virginia Company of London was called, was equally inexperienced and almost as poorly served and faced similarly grueling hardships. A motley band of gentlemen and prisoners, the first settlers were more interested in searching for gold than in the homely task of grubbing a living from the new soil. English grains did not transplant well in American soil, and the settlers were reluctant to adjust to the native diet, mainly Indian corn. Disregarding the instructions of the company, they founded their town on a swampy, malarial site along the James River. More than half the settlers died during the first year, and only the energetic leadership of Capt. John Smith saved the lives of the rest. For the next decade, Jamestown survived under a regime of military discipline.

It had been intended from the first, however, that the English settlers in America, contrary to the practice of all other colonizing nations of Europe, were to "enjoy all liberties, franchises, and immunities . . . to all intents and purposes, as if they had been abiding and born, within this our realm of England," as the original London Company charter declared. Accordingly, in 1619 the company

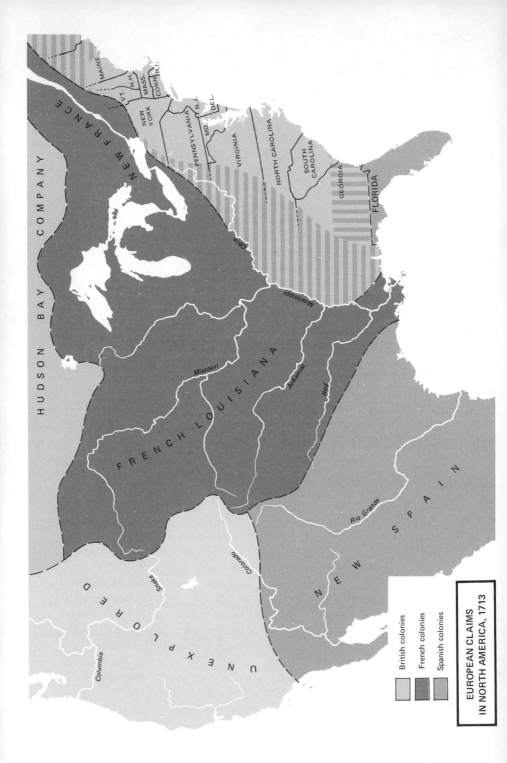

EUROPEAN CLAIMS
IN NORTH AMERICA, 1713

British colonies
French colonies
Spanish colonies

HUDSON BAY COMPANY

NEW FRANCE

MAINE
VT.
N.H.
MASS.
CONN. R.I.
NEW YORK
PENNSYLVANIA
N.J.
DEL.
MD.
VIRGINIA
NORTH CAROLINA
SOUTH CAROLINA
GEORGIA
FLORIDA

Ohio
Mississippi
Missouri
Arkansas
Red

FRENCH LOUISIANA

NEW SPAIN

Rio Grande

Colorado
Snake
Columbia

UNEXPLORED

sent a new governor to Virginia with instructions to call an assembly "freely to be elected by the inhabitants . . . to make and ordain whatsoever laws and orders should by them be thought good and profitable." Self-government was introduced to America that summer with the meeting of the first Virginia House of Burgesses.

At its second meeting in 1621 this assembly was assured by the company that orders would not bind the colony unless ratified by the assembly. The assembly in its turn asserted rights in matters of taxation and administration exceeding even those claimed by Parliament. As a practical matter, however, effective authority continued to rest with the company officials. The time of trials appeared over. Then, in 1622, a surprise Indian raid wiped out virtually all the settlements outside Jamestown. The disaster played into the hands of the opposition to the company leadership. In 1624 the company's charter was revoked, and Virginia became a royal colony, the governor and council thereafter being appointed by the King.

Meanwhile, tobacco made the experiment pay. First raised successfully as a commercial product in 1613—it is said this was achieved by John Rolfe, the husband of Pocahontas—tobacco became an immediately successful money crop with a rapidly increasing market in England. The company officers were concerned lest this new development bring down upon the colony the wrath of King James I, who looked upon smoking as "lothesome to the eye, hatefull to the nose, harmefull to the brain, dangerous to the Lungs." They were concerned also that concentration on the tobacco crop would destroy the possibility of a self-sustaining economy, for it continued to be necessary to supply the colony with foodstuffs from England. Attempts to introduce manufacturing and varied farming largely failed, however, as the artisans and farmers sent over for the purpose deserted their former occupations to benefit from the one main source of profit.

Recruited mainly from the landless English classes, the early settlers of Virginia commonly arrived as indentured servants. They would work for five years in the service of an employer to defray the cost of their passage; thereafter they were freemen and could easily obtain land. There were a few well-to-do Englishmen among the early settlers, who acquired large plantations along the James River. Such holdings were exceptional, however. More representative in the early years were farms of 300 or 400 acres, scattered along the navigable portions of various rivers. These farms were worked by individual families with the assistance of perhaps two or three indentured servants. Black Africans were first brought to Virginia in 1619, but for its first three generations the colony relied primarily on white labor.

Unlike most of the later English mainland colonies, Virginia was not intended as an asylum where refugees might conduct themselves in ways which were considered unacceptably un-English in the homeland. It was the wish of the Virginians to re-create the English countryside as nearly as possible in America, and they did so more faithfully than any of the later colonies. The royally appointed governor and his council comprised almost a local nobility, reserving to themselves the right to wear gold braid and, more importantly, most of the lucrative political positions.

The House of Burgesses was the Virginia House of Commons, elected initially by all adult males but later only by property holders. Justices of the peace, appointed also by the Crown, played much the same key role in local government in Virginia as in England. The Church of England was established in Virginia, and the vestrymen, soon a self-perpetuating group, were responsible for the morals of the community and care of the poor as well as for the upkeep of the church. They shared local responsibilities with the justices and like them were drawn from the "better sort" in the community.

THE FOUNDING OF MARYLAND

In 1632 King Charles I granted a slice of northern Virginia to the court favorite George Calvert, Lord Baltimore, whose son Cecilius two years later succeeded in establishing, on the basis of his own personal resources, the colony of Maryland. Planned as a haven for Catholics from English persecution, Maryland for some reason recruited its population largely from English Protestants. Religious disputes broke out before the first ships, the *Ark* and the *Dove,* had arrived, and thereafter struggle between the Catholic leadership and the Protestant majority raged. A solution was attempted in 1649 in the Toleration Act, which granted religious freedom to trinitarian Christians, but troubles continued and actual civil war broke out during the time of Cromwell and the Great Rebellion in England. The Toleration Act was repealed for a time, and even after it was again passed into law, various acts were passed limiting Catholic political participation.

It had been the intention of Baltimore to fashion a more thoroughly aristocratic government and society than had existed in England for centuries, and he himself devised his charter for this purpose, choosing as his pattern the fourteenth-century charter of the bishop of the palatinate of Durham. As absolute lord and proprietor his ownership of the land was unrestricted, and he possessed the right to make any laws he wished, subject to the "advice, assent, and approbation of the freemen of the province." This arrangement, which gave the Calverts greater authority than kings enjoyed in England, was looked upon as a reasonable application to America of a feudal authority such as had been wielded in the English marches in the medieval time when England had its own frontier areas and endowed lords with great powers in exchange for the performance of military duties.

In America the system faltered at once. Amid the religious struggle, isolated from the seat of royal power, faced with an abundance of land and a shortage of settlers and obliged to seek the approbation of the freemen, Cecilius Calvert soon made new terms with his colonists. The charter terms obliged him to put up with an elected assembly, and in 1639 he assented to its demand that it share with him the right to initiate legislation. Within a dozen years the settled custom had developed of annual sessions, triennial elections, and a two-house legislature, the lower house being composed of freemen whose consent was required for all laws. Maryland and Virginia, created for different purposes under sharply contrasting charters, rapidly developed systems of society and government that were quite similar in major respects, the result of a common culture adjusting to a common geographic setting and to the common social consequences that flowed from its tobacco economy.

SETTLEMENT OF NEW ENGLAND

The addition of 101 souls was lost to Virginia in 1620 when the *Mayflower* missed its course and landed to the north on Cape Cod. Moving across the bay this band of Pilgrims founded a colony which they called Plymouth, after the English city from which they had sailed. As Separatists, the majority of the Pilgrims represented the farthest advance of the Protestant Reformation in early seventeenth-century England. Not content with the separation from Rome which the Church of England had accomplished in the 1530s, the Separatists removed themselves from the Church of England itself and covenanted together in completely autonomous religious bodies. From the point of view of the English church and Crown, this was at least as lawless a course as the refusal to recognize the civil authority of the state. Consequently Separatist leaders were executed, and their followers were driven underground or out of the country.

Those who sailed on the *Mayflower* were enjoined by their pastor, John Robinson, to remember that according to the true religion each man was a priest unto himself and should conduct himself in that spirit. Guided by this injunction and by determination to curb the non-Separatists among them, the Pilgrims, upon planting their colony, drew up the Mayflower Compact promising to abide in their civil affairs by the principle of direct democracy. The Mayflower Compact remains a wonderfully simple and clear-cut demonstration of the democratic tendencies that from the first were inherent in Protestant Christianity. Materially, Plymouth contributed little to the development of New England, and after several generations it merged with Massachusetts. It did, however, initiate many important traditions—symbolized in the *Mayflower,* the Mayflower Compact, Plymouth Rock, and Thanksgiving—by which later Americans came to interpret themselves.

Unlike the Pilgrims, the Puritans of the Massachusetts Bay Company, who began to arrive a few years later, considered themselves unseparated from the Church of England. They thought of themselves as loyal communicants who wished to save the church by purifying it of false Roman Catholic accretions. But despite their professions of loyalty, this reforming zeal made them unwanted by the English church hierarchy and by the Crown, and they therefore removed to New England, where they might build a New Zion, a re-creation of Christianity as it was revealed in the Bible and as they supposed it to have been practiced in the days of the early church.

Much more powerfully placed in England than the Pilgrims, the Puritans succeeded in acquiring from the King a business charter similar to that of the Virginia Company, one which placed their company in complete charge of a large territorial concession. Fearing that the company might fall into the hands of unsympathetic stockholders, radical Puritans among the company shareholders departed from England to Massachusetts, taking their charter with them and so breaking all direct legal connection with the homeland. This questionably legal act placed them, in their own view, in virtual independence of the English Crown. The exodus began in the late 1620s, and the so-called "Great Migration" of 20,000 came in the first generation (6,000 had arrived in Virginia during its first generation of settlement). Then, with the outbreak of civil war in England in 1642, the migration largely ceased. Most New Englanders at the time of the American Revolution were descended from that first migration.

Salem was settled in 1628, and in 1630 a thousand additional settlers, including the company officers bringing with them their charter, settled Boston and other towns. John Winthrop, who dominated the company and the colony for a generation, favored a highly centralized government ruled by himself together with his magistrates. A legislative body called the General Court was created of the magistrates—company officials elected by the stockholders to the board of directors—and of deputies elected by the freemen. The company admitted as freemen only a select group among the adult males who were members of one of the authorized Puritan churches, thereby probably eliminating a majority of the adult males as voters. The issue of whether the magistrates could set aside the votes of the elected deputies resulted in 1644 in the dividing of the General Court into two separate houses.

Local government meanwhile was permitted to develop of itself to an extent. The result was the town meeting, where church members gathered in the meeting house, as the church was called, to decide upon local affairs and to rotate among themselves numerous civic duties. In 1647 the General Court admitted nonfreemen to active, although nonvoting, participation in local affairs. In 1648 nonfreemen were permitted to take part in any town meeting, council, or court proceeding in the colony. In the same year the commonwealth of Massachusetts published its General Laws and Liberties, a conglomeration of General Court legislation, Mosaic law, and altered English common law. Within a generation the colony had changed itself from a company to a commonwealth based on a working compromise between the authoritarian theocratic principles of the leaders and the demands of the majority.

New England Puritanism, although basically Calvinist, did not accept Calvin as an indisputable authority and, among other differences from Calvinism, placed much less emphasis on the doctrine of predestination. The Puritans believed that with Adam's fall all mankind had sinned and deserved everlasting damnation. Christ's sacrifice, however, opened salvation to all who truly loved Christ and desired to seek him. The desire came more readily to some than to others, and none could be certain that he was saved. However, those who had reason to believe they were on the way to grace would be admitted as visible saints if their evidence was acceptable to the congregation.

These saints would band together to worship autonomously under a pastor of their own choosing, as they believed had been the practice in the primitive Christian church. Election was achieved by faith alone and not by good works. Still, good behavior was evidence of sanctification; in practice the Puritans compromised in this matter. They compromised further in 1662 in the Halfway Covenant, which admitted the children of church members to a nonvoting membership in the congregation without evidence of their sanctification, although denying them communion. This covenant marks that decline in Puritan fervor which was a theme of sermons throughout the seventeenth century and into the worldly eighteenth.

The compromise did not extend to open deviation from religious orthodoxy. In 1635 Roger Williams was driven from Massachusetts for questioning the authority of the church, and shortly thereafter Anne Hutchinson was driven after him into exile. Williams, a promising, apparently orthodox minister, caused trouble soon after his arrival when he demanded complete separation from the Church of England and questioned the authority by which the colony had preempted land from the Indians. Then, as if this were not subversive enough, he proceeded to question the authority of the ministry in matters of dogma.

It was the novel contention of Williams that religious truths were not certainly revealed to man in the Bible and that therefore no priesthood was warranted in forcing its dogma upon others. He further argued that men must be brought willingly to religion, that it could not be forced upon them. Anne Hutchinson, on the other hand, was an Antinomian, believing herself to be in direct mystical communication with God. Beyond freeing her from the necessity of submitting to church mediation, this placed her in a position to judge on the eligibility of the Boston ministers, most of whom failed to pass muster. Her following in the colony was so large that in 1636 it succeeded in electing its candidate, Henry Vane, as governor over Winthrop. The orthodox rallied their forces, however, reelected Winthrop the next year, and in 1638 banished Anne Hutchinson forever from the colony.

Williams founded Providence, while Mrs. Hutchinson's party founded Portsmouth. Friction in Portsmouth resulted in the founding of Newport; friction in Providence resulted in the founding of Warwick, and a disharmonious union of the four towns as the colony of Rhode Island and Providence Plantations was officially confirmed in 1663 by royal charter. Founded on the principle of complete religious liberty and, incidentally, household democracy, with the head of each home a voting member of the community, Rhode Island was a precocious manifestation of the libertarianism which was to emerge from the Protestant religious struggles in England in the coming years.

Connecticut was founded mainly by orthodox Massachusetts Puritans and separated peaceably from the mother colony. In 1639 four towns united themselves under the Fundamental Orders of Connecticut, and in 1662 Connecticut received a royal charter, which granted it a remarkably high degree of autonomy and annexed to it the more radically Puritan colony of New Haven. Attempts to colonize upper New England, meanwhile, had been checked by troubles with the Indians and legal disputes over ownership. Massachusetts acquired and then lost title to New Hampshire but managed to win control of Maine and hold on to it throughout the colonial period.

SETTLEMENT OF
THE CAROLINAS

In 1642 rebellion broke out in England against the King, and the English settlement of America was interrupted during the struggle, which continued on until the restoration of Charles II in 1660. During Charles's reign, which lasted to 1685, the second series of colony plantings took place, which resulted in the establishment of New York, Pennsylvania, New Jersey, and North and South Carolina. Interested in colonies mainly as a means of paying off obligations, Charles granted the Carolinas to eight aristocratic supporters in 1663, New York to his brother, the Duke of York, in 1664, and Pennsylvania to William Penn, son of a royal creditor, in 1681.

The intricately aristocratic intentions of the "true and absolute Lords Proprietors" of the Carolinas was indicated in their Fundamental Constitutions, issued in 1669. The colony was divided into three counties and each county in turn subdivided into eight seignories, eight baronies, four precincts, and an indefinite number of large manorial estates. A fixed hierarchy was established of palatine, landgrave, cacique, and so on down to leet men, who, with their descendants, were to remain perpetually in a state of serfdom. At the bottom were the slaves, over whom the masters were given complete authority by law. The Fundamental Constitutions never received the "assent and approbation of the freeman" required by the charter and so never went entirely into effect. However, they remained a guide for the proprietors during the first generation of settlement and a disadvantage to the settlers.

As it turned out, the aristocratic character of the southern portion of the grant, which became South Carolina, was dictated less by the intentions of the proprietors than it was by the geographic environment, which invited the introduction of slaves on a large scale and brought great profits from the culture of rice. In 1719, after endless struggles with the proprietors, the South Carolinians performed a dignified revolution, which was accepted by the English Crown, and the province continued thereafter as a royal colony.

Lacking the marketable cash crop of rice and, more importantly, such port facilities as were provided South Carolina by the Ashley and Cooper Rivers, the northern part of the Carolinas had from the outset a separate history, and after 1694 a separate government. Beyond these difficulties, the North Carolinians faced neglect from their proprietors and hostility from Virginia, with which North Carolina competed to some extent in the tobacco trade. Consequently the development of North Carolina was relatively slow among the colonies and its general economic condition relatively bad.

SETTLEMENT OF NEW YORK

Originally founded by the Dutch as New Netherland in the 1620s, New York was captured in war by the English in 1664. At the opening of the seventeenth century the Dutch were the most powerful maritime people in the world, and they might well have won North America for themselves had their interests not been concentrated elsewhere. The main concern of the Dutch East India Company, however, was wresting the spice trade from the Portuguese and establishing trading centers in the East Indies. Henry Hudson explored the Hudson River and Hudson Bay for the purpose of finding the Northwest Passage which would facilitate the trade with the Far East. Founded in 1621, the Dutch West India Company acquired various American possessions, including for a time Brazil, in addition to settling New Netherland. The company was much more concerned with raiding Spanish and Portuguese towns and treasure ships, however, than it was with establishing flourishing colonies.

The settlers of New Netherland, possessing none of the rights of self-government which their English neighbors enjoyed, suffered under the tyranny or thievery of a succession of governors ending with Peter Stuyvesant, who lost the colony to the English. Also, in a largely unsuccessful effort to attract settlers, the company had offered vast tracts of land, great manorial authority over the tenants, and the title of "Patroon" to any who would bring five hundred families of tenants to New Netherland. As a result of this system and of the more successful English adaptation of it, rural New York was divided into lordly estates where aristocrats ruled the countryside in a fashion not to be seen elsewhere in the Northern mainland colonies.

In the course of war with the Dutch in 1664 the disgruntled colony of New Netherland fell into English hands without a struggle and was turned over to King Charles's younger brother, the Duke of York, under a charter which omitted the usual statement concerning the assent of freemen to the passage of laws. Of all the Thirteen Colonies, New York alone failed to summon a legislature during its first generation of existence. This was made possible in part by an exceptionally able governor, Richard Nicolls, who ruled the colony under "the Duke's laws," a combination of New England, English, and Dutch law. It was made possible in part also by the assent of the Dutch settlers, who had never enjoyed representative institutions in the colony and were better governed and more secure in their rights under the conqueror than they had previously been under their company. The trouble for the government came from English settlers who had moved to Long Island from New England; they complained of the "slavery" of being taxed by a nonrepresentative government. An assembly was finally summoned in 1683.

Meanwhile the Duke of York assigned a portion of his grant, which he named New Jersey, to two friends. One of these sold his portion to two Quakers, and later on the widow of the other sold the rest to a group of proprietors. The subsequent colonial history of the Jerseys was confusing and litigious. The influence of the Quakers tended to predominate in West Jersey, while the Puritan influence was marked in East Jersey, settled mainly from New England and Long Island.

QUAKER PENNSYLVANIA

In 1681 Charles II deeded a large grant of adjacent territory to the English courtier and convert to Quakerism William Penn in lieu of debts owed Penn's father. Already participating in the West Jersey venture, Penn set forth in Pennsylvania on a "Holy Experiment": the establishment of a community based upon the principles of political liberty and religious freedom. It was to be an asylum for Quakers, who were persecuted in England and in all American colonies except Rhode Island, but beyond that it was to be a refuge for those throughout Europe who were persecuted for their religious beliefs.

The Quakers, or Society of Friends, were a religious sect founded by George Fox amid the religious turmoil which accompanied and followed the English civil wars. The Quakers brought Protestantism to its logical conclusion with the announcement of the priesthood of all men and women. Quakerism placed reliance for religious authority not first of all upon Scripture, but upon the divine inner light of each individual conscience. While not original with the Quakers, the doctrine of the inner light was given a uniquely central position in their belief, dispensing with the need for priest, formal church service, or explicit dogma. In colonial America, Quakerism for a time was the dominant religion in Rhode Island, New Jersey, Delaware, Pennsylvania, and North Carolina, and it appeared that it might become the dominant American religion. It lacked organization, however, and subsequently, with the winning of prosperity and social status, it lost its proselytizing zeal, and during the eighteenth century it was overtaken by the more evangelical sects.

Penn presented his design in 1682 in the Frame of Government, which was based upon the belief, blasphemous to the Puritan, that though men might be evil, man was not innately so. "Governments, like clocks," he declared, "go from the motion men give them, so by them they are ruined too. . . . Let men be good, and the government cannot be bad. . . ." He thereupon provided a legislature of two houses, both of them elective, which set about at once to give Penn troubles. Obliged to return to England, Penn for a time lost much of his control over the colony, and his charter was at one point revoked, though it was later restored.

The Frame of Government was altered on several occasions, and finally in 1701 Penn issued the Charter of Privileges, establishing the only unicameral government among the Thirteen Colonies and reasserting the principle of religious freedom. He remained steadfast in his purpose to create the freest and most flourishing of the English mainland colonies. The Charter of Privileges remained the Pennsylvania constitution throughout the rest of the colonial period and provided the liberal pattern, with the coming of the Revolution, for the most democratic constitution of any of the new states. Delaware, meanwhile, had been leased to Penn by the Duke of York for ten thousand years, and early in the eighteenth century it was established as a separate colony.

GEORGIA

The last of the Thirteen Colonies to be established, Georgia, was founded in 1733 by the philanthropist James Edward Oglethorpe, partly to provide a buffer colony against the Spanish in the Floridas and partly to provide an asylum for prisoners in England whose only crime had been indebtedness. This model colony prohibited slavery and rum and limited holdings to 50 acres—restrictive conditions that stunted its growth during the twenty years it remained a private colony. Thereafter, as provided by the original charter, it reverted to the Crown. The idealistic laws were repealed, and the first main development of the colony took place.

ENGLISH EMIGRATION

The little seventeenth-century English nation seems to have achieved the impossible in establishing itself on the long coastline from Maine to South Carolina when one considers that this took place during a century of furious political, social, economic, religious, and military strife at home. Actually, however, it is within the context of this domestic disruption that the great English success on the American mainland is to be understood. Most importantly, the disruption provided the English colonies with an abundant population such as the Dutch had been unable to entice to New Netherland and the much more populous France could not attract to Quebec. Religious discontent, and to a lesser degree economic discontent, populated New England during the absolutist rule of Charles I and the harshly "Romish" regime of Archbishop of Canterbury William Laud.

The Puritan ascendancy in England during the next generation ended the impulse to emigrate to New England, but in turn it served to double the population of Virginia from 15,000 to 30,000 via a new migration which included mainly yeomen and mechanics escaping disorganized conditions in England. This subsequent migration included also a sprinkling of aristocratic Cavaliers. The aristocratic Randolphs established themselves in Virginia during this period, as did the Washingtons. Then, following the restoration of the Stuarts, Pennsylvania gained much of its population from religious refugees, not only from England but also from the Germanies, and so, to a greater or lesser extent, did all the colonies south of New England.

England was not the only nation of Europe that contained discontented subjects, but the English, unlike any other colonizing power, combined persecution at home with toleration abroad. At a time when Catholic subversives at home were being drawn, quartered, and disemboweled before shrieking mobs, Queen Elizabeth was contemplating a Roman Catholic colony in America where English Catholics would be free from persecution and whereby she would be rid of potential enemies of the Crown. The French did not let the potentially subversive Huguenots emigrate to Quebec, nor did the Spanish permit their Jews and Protestants to escape to Spanish America. The English were alone in this tolerant policy, and the result was a thriving population of about 250,000 in the English American colonies by the close of the seventeenth century.

THE ENGLISH REBELLION

The outbreak of the English Great Rebellion in 1642 came in the nick of time to preserve the Massachusetts commonwealth in its independent position. In 1636 Charles I took legal steps to have the Massachusetts charter annulled. He won the court case, but the Massachusetts General Court refused to abide by the decision. The Crown replied by appointing Sir Ferdinando Gorges, a man with large experience in the colonizing of America, as governor general of New England. Gorges had not yet reached there, however, when the rebellion broke out, and soon a Puritan leader, Oliver Cromwell, emerged who had much "pity" for New England and left it in possession of its autonomy.

In a notable instance of New England independence, the colonies of Massachusetts, Plymouth, Connecticut, and New Haven founded the New England Confederation in 1643 on the basis of no authority from England. Organized in defense against the French, the Dutch, and the Indians, the confederation defeated the Narragansett Indians, concluded a treaty with New Netherland, and adjudicated various boundary disputes. It was weakened from the first by intercolonial jealousies, however, and with the revocation of the Massachusetts charter in 1684 it became substantially inoperative, though it continued to exist, theoretically at least, until 1691.

In Virginia the English rebellion resulted in the Royalist Sir William Berkeley's being temporarily deposed as governor, and three Puritans followed him in office during the interregnum. But the Puritan government in England did not stir itself to get rid of Berkeley as a citizen of Virginia or to support the Puritans who followed him. The pro-Royalist assembly refused to be dissolved and instead increased its authority.

In Maryland the English rebellion was the occasion for a rising of Protestants under William Claiborne against the Catholic leadership. The insurgents were in control of the colony for several years, but failed to receive substantial English support, and Lord Baltimore soon regained authority. In 1654 revolt broke out again. The proprietary governor was deposed, and the Toleration Act was repealed. In 1657, however, a personal appeal to Cromwell by Lord Baltimore resulted in the return of his proprietary authority and reenactment of the Toleration Act. Cromwell did envision a "Western Design" to protestantize America, especially in the West Indies, and as a result Jamaica was captured from the Spanish. Beyond that little was done, however, as events absorbed Cromwell's energies in Europe.

THE IMPERIAL SYSTEM

Pressure from Dutch competition in the carrying trade during the period of Cromwellian authority meanwhile resulted in the Navigation Act of 1651. The first general law controlling colonial commerce, the act excluded from trade within the empire the ships of foreign nations. No provision was made for enforcement, however, and the law was widely evaded. In 1660, following the Restoration, a further Navigation Act confirmed the prohibition of foreign ships and restricted to trade within the empire certain "enumerated articles," including tobacco and indigo. In 1663 the Staple Act was passed requiring that all foreign commodities destined for the colonies be landed first in England. In 1668 a Council of Trade was created; in 1675 it was supplanted by a further supervisory agency, the Lords of Trade. Overworked members of the Privy Council, the Lords of Trade were distracted from their responsibilities to the American colonies. Their one main achievement was the creation of the plan for the Dominion of New England.

THE DOMINION OF NEW ENGLAND

English pressure against New England was resumed in 1676, when Edward Randolph was sent to Boston to investigate charges of violations of the Navigation Acts and to consider doing something about the government of Massachusetts before "all hopes of it may be hereafter lost." Following Randolph's hostile report, legal proceedings against Massachusetts resulted in the revocation of its charter in 1684. Thereafter it was governed as a royal colony.

Plans for consolidating New England under central royal authority were worked out, and in 1686 Sir Edmund Andros arrived as governor general of the resulting Dominion of New England. A year later Connecticut, New York, and New Jersey were added to it. No provisions were made for elective assemblies, and Andros prohibited town meetings, except for one meeting annually to elect selectmen and assess property for tax purposes. His efforts to consolidate the region were not altogether effective, but the opposition was even less so, until the coming of the Glorious Revolution in England in 1688.

In 1688, the openly Catholic King James II was driven from the country in a bloodless revolution, and Parliament appointed the Protestant leader of the Dutch Republic, William of Orange, and his English wife, Mary, King and Queen of England. This assertion of parliamentary supremacy was amplified by, among other things, the passage of the Bill of Rights, limiting the power of the King.

The result in America was a series of little glorious revolutions and the passage of a series of colonial bills of rights, all of which the English Privy Council set aside. In Boston, Andros, Randolph, and other dominion officials were jailed, and a government was created which restored the old charter and pledged allegiance to William and Mary. In New York, the Andros administration, headed by Gov. Francis Nicholson, was overthrown in a rebellion led by a German immigrant, Jacob Leisler, who was apparently motivated largely by anti-Catholic sentiment. In Maryland the delay of Lord Baltimore in acknowledging William and Mary led to the overthrow of his authority by a Protestant Association, which controlled the colony for two years. It appeared to many, especially in New England, that a new age was at hand, when "our glorious deliverer," William III, would usher in a new age of liberty.

A good many such expectations were disappointed. Massachusetts was retained as a royal colony, although only the governor was royally appointed and not the magistrates. In New York Leisler was executed and a royal governor appointed in his place. In the long run the most profound impact of the Glorious Revolution upon intercolonial relations probably was that it created an abiding imperial misunderstanding. The English at home saw the revolution of 1688 as vindicating the principle of parliamentary supremacy, throughout the colonies as well as in England. The colonists in America, who had staged their own little revolutions, saw them as vindicating the principle of legislative supremacy, including the supremacy of their own provincial assemblies. This misunderstanding between the homeland and the colonies continued into the eighteenth century until it was settled by the American Revolution.

BIBLIOGRAPHY FOR
CHAPTER 2

Clarance Ver Steeg, The Formative Years, 1607–1763 (1964)
C. M. Andrews, Our Earliest Colonies (1959)
Bradley Chapin, Early America (1968)
George Langson, Pilgrim Colony (1966)
Alan Simpson, Puritanism in Old and New England (1955)
Edmund Morgan, Visible Saints (1965) and The Puritan Dilemma: The
    Story of John Winthrop (1958)
W. F. Craven, The Colonies in Transition, 1660–1713 (1968)
Verner Crane, The Southern Frontier, 1670–1732 (1929)
F. B. Tolles, Quakers and the Atlantic Community (1960)

CHAPTER 3

COLONIAL EXPANSION

THE IMPERIAL ECONOMY

England at the turn of the eighteenth century possessed about two dozen colonies in America, and of these the mainland colonies were by no means the most prized. Sugar had by then supplanted gold and silver as the world's most valuable commodity, more valuable than ever had been those spices of the East that led to America's discovery and exploration. The tremendous expansion of sugar production was continually outrun by the demand, and great fortunes were to be made on small lots of sugar cane—profits to the English Crown, as well as to the planter, that diminished other colonial wealth by comparison. The English settled St Kitts, the first of their sugar islands, in 1623. Barbados was settled several years later, and then additional small islands such as Nevis and Montserrat. Admiral William Penn, father of Pennsylvania's founder, captured Jamaica, largest of the English Caribbean possessions, in 1655.

The West Indian planter tended to think of himself as an Englishman away from home who would eventually return to the homeland, purchase land in the country, and take the seat in Parliament to which his new landed estate would virtually entitle him. Planters in Virginia and South Carolina thought likewise in the early stages of colonization perhaps, but they were clearly no longer of that mind by the middle of the eighteenth century. This contrast in outlook came from the Virginians' and Carolinians' being attached to a new continent as the West Indian planters were not.

The West Indian planters consolidated their holdings into fewer and larger plantations and soon came to the limit of their opportunities; the continental planters, constantly extending their holdings, did not begin to see the end of the opportunities lying westward. Early English West Indian history followed a course similar to that of the English mainland colonies, including defiant Puritanism in religion and defiant democracy in politics, but with the completion of

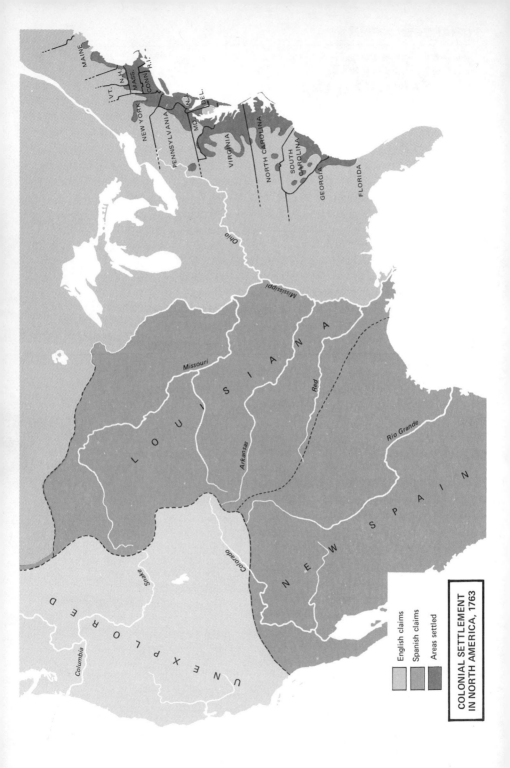

COLONIAL SETTLEMENT
IN NORTH AMERICA, 1763

English claims

Spanish claims

Areas settled

MAINE

N.H.

VT.

MASS.

R.I.

CONN.

NEW YORK

PENNSYLVANIA

N.J.

DEL.

MD.

VIRGINIA

NORTH CAROLINA

SOUTH CAROLINA

GEORGIA

FLORIDA

Ohio

Mississippi

Missouri

L O U I S I A N A

Arkansas

Red

Rio Grande

N E W   S P A I N

Colorado

Snake

Columbia

U N E X P L O R E D

settlement and the consolidations of plantations, all this changed. The slave population increased, the white population decreased, and a good many of the most successful planters did in fact go home to England.

One result of this tendency was a rising West Indian political strength in England in the eighteenth century. By mid-century more than forty members of Parliament had a vested interest in West Indian sugar and therefore in any legislation that would be to its benefit. The tobacco planters of the Chesapeake and the rice planters of South Carolina had no such representation, not to speak of the farmers in the mainland areas which produced little that the English government thought to be of value. In the imperial scheme, therefore, the mainland colonies in the eighteenth century were almost bound to get the worst of it, however much the English government might intend to be fair all around.

The most egregious example of this favoritism was the Molasses Act of 1733, which, among other things, placed a prohibitive tax on molasses imported to the mainland from the non-English West Indies. The purpose of the tax was not to protect the molasses trade of the English West Indies, for these colonies used up their own molasses production in their own rum industry. Its purpose was to deprive New England, and especially "mobbish Boston," of the molasses necessary to compete with the West Indian rum industry on the mainland rum market. This striking example of partiality in the imperial system was softened, characteristically, by the fact that little was done to enforce it.

MERCANTILISM

England, in common with other colonizing nations, attempted to govern its colonies according to a set of notions that go by the name of mercantilism. During the three-quarters of a century before the Revolutionary War, England and France were at war with each other almost half the time, and mercantilism was essentially economic warfare. The agricultural and industrial revolutions had not yet demonstrated their ways of increasing productivity, and it was therefore assumed that a nation could substantially increase its riches only at the expense of another nation or through colonial acquisitions. Colonies should be so regulated as to prevent their most valuable products from escaping into foreign hands, and most particularly into enemy hands in time of war. Colonies should further serve to make the empire as a whole self-sufficient, for purposes of national security, by producing raw materials not available at home. On the other hand, colonies should not injure the economy of the homeland by duplication and competition.

So far as the mainland was concerned, South Carolina produced rice, which was not grown in England, and, on the basis of bounties paid by England, indigo for dyes. Virginia and Maryland produced tobacco, which was prized on the world market; therefore the Chesapeake received special economic consideration, including a prohibition against tobacco growing in England. Newfoundland served admirably in the fishing industry, which was additionally prized as the nursery of the British Navy. For the rest there was not so much to be said from the English point of view. North Carolina and New England produced naval stores—pitch, tar, and timber—which served to strengthen British sea power; and the middle colonies of New York, New Jersey, and Pennsylvania grew the food and raised the horses needed in the colonies to the south that were devoting their attention to cultivating the prized staple commodities. Each area had its part to play in the imperial economy. But to English eyes the parts played by New England and the middle colonies were relatively humble ones, and increasingly in the eighteenth century, these areas came to engage in manufacturing pursuits that competed with English interests.

The effort to regulate all for the good of the whole which began with the Navigation Act of 1651 continued into the eighteenth century. The Navigation Act of 1660 originally prohibited the export from the empire of sugar, tobacco, cotton, and dyestuffs. Later rice, molasses, naval stores, beaver skins, furs, and copper were added. Then, as the colonies increased in population, Parliament enacted a new kind of mercantilist legislation to regulate their economic activities. Initially important as sources of raw materials, the colonies became important as markets for English manufacturers; when this happened, laws were passed discouraging the colonists from making for themselves what they would otherwise buy from England.

In 1699 the Woolens Act was passed, prohibiting intercolonial commerce in woolen goods. In 1732 the Hat Act was passed prohibiting intercolonial commerce in hats. In 1750 the Iron Act was passed prohibiting the construction of new slitting and rolling mills, plating forges, and iron furnaces. These acts naturally annoyed the colonists, but apparently they did not feel the need to obey them. Indeed, the assemblies of Massachusetts, New York, and Pennsylvania passed legislation encouraging the construction of new iron mills after the parliamentary prohibition had gone into effect.

In an effort to enforce its economic regulations, Parliament in 1696 passed a new Navigation Act giving greater power and responsibilities to customs officers and naval officers in America and imposing fines upon colonial governors who failed to enforce the laws. In the same year the Lords Commissioners of Trade and Plantations, known as the Board of Trade, were created as an advisory board of Privy Councilors and English merchants to oversee imperial trade. This agency gave comprehensive and detailed attention to colonial affairs, and Treasury officials, Admiralty officers, the War Office, and the Secretary of State for the Southern Department all concerned themselves with colonial matters in one connection or another.

Altogether, however, it amounted to something less than a comprehensive and effective system. During the first half of the eighteenth century the English government proceeded on the assumption that its imperial laws were not really enforceable and that anyway, things were going along all right as they were. This was the spirit behind the policy, associated with England's first Prime Minister, Robert Walpole, known as "salutary neglect." Under this dispensation colonists obeyed or violated regulations pretty much as it suited them.

THE COLONIAL ECONOMY

The great majority of mainland colonists made their livings by farming, and from frozen Maine to sultry South Carolina America offered a wider range of agricultural pursuits than Europe provided. Agriculturally the colonies were divided into rather distinct regions: timbered and rocky New England; the fertile bread colonies of New York, Pennsylvania, New Jersey, and Delaware, where the main production was foodstuffs and livestock; the Chesapeake region of Maryland and Virginia, concentrating on tobacco; the South Carolina rice fields; and the backcountry, including most of North Carolina and the western areas of the colonies generally, which engaged mainly in subsistence farming.

Richest of all these farming areas were the rice fields of South Carolina. Slave labor was the indispensable basis there from the first, since the wretched, lethal conditions in those malarial swamps did not invite any workers who had a choice in the matter. Rice plantations were found to be most efficiently operated on a relatively small scale, and the major planters owned a number of these, each with its slave force under the direction of an overseer.

To escape the fevers, those who could afford to do so withdrew for six months of the year to the city of Charleston, which became an extraordinarily exclusive and prideful community. By contrast to the rich rice swamps, the South Carolina backcountry provided for little more than subsistence farming until the introduction of cotton, and the colony was divided between "opulent and lordly planters, poor and spiritless whites, and vile slaves." Charleston supported also a merchant aristocracy, and the planters themselves engaged in commercial enterprises.

In good times tobacco might be profitably grown in the Chesapeake region both on small farms and on vast plantations, but as a hand crop it required much labor, and therefore only slave owners did really well with it. The amount of land was less important than the amount of labor, for the acreage devoted to its planting was small, even on large plantations. Its culture rapidly exhausted the soil, however, and land-hungry Virginia planters acquired up to as much as several hundred thousand acres of land.

Unlike the South Carolina planters, the Virginia planters lived on their land and generally superintended the operation of their own plantations. The plantations were directly connected with England by water transportation, and the planters dealt directly with English factors. The idea, later current in the South, that a gentleman did not engage in trade was not current among the colonial planter gentry. No need for a middleman existed in colonial Virginia and Maryland, and therefore no towns of any size developed in the region.

New York and Pennsylvania were economically the most varied of the colonies. Albany, New York, remained the fur-trading center it had been since the Dutch had enlisted the services of the Iroquois nations. Pennsylvania led in the iron industry, which existed to some extent in all colonies. The lumber industry was important throughout the area, and Philadelphia and New York City were engaged in a wide variety of manufactures. Grain, horses, and cattle for the Southern mainland colonies and the West Indies made up the greatest part of the export trade.

Throughout most of New England, except for limited areas such as the Connecticut Valley, the land was suitable only for subsistence farming, and those who were ambitious to rise above the level of plain if ample subsistence moved into areas of activity other than farming. Forests were among New England's most obvious assets, and shipbuilding early became a leading industry, and with it fishing and shipping. New England constructed ships for English purchasers suitable for transatlantic voyages. New England merchants, however, concentrated their energies in the coastal and West Indian trade, where geographically they held the advantage over their English competition.

The idea that there existed a triangular trade by which New England merchants traded rum for slaves in Africa, slaves for molasses in the West Indies, and molasses for rum in Boston is a myth, based upon a very few instances of such a voyage. Rhode Island merchants did engage in a fairly sizable slave trade, but on the whole New England merchants, such as the Browns of Providence and the Hancocks of Boston, preferred the substantial and safer returns to be found closer to home.

Farming generally, and frontier farming especially, was conditioned by the abundance of land, the lack of profitable markets, and the medieval farming methods that the American farmers brought with them from England. Foreign observers were almost uniformly severe in their criticism of colonial farming, reserving their praise for non-English settlers such as the Swedes and the Germans. From the Indians the Americans learned not only to grow corn, which remained the staff of life throughout the colonial and well into the national period, but also to avoid the necessity of clearing the land by simply girdling the trees and allowing them to rot by themselves and blow down. Intertillage—the growing of a variety of crops in the same fields—was also adopted from the Indians. But beyond what he was taught by the Indians the frontier farmer did not go far. Draft animals and farm implements were rare. Plows were of wood and did no more than scratch the surface. Owing to the easy availability of land the farmers stripped the soil with no concern for saving its fertility until finally, by the close of the colonial period, soil exhaustion in the tobacco region did produce a notable crop of scientific farmers, including George Washington and Thomas Jefferson.

Foreign observers bestowed upon colonial cities some of the praise they withheld from colonial farms. The spectacle of a developed metropolis in the American wilderness rarely failed to evoke surprised admiration. By the middle of the eighteenth century Philadelphia had supplanted Boston as the major colonial city, and its broad and busy streets and handsome architecture were matters for wonder. Philadelphia was founded in 1683; by the eve of the Revolution, with a population of more than 30,000, it was about as large as any city in Great Britain except London. In population New York followed Philadelphia at the close of the colonial period with a population of about 22,000, and after it came Boston with 17,000. Although Boston had decisively lost its standing as the metropolis of the colonies, New England contained a much larger urban population than any other region, with a number of lesser cities and towns, of which Newport was the largest. These cities in the wilderness gave evidence of a complexity and maturity in American colonial society which the English government failed to take into account.

IMMIGRATION

The most important colonial developments during the first half of the eighteenth century went largely unnoticed in England because they caused no imperial crises. The main change was the change in size. Between 1700 and 1775 the population of the colonies increased roughly ten times, from about 250,000 to about 2,500,000. During the same period the population of England increased by less than 30 percent. On the eve of the Revolution Englishmen at home still outnumbered those in the mainland colonies 3 to 1, but colonial leaders were aware that the day would come when America would outstrip England, and they were made the more confident and assertive by their awareness of America's growing importance within the empire.

In addition to the natural increase in population—in a farming age when large families were economic assets—America gained heavily by two waves of free immigration, one from northern Ireland and one from Germany and Switzerland, and by the great increase in the African slave trade beginning in the last quarter of the seventeenth century. During the seventeenth century thousands of lowland Scots had been settled in northern Ireland for the purpose of bringing it more firmly under Protestant English control, but as Presbyterians these Scotch-Irish were made to suffer the same political and legal disabilities as did the native Celtic Catholics. Beyond that, again in common with the native Irish, the Scotch-Irish suffered from discriminatory economic legislation, especially the Woolens Act of 1699. Unlike Massachusetts or Pennsylvania, Ireland was close enough to England that the Navigation Acts could be enforced, and with devastating effect. The consequences were mass starvation and an eighteenth-century migration to America of perhaps 300,000, beginning in the second decade of the century.

The first main migration was to New England, but the stony welcome received by the Irish Presbyterians persuaded later groups to choose the middle and Southern colonies. New York welcomed them as New England did not, for the large landholders were eager to attract tenant farmers, but New York gained a bad reputation for victimizing the immigrants and for preventing them from acquiring their own land.

The most hospitable port, and the one through which most of the Scotch-Irish passed, was Philadelphia. From there many were sent to the Southern colonies, while others took advantage of the favorable Pennsylvania land policy to acquire farms to the west. Their westward advance was halted by the Appalachian Mountains and the Indians who occupied them. Coming up against these mountains the settlers turned southward and, beyond the reach of the seaboard government, took up land without much regard for the matter of legal titles.

Migration from Germany began in the late seventeenth century in response to the promotional work of William Penn, but the large-scale migration from both Germany and Switzerland began with that of the Scotch-Irish in the second decade of the eighteenth century. Many of the Germans were refugees from religious persecution, and these tended to arrive in religious congregations under the leadership of their pastors, as had the New England Puritans originally. Like the Scotch-Irish the Germans settled in all the colonies south of New England, but they concentrated in Pennsylvania where they were able to acquire land on attractive terms. By the close of the colonial period they made up about one-third of the entire Pennsylvania population.

Held together by their distinctive language and religious beliefs, they formed closed societies of their own within the dominant Anglo-American society. The Scotch-Irish, lacking the barriers of language and religion, were less exclusive. But even they were "clannish, contentious, and hard to get along with," in the view of the older settlers, and did not readily assimilate.

In addition to these main waves of migration, American society was increased by a small but significant influx of Welsh Quakers, French Huguenots, and Iberian Jews, and the latter two groups exerted a considerable influence on the character of the colonial cities where they were concentrated.

By the eve of the Revolution, as a consequence of these population movements, there existed in all the colonies from New York to Georgia a separate western society, largely non-English, certainly nonmembers of the established Church of England, and generally at odds with the seaboard community over matters of religion, taxation, representation, and Indian defense. Even before they had won their independence from England, the English colonies had acquired their own colonial regions, and in a number of cases these were suffering many of the same abuses that the seaboard communities complained of suffering in the hands of the British government.

SLAVES FROM AFRICA

By far the largest group of immigrants—several times as numerous as all other immigrants together in the eighteenth century—were the African slaves. The first twenty of them were brought to Jamestown aboard a Dutch vessel in 1619, and by mid-century there were 300 in the colony. The legal status of these Africans was at first unclear, but gradually, over a forty-year period, the laws of Virginia adapted themselves to the institution of slavery, and legislation was passed encouraging its increase. By 1671 there were 2,000 slaves in the colony together with 6,000 indentured servants.

Early in the eighteenth century the ratio of blacks to whites in Virginia stood at 2 to 3. The black population continued to increase more rapidly than the white down to the close of the American Revolution, when slaves may for a time have been in the majority in Virginia. Then, with the collapse of the tobacco crop, the trend reversed itself. By the eve of the Civil War Virginia's 500,000 slaves made up about one-third of its population. Virginia remained the state with the largest absolute slave population, but the states of the Deep South all came close to overtaking it.

South Carolina had black slave labor from the start, and by the second decade of the eighteenth century the slaves in the Carolina low country far outnumbered freemen. The stoop labor in hot, humid, malarial rice fields under the eye of hired overseers was too abhorrent for any free labor system, and slavery thrived in South Carolina more luxuriantly than anywhere else in the colonies.

During the eighteenth century the supply of slaves tended to exceed the demand, and after independence all thirteen states took early occasion to prohibit the African trade. Georgia and South Carolina later reopened the trade, but after 1808 it was prohibited by national law. Slave buyers thereafter were obliged to rely on the interstate slave trade or on slaves smuggled from Africa. The slave trade was an aspect of the peculiar institution that Southerners themselves preferred to overlook. Much was said of the advantages of Christianity and civilization awaiting the blacks who survived the middle passage, but of the voyage itself as little was said as possible.

The status of the slave was ambiguous, for he was at the same time a human being and a piece of property. As a Southern judge explained the matter, a slave was "not in the condition of a horse. . . . He had mental capacities, and an immortal principle in his nature." The law did not "extinguish his high-born nature nor deprive him of many rights which are inherent in man." The only right that received clear legal recognition, however, was the right to life. An owner who killed his slave was a murderer in the eyes of the law, and the law sometimes dealt with him as such. If the death was the accidental consequence of brutal discipline, the master might still be sentenced for murder. But the slave could not hold property, marry, or make any form of contract without his master's permission. And if he made a contract with his master, to work out his freedom for instance, his master was not bound to honor the contract when the terms had been satisfied.

Indians had been enslaved by English as well as Spanish settlers, but the Indian slaves had proved unmanageable, and efforts to acquire them had gradually ceased. It was not so much that the Indians rebelled against slavery itself as that they rebelled against a methodical schedule of work under any circumstances. Slavery was widely practiced among American Indian nations, just as it was among African nations. But the idea of private property, including private ownership of slaves, was alien to the Indians, just as was the work ethic of the American slave owner.

Africans, on the other hand, were familiar with both the concept of private property and that of communal ownership of property. Furthermore, agriculture, manufacturing, and trade were pursued in recognizably similar ways in the American colonies and much of west Africa. The African was equipped by his African experience to understand what was expected of him in the American system, however little he might be inclined to follow through.

To the extent that it was possible to eradicate the African heritage of these slaves, the system was designed to do so. Slaves had customarily been separated from tribal associates in the process of their enslavement and sale in Africa, and in America they were resold as miscellaneous individuals into a new social system. The separation of mothers from children was a routine aspect of the slave trade, and thereafter any fraternizing of groups of slaves was viewed with suspicion by owners and overseers. The family was the basic unity of society throughout most of Africa, but under the American slave system the family received no general recognition and protection. Efforts to christianize the slaves were highly successful, and thereafter black ministers tended to discourage their people from un-Christian practices such as the performance of indecorous traditional African dances.

But it was evidently not possible to eradicate the African heritage, which flourished richly in the most thoroughly black regions of the Caribbean and, in modified forms, wherever blacks were assembled together in the American colonies. Down to the Revolution, slavery existed in all the English colonies in America, but except for limited areas in the North, such as parts of Long Island, sizable black work forces were limited to the region from Maryland and Delaware southward. It was especially in this region that society as a whole was influenced both by the institution of slavery and by black culture, as that culture reshaped itself in white America.

The most creative contributions of black culture to American society were in music. Jefferson wrote of the blacks in *Notes on Virginia* that "in music they are more generally gifted than the whites, with accurate ears for a tune and time, and they have been found capable of imagining a small catch. . . . The instrument proper to them is the *banjar,* which they brought hither from Africa." Black slaves created work songs for themselves in the fields and hymns for their religious services. Although Negro ministers might oppose African dances on moral grounds, music that encouraged work and religion was approved of by white owners and black ministers alike.

Slaves introduced what Jefferson called the *banjar* together with the bones (polished small rib bones of sheep held between the fingers and played like castanets). Slave groups worked up routines accompanied by banjo and bones and other makeshift instruments. These became a form of entertainment patronized by plantation owners. In the course of the nineteenth and twentieth centuries, during the eras of the minstrel show and of ragtime and jazz and swing and soul music, black America was to exert a powerful and enduring influence not only on American society but on Western culture as a whole.

The conditions of slavery varied widely, depending on job and region—domestic servants in New York or Boston, field hands in Virginia, and those in South Carolina rice fields had very different lives—and depending on the will of the individual master. Whether slaves were better or worse off in Anglo-America than in Latin America is a subject that has been much discussed. In general it appears that the Anglo-Americans had greater racial consciousness than the Latin Americans. Miscegenation was taboo (although commonplace) in the English colonies to an extent that it was not in Latin American societies. On the other hand, humanitarianism may have been a greater influence in Anglo-American slave societies than in those of Latin America, at least from the Revolutionary era on.

Still, the system remained that of slavery, and ultimately it was the whip, or the fear of the whip, that made the system go. Good business sense might deter the planter from inflicting crippling punishments. Compassion might move him to moderate discipline at the cost of his profits. The planter might place the slave on a modified wage basis to give him greater incentive or ultimately give him his freedom. But fear, and most particularly fear of the whip, was the indispensable principle. It is true that this rule also applied to a considerable extent to white indentured servitude, but indentured servants were not racially degraded, their servitude was not perpetual, and escape from intolerable conditions was for them a more practical possibility than it was for the black slave.

COLONIAL CLASS SYSTEMS

Above the level of slavery and indentured servitude, American society was yeasty with democratic tendencies, by British standards, to the continual distress of the ruling classes. Eighteenth-century colonial society looked to England for its patterns of behavior, including that of New England, which by then had lost much of the impulse to maintain a New Zion. English society was aristocratic, and accordingly American society was also aristocratic to the limited extent that highly unfavorable conditions permitted. Americans thought naturally in terms of ranks and stations, and since most of America was rural, it was the rural English class system that was emulated. To begin with, however, class lines were less rigid in England than on the European continent, and in America they were much harder to maintain than in England.

Attempts to create a formal aristocracy if not a nobility were made in upper New England, New York, Maryland, Virginia, and the Carolinas, but never with any great success. The nearest approaches to success were in New York, with its great landed estates, and in South Carolina, with its rich rice lands. When Lord Saye and Sele and other Puritan aristocrats offered to emigrate to New England if the government could be reformed to provide for a hereditary house of lords, John Cotton was delegated the task of explaining to them that there was only one upper class of gentlemen in Massachusetts, of which he and its other leaders were members, and it was not intended that another class should be raised above them.

On the other hand, in Massachusetts as elsewhere, the attempt was made to observe fine class distinctions. The Massachusetts General Court in 1651 prohibited "excess in Apparel . . . especially amongst people of mean condition," going on to express its "utter detestation and dislike that men or women of mean condition should take upon them the garb of Gentlemen." The difficulty remained of deciding who fit where. In every settled community there existed the "better sort," consisting of planters and merchants and, in New England, the ministry; beneath these "gentle folk" were the "middling sort," yeomen, small merchants, and successful craftsmen; then came the "plain people," the subsistence farmers and artisans; beneath them were the "meaner sort," indentured servants, tenant farmers, drifters; and finally, at the bottom of the scale, there were the Negroes, virtually all of whom were enslaved in the Northern as well as the Southern colonies.

Titles were of importance to people in fixing these distinctions, but they could not be exactly applied. "Esquire" was a title reserved for councilors and magistrates. "Squire" generally referred to a broader group including justices of the peace. "Gent." followed the name of a larger classification of members of the well-born ruling social group, often including ministers. "Goodman" was the customary form of address for the substantial yeoman or artisan, with "Goodwife" for his wife. "Mr." was a decided cut above "Goodman" as a mode of address, and in at least one case a Bostonian was officially deprived of the right to be addressed as "Mr." in punishment for a criminal offense. The established churches were among the strongest supports to class distinctions, often ranking the community precisely by order of seating arrangement.

Politically, most of the colonies were relatively democratic by English standards, although this varied widely in the colonies as indeed it also did in England. The vote was limited to free white male property holders, the assumption being universally held that only those persons had a right to take part in the political life of the community who had a "stake in society." The property qualification ranged from 25 to 100 acres in most colonies, although in South Carolina it was 300. Personal property met the requirement in some colonies. There were further restrictions based on religion, especially against Catholics and Jews, and there were other antidemocratic circumstances such as distance to the polling places, which might be as much as a day's journey from the voter's residence, plural voting, and the practice of voting by voice.

PROVINCIAL POLITICS

Apparently, however, the election laws were less undemocratic than was the spirit of the people. The voting restrictions do not seem to have been seriously regarded in many areas; Governor Hutchinson of Massachusetts complained that "there is scarce ever any inquiry" into the qualifications of the voters. But the fact was that the overwhelming majority of the people did not vote, whether or not they were qualified to do so. Consistently in Massachusetts and Connecticut before and during the Revolution, the major issues were decided by about 2 percent of the population, or about one out of eight legal voters. Men in colonial America, unlike their descendants in the nineteenth century, were willing to leave political matters to their betters.

Colonial political history in the eighteenth century was a continuous struggle between the assemblies and the governors, with the advantage generally going to the assemblies. Despite the authority and social prestige of the governors and the power they received from patronage and from the support of their councils, their fiats were often nullified in practice. The distance from England was a source of weakness, and the viceroys were subjected to strong pressures not to violate the feelings of the best people of the community. In most of the royal colonies the governors were subjected to economic pressures as well. Except in Georgia and Virginia the governor was dependent for his salary upon grants of money by the assembly, and the assemblies followed the practice of paying the governor in annual grants in order to limit his independence.

Within the assemblies no clear permanent party lines developed during the colonial period. In New England the assemblies tended to divide on the issue of paper money, between the large merchant interests, against it, and the farmers and lesser merchants, for it. In New York politics remained chiefly a struggle for power among the leading families, with New York City providing a disturbingly democratic element. In Pennsylvania the Quakers, with German support, controlled the assembly until the middle of the century against the proprietors, who by then had joined the Anglican Church. In contrast to New York, Pennsylvania was democratic in the countryside and oligarchic in Philadelphia. In the tobacco colonies the division was chiefly between the large and small planters, and in South Carolina the chief contests were between the merchants and the major planters, the plain people being largely unrepresented.

Most of the colonial assemblies, in their turn, experienced growing western opposition to seaboard control in the decades before the Revolution. In three colonies, Pennsylvania, New York, and North Carolina, the opposition broke into active if ineffective insurrection. Latent western opposition in Massachusetts later erupted into Shays' Rebellion, during the period of the Articles of Confederation. Western resentment fed on complaints of overtaxation, support of an established church most westerners did not attend, underrepresentation, unreasonable legal expenses, graft, government influence in land speculation, and inadequate Indian defense.

In New York the tenant farmers rose in arms against their landlords to be suppressed swiftly by British redcoats. In Pennsylvania the unwillingness of the assembly to defend the frontiers inspired the abortive march of Paxton's Boys on Philadelphia. In North Carolina the western Regulators were defeated at the Battle of Alamance, but they were not without their effect on North Carolina politics. One result was the manifestation of strong loyalist sentiment in western North Carolina during the Revolution. Another was the development of militant democratic sentiment among the westerners, a sentiment which the eastern Whigs felt obliged to appease in drawing up the first state constitution.

Western South Carolina enjoyed no regular government at all to the very eve of the Revolution. Only in 1769, in response to desperate western appeals, did the South Carolina Assembly finally create four grossly underrepresented western counties. The aristocratic patriots of South Carolina, while fighting England in defense of their liberties, refused to make any substantial concessions to western demands. Elsewhere, however, eastern patriots seeking unity against England with the approach of the Revolution were willing to satisfy some of those grievances of westerners that were so embarrassingly similar to their own.

BIBLIOGRAPHY FOR CHAPTER 3

Clarance Ver Steeg, The Formative Years, 1607–1763 (1964)
L. B. Wright, The Cultural Life of the American Colonies (1957)
M. L. Hansen, The Atlantic Migration, 1607–1860 (1940)
G. L. Beer, The Old Colonial System (1912)
J. Pope-Hennessey, Sins of the Fathers (1967)—the colonial slave trade
Ola Winslow, Meetinghouse Hill (1952)—the New England community life
S. E. Morison, The Intellectual Life of Colonial New England (1956)
Carl and **Jessica Bridenbaugh,** Philadelphia in the Age of Franklin (1942)
Carl Bridenbaugh, Myths and Realities: Societies of the Colonial South
    (1952)
C. S. Sydnor, Gentlemen Freeholders (1952)
R. E. and **B. K. Brown,** Virginia, 1705–1786: Democracy or Aristocracy?
    (1964)
W. D. Jordan, White over Black (1968)

CHAPTER 4

THE IMPERIAL CRISIS

WARS WITH FRANCE

In bringing to the throne of England William of Orange, the archenemy of Louis XIV of France, the Glorious Revolution of 1688 marked the beginning of the so-called "second Hundred Years' War" between France and England—a series of wars including the War of the Spanish Succession, the Seven Years' War, the American Revolutionary War, and the wars of the French Revolution and finally terminating in 1815 in the defeat of Napoleon at Waterloo. These wars were fought out in Europe and around the globe, in Africa, India, the West Indies, and North America. It was in the context of this long Anglo-French struggle that the British government developed the policy toward its American colonies which led to the American Revolution. It was in the same context that the American revolutionists were able to secure the French support which was essential to their military success. And finally, it was in the same context that the victorious revolutionists were given the relative freedom from outside interference necessary for the establishment of the new nation.

France had gained its initial foothold on the North American mainland a year after the founding of Jamestown with the settlement of Quebec on the St. Lawrence River in 1608. Quebec was founded by soldiers and missionaries, and the history of French Canada thereafter was the history of soldiers, missionaries, and fur traders, rather than of settlers. Persecuted Frenchmen, the Huguenots, departed for America, but they went to the English rather than the French colonies. In 1689 there were not more than 20,000 Frenchmen in America, as compared with 200,000 or so in the English mainland colonies, and this disparity increased during the eighteenth century.

During time of war English colonists became reluctant militiamen who would only serve for short terms and who were untrained as soldiers. They proved themselves to be first-rate fighters on many occasions, but they often refused to fight beyond the boundaries of their own colony or during the seasons when they were needed on the farm. The unsoldierly conduct of many American militiamen during war was one of the reasons why the English government set forth with such confidence in 1775 to suppress the rebels. Military men who had fought in America advised the government that the colonials could be counted on to put up an ineffectual resistance.

The French empire in Canada followed the course geographically marked out for it, down the St. Lawrence River to Montreal and on to the Great Lakes. Then, following the rivers of the Ohio Valley, the French continued down the Mississippi, founding New Orleans and claiming a vast, undiscovered area of Louisiana for France.

The French settlements in the Ohio Valley were communities of farmer-soldiers, men who farmed chiefly as a means of supporting semi-military establishments. Concerned with fur trading rather than farming, the French colonists were in a better position than the English to win support from the Indians, and they strengthened this attachment by intermarriages. The Algonquin Indians were a great source of strength to the French. The Iroquois, by contrast, supported the English mainly because their Algonquin enemies were on the other side, and the Iroquois therefore proved much less dedicated allies during four wars with New France.

The first of these, King William's War, began in 1689, when William of Orange was crowned King of England. The world conflict of which this was a part was temporarily concluded in 1697. War was resumed in 1702, and the American phase, Queen Anne's War, was small-scale and sporadic on both sides. Aside from the border colonies of New England and the Carolinas, the colonials may hardly be said to have involved themselves.

Thirty years of peace followed the conclusion of Queen Anne's War in 1713. The next one, King George's War, 1740 to 1748, also was small-scale and inconclusive in America, except for one successful major campaign, the conquest of Louisbourg by a large New England force. The return of Louisbourg to France at the conclusion of hostilities served to dampen enthusiasm among the colonists for further such heroic exertions in the decisive war that was soon to come.

Unlike its predecessors, the French and Indian War—the American phase of Europe's Seven Years' War, 1756 to 1763—had its origins, not in a European declaration of war, but in conflict which developed between contending French and English colonials in the disputed Ohio Valley in 1754. From the beginning the scale of fighting in America was much greater than in any of the previous wars, and for the first three years the major victories were all on the side of the French.

Then the masterful William Pitt, as Prime Minister of England, took command of a conflict which had spread to the continent of Europe and to the subcontinent of India. European allies financed by England drew off French troops. The colonial and the English armies were both greatly augmented, and England moved on the offensive. On September 13, 1759, Quebec fell in the decisive battle of the war in America. Although the general war continued for four more years, the great battle between the forces of Wolfe and those of Montcalm, as it proved, settled the issue on the North American mainland.

At the close of the French and Indian War, for the first time in English colonial history, no major power arrayed itself along the English frontier. Until then the presence of the French enemy had created to some extent a colonial reliance upon English redcoats. The defeat of New France freed the colonists of this need for military support, and Britain removed the one force which had made the British connection essential to the colonials. "With the fall of Quebec," wrote the historian Francis Parkman, "began the history of the United States."

COLONIAL REORGANIZATION

At issue as the British brought the Seven Years' War to a victorious close in America was the question of whether to retain French Canada or the French sugar island of Guadaloupe at war's end, it being understood that one or the other would have to be returned to France. The issue was a dangerous one. "The having all North America to ourselves by acquiring Canada dazzles the eyes," wrote a "Gentleman from Guadaloupe" in 1761, "and blinds the understandings of the giddy and unthinking people . . . yet it is easy to discover that such a peace might ruin Britain. . . ." Indeed, to the gentleman from Guadaloupe the folly of creating a united North America was clear as day, for "such a country at such a distance could never remain long subject to Britain . . . they are always grumbling and complaining against Britain, even while they have the French to dread, what may they not be supposed to do if the French is no longer a check on them. . . ."

To this argument the affable American colonial agent in Britain, Benjamin Franklin, felt obliged to take exception. Such fears of American independence were groundless, he argued. On the contrary, the acquisition of Canada would serve to remove imperial stresses which already were beginning to appear. The opening of Canadian farmland, Franklin explained, would serve to consume colonial energies and so delay the day when declining agricultural opportunities might force Americans into lines of economic activity which would compete with English manufacturing and commercial interests.

After an extended debate Parliament, pressured by the West India sugar interests, which opposed bringing the rich French sugar island into the empire, returned Guadaloupe and retained Quebec. Thirteen years later, as the gentleman from Guadaloupe had predicted, the American colonists declared their independence from England. By that time some Englishmen were calling on their government to return Canada to France and "turn the French Indians loose" on the colonists again, but these men had become wise too long after the fact.

Guadaloupe would have brought immediate revenue to Britain. Canada brought heavy expenditures and these, moreover, to a government which already had gone deeply in debt to finance the most expensive war in its history. Nor did the removal of French power permit military economies to the extent anticipated, for the former Indian allies of France remained on the rampage, and England faced the expensive prospect of subduing the conquered regions.

The prospect was the more dolorous to members of Parliament in that the main source of revenue for the government remained the land tax, which bore with disproportionate weight upon members themselves. Naturally they were concerned to find some means of distributing the burden more equitably, and so they were led to consider taxing those American colonists who, as it turned out, had been the chief beneficiaries of the war. It had never been a part of the British mercantilist practice to supplement the national revenue through taxation of the colonists, and the Grenville administration, which assumed power in England in 1763, did not altogether admit to such a motive. It argued, rather, that the military helplessness of the colonies required Britain to retain troops in America and that, such being the case, it was entirely reasonable to have the colonists support through taxation a part of the burden of their own defense.

The time seemed propitious, in fact, for a general overhauling of the imperial system. In their contribution to the war effort the colonies had done much less than might reasonably have been expected of them. Worse than that, colonial merchants had extended the length of the war by trading briskly with the enemy throughout the conflict. On the other hand, the efforts of the British government under Pitt to exert greater control over the colonies and to suppress smuggling had provided valuable experience which could be made use of in time of peace.

Previously the Navigation Acts had been but indifferently enforced, partly because effective enforcement seemed to involve insuperable difficulties and prohibitive expenses. The fact that successful smugglers late in the war were making up to 4,000 percent profits, however, indicated the surprising extent to which this trade had been suppressed. Thus faced with serious postwar problems and at the same time armed with valuable wartime experience in meeting them, the British government set forth to put the whole empire in good operating order.

George III came to the throne in 1760, and it was he more than anyone else who was responsible for the new imperial policies which led to the Revolution. But until the Boston Tea Party offended him, George was not altogether unsympathetic to the colonial point of view. Until then he certainly did not associate himself with any aggressively coercive colonial policy. The trouble with George III was that he was much more concerned with small matters of domestic politics than with the great imperial problems and that he therefore neither informed himself thoroughly on imperial matters nor appointed able and well-informed men to carry out the new programs. It was his main purpose to recover the royal authority which his two predecessors had let pass into the hands of Parliament. Conceding the sovereignty of Parliament, he set forth to build a King's party in the House of Commons through which he could rule the nation.

Opposition to these royal pretensions came from various discordant factions led by ambitious and powerful lords and known as the Whigs. There was a certain Tory element in Parliament which always automatically voted on the side of the King, on the grounds that it was disloyal and blasphemous to do otherwise. To this group George III added enough followers to gain control of the House of Commons, by using the royal patronage, by conferring numerous titles, and by influencing elections, especially in the rotten boroughs where members were elected by a handful of votes. British politics under these circumstances were intensely personal, picayune, and not characteristically divided by great issues. Who got a local franchise was apt to seem more important at the moment than how to handle the Indian problem in America.

Upon coming to the throne in the midst of the war, George III dismissed the brilliant and experienced William Pitt as Prime Minister and started shuffling his cabinets busily. There was the Newcastle ministry until 1762, the Bute ministry until 1763, the Grenville ministry until 1765, the Rockingham ministry until 1766, and the Pitt-Grafton ministry until 1770. By that time George III, firmly in control, was able to place the pliant Lord North in office and keep him there until he was forced out by the disastrous conclusion of the American Revolution.

Of these men Pitt was much the best equipped to deal with the problems of empire. Unfortunately he was taken by seizures of insanity several months after assuming office and for some time thereafter took no part in the conduct of the government. George III himself was suffering the early stages of those recurring fits of madness which later on incapacitated him altogether, and a number of the Friends of America in Parliament, since they got drunk nightly on port wine, must have suffered terrible hangovers during debates. Because of these circumstances the American colonies did not receive the consideration their importance to England warranted.

INDIAN UPRISINGS

The most immediately pressing American concern at the close of the French and Indian War was the Indian problem. There were three main Indian language groups along the Anglo-American frontiers: Muskhogean, Algonquin, and Iroquois. The Muskhogean Indians occupied the Southern frontiers, and of the tribes in this group the Creek nation was the most formidable, occupying the territory from Georgia to the Mississippi. Too loosely organized for any effective counterthrust against the white colonists, the Creeks occasionally united even less effectively with the neighboring nations such as the Seminole, Catawba, Chickasaw, and Choctaw against the white invaders.

Later, however, during the Revolutionary era, the Creeks gained a remarkable leader in Alexander McGillivray, the son of a Scotch-Indian trader who, through the matrilineal system, could claim status as a full-blooded Creek. Accepting pay simultaneously from the English, the Spanish, and the Americans, McGillivray played one off against the other so effectively that he secured the sovereignty of the Creeks for a generation after the Northern tribes had been settled on reservations.

To the north the Algonquin Indians occupied most of Canada and the Ohio Valley and all of New England. Their firm alliance with the French had been secured early by the French interest in fur trading and the relative lack of French interest in farming. The traditional enemies of the Algonquins were the Iroquois confederacy of Cayuga, Mohawk, Oneida, Onondaga, and Seneca tribes in upper New York. The English inherited the alliance the Dutch fur traders had earlier made with the Iroquois, but they never succeeded in controlling their Indian allies as effectively as the French did theirs.

In 1763 the Algonquins found a leader in Pontiac, a chief of the Ottawas, and he was aided by the mystical Delaware Prophet, who envisioned a vast Indian confederacy extending across the language groupings. No alliance with the Southern Indians was achieved, and the fragmenting tendencies of tribal custom prevented Pontiac from holding his local alliance together for long. Northern Indians rose up in the Conspiracy of Pontiac, however, and in 1763 his warriors succeeded in capturing every English fort west of Fort Niagara but the one at Detroit.

The uprising was not put down until 1765. In the meantime a hastily prepared proclamation of 1763 was issued by George III dealing with the Indian problem as well as all the territory acquired from France. Civil governments were established in Quebec, East and West Florida, and the island of Grenada, and a line was drawn down through the Appalachian Mountains beyond which land was not to be granted and settlers were not to go.

The proclamation was protested by Americans on various grounds but most seriously on the ground that it deprived colonies of their rights to territories which were assigned them in their charters. Most directly affected were Virginians and Pennsylvanians, including Franklin and Washington, who had invested in land companies in the Ohio Valley. These objections were tempered, however, by the belief, which Washington shared with others, that the proclamation was no more than an emergency measure which would be rescinded when the crisis was past. Only later did it come to be looked upon as part of a comprehensive plan to coerce the colonies.

THE SUGAR ACT AND
THE STAMP ACT

Even before the Pontiac rising the English government had decided to maintain 10,000 troops in America for Indian defense and to maintain order among the newly acquired Spanish and French populations, and the government considered it reasonable to expect the American colonies to assume from a third to a half of the expenses involved. One means of achieving this was the added revenue that would derive from strict enforcement of the trade laws. The navy was given greater authority to inspect trading vessels, and crews were given half the prize money for the capture of smugglers.

The greatest source of revenue lost to the Treasury through smuggling was in the rarely collected tax on non-English molasses, and in 1764 the Sugar Act was passed to remedy this. The Sugar Act, which taxed a variety of commodities brought into the colonies from foreign areas, lowered the duty on molasses from 6d. per gallon to 3d. in order to permit the trade to continue, and then Parliament passed a series of enactments increasing rewards, facilitating searches and seizures, and providing legal immunities for enforcement officers.

The news of this act, according to Governor Bernard of Massachusetts, "caused a greater alarm in this country than the taking of Fort William Henry did in 1757." New England merchants were sure that the act would destroy their vital trade with the non-English West Indies, and they argued this point convincingly and at length in memorials to Parliament, amid deepening depression conditions. Similar memorials were sent by merchants from the middle colonies and from Charleston. The Massachusetts Assembly passed a resolution declaring the act to be a violation of the principle of no taxation without representation and calling for united colonial opposition to it.

The Massachusetts resolution was not effective in achieving its purpose because, in the first place, the act injured few economic interests in the colonies south of Pennsylvania and, in the second place, the merchants who were most directly concerned did not want to argue their case in the inflammatory terms of their rights as Englishmen. They were much happier appealing to the business sense of Parliament by demonstrating that large business losses would be suffered by England from the resulting decline in purchasing power in the American market for British goods. But while the merchants were waiting for their bread-and-butter arguments to sink home, the Sugar Act, according to James Otis of Massachusetts, "set people to thinking, in six months, more than they had done in their whole lives before."

Following the Sugar Act, Parliament passed the Colonial Currency Act, prohibiting the use of bills of credit as legal tender and so threatening to deprive the colonies of their main form of currency. Then in 1765 Parliament managed to alienate the colonies completely, as it had failed to do with the Sugar Act, by passing the Stamp Act. Passed after a dull and perfunctory discussion, this act provided that colonial expenses would be defrayed in part by taxes in the form of stamps or stamped paper to be paid for in specie and to be required for the handling of numerous items, including newspapers, business documents, and legal papers.

Unlike the Sugar Act, the Stamp Act was a direct tax for the exclusive purpose of revenue, and again unlike the Sugar Act, it struck at practically everybody of consequence in all the colonies and with special force at the most influential members of society: the merchants, the planters, the lawyers, and the newspaper editors. The colonists were virtually unanimous in their conviction that such taxation, by a Parliament in which they were not represented, was unconstitutional, and they rose angrily to prevent it. Parliament had considerately provided a period of grace before the law would go into effect. It never did go into effect.

In the Virginia House of Burgesses Patrick Henry was successful, after a close fight, in passing a series of resolutions denouncing taxation without representation and recalling to the English government the "liberties, franchises and immunities" which Americans possessed by virtue of being Englishmen and also by their charter rights. The resolutions, in company with a number which failed to pass the house, were at once circulated through the colonies. Then in "mobbish Boston" radicals staged violent anti-Stamp Act demonstrations which the authorities were powerless to restrain. In Rhode Island a mob drove the King's officers from their houses.

Riots spread through the colonies. Stamp officials were tarred and feathered, and a new political force, the lower-middle-class Sons of Liberty, made its appearance. The Sons appeared in all thirteen colonies, and everywhere they received strong aristocratic support. In New York, De Lanceys and Livingstons sponsored them, and in South Carolina Henry Laurens, mobbed by rioters in the middle of the night, identified nine aristocratic acquaintances of his beneath the "soot, sailors habits, slouch hats &c." Meanwhile colonial leaders assembled in New York in the Stamp Act Congress to resolve that the act had "a manifest Tendency to subvert the Rights and Liberties of the Colonists."

Amazed and shocked by the violent American reaction, Parliament, which had passed the act with no expectation that it would arouse great commotion, repealed it by a vote of more than 2 to 1 four months after it was supposed to have gone into effect. Beyond that, Parliament repealed the Sugar Act and reduced the molasses duty to a penny. A declaratory act that accompanied the Stamp Act repeal asserted Parliament's right to tax the colonists, but this point was disregarded amid the rejoicing over the repeal. The Quartering Act, passed at the time of the Stamp Act, provided under certain circumstances for the quartering of troops in privately owned barns, taverns, inns, and unoccupied houses. Its continued operation caused trouble in Massachusetts and New York, but the colonists generally took the view that they had won their point and all was well.

AMERICAN NEWSPAPERS

Nevertheless, the Stamp Act crisis left lasting changes in American society that boded ill for the well-being of Britain's American empire. In the course of the crisis radicals gained control of the Massachusetts Assembly under the leadership of James Otis and of the Virginia House of Burgesses under the leadership of Patrick Henry, and the Sons of Liberty stayed in existence. Afterwards they alienated many of their original aristocratic sponsors by their violence and the radicalism of their demands, which included broadening of the suffrage and other political and social reforms, but they continued on under more plebeian and more radical leadership in the urban centers of the Northern colonies, corresponding with each other and looking for ways to cause further trouble.

Originally the colonists had been virtually united in their opposition to the Stamp Act, but they were never united again. The issue was drawn by the lawless and violent manner in which the act had been opposed. Sides were taken on this issue, and roughly the same sides later divided into the Revolutionary patriots and the Tory loyalists.

The Stamp Act crisis brought the American newspaper into existence for the first time as an independent political force. Previously the colonial newspapers, beginning with the *Boston News Letter* in 1704, had been published "by authority" and had served as the official organ of the government. Their editors, if they wished to stay out of jail, had done nothing to bring themselves unfavorably to official notice. In 1733 the cause of freedom of the press had won a victory when John Peter Zenger, editor of the *New York Weekly Journal*, was acquitted of the charge of libeling the governor of the colony. Acquittal was on the grounds—not acceptable at that time in English common law as a defense against libel charges—that the statements had been true.

The Zenger case had had no direct effect on the law of the land, but subsequently all colonies passed laws giving juries, not judges, the right to determine libel. Until 1765, however, newspapers ventured little into political controversy. Then, injured more by the Stamp Act than perhaps any other element in the colonies, they struck out with political cartoons and ringing editorials which were widely circulated and widely popular. Having had this first taste of power, the newspapers remained in the forefront of controversy. The large majority of them continued to take the radical side and later supported the Revolution.

THE AMERICAN
LEGAL PROFESSION

It was during this period that the American lawyer rose suddenly to achieve a political power probably uniquely great among the nations of the world. Until the middle of the eighteenth century the role of lawyers was a minor one and their position in society was quite low. Yet twenty-five of the fifty-six signers of the Declaration of Independence were lawyers, and so were thirty-one of the fifty-five who attended the Constitutional Convention. Life in seventeenth-century America had been too simple for the complexities of the common law, but during the eighteenth century the westward expansion, with its endless opportunities for litigation in land law, provided incentives for the legal profession, as did the growth of commerce.

Most illustrious among the common people who chose the law as an avenue of advancement was John Adams, who made the decision after some hesitation. "The study of law," he wrote a friend, "is indeed an avenue to the more important offices of State and the happiness of human society is an object worth the pursuit of any man. But the acquisition of these important offices depends upon many circumstances of birth and of fortune, not to mention capacity, which I have not and I can have no hopes of being useful in that way." The American Revolution did much to prove John Adams wrong, freeing America from aristocratic English control and placing American lawyers firmly in the seats of power. Ambitious American lawyers brought the law to the side of liberty and the Revolution. Once in power, these lawyers just as effectively sided with property and position against the threatening advance of democracy. The history of the American bar helps to explain why the Revolution came in the first place and why it then took the moderate course that it did.

THE TOWNSHEND ACTS

There remained for Parliament that same English debt and those continuing expenses of maintaining soldiers in America. With Pitt's withdrawal from the Pitt-Grafton cabinet which succeeded that of Grenville, the real leader became Charles Townshend, serving as Chancellor of the Exchequer and therefore responsible for preparing the 1767 budget. He took an unusually supercilious view of the American colonists, and he thought it would be a clever idea to take advantage of a distinction which he mistakenly thought the colonists made between internal and external taxes, internal taxes being those placed on goods within the colonies and external taxes being those placed on goods as they were being imported. In 1767, therefore, against the advice of other members of the cabinet, Townshend introduced the Townshend Acts, placing import duties on English painters' colors, lead, paper, glass, and tea in order to raise a rather paltry £40,000 in annual revenue. In addition a Board of Customs Commissioners was created, which proved far more effective than had the older Naval Office, and the New York Assembly was suspended until it complied with the Quartering Act.

For a time Townshend appeared to have won his point. The New York Assembly knuckled under with an appropriation for quartering the soldiers; colonial leaders, who had been shocked by the Stamp Act riots, held back for a time; and merchants, deciding that they would not be materially injured by the duties, showed no disposition to stand irresponsibly on principle. For six months after passage of the duties there was calm before the storm. Then the storm broke, with the publication by the wealthy and rather conservative Quaker lawyer John Dickinson of *Letters from a Farmer in Pennsylvania*, the most influential of all pre-Revolutionary tracts before the writings of Thomas Paine. Concerned to resolve the conflict rather than inflame it, Dickinson tried to prove that the taxes were constitutionally incompatible with the British imperial system. Edmund Burke had spoken admiringly of the Americans as "smatterers" in law, and the legalism of Dickinson's argument was typical of the American approach to the problem. His essays were immediately acclaimed on both sides of the Atlantic, and a whole literature of writings began to appear in their support.

Two months after the appearance of Dickinson's *Letters* the Massachusetts Assembly, under the direction of Samuel Adams, drafted a circular letter and sent it to the other colonial legislatures protesting the new duties. The assembly was ordered to rescind the circular letter, and when it refused by an overwhelming vote to do so, it was dissolved. A law was passed which provided that persons suspected of treason would be sent to England for trial, and two additional regiments were sent to Boston. The Boston town meeting remained in operation, however, and the Boston merchants were finally moved to accept a Non-Importation Agreement boycotting the goods covered by the Townshend duties. The merchants of New York and Philadelphia reluctantly followed suit. The Virginia House of Burgesses passed the Virginia Resolves against the duties and against the law providing for trying Americans in England. It then adopted nonimportation and was accordingly dissolved.

THE COERCIVE ACTS

The colonists never regained the first fine careless rapture of their opposition to the Stamp Act, though. The merchants not only moved reluctantly but were sometimes caught at violations by the Sons of Liberty, who made themselves the chief enforcers of nonimportation. In Boston in 1770, excitement momentarily reached a new pitch when redcoats fired on a mob, killing five people, but outside Massachusetts this "massacre" caused little commotion. Meanwhile Lord North had taken office as Prime Minister and decided that a tax on English goods was prejudicial to English interests. He pushed a measure through Parliament repealing all the duties except that on tea, which was retained, George III wrote, "to keep the right" in the matter of parliamentary authority.

In the colonies cannons exploded in celebration, as they had after repeal of the Stamp Act, and to most people all seemed well. Nonimportation was broken first by New York, which had suffered most from it—a defection which the New York Sons said would be "a stench in the nostrils of every true-born American, till time is no more." Amid a halfhearted boycott on tea and the shrill frustration of radicals such as Samuel Adams, three years of relative quiet descended upon the empire. Imperial affairs were critically disrupted neither by the burning of the British revenue boat *Gaspee* in Rhode Island nor by British assumption of the responsibility for paying the salaries of the governors and judges in Massachusetts. Radicals, meanwhile, organized committees of correspondence to achieve intercolonial unity while they awaited opportunity for new assaults against the home government.

Opportunity came in 1773 in the form of the Tea Act, bestowed by the British government upon the East India Company, with its needy stockholding following in Parliament. Under this act the East India Company was permitted to ship tea directly to the American colonies and so avoid the English duties. This piece of favoritism enabled the company to undersell even native American smugglers on the American market. Sharp protests were heard from Charleston, Philadelphia, and New York, and then from Boston came the splash heard around the world. Radicals, disguised as Indians, boarded East India Company ships in Boston Harbor. They dumped a fortune in tea into the bay, and revolution was in sight. This violation of the natural right of private property, which shocked many colonists, roused Parliament to a righteous fury and resulted in the Coercive Acts, or as the Americans called them, the Intolerable Acts. These in turn roused the colonists to call the First Continental Congress for the purpose of organizing against England.

The Coercive Acts consisted of the Boston Port Bill, closing the port to trade until *somebody* paid for the tea; the Massachusetts Government Act, arbitrarily altering the provincial government in violation of charter rights; the Administration of Justice Act, permitting the trial in England of persons accused of any serious crime in a colony; and a new Quartering Act, making local authorities responsible for the quartering of troops in areas to which they were sent if barracks were not available. Additional troops were sent to New England, and General Gage was made governor of Massachusetts "to put the rebels in their places."

At the same time, although independently of the Coercive Acts, the Quebec Act was passed, incorporating the Ohio Valley into the province of Quebec in violation of colonial charters and extending wide religious and political liberties to the Catholic French Canadians. The Quebec Act, except perhaps for the extension of the province to include the Ohio Valley, was an honest implementation of promises made the French in the Treaty of Paris of 1763. The colonists, however, had good reason to suspect that this act was an attempt to destroy colonial independence by building up Canada as an opposing force, and they lumped it together with the rest of the acts in their minds as part of a comprehensive program of coercion.

The Quebec Act may have been motivated by the intention to divide and thereby conquer; the Coercive Acts certainly were. Under them the British government singled Massachusetts out for discipline, apparently supposing that other colonies, since they were not affected, would keep fairly quiet while Massachusetts was being made an example of. Events quickly pointed up the error in this reasoning. Pamphlets appeared, such as Jefferson's *A Summary View of the Rights of British America*. Resolutions of sympathy were passed in various cities, and the Sons of Liberty went into action with their committees of correspondence. The New York Sons called for a renewal of nonimportation, and the Virginia House of Burgesses, meeting in a tavern after being dissolved for approving something Thomas Jefferson said, did likewise.

Faced with this new radical challenge, the conservative New York oligarchy bypassed the New York Committee of Correspondence and organized its own group, the Committee of Fifty-one. This committee defeated the radicals partly by holding meetings in the early afternoon when workingmen found it hard to attend. It moved to circumvent the committees of correspondence by calling for the meeting of a continental congress. Such a congress, according to conservative calculations, would be controlled by prudent men who could act in unison to curb radical elements in individual colonies. These calculations left out of account the incendiary radicalism of the Southern aristocrats, especially the new order in Virginia. They left out of account also the increasingly bellicose program of the British government, which was rapidly driving moderates into the radical camp.

BIBLIOGRAPHY FOR CHAPTER 4

C. M. Andrews, The Colonial Background of the Revolution (1931)
L. H. Gipson, The Coming of the Revolution, 1763–1775 (1954)
Ian Cristie, Crisis of Empire (1966)
L. B. Namier, England in the Age of the American Revolution (1930)
G. L. Beer, British Colonial Policy, 1754–1765 (1907)
Bernard Bailyn, Ideological Origins of the American Revolution (1966)
E. S. and H. M. Morgan, The Stamp Act Crisis (1953)
A. M. Schlesinger, Sr., Prelude to Independence: The Newspaper War on Britain (1958)

CHAPTER 5

THE AMERICAN REVOLUTION

THE CONTINENTAL CONGRESS

Thehe colonists responded to the Coercive Acts with the First Continental Congress, which met in Philadelphia in September 1774, representing all the Thirteen Colonies except Georgia. The first victory went speedily to the radicals with the endorsement of the Suffolk Resolves, drawn up by the people of Suffolk County, Massachusetts, including Boston, calling for a preservation of the people's liberties. The conservatives, hurrying to stave off disaster, joined in support of a plan proposed by Joseph Galloway of Pennsylvania, providing for an American parliament, inferior to the British Parliament but in charge generally of intercolonial matters. Any legislation affecting America would require concurrence of both parliaments. The Galloway Plan was similar to the Albany Plan proposed by Franklin in 1754 to unify the colonies in the face of the French threat. It was similar also to plans later suggested by a number of other men including Jefferson and John Adams. One objection to Franklin's proposal had been that Parliament would not accept it, and there was still no assurance, and probably no likelihood, that Parliament would accept the Galloway Plan. In any event, it was rejected by a vote of six colonies to five, and from that point on the radicals had it their own way.

A Declaration of Rights and Grievances was passed criticizing Parliament for a whole catalog of errors, and an association was created to enforce the cessation of all trade with England and the British West Indies, the voters in all communities being charged with electing committees to enforce the boycott and, after September 1775, nonexportation as well. A job lot of petitions and memorials was then composed, and the Congress adjourned, voting to meet again the following May if grievances had not been redressed by that time.

Conservatives still hoped for a middle road out of the crisis, but the radical Patrick Henry departed from Philadelphia happily convinced that a situation had been created from which war would certainly result, and the Battle of Lexington

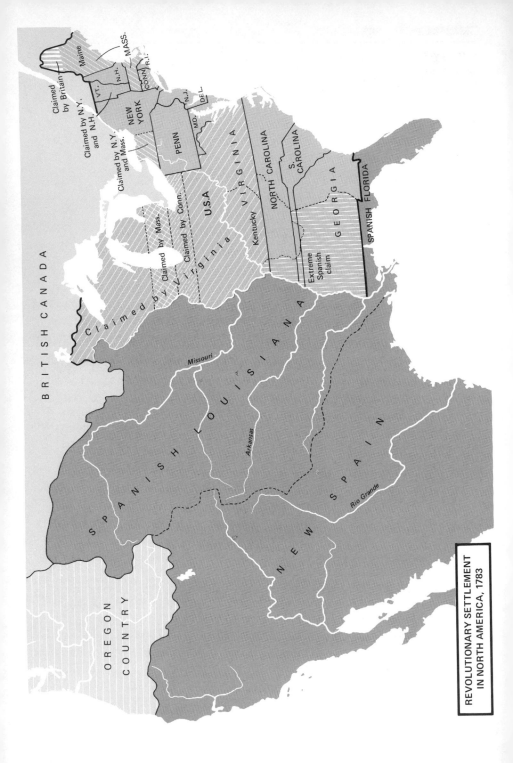

REVOLUTIONARY SETTLEMENT
IN NORTH AMERICA, 1783

BRITISH CANADA

Claimed
by Britain

Claimed by N.Y.
and N.H.

Claimed by N.Y.
and Mass.

Maine

MASS.

N.H.

VT.

CONN.

R.I.

NEW
YORK

N.J.

DEL.

PENN

MD.

VIRGINIA

U.S.A

Claimed by Mass.

Claimed by Conn.

Claimed by Virginia

Kentucky

NORTH CAROLINA

S.
CAROLINA

GEORGIA

Extreme
Spanish
claim

SPANISH FLORIDA

S P A N I S H   L O U I S I A N A

Missouri

Arkansas

N E W   S P A I N

Rio Grande

OREGON
COUNTRY

and Concord occurred three weeks before the meeting of the Second Continental Congress to prove him right. When it met in May 1775, the Second
Continental Congress was faced with the fact of war, and it continued on as the
wartime government of the Thirteen Colonies until replaced in 1781 by the
government of the Articles of Confederation.

In April 1775, General Gage sent troops to Concord to confiscate rebel
military stores. The mission was accomplished at the cost of 273 dead and
wounded as the redcoats ran the gauntlet of minutemen from Concord back to
Boston. On May 10, the day the Second Continental Congress convened, Ethan
Allen captured Fort Ticonderoga, and two days later Benedict Arnold captured
Crown Point. In June the capture of Breed's and Bunker Hills in Boston cost the
British more than a thousand casualties. British reinforcements had arrived,
increasing British troops in America to about 10,000. In June the Congress
named George Washington commander in chief of the Continental forces. Sub-
ordinate generals were later named, and provision was made for the creation
of a navy and for the issuance of letters of marque and reprisal for privateers.
Congress then drew up the Olive Branch Petition expressing its loyalty to the
King.

More than a year passed before the revolutionists were driven to abandon
their hopes for reconciliation and declare their independence of England, yet at
no point during that period did the British government give them any basis for
hoping that their main demands would be met. In England their cause was
supported by William Pitt, now Lord Chatham, James Fox, and Edmund Burke.
But Pitt, though he praised the Continental Congress as a valuable addition to
the imperial system, insisted that the colonies recognize the theoretical right of
Parliament to tax them, which the revolutionists were bound not to do; and
apart from this, Chatham, Fox, and Burke were powerless amid outraged public
opinion and in a Parliament by now securely controlled by George III and Lord
North.

Several months before Lexington and Concord Lord North presented the
government's offer: the colonies would not be taxed if they themselves would
raise the funds for their administration and for their share in the common
defense. The offer conceded nothing concerning the English right to tax its
colonies, nor did it propose withdrawing troops from the colonies. It served only
to convince the rebels of the hopelessness of negotiation. The Continental
Congress made no further formal attempt at reconciliation. Held together by no
traditional loyalties except English loyalties, the revolutionists continued to toast
the King and argue for their English liberties as they armed for independence.

INDEPENDENCE

Thomas Paine, recently over from England, broke the cake of custom early in
1776 with his *Common Sense,* presenting the natural-rights argument for revolu-

tion and attacking monarchy in general and the "royal brute" George III in particular. This first published argument for independence was read everywhere in the colonies within a month and exerted an immense influence. In June Richard Henry Lee presented before Congress a Virginia resolution calling for outright independence. After a sharp debate the resolution was approved by a vote of 7 colonies to 5, and a committee was appointed to draw up a declaration of the fact. On July 2 the Congress announced to the world that "these United Colonies are, and of right ought to be FREE AND INDEPENDENT STATES," and two days later the Declaration of Independence was formally signed.

As author of the Declaration Jefferson presented the natural-rights argument for revolution, and in the view of the signers it was a self-evident one. All men, they believed, were created equal, not in native ability or in their share of the world's goods or in their right to participate in government, but in their equal possession of God-given rights to life, liberty, and property. Governments were formed for the purpose of securing these rights for them. The government that failed of this purpose lost its reason for being. The social-compact theory of government in the argument was derived from English and European writers such as John Locke and Samuel Pufendorf, but it was strengthened in America as nowhere else by actual experience. From the Mayflower Compact to the establishment of the latest frontier community, men had joined together in a state of nature to form governments on the basis of written social compacts. What was theory to European philosophers was common practice to American settlers.

Although undeniably a revolutionary document, the Declaration presented a more conservative argument, in the minds of its signers, than would appear from a modern reading of it. By "consent of the governed" the signers meant consent of the property-holding taxpayers. By "pursuit of Happiness" the signers meant the right to do with their property as they liked, subject to such necessary limitations as they placed upon themselves through their governments.

That the signers viewed the words of the Declaration in this rather conservative light is demonstrated by the conservative state constitutions they proceeded to draw up. The phrase "pursuit of Happiness" was a Jeffersonian touch which gave warmth to the document while in no way binding the signers or the new nation (although the phrase afterwards crept into various state constitutions, where it remained as a perplexing problem for the state courts). But the Declaration, whatever the sober intentions of its signers, was inescapably a revolutionary document, and although it bound no one to anything but independence, it remained as a consecrated statement of revolutionary purpose to which American radicalism thereafter could always appeal.

THE STATE CONSTITUTIONS

Ten of the states completed their constitutions within the year. New York and Georgia followed in 1777 and Massachusetts, the only state to submit its constitution to the people for ratification, in 1780. Most of these documents were basically republican translations of the colonial charters, with bills of rights added. Where they departed from precedent it was generally to weaken the executive and strengthen the assembly, liberty being associated in the patriots' minds with assemblies, tyranny with kings and governors.

The most radical constitution, that of Pennsylvania, created a one-house legislature, annually elected and sharing administrative authority with a plural executive. Without having to depart far from the Charter of Privileges of 1701, the Pennsylvania constitution expressed the radical Whig belief that government ought to represent the unobstructed will of the people. The most influential of the conservative constitutions, that drawn up for Massachusetts mainly by John Adams, demonstrated the conservatives' fear of faction, whether of the popular majority or of the privileged minority. It provided for an independent judiciary, a strong, indirectly elected executive, an upper house designed to represent property interests, and a lower house representing the people and holding power to levy taxes. The judiciary, the executive, and each legislative house held separately the right to veto, to check and balance the conflicting factions in society.

Perhaps the most significant innovation in most state constitutions was the addition of those bills of rights which the Privy Council had denied the colonies. The first of these, and the model for the first nine amendments to the federal Constitution, was the Virginia bill of rights, chiefly written by the libertarian aristocrat George Mason. Proceeding from the Lockean compact theory of government, the Virginia bill of rights listed the liberties necessary to a free people: prohibition of hereditary offices, an independent judiciary, no taxation without representation, trial by jury, the right of the accused to confront opposing witnesses, his right to refuse to testify against himself, prohibition of general warrants for searches and seizures, prohibition of excessive bail, freedom of the press, the right to bear arms, subordination of military to civil power, and the free exercise of religion according to the dictates of conscience. Mason's eloquent list influenced French revolutionary thought more than perhaps any other document of the American Revolution. It demonstrated a concern for individual liberty among slaveholding aristocrats in the eighteenth century such as was rarely matched by equalitarian democrats in the nineteenth.

One general trend which exerted a democratizing influence on state governments was the removal of state capitals inland. It had been Jefferson's opinion that in theory the western counties of Virginia had their fair share of representation, but that in practice the distance to Williamsburg meant that they were consistently underrepresented. In 1776 Jefferson proposed the transfer of the capital to Richmond, and the move was approved three years later. North Carolina and Georgia, with no regular permanent capitals before the war, established them inland at Raleigh and Augusta. The capital of South Carolina was moved from Charleston to Columbia in 1789. The trend was slower in the Northern states, New York and Pennsylvania each delaying for two decades.

Each state was an independent nation over which the Continental Congress had no legal authority. Congress decided on the number of troops each state was supposed to contribute to the war, but the state was under no legal obligation to comply. Similarly Congress requisitioned the states for money and then took what it was given, which was never nearly enough. With victory in sight the war was nearly lost in 1781 for lack of money, until Congress was rescued by the newly appointed superintendent of finance, Robert Morris. Congress assumed command of the Continental Army and the direction of foreign affairs, but in domestic political matters it could no more than recommend and hope.

THE REVOLUTIONARY WAR

From first to last the War for Independence was a remarkably chancy fight. The probable outcome was always in doubt until after Yorktown in 1781, the struggle was marked over and over again by very close shaves, and, in the context of eighteenth-century warfare, it was full of imponderables. In the age of enlightened despotism nobody had been expected to fight for love of country. The people had had nothing to do with the many wars of the age, which had been fought by highly disciplined professional soldiers maneuvering in set formations under the suspicious scrutiny of their officers.

Had the Americans played by these rules, England would have made short work of Washington's amateurs with its professional army and overwhelming naval superiority. With this disproportionate power the British were able to take major Northern cities with relative ease, and had they been content with this, they might have just held on and in time stopped the rebels short of complete independence. They had orders to put down the rebellion, however, and when they moved into the country to accomplish this, they were subjected to guerrilla tactics of farmer-soldiers which they were not trained to cope with.

Conflicting loyalties confused the struggle throughout. The Americans were bitterly divided between patriot and loyalist; at least 80,000 loyalists and perhaps more fled the country in the course of the Revolution. The Southern planters were largely united on the patriot side, but in the Northern states, except among the merchant gentry, the aristocratic leadership was predominantly loyalist, while many frontier regions were overwhelmingly antipatriot. But the loyalists were unable to unite and organize a clearly understood program behind forceful leaders, which the patriots did. England also was divided on the Revolution. There were Friends of America not only in Parliament but also in the

British Army, many officers being unwilling to fight against their countrymen in America. Doubt concerning the reliability of British soldiers was a major British motive for relying heavily on Hessian mercenaries.

To the British went the advantage of the centrally organized government pitting itself against a league of independent states, but this advantage was offset by the corruption and incompetence of Lord North's government. The venality and incompetence of the Admiralty under the loathsome Lord Sandwich is generally regarded as unique in the annals of the British Navy, and the War Department was mismanaged by Lord George Germain, who, among his many disqualifications for the position, had himself been cashiered from the army for cowardice. The Americans had their share of incompetents and cowards also, but in George Washington they possessed the incomparable leader of the age. Washington's greatness as a national leader and the resulting confidence which even the Continental Congress came to place in him did much to offset the lack of a true central government and a national tradition and so made victory possible.

Driven from New York in the summer of 1776, Washington raised the perilously low morale of the army the following winter with brilliant sallies at Trenton and Princeton. The initiative nevertheless remained with the British on the basis of their great naval and military superiority, and in the spring of 1777 Lord Germain approved a campaign to end the war by dividing the colonies at the line of the Hudson River. General "Gentleman Johnny" Burgoyne was to move south from Canada by way of Lake Champlain, Col. Barry St. Leger was to move east from Lake Ontario, Gen. William Howe was to send a detachment north along the Hudson, and the three forces were to converge on the American Northern army and destroy it. Several things went wrong. St. Leger met the Mohawk Valley militia and retreated into Canada, Howe was unable to act until it was too late, and a sizable force sent by Burgoyne to collect needed military supplies was beaten by the Green Mountain Boys at the Battle of Bennington.

Burgoyne's delayed advance permitted the strengthening of the Northern army, and at the Battle of Saratoga Burgoyne surrendered his entire army of 5,000. This proved to be the decisive battle of the war, for it did much to convince the French to come in on the American side. Howe, meanwhile, had captured Philadelphia, and Washington retreated to spend that famous bitter winter in Valley Forge, the summer soldiers and sunshine patriots having by then deserted in large numbers. A year of indecisive fencing followed, during which the British, having failed in their main Northern attempt, shifted their attention to the South.

THE FRENCH ALLIANCE

From the first the revolutionists had looked upon French military assistance as a likely possibility, and four months before their Declaration of Independence they sent Silas Deane to Paris to see what could be arranged. The French responded with generous supplies of cannon, guns, gunpowder, and clothing. In September Deane, Benjamin Franklin, and Arthur Lee were appointed to negotiate a commercial treaty with France, and a half dozen other European states were similarly sounded out. Nothing was achieved until news arrived of the Battle of Saratoga and of new favorable terms of settlement being considered by the British government. In February 1778, a treaty of alliance was concluded providing that if France were drawn in, it would make American independence the essential object of the war and neither nation would make peace with England before consulting the other. A commercial treaty was also concluded. France entered the war in June; Spain followed in 1779 and Holland in 1780.

The French were to play the major part in the eventual American victory, but they were woefully slow in arriving. The British captured Savannah in September 1778, and royal government was returned to Georgia. In 1780 they launched the main Southern campaign with Sir Henry Clinton's capture of Charleston and General Cornwallis's devastating defeat of the American army under Horatio Gates at Camden. Then, with everything apparently going their way, British cavalry forces with Tory supporters moved overboldly into the backcountry and were annihilated at Kings Mountain, ruining Southern Tory morale and raising up bands of farmer-fighters under Andrew Pickens, Thomas Sumter, and Francis Marion. Gates was replaced by the able Gen. Nathanael Greene, and the British, defeated at Cowpens and weakened by a costly victory at Guilford Courthouse, were driven back to the coast. At this encouraging point the French joined in with the military and naval support needed to win the American war.

General Rochambeau arrived in Newport with 6,000 men in the summer of 1780 and waited there a year for the arrival, essential to his usefulness, of the French fleet under the command of the Comte de Grasse. In August 1781 Grasse sailed for the Chesapeake, a Franco-American army moved southward from New York, and by the end of September the French fleet and combined French and American forces of 16,000 had Cornwallis penned up at Yorktown. On October 19, 1781, he surrendered his entire force. The war in America was over, except for frontier fighting in the Northwest and a general mopping up of American merchantmen by the British Navy.

Defeat in America discredited the personal rule of George III, toppled his Minister, Lord North, and brought the Friends of America to power in time for them to conclude the hostilities with a treaty which gave the United States terms much more generous than they had any good reason to expect. But the treaty negotiations were complicated, to say the least, by the French alliance and the further alliance between Spain and France.

Congress appointed a commission to negotiate the peace by consultation with the French. Suspicious, with good reason, that the French intended to appease Spain at American expense, the commission—John Adams, John Jay, and Benjamin Franklin—violated its instructions by entering into negotiations directly with England. The resulting agreement was signed in November 1782; faced with an accomplished fact, the French negotiators accepted the terms and they went into effect September 3, 1783, when the Peace of Paris was concluded, bringing the general war to a conclusion. By the terms of this treaty Britain acknowledged American independence and conceded to the United States the territory extending north to the Great Lakes, west to the Mississippi, and south to the Floridas, which England returned to Spain. The treaty was based on extremely sketchy geographic knowledge, however, and in important matters it was ambiguously worded. It took sixty years of diplomatic negotiation to decide what it meant.

THE ARTICLES OF CONFEDERATION

Once independence had been decided upon, nobody supposed that the Second Continental Congress, summoned for quite a different purpose, was a suitable government for the new nation. The Virginia resolution of June 1776, while calling for independence, called also for a plan of confederation to be prepared and transmitted to the colonies, and Congress appointed John Dickinson to prepare the plan. His committee returned a month later with a report which for more than a year was not acted upon because of the military situation and also because of disagreements among the states. They mainly disagreed over whether Western lands belonged to the states with charter rights to them or belonged to the nation as a whole. In November 1777, however, thirteen Articles of Confederation and Perpetual Union were submitted to the states for ratification.

The Articles provided for a unicameral Congress in which each state would have one vote. The Congress possessed the power to declare war, make peace, control foreign policy, appoint military officers, regulate Indian affairs, fix standards of weights and measures, determine the value of coins issued by the states as well as by the national government, and decide on interstate disputes. On all decisions of importance approval by nine states was needed, and on all amendments to the Articles unanimous agreement of the states was required. No executive branch was created except for a Committee of the States, each being represented by one delegate. Drawn up chiefly by the conservative Dickinson (who had refused to sign the Declaration of Independence on the ground that there still remained lines of legal argument to be explored), the Articles put into writing the authority that the Second Continental Congress had already assumed. They were therefore not in themselves any matter for controversy, except among those nationalists who clamored for a stronger central government.

The disposition of the Western lands remained at issue, however, the argument of the states without Western claims being that these belonged to all who were fighting the common fight. If the charter claims had been honored, Virginia would have had the right to rule a territory, extending to the Great Lakes, greater than that of all the other states combined. The Articles were speedily approved by most of the states, but Virginia's Chesapeake neighbor, Maryland, held out on the Western lands issue until its point was won. New York, with the weakest claims to Western land, conceded first, Virginia capitulated in January 1781, Maryland signed a month later, and the Articles went into effect.

CRISES OF THE CONFEDERATION

At the outset the period of the Confederation appeared to be opening upon an age of triumph. It began brilliantly with the decisive victory at Yorktown, lifting the American states from a long, doubtful contest into a world of astonishing promise. When the generous treaty of peace was concluded two years later, it seemed that the world was to be edified by a new nation of noble Romans guiding their own self-reliant republican destinies by the pure light of Scripture and by the self-evident truths of the Declaration of Independence. Freed from the restrictions of the British imperial system, American enterprise saw boundless possibilities for profit in commercial agriculture, commerce, manufacturing, banking, road and canal building, and land speculation. Before the Revolution the royal governments had been the selfish guardians of British interests. The governments were now in the hands of the people and so could be trusted to help the people to enrich themselves.

Such buoyant hopes were bound to be deflated in the course of everyday events. Not everybody shared the widespread enthusiasm for the new republican ways or for independence, and even at the moment of victory many of those who had worked hardest for the cause had good reason to suspect the new system of inconstancy. At the close of the war the army, unrewarded and ill-cared-for, was ominously restless. The older aristocracy, momentarily discredited, still held great power in most of the states, and after the war it was daily strengthened by returning loyalists.

Peace had hardly been declared when republicanism was threatened by the army. Its main force was wintering at Newburgh on the Hudson at war's end, idle and exasperated by lack of supplies and the failure of Congress to fulfill pledges. The officers had been promised half pay for life, after the European custom, but Congress delayed taking official action. As the army grew increasingly restless, right-wing politicians like Alexander Hamilton came to view it as a potentially useful political instrument. The narrowly aristocratic Gouverneur Morris was enthusiastic about such a prospect. He wrote John Jay that he was "glad to see things in their present train. Depend on it, good will arise from the situation to which we are hastening . . . although I think it probable that much of convulsion will ensue, yet it must terminate in giving government that power, without which government is but a name."

The crisis reached its climax in March 1783 with the circulation of the anonymous Newburgh Address. Were the men in the army to be the only sufferers in the Revolution? It would not be so "if you have sense enough to discover, and spirit enough to oppose tyranny under whatever garb it may assume; whether it be the plain coat of republicanism, or the splendid robe of royalty. . . ." If there was any real danger of a coup d'etat in an antimilitaristic nation of armed men, it was ended by Washington's admonitory address to his officers, who thereafter disbanded peaceably without waiting for their demands to be met. Widespread fear of the military was aroused all over again when the Society of the Cincinnati was organized as a hereditary secret order of the officers of the Revolution. Sam Adams was convinced that it was an attempt to establish, in as short a time as had ever been known, a military aristocracy, and radical enlisted men hurried to organize their own Sons of St. Tammand or Tammany Societies in opposition. In time one of the Tammany organizations did develop into a permanent political power, but the Cincinnati proved to be no more than another bogeyman for Sam Adams and others of like mind.

There remained the problem of the common soldiers. In Pennsylvania about eighty soldiers, ill-treated and unpaid, marched to Philadelphia, got drunk, and surrounded the building where Congress was convened. Congress suffered fear and embarrassment, fled to Princeton, and finally took up quarters in New York. It made known its attitude toward the military by defeating a bill to create a permanent standing army of 896 men. It authorized instead a permanent force of eighty men, twenty-five at Fort Pitt and fifty-five at West Point. The officers were finally voted five years' pay, but Congress did nothing of a like nature for the enlisted men, although individual states responded to their demands.

While the end of the war brought vast new economic opportunities for American businessmen, it also ushered in a commercial depression of continental proportions, and this was compounded by the merchants, who continued to import large amounts of goods at continually falling prices. In 1785 there was a sharp decline in prices for American agricultural produce. Then depression passed over into recovery. By the eve of the Constitutional Convention the nation had entered upon good times and was launched upon the worldwide commercial enterprise which independence had promised. The period of the Confederation was the occasion for the depression, which created sentiment in favor of a strong central government; it was also the time of return to prosperity, which helped to launch the constitutional venture so auspiciously.

Although businessmen roundly denounced the thirteen democratic states and the weak Confederation for practices inimical to a sound economy, the politics of the time were generally favorable to business except in the realm of financial legislation. In the area of interstate trade the state governments showed an impressive spirit of restraint; the main tendency of the duties was to protect against foreign rather than interstate trade. There were acrimonious disputes over the location of state borders, but these were peacefully settled.

Most impressively, the problem of Western lands was settled with the acquisition of the national domain from the states and with the creation by Congress of an orderly system for land sales, settlement, territorial government, and eventual statehood.

By the Ordinance of 1785 government lands were divided into townships 6 miles square, which in turn were subdivided into thirty-six sections of 640 acres. They were to be sold alternately by townships and by sections at $1 per acre. The Ordinance of 1787 established government for the territories and created the method of achieving statehood. The initial government, appointed by the Congress, consisted of a governor, a secretary, and three judges. When the territory supported 5,000 adult males, they would be permitted to elect a legislature, which would in turn nominate a legislative council, while administration of the territory would remain in the hands of the appointed governor. At that stage the territory would be entitled to a nonvoting delegate to the Congress. When the total population reached 60,000, the territory might call a convention, draw up a constitution, and submit it to Congress, which then had the authority to admit the territory as a state on an equal political basis with the original states.

With this Northwest Ordinance, it has been said, the American government fundamentally solved the problem upon which the British empire had broken. Early settlement of the Northwest Territory, meanwhile, was expedited little by the Ordinance of 1785 and much by grandiose schemes of land speculators. The Ohio Company was chief among the companies and individuals acquiring vast tracts of land, often on the claim of their being just rewards for Revolutionary War services. As it turned out, few made substantial profits on these schemes, but the activities of the companies resulted in the rapid settlement of what became the state of Ohio.

SHAYS' REBELLION

The yeoman farmers had been the main force of the armies during the Revolution, and they were the chief basis of society in the Confederation period. They were the most numerous voters, and they demanded that their grievances be met. Their economic demands were simple. They lived as they had always lived, in a subsistence and barter economy. They had debts and taxes, and they lacked the money to pay them. They were forced to bear a disproportionately heavy share of the tax burden through the payment of poll taxes, and foreclosure and perhaps debtors' prison awaited those who could not meet their obligations.

Their remedy was cheap money, as it had always been. In colonial times the Privy Council had consistently fought the issuance of paper money. The Revolution, however, had been financed in large part by state and continental paper currency, which quickly became worthless and was no longer in use by the close of the war. Upon the ruins of the paper-money system the creditor group established a hard-money policy which enhanced the value of the debts owed to it by the people, the states, and the Confederation government. In all states the growing opposition of the small-farmer debtor classes was inflamed by the sharp price decline in agricultural goods in the mid-eighties.

Demands for paper money became the center of controversy in all states, and seven states responded by issuing it. In New York, New Jersey, South Carolina, Rhode Island, and Pennsylvania the money was based on land and served a need which was not met again until the establishment of federal farm loan banks in the twentieth century. In some states the paper-currency system was used to fund state and national debts. In states where the merchants complied with the law willingly, the measures worked well enough. Debtors found the opportunity to pay their creditors, and the paper money held its value. In states where the measures were fought by the merchants, notably in Rhode Island, the consequences were disastrous to creditors and debtors alike.

The central and western farmers of Massachusetts, struggling to hold their farms and stay out of debtors' prison, received no satisfaction from their legislature. In some western districts there remained no single citizen who could meet the property qualification for representatives, and those districts were obliged to go unrepresented. Slow to revolt in the period before the Revolution, these western farmers had been trained by Boston and Sam Adams to organize and fight. In 1786 they rose again. They took possession of the courthouse at Northampton and at Worcester. They drilled and marched, and at Springfield, under the command of Daniel Shays, they clashed with the state militia and retreated in disorder. Through a dismal winter bands of insurgents wandered about the countryside. By spring the remnants had returned to their homes, and Shays' Rebellion was at an end. Congress in the meantime cautiously began to raise troops, asserting the need for frontier protection against Indians. It moved too slowly and timidly, however, to be of any assistance to the state of Massachusetts, whose militia proved amply sufficient for the purpose.

Shays' Rebellion, ineffectual as it proved to be, was a straight-out example of violent class struggle, and it struck fear into the hearts of the old Whig revolutionists. The rights of property were threatened, and everywhere the call went out for a sober counterrevolution. Until the eruption of Shays' Rebellion the aristocratic Rufus King had been an enthusiastic and powerful leader of the opposition to all attempts to give greater authority to Congress, but in 1787 he wrote, "Events are hurrying us to a crisis; prudent and sagacious men should be ready to seize the most favorable circumstances to establish a more perfect and vigorous Government." From the time of the rising of the western farmers of Massachusetts, King was a staunch Federalist. The nation had triumphed over England, and it had triumphed over its own army. The moment was at hand when it must stir itself to triumph over the unruliness among the masses of its people.

BIBLIOGRAPHY FOR
CHAPTER 5

E. S. Morgan, The Birth of the Republic, 1763–1789 (1956)
J. R. Allen, A History of the American Revolution (1969)
Howard Peckham, The War for Independence (1958)
J. C. Miller, Triumph of Freedom (1948)
Eric Robson, The American Revolution (1955)—a British viewpoint
Carl Becker, The Declaration of Independence (1922)
P. H. Smith, Loyalists and Redcoats (1964)
R. B. Morris, The Peacemakers (1965)
J. F. Jameson, The American Revolution as a Social Movement (1926)

CHAPTER 6

FOUNDING THE REPUBLIC

THE CONSTITUTIONAL CONVENTION

Even while the Articles were under consideration some of the revolutionists were dedicating their efforts to the cause of a more centralized government. None were in such a good position to appreciate the need for one as the army officers who had to deal with the Second Continental Congress. Among these men, whose profession naturally imbued them with respect for authority, Washington and his aide Hamilton were early converted to a belief in a strong central government. In 1785 there was a conference at Washington's home, Mount Vernon, on a dispute between Maryland and Virginia over water rights on the Chesapeake, which had vexed relations between them for 150 years. No agreement was reached, but it was decided at the meeting that the time had arrived for a general conference of the thirteen states to discuss interstate problems, especially those in the commercial field.

The result was the Annapolis Convention in 1786, attended by representatives of only five states: Delaware, New Jersey, New York, Pennsylvania, and Virginia. Four other states appointed delegates who, for one reason or another, failed to show up. The Annapolis Convention discussions broadened into consideration of the weakness of the Articles generally, and out of this came a call, suggested by Hamilton, for an interstate meeting to be held the next year at Philadelphia to think over the whole nature of the national government and propose reforms for the consideration of the Congress and, after its approval, the state legislatures.

The delegates to this Philadelphia meeting were selected by the state legislatures at a time when Shays' Rebellion was causing men of substance everywhere to fear for their safety. The legislatures, following the example of Virginia, rose to the occasion by appointing the most prominent and respected citizens of their states. Substitutions had to be found for some who refused the offer, but the substitutions, though men of smaller reputations, proved to be safe appointments. The few radicals among the delegates were right-wing radicals holding monarchist or ultra-aristocratic views, such as Alexander Hamilton. The majority were in close agreement on the nature of the problem, and except where the question of representation of the states entered in, the delegates did not disagree widely on the nature of the solution.

Except for a surprisingly large number of men still in their twenties, the delegates were patriots who had fought for American independence. Some of them had signed the Declaration of Independence, and it is not to be supposed that they had repudiated their earlier views on the natural rights of man. But now they faced a new problem, during new times, of making rather than breaking. After all, the revolutionary state governments of 1776 had not relied on self-evident truths in constructing workable instruments of government, and the founding fathers had even less reason to do so. "Experience must be our only guide," the delegates were warned by the conservative John Dickinson, who at a similar stage in the French Revolution would have long since lost his ninth life. "Reason may mislead us," he further warned.

The delegates wanted a system of government strong enough to protect property interests but not strong enough to deprive the states of authority or the citizens of liberty. It was essential that such a government be kept from the control of "faction," whether popular or aristocratic. The aristocratic delegates had seen and read enough to know that unlimited power in the hands of an aristocratic faction would lead to corruption just as surely as if it were in the hands of the people, and they wanted a government which could withstand their own overweening passions as well as those of the people; but the popular threat was uppermost in their minds.

In meeting the problem, the delegates used the Articles of Confederation as their chief working model and took a great deal from them bodily. They also had at their disposal thirteen working models of republican government, and the experiences of the state governments were frequently drawn upon. The key to the resulting document was its mechanism for avoiding what James Madison, the convention's most influential member, called "the accumulation of all powers, legislative, executive, and judiciary, in the same hands, whether of one, a few, or many, and whether hereditary, self-appointed, or elective."

The Senate and the House of Representatives were designed to balance wealth against popularity as well as to balance the large states against the small states. The President could veto legislation, and the legislature by a two-thirds vote could still pass it into law. An independent judiciary was established, headed by a Supreme Court which at least some delegates assumed would have the right, contrary to practice elsewhere in the world, of declaring congressional laws unconstitutional. A separate principle of selection was devised for each branch of the government. The House was to be elected by the people as the states directed. The Senate was to be appointed by the state legislatures. The President was to be chosen by special electors whom the states might designate as they saw fit. All branches of the government would be bound by the Constitution, which imposed specific limitations on the powers of them all and declared itself to be the supreme law of the land.

The one main disagreement in the convention, and one that threatened for a time to disrupt it altogether, concerned the basis of representation in the proposed government. The less populous states desired representation by states, as in the Congress of the Confederation, and the more populous states demanded the apportionment of representation by population. Virginia, having led in the calling of the convention, presented the plan of government that remained substantially the basis for discussion in the convention. The Virginia Plan, largely the work of James Madison, called for a two-house legislature, both houses to be apportioned according to population, an executive, to be elected by Congress, and a federal judiciary headed by a Supreme Court.

Against this proposal William Paterson of New Jersey presented a plan for a unicameral legislature, in which each state would have one vote, and a plural executive, to be elected by Congress. Where this New Jersey Plan departed from the existing system was in giving its Congress increased authority over finance and commerce and in creating a national judiciary. The solution of electing the upper house by states and the lower house by population ended the one conflict which might have broken up the convention.

During the fight for ratification additional restrictions were demanded, and these were incorporated into the Constitution during the first federal administration in ten amendments. The first nine of these comprised a Bill of Rights limiting the power of government over the private citizen. The tenth specifically reserved to the states all powers not delegated to the federal government. The convention had rejected such a Bill of Rights when George Mason proposed one during the final sessions. The delegates apparently voted the proposition down because they felt that such an addition would merely duplicate existing state bills of rights and because it was late and they wanted to go home, not because they opposed a Bill of Rights on its own merits.

At each step of the way the Constitution was altered to meet specific, practical objections. In the course of meeting them, as Madison said, it was "forced into some deviations from that artificial structure and regular symmetry which an abstract view of the subject might lead an ingenious theorist to bestow on a Constitution planned in his closet or in his imagination." Nevertheless, the deviations were not permitted to do violence to the basic political principles of the eighteenth century, those of republican, libertarian, antidemocratic, American whiggery.

The final draft might well have been more aristocratic than it was. There were a number of delegates who wanted the President to be elected for his lifetime. At one time four states voted for such a provision, and alternative terms of twelve and fifteen years received serious consideration. Property qualifications for legislators were abandoned only because the problem appeared too difficult to arrange nationally. The majority of delegates favored apportionment of representation in the House according to wealth as well as population. This arrangement was discarded largely because of the difficulties involved in measuring wealth. It was generally agreed that new states should be admitted to the Union, but it was by no means agreed that they should be admitted on a basis of equality with the older ones. The Constitution remained ambiguous on this point, and some delegates hoped it would be interpreted in such a way as to leave political control permanently with the Atlantic states.

In drawing up an entirely new Constitution, the Convention had exceeded the authority given it by the Confederation Congress, and now it was faced with the difficult task of persuading the nation to accept what it had done. Realizing that a major source of opposition would probably be the state governments, which the Constitution would deprive of sovereign powers, the convention decided to bypass the state legislatures in seeking national approval by calling for special ratifying conventions in the states. It further provided that when nine states had so ratified, the Constitution would become the law of the land.

The delegates who had remained throughout the convention and signed the document—about one-third had abandoned the project or had remained to oppose it—hurried home to lead the fight for ratification. Most of the smaller states ratified with little opposition. The doubtful contests were fought in the large states, especially New York and Virginia. New York ratified by a narrow margin after a bitter struggle which produced the classic *Federalist Papers* by Alexander Hamilton, James Madison, and John Jay. News of this victory was rushed to Virginia in time to influence its decision to ratify. North Carolina and Rhode Island delayed ratification until after the first federal government had taken office in 1789, and Rhode Island, the one state which had not participated in the convention, joined the Union only under the coercion of the neighboring states. It remained to be seen what form of government would result from the implementation of this unique, concise, and in many respects ambiguous document, the Constitution of the United States.

THE GREATNESS OF GEORGE WASHINGTON

Among the makers of the modern world two political leaders, Washington and Lenin, remain unrivaled by any third in their vast and enduring influence. Each brought to triumph an improbable revolution out of which emerged a nation that in time would dominate half the globe. It is said that forces and not men make history; yet without the leadership of these two men the revolutions which created American democracy on the one hand and Russian communism on the other would not have succeeded. Beyond winning the Revolution and establishing the republic, Washington, by his mere presence as presiding officer of the Constitutional Convention, influenced the shaping of the new government; for the men of the convention acted on the assumption that he would be the nation's first Chief Executive and as such would invest the government with an immense prestige which would greatly facilitate its general acceptance.

It is difficult to keep in mind the fact that Washington was the one man who was indispensable to the task of founding the federal government. He seems strangely aloof from the struggles which marked his two administrations, asserting himself only at the close of his Presidency to present his Farewell Address, prepared for him by Alexander Hamilton. Political activity appears to have been directed almost entirely by his subordinates, chiefly Hamilton and Thomas Jefferson. The all-important fact, however, is that these other men were able to act out their parts as they did because Washington gave the government the strength to withstand the desperate factionalism of the opening years.

Already canonized for his role in the Revolutionary War, Washington was a unique political force by the time he served as president of the Constitutional Convention. As President of the United States he was the one man who could command a loyal opposition. Jefferson became the leader of the party which sought to defeat the program of the Washington administration; yet of the leader whose program he opposed Jefferson later wrote, "On the whole, his character was, in its mass, perfect, in nothing bad, in few points indifferent; and it may truly be said, that never did nature and fortune combine more perfectly to make a man great, and to place him in the same constellation with whatever worthies have merited from man an everlasting remembrance."

THE HAMILTONIAN SYSTEM

It was Washington's intention to select his advisers from the wisest and best part of the nation and to rule on his own responsibility by the light of their wisdom. He selected Hamilton, his trusted former military aide from New York, for Secretary of the Treasury, and Jefferson, the Minister to France, for Secretary of State. His other appointments were of comparatively little consequence, and as it turned out, Jefferson's influence was greater after he had resigned from the Cabinet and become leader of the opposition. It was Hamilton's program that Washington accepted as the basis for his administration.

Hamilton believed that the British royal government more nearly approached perfection than any other that history recorded. By comparison the American federal republic, to his way of thinking, was ramshackle and feckless. It rested upon the will of the people, which was to say upon the will of a great beast, senseless, self-seeking, and always dangerous to the stability of society and the security of property. The salvation of the republic lay in the creation of a responsible aristocracy whose interests would be inextricably associated with the maintenance of a strong central government. The aristocrats would be every bit as venal and self-seeking as the common people beneath them, but theirs would be a socially useful avarice, serving to strengthen the government and maintain order.

Hamilton's economic measures—economic in character but also political in intent—were passed during the first two years of Washington's administration. Hamilton called for the assumption by the federal government of the debts incurred by the states during the Revolution. These were to be funded together with the debts incurred by the Continental Congress and the government of the Articles of Confederation, and the consolidated debt was to be made redeemable in new government bonds at par value, even though at that time state and national bonds sold on the market for but a fraction of their par value.

Opponents of the scheme argued the injustice of allowing speculators thus to make huge profits at the expense of the original patriotic holders of the bonds, the nation as a whole, and the states that had already paid off their wartime indebtedness. Hamilton argued in reply that the scheme was necessary to secure the credit of the nation. He further believed that the system would make good citizens of the economically powerful speculators who held the new government bonds and that when their holdings of state bonds had been nationalized, their loyalties would be nationalized correspondingly. Hamilton had declared that it was "a fundamental maxim, in the system of public credit of the United States, that the creation of debt should always be accompanied with the means of extinguishment." In his funding measures, however, he provided only for payment of interest, not for payment of the debt itself, its perpetuation being essential to his system.

Successful in his funding program, Hamilton was also successful in creating the Bank of the United States, which would handle government money, would have a controlling influence on state banks, and, again, would attach to the national government the interests of the mercantile community, which would provide the main stockholders for the bank. The bank bill called for a subscription of 10 million dollars, one-fifth to be held by the government, giving it one-fifth representation on the board of direction, and the rest to be subscribed privately. Finally, Hamilton instituted a series of excise taxes for the financial purpose of supporting the government and for the political purpose of impressing the power of the government upon the tax-paying population.

Hamilton also proposed, in his Report on Manufactures, a tariff high enough not only to raise revenue but also to protect American industry. This, he argued, would make the nation self-sufficient in time of war, provide markets for domestic farm produce, and provide employment for women and children of "tender years." In this he was frustrated, although a moderate tariff measure was passed in 1792. He faced the difficulty that his staunchest supporters, the commercial interests, opposed a tariff that would interfere with trade.

Amid the political storms it aroused, the Hamiltonian program succeeded brilliantly in its economic purpose of restoring the public credit. The new government bonds were soon selling at above their par value, commerce expanded rapidly, and the nation entered a period of heady prosperity. In his political views Hamilton was a reactionary, quite out of tune with the times. In his economic views he was a creative statesman; he fashioned a practical program for a developing nation against which the economically reactionary Jeffersonians and Jacksonians were to struggle fruitlessly during the following generations.

PARTY CONFLICTS

Among the unlooked-for developments under the new Constitution, perhaps the most unwelcome was the appearance of the two-party system, which Hamilton's controversial program brought into being. "There is nothing I dread so much," John Adams wrote during the Federalist period, "as the division of the Republic into two great parties, each under its leader. . . . This, in my humble opinion, is to be feared as the greatest political evil under our Constitution." Adams had more reason than most to dislike political parties, but his sentiments toward them were shared by all the leading political figures of the time, including those masters of party organization Hamilton and Jefferson.,

Each of these two men thought of himself, not as a party leader, but as a champion of rightly constituted government. Each thought of the other as the chieftain of a dangerous faction, subversive of good public order, a threat to the state. That was Jefferson's point of view when in his first inaugural address he said, "We are all Republicans; we are all Federalists." He meant that "faction" had been defeated and that the country henceforth would be in the hands of a truly national government rather than a party one. The bitterness of politics in the 1790s fed on the assumption that the fight was to the finish for permanent control of the nation. The assumption proved correct, for the Federalists never recovered from their defeat in 1800, partly because of the desperate spirit engendered by the assumption in the first place. Two generations passed before Americans came to accept organized political parties as a regular part of constitutional government.

In retrospect the division between Federalists and Republicans, or Anti-Federalists, can be detected in the *Federalist Papers,* chiefly written by Madison and Hamilton during the New York fight for ratification. Although the coauthors worked effectively together, they actually produced two separate attitudes toward the Constitution. Madison's argument revealed the document as creating a balanced, limited government drawing its authority from the people. Hamilton defended it as the plan for an effective administrative organization which would further the national interest and protect property against injudicious political acts by the states. These divergent points of view had created no issues in the Constitutional Convention, because Hamilton was in such a feeble minority position that he contented himself with announcing his position and standing aside while the convention as a whole worked out a plan alien to his views and in harmony with those of Madison.

Conflict between the mercantile and agrarian interests was inevitable, but it was Hamilton's militant partisanship that split them into irreconcilable factions. He gathered in the speculators' support by granting them opportunities such as they had never anticipated. Within twenty-four hours of Hamilton's first financial report the value of government securities had risen by 50 percent, speculators were running to the woods to buy securities from the common people before the news spread, and congressmen, about half of whom were probably holders of public securities, were beginning to speak of assumption at par as the minimum requirement of honesty.

Hamilton's program drove into the opposition agrarian leaders who had been nationalistic supporters of the Constitution and the Judiciary Act of 1789, which created the national judiciary. Neither Madison nor Jefferson had opposed federal assumption of the states' debts on some basis. Neither, for that matter, had given systematic attention to financial questions. Some of their planter colleagues had, however, and the naked ruthlessness of Hamilton's program caused the landed interest to side at once with the political economics of such agrarian writers as John Taylor of Caroline.

The agrarians argued the injustice of enriching speculators at the expense of the nation, and beyond that they argued the evil of maintaining the debt for what amounted to purposes of political bribery. It should be paid off. They objected to the bank as a government-authorized monopoly which similarly would lend itself to political corruption. The government, they argued, should conduct itself like an honest business house and economize for the purpose of paying its debts. It should also do so as a useful exercise in self-limitation of powers. It should be beholden to no particular group in the nation and should benefit no particular group, least of all the small speculating interest as compared with the great farming majority.

When Hamilton's program divided the commercial North from the agrarian South, it also crystallized a long-standing contrast in political outlook between New England and the Southern states. New Englanders were proud of their township, county, and state government regulations, which the people themselves maintained for the good of the whole. They spoke glowingly of the "steady habits of New England, which habits were formed by a singular machinery in the body politic." But to the Southern agrarian aristocrats, living as they did in comparative isolation on splendid, self-sufficient estates, such complicated machinery of government seemed like the wheels and cogs of tyranny. The planters believed in centralized government for their own plantations; otherwise the best government was the one that governed least.

The first political parties were divided more clearly by divergent political theories than was perhaps ever again the case in the nation's history, and appropriately the opposing leaders were dramatic contrasts to each other personally. Hamilton was a short, dapper, handsome, and vigorously forceful man who had been born under disadvantageous circumstances—the bastard son of a Scottish peddler, as the hostile John Adams had put it. He leaped to prominence by virtue of his energy and brilliance, becoming General Washington's aide during the Revolution at the age of twenty and then the leading figure behind the calling of the Constitutional Convention. By his thirty-fifth year he had single-handedly established the economic basis upon which the new government would rest. An almost arrogantly honest man, Hamilton created a system founded upon a firm faith in the fundamental dishonesty of man.

Against him Jefferson, a descendant of the aristocratic Randolph family, became the chief philosopher and spokesman for government based upon faith in the ability of men to govern themselves. A tall, homely, shambling figure of a man, Jefferson was probably not Hamilton's match in logical argument, and certainly not his match in the grasp of economic realities. The range of Jefferson's inquiring genius, however, made Hamilton's thinking appear narrowly provincial by comparison. A brilliant product of the Age of Enlightenment, Jefferson was a lawyer, statesman, political theorist, agricultural scientist, natural scientist, inventor, architect, classical scholar, educator, musician, and man of letters. Awkward in public speech, he was a master literary stylist; his writings remain among the most eloquent expressions of continuing American ideals. In different ways both Jefferson and Hamilton rather despised the arts of politics, and both were masters of political manipulation. Jefferson's politics were on the side of popular rule, however, and they were destined to triumph.

Hamilton began to initiate his program while Jefferson was still abroad, and it was Madison in Congress who rose first in opposition. Under his leadership the Anti-Federalists opposed Hamilton's assumption program and put forward an alternate proposal which would reward the original bond holders rather than the later speculators. Hamilton's assumption measure was defeated in the House, and its eventual passage was made possible only by a bargain with Jefferson. Jefferson, just returned from France, exchanged his influence in favor of Hamilton's measure for Hamilton's influence in favor of locating the national capital permanently in the South. After making this bad bargain, Jefferson and Madison were in a weak position to fight the excise taxes, which they disapproved of, because they were necessary to the financing of the funding program.

It was the creation of a national bank which they made the chief issue, arguing not only that it was dangerous and unjust but also that it was unconstitutional, no specific provision having been made in the Constitution for a federally chartered bank. In reply Hamilton argued that Congress had the "implied power" to establish such a bank, since the bank was necessary to the performance of functions which were specifically authorized by the Constitution.

THE FRENCH REVOLUTION

The extraconstitutionality and novelty of the two-party system was sufficiently shocking in itself to eighteenth-century statesmen, but the shock was compounded by violent revolutionary influences imported from France. On May 5, 1789, a month after the first Congress of the new federal government took up its duties, the Estates-General met in France for the first time in 175 years. Revolution swiftly followed, and Americans gave it an enthusiastic welcome, in fact took positive pride in it. They congratulated themselves that the more enlightened part of the Old World was taking a lesson from the New. But as the revolution grew increasingly violent, American conservatives became increasingly critical. They read Edmund Burke's *Reflections on the Revolution in France* and became convinced that the old champion of the American cause was right again. Americans began to take sides and argue heatedly about France. The argument remained largely academic until war broke out between France and England in 1793.

The French government, already at war with Austria and Russia, opened the year by executing the King, then declared war against Great Britain, Holland, and Spain and invited the peoples of Europe to rise up against their rulers. In November it announced the abolition of the worship of God and the organization of the cult of reason.

Within a few months of the French King's execution Citizen Genêt arrived in the United States as the new French Minister to America. His orders were to make what capital he could of the fund of republican enthusiasm in America and of the military alliance of 1778, which still bound the United States to support France in war. Genêt was greeted with enthusiastic mass demonstrations wherever he went, and apparently became convinced that he, rather than Washington, represented the will of the American people. He busied himself with projects to make American men and resources felt on the French side. His irresponsible conduct was acutely embarrassing to Jefferson, who finally asked the French government to relieve Genêt of his duties.

Fast on the heels of the French declaration of war the first of the Democratic Societies appeared in Philadelphia, and they spread rapidly throughout the Union. Although less violent and more law-abiding than the old Sons of Liberty, these societies were disturbingly democratic in their behavior, and some of them functioned without the restraining influence of upper-class leadership. They were patterned upon the revolutionary Jacobin clubs in France, and they made Citizen Genêt's travels through America one long triumphal march.

In 1794 the Reign of Terror was at flood tide in France, and in that year farmers in western Pennsylvania demonstrated against the newly imposed excise tax on whiskey. They raised liberty poles, held mass meetings, and rioted. The violence lacked direction, however, and failed to win support from the law-abiding and essentially middle-class Democratic Societies outside the immediate region.

Washington nevertheless was convinced that the Democratic Societies were behind these whiskey rebels, and although he himself was a member of the Society of the Cincinnati, he did not suppose that anything could be "more absurd, more arrogant, or more pernicious to the peace of society, than . . . self created bodies . . . endeavoring . . . to form themselves into permanent censors . . . endeavoring to form their *will* into laws for the government of the whole. . . ." He sent Col. Alexander Hamilton after the rebels at the head of an absurdly large militia. By the time Hamilton had reached the scene, the local authorities had stepped in and there was no organized opposition to attack. Cheated of his glory, Hamilton nevertheless charged ahead, making arrests and calling for "rigor everywhere." Under the impact of Washington's opposition and Genêt's absurdities, the rather flimsy Democratic Societies disintegrated, but the harsh suppression of the very little rebellion damaged the reputation of the administration and played into the hands of the opposition.

The wars of the French Revolution were full of both opportunities and dangers for the new federal republic. They distracted Europe from America while the United States was establishing itself, and at the same time they opened up great commercial opportunities to a neutral nation. Under the terms of the Franco-American treaty of 1778 France might have asked America to enter the war, but the United States was more valuable to France as a neutral supplier of the French West Indies.

The difficulty here for the United States was a difference of opinion between France and England as to the trading rights of neutrals. The French and the Franco-American treaty permitted the trade of neutrals with belligerents except in contraband, which did not include food and naval stores. The British, who had not accepted this dictum, issued orders-in-council in 1793 to bring in all ships carrying goods to French ports. Early the next year three hundred American vessels were captured in the Caribbean under these orders. News of the captures further aroused Americans, who already were convinced that the British were inciting the Indians against America in the Northwest, and the ensuing war crisis persuaded Washington to send John Jay to England to secure the peace with England which was so necessary to the new republic.

By the terms of the resulting Jay Treaty of 1794, Great Britain agreed to evacuate forts on American soil in the Northwest and to pay compensation at some future time for the capture of American vessels. Trade with the British West Indies was permitted, but on conditions which were unacceptable to the United States Senate. On the other hand Britain retained fur-trading rights with the Indians on American soil, and the British conceded nothing to the American claims concerning trading rights of neutrals. After some hesitation Washington submitted the treaty to the Senate, fearing that war with England would result from refusal to sign it, and the Senate, amid the angry outcries of an indignant public, approved it by barely more than the necessary two-thirds majority. The Jay Treaty was followed in 1795 by a highly popular treaty with Spain, arranged by Thomas Pinckney of South Carolina, settling the northern boundary of Spanish Florida at 31° and opening the Mississippi, including the port of New Orleans, to American trade.

THE ADAMS ADMINISTRATION

Declining to serve for a third term, Washington opened the way in 1796 for the party contests which had been checked to some extent by the great regard in which he was still held. Jefferson, as the acknowledged leader of the Anti-Federalists, was their obvious candidate. Among the Federalists a split had developed between Hamilton of New York, who had already resigned as Secretary of the Treasury, and Vice President John Adams of New England. Adams won the candidacy against the opposition of Hamilton, and by a margin of 71 electoral votes to 68 he won the Presidency. In this as in other early elections the presidential electors were chosen by the state legislatures, and no election campaign was waged in the modern sense. The opposition candidate, Jefferson, since he received the second largest vote, won the Vice Presidency in place of the Federalist candidate, Thomas Pinckney—a peculiar situation which was prevented from repeating itself by the Twelfth Amendment to the Constitution, passed in 1804.

Within the limitations of his own view of his office, the crotchety Adams was fairly effective as President. In foreign affairs he took a realistic and independent view of America's interests, successfully withstanding the pro-British influences within his party as well as the pro-French efforts of the opposition. In domestic politics he successfully resisted the intrigues of the politically astute Hamilton, and in 1800 he was still the head of his party and in a good position to win reelection. His distaste for politics and his distrust of popular rule, however, limited his effectiveness in a time of bitter party strife. He did little to organize his party behind him or to rid his administration of the Hamiltonian faction which opposed him, and unlike Washington, he often absented himself from the capital for months at a time, remaining almost completely out of touch with his subordinates.

The most trying problems of Adams's administration, as of Washington's second term, were in foreign affairs. Angered by the Jay Treaty, the French had stepped up their attacks on American commerce, and they refused to accept the Minister Adams appointed to the French court. To avoid a war with France, which would have been highly popular with the Hamiltonian faction, Adams sent a diplomatic mission to the French government. The members of the mission were told that they could not begin diplomatic discussions until they paid bribes to French officials, a fairly common European practice. The Americans indignantly refused and sent a report back to President Adams, and he submitted it to Congress, except for the names of the French agents involved, whom he listed as Messrs. X, Y, and Z. The report of the "XYZ Affair" was published and set off a national salvo of martial indignation, precipitating an undeclared naval war with France and rousing Congress to pass the Alien and Sedition Acts.

The acts, unsponsored by the administration, were passed partly out of fury and partly for Federalist party advantage. Their purposes were to curb the political power of the new immigrants, who, it was noted, tended overwhelmingly to vote Republican, and to curb criticism of the government by the opposing press as well as by private citizens. The three Alien Acts extended the residence requirement for citizenship from five to fourteen years and empowered the President to jail or deport undesirable aliens. The Sedition Act provided fines and jail sentences for anybody who wrote or said something "with intent to defame . . . or bring into contempt or disrepute" any member of the government. No aliens were prosecuted under the Alien Acts, but more than two dozen men, most of them newspaper editors, were jailed under the Sedition Act.

The Jeffersonians tried to combat this repressive legislation with the Virginia and Kentucky Resolutions, written by Madison and Jefferson, who argued the unconstitutionality of these laws and suggested that the states had the constitutional authority to nullify them. They were disappointed in the hope that other state legislatures besides those of Virginia and Kentucky would pass similar resolutions, and their resolutions probably had little effect on the presidential election that followed. They were to have a much greater political impact more than a generation later, when John C. Calhoun resurrected them in defense of the Southern states-rights argument.

In this atmosphere of mutual suspicion John Adams in 1800 ran for reelection against Jefferson. As it turned out, none of the bitter issues of the time had a perceptible influence on the outcome of the election. Outside the state of New York, Adams was given a few votes more than he had received in 1796. He nevertheless lost the election because New York, which until then had voted solidly Federalist, was captured by the opposition under the direction of Tammany Hall and the brilliant political leader Aaron Burr. New York voted for Jefferson, with Burr as his running mate, and by that margin the Presidency changed from Federalist to Republican hands. Since Burr and Jefferson received the same number of electoral votes, the House of Representatives had the constitutional right to choose either man as President. Congress finally did name Jefferson President-elect, but for a time it appeared that the anti-Jeffersonians might deprive him of the office. This situation also was made impossible in the future by the Twelfth Amendment to the Constitution.

Thus narrowly slipped into office, Jefferson launched quietly upon what he afterwards liked to speak of as a revolution. Adams, meanwhile, as his last act in office, launched a counterrevolution of his own by appointing stout Federalists to newly authorized judicial posts, and most importantly by appointing John Marshall Chief Justice of the Supreme Court. Marshall was to outlast four Presidents in that position and to entrench federalism in the courts for a generation after it had been driven from the executive branch of the government.

BIBLIOGRAPHY FOR CHAPTER 6

J. C. Miller, The Federalist Era, 1789–1801 (1960)
Max Farrand, The Framing of the Constitution (1913)
R. A. Rutland, Ordeal of the Constitution (1966)
The Federalist Papers
L. D. White, The Federalists (1948)—an administrative history
Adrienne Koch, Power, Morals, and the Founding Fathers (1961)
Marcus Cunliffe, George Washington, Man and Monument (1958)
M. J. Dauer, The Adams Federalists (1953)
S. G. Kurtz, The Presidency of John Adams (1958)
Russel Nye, Cultural Life of the New Nation, 1776–1830 (1960)
P. A. Varg, Foreign Policies of the Founding Fathers (1963)
Bray Hammond, Banks and Politics (1957)
J. M. Smith, Freedom's Fetters (1956)—the Alien and Sedition Acts

CHAPTER 7

THE JEFFERSONIAN ERA

JEFFERSONIAN REPUBLICANISM

Jefferson's first inaugural address, with its faith in a libertarian society founded upon a self-reliant yeomanry and maintaining itself in perfect equipose within the balanced government of the Constitution, is the classic document of eighteenth-century republicanism. Jefferson took the occasion to present "the essential principles of this government, and consequently those which ought to shape its administration." His republicanism breathed the old-fashioned Whig spirit of John Locke. It comfortably retained Locke's mutually contradictory tenets of majority rule and inalienable personal rights. Like Locke, Jefferson could incorporate this inconsistency in his beliefs because although his conception of individual rights was vivid and specific, his conception of majority rule was hazy and general and not altogether distinguishable from the idea of "the common good."

Jefferson was far from being a democrat in the sense that the word came to be used in the nineteenth century. In his view, the first requirement of government was not that it be completely representative, but that it be limited. Although he viewed human nature more optimistically than most of his colleagues, he believed with them that power inevitably corrupted and that liberty was secure only where power was limited. To the extent that government was necessary, it should be controlled by the people immediately affected, so far as possible. State governments should not assume the responsibilities which the counties could discharge, and the national government should accept as a self-limiting duty "the support of the State governments in all their rights, as the most competent administrations for our domestic concerns and the surest bulwarks against antirepublican tendencies." Although later interpreted by Southerners simply as a states-rights advocate, Jefferson was more truly an advocate of localized authority generally than a champion of state sovereignty.

It was the agrarian basis of American society, in Jefferson's view, that made the continuance of republican institutions possible. The yeoman farmer was the key to a free society. On the one hand, owning his own land and supplying most of his own wants, he represented the freest class of men on earth. On the other hand his position in society did not give him the power to tyrannize others. And beyond this, despite his distaste for Rousseau's romanticism, Jefferson cherished a very nearly mystical faith that "those who labor in the earth are the chosen people of God, if ever he had a chosen people," and that "corruption of morals in the mass of cultivators is a phenomenon of which no age nor nation has furnished an example."

The yeomanry ought to be charged with controlling their own local affairs and choosing the representatives who would speak for them in the larger areas of activity with which they were unfamiliar. Those who guided the national destinies, in Jefferson's view, should be drawn from the natural aristocracy, chosen not on the basis of having been born to high station, but on the basis of a natural superiority in virtues and talents whatever their original station in life. Jefferson proposed a system of education which would bring forth this natural aristocracy by giving all boys a grammar school training—girls did not figure significantly in the Jeffersonian system—and then, through successive weedings out, bringing to college training at state expense the select group which had demonstrated its ability to assume the main national responsibilities. Jefferson's efforts to create such an educational system in Virginia failed, and the equalitarian educational system which later developed in democratic America, in the contrast it presents to the Jeffersonian system, is one good measure of the contrast between democracy as Jefferson understood it and democracy as it turned out to be.

JEFFERSON'S FIRST ADMINISTRATION

As President, Jefferson set out at once to quiet the sectional conflict which had dominated the campaign by making his inaugural address conciliatory and by appointing New Englanders as Attorney General, Secretary of War, and Postmaster General. For the two most important posts he chose two of his most brilliant Republican colleagues. James Madison, the architect of the Constitution, became Secretary of State, and Albert Gallatin of Switzerland and Pennsylvania became Secretary of the Treasury.

In replacing Federalist appointments, Jefferson moved slowly out of regard for Federalist sensibilities and out of a distaste for the job, noting that "whenever a man has cast a longing eye on offices, a rottenness begins in his conduct." He did not extend his forbearance, however, to the "midnight judges" whom Adams had crowded onto the bench during his last hours and minutes in office. Jefferson's own brief and highly successful experience as a lawyer had left him distrustful of the law as a guardian of liberty, and the judicial tyranny which the Sedition Act had unleashed was fresh in his memory. He set forth at once, therefore, to try to replace Adams's appointments with his own and then to repeal the Judiciary Act of 1801, which had created these new positions.

Jefferson's anger at the midnight appointments was heightened by the appointment of his hated cousin John Marshall as Chief Justice, and Cousin John lost no time in getting in his own hard licks. At the first session of the Supreme Court Marshall handed down the decision in the case of *Marbury v. Madison,* dealing with a midnight appointment, Marbury, from whom Secretary of State Madison had withheld the position. The case appears to have been contrived in order to allow Marshall to lecture Jefferson through the medium of judicial opinion and, more importantly, to enable Marshall to assert the authority of the Supreme Court to declare federal laws unconstitutional. Until that time the Supreme Court had ruled against no federal law, and it was by no means clear that the Constitution gave the highest court that power.

After finding Madison's actions legally indefensible, Marshall went on to declare that Marbury nevertheless could not gain his just deserts by applying to the Supreme Court for them. The authority by which Marbury had attempted to do so had been the Judiciary Act of 1789, which, Marshall ruled, was constitutionally faulty in this regard. It was "emphatically the province and duty of the judicial department to say what the law is," and "a law repugnant to the Constitution is void." The relevant clause of the Judiciary Act was therefore declared unconstitutional, and Marbury could not receive satisfaction.

This first case in which the Supreme Court asserted the right to declare a federal law unconstitutional was cleverly contrived to give no one a practical interest in challenging the decision. Having made his point, Marshall never again attempted to assert this authority. The next time the Supreme Court did so was 1857, in the Dred Scott decision, which was followed by an enormous uproar and then civil war.

Jefferson, no doubt with Marshall in mind as an eventual victim, acted through his congressional leaders to impeach Federalist judges, beginning first with an obvious incompetent by reason of insanity. Successful in this, House Republicans impeached a Supreme Court justice, Samuel Chase, who had conducted sedition trials in a most violently injudicious manner. Tried by the Senate, Chase was found innocent of crimes and misdemeanors. With this defeat the Jeffersonians gave up the fight, and federalism continued its guardianship of the nation from its vantage point in the federal judiciary.

Jefferson had much better fortune elsewhere during his first administration. He freed those imprisoned under the Sedition Act and returned them their fines. As for the United States Bank, he was content to tolerate it until its charter expired in 1811. He applied himself, however, to ridding the nation of its debt, reducing the personnel of the government, shrinking the army, stopping naval construction, but at the same time removing excise, stamp, and land taxes.

Aided by the removal of the national capital in 1800 from urbane, aristocratic New York to the Washington, D.C., mud flats, he eliminated most of the ceremonies of his office to conform to his views on proper republican simplicity.

His pure theory was subject to the corruptions of power, however, as he himself predicted it would be. In 1802 he wrote Secretary of the Treasury Gallatin that since all banks were evil whether chartered by the nation or the states, "between such parties the less we meddle the better." But the next year he wrote Gallatin, "I am decidedly in favor of making all the banks republican by sharing deposits with them in proportion to the dispositions they show." Still, during his first administration he was probably as successful in putting his ideas into action as any President has ever been. To a friend he wrote, "The path we have to pursue is so quiet that we have nothing scarcely to propose to our Legislature. A noiseless course, not meddling with the affairs of others, unattractive of notice, is a mark that society is going on in happiness." Of all federal administrations in the nation's history, the first Jefferson administration governed least, a circumstance made possible by Jefferson's own great political skill as well as convictions and, with notable exceptions such as his fury against the midnight judges, by his imperturbable tolerance and forbearance.

During his first term Jefferson sinned seriously but once against his eighteenth-century republican decalogue. The opportunity to buy the province of Louisiana from France presented itself to him, and despite the absence of explicit constitutional authority, he hurried to do so. Until 1800 Louisiana had been in Spanish hands, and Jefferson had thought that from the American point of view there could be no better custodian for it "till our population can be sufficiently advanced to gain it from them piece by piece." In 1800, however, Spain returned it to the France of Napoleon Bonaparte, and when this dangerous development occurred, Jefferson moved to acquire for the United States at least the port of New Orleans, which was vital to the Mississippi trade of the Northwest. In 1802 Spain, still actually in occupation of New Orleans, suspended the American right of deposit there, and amid demands for war Jefferson sent James Monroe to Paris to help the American Minister, Robert Livingston, persuade Napoleon to sell New Orleans.

The French armies had been demolished by disease and native insurrection in Santo Domingo, and the resumption of hostilities impended in Europe, and so Napoleon decided to cut his American losses and sell all of Louisiana to the United States for 15 million dollars. The surprised American negotiators accepted, and the United States almost doubled its territory. Jefferson, the strict constructionist, with no specific authorization in the Constitution for such an act, rushed the measure through Congress before Napoleon could change his mind, later justifying the purchase as a response to a "higher obligation" than that of written laws.

For Jefferson the acquisition of Louisiana meant room for indefinite expansion of that farming population which in his view was the one firm foundation for republican institutions. To embittered New England Federalists, who had visions of new states rising up in the West to overwhelm New England's already waning power in the Union, it was a ruthless violation of the Constitution and one which presaged the end of the republic. As the election of 1804 was to show, however, Jefferson's program of sweet reasonableness was beginning to subvert even that stronghold of Federalism in 1804, running against the Federalist candidate C. C. Pinckney of South Carolina, he won the electoral votes of every state except Connecticut and Delaware.

WESTERN EXPANSION

While many New Englanders would have been happy to see the West depart from the Union to form some kind of savage nation of its own, many Westerners were on their part willing to end their unfriendly and seemingly unrewarding connection with the Eastern states. The trans-Appalachian settlements, which in 1800 numbered 386,000 souls, had had their first beginnings on the eve of the Revolution, after the suppression of Pontiac's Conspiracy. In the early seventies two Virginia land speculators, James Robertson and John Sevier, led separate parties of settlers into what was then western North Carolina and later eastern Tennessee, creating the Watauga Association as their governing body. In 1775 Richard Henderson of North Carolina organized the Transylvania Company, which made settlement in what later became part of Kentucky. The history of these early settlements was marked by bickering among the settlers, very high-handed and legally questionable tactics on the part of their leaders, and constant jurisdictional disputes with the mother states and later with the government of the Confederation.

Ohio Territory in the Northwest, by contrast, was settled in a relatively orderly manner under the terms of the Ordinance of 1785 and that of 1787 and under the direction of various state governments and authorized land companies. Connecticut retained a portion of northern Ohio, the Western Reserve, where New England society was transplanted under the auspices of the Connecticut Land Company and Moses Cleaveland. Virginia retained a military district in southern Ohio, chiefly for the purpose of rewarding Revolutionary War veterans. Southeastern Ohio went at bargain rates to the Ohio Company on the basis of a complicated piece of chicanery involving the creation of a second company, the Scioto Company, in which congressmen held stock. The Scioto Company earned nothing but scandal, and the backers of the Ohio Company failed to make the huge profits anticipated. The settlement of Ohio meanwhile proceeded briskly.

The early history of the New West was marked by struggles with the states and the United States that repeatedly threatened the dismemberment of the new nation. The key to Western settlement was the port of New Orleans, which controlled the whole Western system of water transportation. In 1785 the Confederation Congress authorized the New Yorker John Jay to arrange a treaty with Spain. The resulting Jay-Gardoqui Treaty exchanged commercial concessions in Spanish ports, which would aid principally New England and the middle states, for an American agreement to surrender its claims to the use of the Mississippi for twenty-five years. Although the treaty failed of ratification, seven states voted in its favor, and Westerners began seriously to consider the Spanish offer to admit them to the Spanish empire.

In these circumstances Tennessee ruled itself as the independent nation of Franklin for five years before it settled upon a working arrangement with the Union, and then it accepted as its chief leader John Sevier, upon whom the federal government had not yet bestowed an official pardon for his leadership of the Franklin independence movement. Tennessee in 1796 elected as its first senator William Blount, who proceeded to conspire to capture Louisiana Territory and the Floridas for Great Britain. Expelled from the Senate for high misdemeanor, Blount was enthusiastically received in Tennessee and elected presiding officer of the state senate.

James Wilkinson was almost constantly involved in a bewildering variety of conspiracies from the time of his early career under Horatio Gates and Benedict Arnold until his opium-induced death in 1825 while representing the American Bible Society in Mexico; yet his justly deserved reputation as a traitor did not prevent him from receiving a Jeffersonian appointment as governor of Louisiana Territory, at a time when he was in the pay of the Spanish government.

Wilkinson was also involved in the most famous of the Western intrigues, the schemes of Aaron Burr, apparently to form some sort of independent Western nation. Burr, politically discredited by his duel with Hamilton in 1804 and out of favor with Jefferson, had apparently already involved himself in a scheme to separate New York and New England from the Union. Failing in this, he moved west to investigate the possibilities of establishing a Western empire under either British or Spanish patronage. Wilkinson, with whom he plotted, betrayed him to Jefferson, and in 1807 Burr was tried for treason by John Marshall. Burr had failed to repudiate the efforts of those politicians who in 1801 had attempted to make him President instead of Jefferson, and now, six years later, Jefferson became a thoroughly vindictive prosecutor of Burr. But Marshall turned the trial into a judicial attack on Jefferson and, incidentally to this, secured Burr's acquittal. The precedent established by Marshall, in requiring the prosecution to provide evidence it could hardly have obtained, made future conviction for the crime of treason a near impossibility, and from then on the courts had to try traitors for espionage instead. With Louisiana and New Orleans in American hands and with Tennessee, Kentucky, and Ohio admitted to statehood meanwhile, the Burr trial brought a close to the era of Western conspiracies.

The first Western state, Kentucky, drew up its constitution and entered the Union in 1792 after a sharp struggle in which representatives of the major property-holding interests substantially defeated the radical democrats. Drawing their program from the Pennsylvania constitution of 1776, the radicals fought for manhood suffrage, abolition of slavery, a one-house legislature, popular election of all local officials, and the omission of a bill of rights. Opposition to a bill of rights was based partly on the protection such a bill would give to slavery as a form of private property. Partly, however, the radicals rejected it as an undemocratic restriction on the will of the people. For democrats in Kentucky as elsewhere in the West, democracy meant the full implementation of the will of the majority, unobstructed even by those guards to individual liberty which in the Jeffersonian view served the first purpose of government. This was to prove the fundamental difference which divided libertarian Jeffersonian republicanism from majoritarian Jacksonian democracy. In 1792, however, the Kentucky conservatives carried the day.

By democratic standards the Tennessee constitution of 1796 improved on the Kentucky model, but it was Ohio, in 1803, that set the pattern for democratic government for the coming age of Jackson. Ohio extended the ballot to all white male taxpayers resident in the state for a year. Both governor and legislature were popularly elected, and all town and township officers were chosen annually by the people. The legislature rather than the governor chose judges. Subsequent constitutions of new Western free states tended to follow this Ohio model.

JEFFERSONIAN NEUTRALITY

Absolutely essential to the Jeffersonian system was an immaculate isolation from Europe in the areas of politics and war. The system did not admit of the maintenance of a large army and navy, because these would theaten the liberties of the people and impose burdensome taxes upon them.

Jefferson demonstrated that he was no pacifist during his first administration by refusing to pay tribute to the pirate rulers of North Africa, as European nations did and the United States had formerly done. He ordered the bombardment of Tripoli, which led to a treaty with Tripoli meeting American conditions. At the same time, Jefferson held to the idealistic view that wars were unreasonable and, for United States, unnecessary. The United States could remain neutral during Europe's wars, and it could force Europe to respect its neutrality by the peaceful and reasonable method of imposing sanctions on the violator. The famous Jeffersonian rule was friendship with all nations and entangling military alliance with none. It was true that the birth of the republic had been achieved through the original sin of a permanent entangling military alliance with France. Nevertheless, once independence had been achieved, Jeffersonians as well as Federalists wished to conduct themselves whenever they could as if no such alliance existed.

This had proved difficult for Washington and Adams, but Jefferson inherited from Adams the final settlement with France and a period of diplomatic calm in which to create his "quiet" system of government. Following his triumphant reelection, Jefferson embarked with understandable confidence upon a second administration during which his quiet system was to be wrecked beyond recovery by international storms he mistakenly supposed he could control.

In 1805 Lord Nelson broke French naval power at Trafalgar, and two months later Napoleon defeated the combined Austrian and Russian armies at Austerlitz. In the stalemated war of attrition that followed, between the mistress of the seas and the master of the continent, neutral trade was harried and destroyed by authority of British orders-in-council and Napoleonic decrees, inflicting terrible depredations upon American commerce. Since Britain controlled the seas, that nation was the more effective in carrying out confiscations, and to this violation of American neutrality it added the kidnapping of American sailors into the British Navy. Impressment, as the practice was called, was vital to the manning of the British Navy, given the uninviting conditions of navy life, and since there often was no good way of distinguishing American from British sailors, the English government refused to guarantee the security of Americans from being accidentally impressed.

In 1807 the British warship *Leopard,* in search of deserters, intercepted the American frigate *Chesapeake.* When the commander of the *Chesapeake* refused to permit a search party on board, the *Leopard* opened fire, boarded the ship, and removed some alleged deserters. That the United States would declare war immediately seemed to many to be a foregone conclusion, but Jefferson had other plans. He was ambitious to give an enlightened demonstration of the superior effectiveness of peaceful coercion over war. He therefore replied to the *Leopard-Chesapeake* affair with the Embargo Act, closing all American ports to foreign trade, in the confidence that this would starve England into submission before it had destroyed the American economy.

When, after fourteen months of desperate economic depression, Jefferson's expectations were still disappointed, he consented to replacing the Embargo Act with the Non-Intercourse Act. This act opened trade with all countries but England and France and promised to open trade with either of those countries when it would cease its attack on American shipping. Then Jefferson, "panting for retirement," departed for his plantation at Monticello, turning the problem over to his Virginia neighbor, close friend, and chosen successor President Madison, who defeated C. C. Pinckney by 122 electoral votes to 47.

Under Madison, failure of the Non-Intercourse Act was followed by passage of Macon's Bill No. 2, ending nonintercourse but promising to revive it against France if Britain rescinded its orders-in-council or against Britain if Napoleon rescinded his decrees. The wily Napoleon persuaded Madison to restore nonintercourse with England by announcing the revocation of the disputed decrees without, apparently, the least intention of ceasing their enforcement. At that point an unlikely turn in the weather suddenly created for the first time the conditions under which the Jeffersonian policy of peaceful coercion might have proved effective. The British winter of 1811–1812 was the worst in a century and a half, and during that winter Napoleon extended his continental system against England with increasing effect. The American market was vital to England as never before, and in June, 1812, the British suspended the orders-in-council. Five days previously and weeks before word could be received of the British capitulation, Congress had declared war on England.

ORIGINS OF THE WAR OF 1812

From the embargo in 1807 until the winter of 1811–1812, the Jefferson-Madison programs of economic coercion had consistently damaged the American economy much more seriously than that of either Britain or France. Until the embargo American shippers, despite both British and French harassment, has been making unprecedented profits from neutral trade. When England's control of the seas increased after Trafalgar in 1805, neutral trade became much safer for neutrals who would submit to British inspection and regulation, as American shippers were glad to do, considering the profits involved. Then that Virginian in the White House put an end to this traffic, plunging New England and New York into depression and permanently ruining many of the smaller shippers.

Depression struck also in the South and the West, but the brunt of the embargo was sustained by the Northeast, where Federalism had lately been dying out. Now Federalism surged up again, and state legislatures hurled defiance against the federal government in terms reminiscent of those Virginia and Kentucky Resolutions of Madison and Jefferson a decade earlier. The rapid spread of secessionist sentiment from New York north did not go unnoticed in England, where many had never accepted American independence as final. The possibility that Jefferson and Madison might drive New York and New England back into the British Empire made at least some English governmental officials wholly enthusiastic supporters of the Jeffersonian policy.

Nothing had happened by 1812 to reconcile most of the Northeast either to a continuance of the program of economic coercion or, even worse, to waging war with England in support of it, and that section of the country voted heavily against the declaration of war (the maritime areas of the Northeast, however, voted in its favor). The measure passed by a large margin on the strength of its popularity in the South and the West. The division of sentiment was reflected also in the election of 1812, when Madison, the mild leader of the "war party," won reelection on the basis of Southern and Western votes against DeWitt Clinton of New York, who carried every state in the Northeast but Pennsylvania and Vermont. Though ostensibly a war for "Free Trade and Sailors' Rights," the War of 1812 was most popular in those areas least affected by British regulation and impressment.

In the South and West the war was popular on patriotic grounds, for American sovereignty obviously was being violated, but there were also more tangible reasons for its popularity. In the Northwest the Indians had been removed from more than 100 million acres of land by treaties they did not entirely understand. They were spoiling for a fight, and in 1811 the Shawnee Chief Tecumseh announced the beginning of a general organization of Northern and Southern tribes against further white penetration. The governor of Indiana Territory, William Henry Harrison, answered the challenge by moving against the Shawnees during the temporary absence of Tecumseh, only to be surprised by the forewarned Indians. In the resulting Battle of Tippecanoe, Harrison drove them back and burned their Prophetstown, but at the cost of heavy casualties and without breaking Tecumseh's power.

The frontiersmen, meanwhile, were absolutely convinced that the English in Canada, guided by their fur-trading interest and their hatred of the United States, were supplying the Indians with arms and sending them against the Americans. The battle of Tippecanoe therefore inflamed anti-British feeling on the frontier and aroused frontiersmen to demand a war with Britain, a war which would not only end the Anglo-Indian menace but also result in the American conquest of Canada. And while anti-British feeling was combining with land hunger to make this war popular in the Northwest, anti-Spanish feeling combined with land hunger to make war popular on the Southern frontier, where the Floridas, under weak Spanish administration, had become nests of pirates, international adventurers, raiding Indians, and runaway slaves. In the elections of 1810 this Western war sentiment sent to Congress from the Western regions the "war hawks," who elected their leader Henry Clay as Speaker of the House and launched the campaign which ended with the declaration of war.

THE WAR OF 1812

The unhappy experience of the United States with its state militia during the Revolutionary War had done nothing to diminish confidence in the system. With an ill-trained standing army of less than 7,000 men, the militia remained the main line of defense, and one which unhappily sorted well with the leadership it was given. Theoretically there were 694,000 of these "swords of the Republic," but despite repeated appeals to them to act accordingly, there were never more than 35,000 men in the war. This was hardly sufficient even against the motley opposition that England could spare from the Napoleonic conflict, but in addition, the campaigns were hopelessly bungled by the superannuated commanders.

The Americans having no chance of matching the British Navy in sea battles, attack on Canada was obviously dictated, and a three-pronged attack was planned—from Detroit, Niagara, and Lake Champlain. But at the outset Gen. William Hull was outmaneuvered by the British and surrendered Detroit to a force half the size of his own, losing his personal belongings in the process, along with the army war plans. At Niagara the New York militia quit the fight when it crossed the border. At Plattsburg on Lake Champlain the militia made a 20-mile hike, decided that was enough, and went home.

These demonstrations of ineptitude taught the Americans enough to make possible the winning of some of their subsequent battles under new commanders, notably the stirring American triumph at Niagara in the Battle of Lundy's Lane. Paradoxically, however, the real saving of the American cause was due, not to military victories, but to naval exploits. At the outset the American Navy gained spectacular victories at sea in one encounter after another, based on the heavier broadsides of the American ships and the better spirit of the volunteer American crews. But soon the British bottled up the American Navy in American harbors, where it remained for the rest of the war. Of much greater strategic importance were the tour de force of Oliver Hazard Perry in building a fleet on Lake Erie, which gained control of the lake for the United States, and the naval victory of Thomas Macdonough on Lake Champlain, which gave the United States an almost invulnerable position along the eastern Canadian border. It was the strong position of the nation's freshwater navy that mainly decided the British government in favor of moderate peace terms.

Checked in Canada, the British, in the final stages of the war, used their naval superiority to invade the Chesapeake and burn Washington, D.C., while a further expeditionary force landed at New Orleans. There it met a large collection of militia under the direction of Andrew Jackson, fresh from victory at the Battle of Horseshoe Bend, where the power of the Creek nation had been decisively broken. The British frontal attack against Jackson's fortified position resulted in more than two thousand British casualties to seventy-one for the Americans. As it turned out, the Battle of New Orleans occurred two weeks after the peace treaty had been signed at Ghent and so had no military value. It served, however, to wipe out memories of the many past defeats and usher in a period of perfervid patriotism.

POSTWAR RECONSTRUCTION

The home front had proved every bit as incompetent in the struggle as the front lines. The Bank of the United States had been allowed to die upon the expiration of its charter in 1811, and the war had resulted in inflation and a public debt of 127 million dollars. Jeffersonian opposition to an extensive federal road- and canal-building program without specific constitutional authorization had contributed to the breakdown of wartime transportation. The Jeffersonian military policy had disastrously weakened the nation at a time when the national security was in peril. And the Jeffersonians, who preached that those governments were best which governed least, had proceeded to govern New England commerce into extinction.

In 1814 the experimental American federal republic seemed to many to be about to fall apart, and Massachusetts sent out a call for a convention of New

England representatives to discuss how that maligned and injured section should conduct itself in the course of this dissolution and possible conquest. Meeting at Hartford, Connecticut, the convention proceeded with moderation, given the circumstances; it did not propose secession, but simply a number of constitutional reforms. Its emissaries had no sooner been dispatched to Washington, however, than the incredible news came of Jackson's overwhelming victory at New Orleans and of the Treaty of Ghent with England, restoring to the United States all it had lost in the war and bringing the conflict to a close. Under the circumstances the emissaries had the discretion not to present their proposals, but in the ensuing rush of nationalism they and their confederates in New England were given ample reason to regret their most ill-timed action.

As for the Jeffersonians, the war obliged them to repudiate their main political tenets one after another. Wartime financial chaos resulted in the passage of a bill chartering a second Bank of the United States, and it was signed reluctantly by President Madison, "Public Judgement necessarily superceding individual opinion." The nation emerged saddled with debt, and therefore with what the Jeffersonians called "monocratic" bondholders, to an extent hardly anticipated in the days of Hamilton.

The Jefferson policy of commercial warfare had resulted in the rapid development of American industry, especially the textile industry made possible by the temporary absence of British competition. At war's end the British attempted to destroy America's infant industries by dumping their own goods on the American market at reduced prices. The United States retaliated by passing a protective tariff such as Hamilton had earlier fought in vain to push through Congress. The Jeffersonians themselves, who had once urged America to leave its shops and mills in Europe, were brought to the support of at least moderate protection of American industry to give the nation a degree of economic independence from Europe that it had formerly lacked. The war had dramatized America's bad roads, and the Jeffersonians were now in favor of federally sponsored internal improvements, demanding only that they be authorized by a constitutional amendment. By 1816 this demand, wrote Jefferson himself, was "almost the only landmark which now divides the Federalists from the Republicans."

In this Jefferson was generous to a slain opponent. The Federalist party had in truth become a narrowly sectional party—cranky, obstructionist, and somewhat theocratic. From the time of its secessionist grumblings at the Louisiana Purchase, its leadership had become more and more narrowly provincial. During "Mr. Madison's War," not only had the Federalist party resisted all efforts to bring New England into the struggle, but Federalists had traded openly and briskly with the enemy. The Federalists climaxed their recalcitrance with the Hartford Convention. They continued their struggles into the twenties, winning victories locally and harassing the Republicans nationally, but as an effective national political party they had destroyed themselves.

The triumphant conclusion of the war, meanwhile, was almost as disastrous to the spirit of Jeffersonian republicanism as it was to the old Jeffersonian program, for the boastful nationalism of the time affected even the Virginia dynasty. In 1816 the third successive Virginian, James Monroe, was elected President almost by acclaim, and four years later he swept the nation with but one dissenting electoral vote. A comparison of Monroe's first inaugural address with those of Jefferson and Madison is instructive. Theirs had both been chiefly concerned with the problem of defending individual liberty in a national state. Both Jefferson and Madison had been concerned also to conciliate sections of the country which evinced the disposition to fly off into independent nations of their own if things did not go according to their liking. Not so Monroe:

> **To whatever object we turn our attention, whether it relates to our foreign or domestic concerns, we find abundant cause to felicitate ourselves on the excellence of our institutions. . . .**
>
> **Such then is the happy Government under which we live—a Government adequate to every purpose for which the social compact is formed. . . .**
>
> **Never did a government commence under auspices so favorable, nor ever was success so complete. If we look to the history of other nations, ancient or modern, we find no example of a growth so rapid, so gigantic, of a people so prosperous and happy . . . If we persevere in the career in which we have advanced so far and in the path already traced, we can not fail, under the favor of a gracious Providence, to attain the high destiny which seems to await us.**

BIBLIOGRAPHY FOR CHAPTER 7

Marshall Smelser, The Democratic Republic, 1801–1815 (1968)
Noble Cunningham, The Jeffersonian Republicans (1957)
Adrienne Koch, Jefferson and Madison: The Great Collaboration (1950) and The Philosophy of Thomas Jefferson (1943)
D. J. Boorstin, The Lost World of Thomas Jefferson (1948)
J. E. Charles, The Origins of the American Party System (1956)
G. D. Luetscher, Early Political Machinery (1903)
Merrill Peterson, The Jeffersonian Image in the American Mind (1960)
Gilbert Chinard, Thomas Jefferson (2nd ed., 1939)
J. S. Young, The Washington Community, 1800–1829 (1966)
Bradford Perkins, Prologue to War (1961)
H. L. Coles, The War of 1812 (1965)
D. H. Fischer, The Revolution of American Conservatism (1965)

CHAPTER 8

THE ERA OF GOOD FEELINGS

ECONOMIC CHANGE

t is customary to speak of Monroe's two administrations, from 1817 to 1825, as the Era of Good Feelings—a thoroughly inappropriate phrase to describe an age of confused politics and desperate politicians. During Monroe's tenure the nation suffered the worst depression it had ever experienced. Then, in the midst of that depression, it was frightened by sudden intimations of a coming civil war, during the congressional debates on slavery inspired by the proposed admission of Missouri to the Union as a slave state.

The period was an Era of Good Feelings in the superficial sense that organized opposition to the Jeffersonian Republicans collapsed after the suicidal Federalist Hartford Convention, and Monroe, as a consequence, won by a landslide in 1816 and won again without any opposition whatever in 1820. "Era of Good Feelings" refers also to the heady spirit of nationalism which filled the country following the surprising American victory at New Orleans and favorable peace terms at Ghent. The period of trial was over. The republic was established, and Monroe, dressed in the high-top boots and white periwig of Revolutionary times, presided above the fight as a symbol of the republic itself, a nation certain of itself at last. This nation, however, was caught in the throes of turbulent economic and geographic change and in the clutches of politicians who, released from the restraints of party discipline, were trying to claw their way savagely to the Presidency by 1825.

So swiftly was the nation expanding and changing that politicians found it impossible to measure the true interests of the sections they represented. In 1816 John C. Calhoun of South Carolina was an outstanding champion of the nation's first protective tariff, while Daniel Webster of Massachusetts was its staunch opponent. Twelve years later Webster was the leading Senate spokesman for the high protective tariff, and Calhoun was the author of the *South*

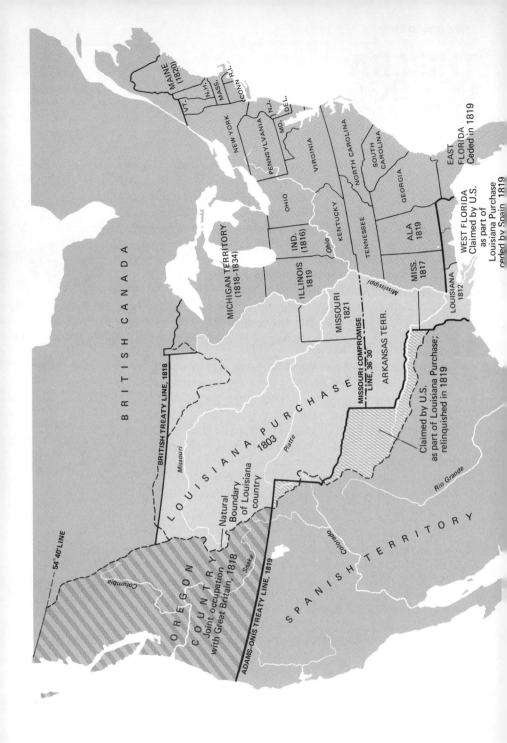

MAINE
(1820)
VT.
N.H.
MASS.
CONN. R.I.
NEW YORK
PENNSYLVANIA
N.J.
DEL.
MD.
VIRGINIA
OHIO
IND.
(1816)
KENTUCKY
NORTH CAROLINA
SOUTH CAROLINA
TENNESSEE
GEORGIA
ALA
1819
MISS.
1817
LOUISIANA
1812

EAST
FLORIDA
Ceded in 1819

WEST FLORIDA
Claimed by U.S.
as part of
Louisiana Purchase
ceded by Spain 1819

MICHIGAN TERRITORY
(1818–1834)

ILLINOIS
1819

MISSOURI
1821

Mississippi
Ohio

MISSOURI COMPROMISE
LINE, 36° 30'

ARKANSAS TERR.

Claimed by U.S.
as part of Louisiana Purchase;
relinquished in 1819

BRITISH CANADA

BRITISH TREATY LINE, 1818

LOUISIANA PURCHASE
1803

Missouri

Platte

Natural
Boundary
of Louisiana
country

Rio Grande

54° 40' LINE

OREGON
COUNTRY
Joint occupation
with Great Britain, 1818

Snake

ADAMS-ONIS TREATY LINE, 1819

Columbia

Colorado

SPANISH TERRITORY

Carolina Exposition, threatening to nullify within the state of South Carolina the tariff that had been passed that year.

Webster originally opposed the tariff as a spokesman for the dominant commercial classes in New England, since the merchants, who had earlier been instrumental in defeating the Hamilton tariff proposals, naturally were opposed to a tax on trade. Even while Webster was fighting the tariff, however, New England's industry was beginning to rival its commerce in importance. While the War of 1812 had ruined New England shipping, it had created a protected market for American manufactures. Prominent Boston merchants had thereupon entered the textile industry on a large scale and with such success that they continued to make large profits in the postwar period, even under the pressure of British competition. By 1828 the transition had largely taken place. New England was by then the most industrialized area of the nation, and Webster, always the fiery champion of the upperdog, made himself industry's most eloquent spokesman.

Calhoun's early support of the tariff had been based on nationalist sentiment and also on the expectation that South Carolina would soon develop an important cotton textile industry which would benefit from protection. Even in 1816 the dominant opinion in South Carolina probably was against the tariff, but Calhoun was a logical man, and logic was on his side. South Carolina was a leading producer of cotton and also possessed everything else necessary to make it a leading textile center: cheap slave labor, sources for skilled labor among the German and Scotch-Irish settlers in the piedmont, plentiful water power, and a commercial metropolis.

In 1828 it still had all of these things, but no textile industry was resulting from them. South Carolina was therefore dependent for its livelihood on cotton exports to England and France, and tariff protection meant only rising costs of manufactured goods sent down from the North. By that time, although the nation's first railroad line was yet to be completed, the main national pattern of economic development had established itself, and politicians in all sections could speak on economic matters with assurance. The relationships between the sections themselves, meanwhile, were altering unpredictably as the West emerged suddenly to rival the Northeast and Southeast in political importance.

THE MARSHALL COURT

To the Hamiltonian nationalism of the postwar tariff and banking legislation was added the Hamiltonian nationalism of the Supreme Court under Chief Justice John Marshall. The Marshall Court decisions tended consistently to strengthen the power of the federal government over the states and at the same time to secure the protection of property rights against government regulation and to secure vested interests against free competition. Although Marshall never again attempted to set aside a federal law after *Marbury v. Madison,* his

Court declared state laws to be unconstitutional in thirteen cases from *Wilson v. Mason* in 1801 to *Worcester v. Georgia* in 1832. In this he was clearly following the intention of the founders, as had been by no means so clearly the case when he invalidated part of a federal law in *Marbury v. Madison.*

Unleashing judicial decisions like thunderbolts throughout his long tenure as Chief Justice, the gentle and kindly John Marshall was a veritable Wizard of Oz in the contrast between his public personality and his private one. Unaffectedly democratic in his tastes and habits, he was committed intellectually to the view that society could remain in good order only so long as it remained in the capable hands of "the wise, the rich, and the good." During most of his career on the Court, the majority of his fellow members were appointees of Republican Presidents, placed on the Court to fight Marshallian federalism. And Marshall took one after another of these capable men in hand and brought them up to become his dedicated followers, aided by the fact that the Supreme Court, as a centrally national institution, would tend to form the thinking of its members along centrally national lines.

The most famous and controversial of his rulings against the states was in *McCulloch v. Maryland* in 1819, prohibiting the state of Maryland from taxing the Maryland branch of the United States Bank. The Constitution has nothing to say about banks or about federal power to charter any corporations, and it might therefore be concluded that under the Tenth Amendment these powers are reserved to the states. The Constitution does, however, empower Congress "to make all laws which shall be necessary and proper for carrying into execution the foregoing powers." To Marshall, in *McCulloch v. Maryland,* this meant, "Let the end be legitimate, let it be within the scope of the constitution, and all means which are appropriate, which are plainly adapted to that end, which are not prohibited, but consist with the letter and spirit of the constitution, are constitutional."

Having thus sweepingly established the authority of the federal government to charter the bank, Marshall went on to declare invalid the Maryland tax. The states were not empowered to destroy a federal instrumentality, and the power to tax was the power to destroy. Marshall made no distinction between a tax which was indeed destructive in intent, such as the Maryland one, and other state taxes which were neither destructive nor discriminatory. The result of this sweeping decision was that the doctrine of government instrumentalities' immunity from taxation, so fruitful of administrative difficulties, became firmly imbedded in constitutional law.

Business won constitutional protection against state interference in 1810 to an extent never contemplated by the founding fathers when, in the Constitution, they prohibited the states from passing laws "impairing the obligation of contracts." The original intent appears to have been to keep the states from impairing contracts between private persons. In *Fletcher v. Peck,* however, Marshall cited the contract clause as his authority to prohibit the state of Georgia from repealing a state enactment involving the corrupt Yazoo land sales, by which land speculators had received millions of acres of valuable land for about 1½ cents an acre.

Then, in 1819 in *Dartmouth College v. Woodward,* the state of New Hampshire was prevented from altering the charter the college had received in 1769 from George III. Thus the Court decided that states cannot alter contracts made with private persons and, further, that a corporate charter is a contract. This decision brought business corporations under the broadened protection of the contract clause. The importance to free enterprise of the decisions involving corporations has probably been overemphasized however. At the time few business corporations existed. It was only later in the century that the importance of the Dartmouth College decision as a protection to vested interests became manifest, and by that time corporation lawyers had found an even better legal protection in the "due process" clause of the Fourteenth Amendment.

The Marshall Court decided on only three cases involving the constitutional authority of the federal government to regulate interstate commerce, the most famous of which was *Gibbons v. Ogden* in 1824. Marshall's decision in this case was a popular one because it invalidated a state-authorized shipping monopoly, on the grounds that it came in conflict with a federal coasting license law. He firmly asserted the sovereign power of the federal government to regulate interstate commerce. He further defined control over commerce to comprehend government supervision over the product from point of origin to point of destination. By noticing the fact of an applicable federal licensing law, however, he spared himself the necessity of asserting the exclusive authority of the federal government in the area of interstate commerce As in other of his decisions, his assertions of wide federal authority escaped serious challenge because he based his adjudication on a different and narrowly technical ground. Marshall was by all odds the nation's most powerful advocate of nationalism in the postwar period, which is not to say that his deviously forthright decisions always contributed to the good feelings of the era.

THE MONROE DOCTRINE

Postwar nationalism achieved its happiest expression in the field of foreign affairs under the direction of Monroe's fretfully undiplomatic Secretary of State John Quincy Adams. Chief among the nation's diplomatic triumphs were the Spanish-American Transcontinental Treaty of 1819 and the Monroe Doctrine of 1823, each of them related to the fact of rapidly failing Spanish power in America. The first quarter of the nineteenth century saw the disintegration of the Spanish empire in America as Spain became distracted by internal revolution and Napoleonic and British invasions. Forced to cede Louisiana to France in 1800, Spain lost all of mainland Latin America within the next generation to patriotic revolutionary forces, except for the Floridas, which were wrested away by the United States.

Stretched across the river systems that gave Alabama and much of Georgia access to the ocean, the Floridas had early been, with New Orleans, objects of American desire. An ingenious interpretation of the terms of the purchase of Louisiana permitted the Americans to persuade themselves that they had purchased West Florida with it, but the always land-hungry Jefferson was unable to persuade the Spanish. Madison was in a better position to do something about the Floridas as near anarchy in Spanish America came to accompany the revolution in Spain. The United States occupied part of West Florida in 1810, and at Madison's direction Congress followed up with the declaration, directed chiefly against Britain, that the United States "cannot, without serious inquietude, see any part of the said territory [of the Floridas] pass into the hands of any foreign power." The United States occupied the rest of West Florida in 1813.

In 1817 the Spanish Minister Luis de Onis sat down with Secretary of State Adams to a series of discussions which Onis protracted for more than a year with the aid of successive new documents from the bottomless Spanish archives in the vain hope of receiving assistance from the European powers. In 1818, however, Andrew Jackson hurried the Spanish to a decision by invading East Florida in pursuit of marauding Seminole Indians. In 1819 the Spanish agreed to the Transcontinental Treaty, ceding to the United States all of the Floridas, finally acknowledging American possession of Louisiana Territory, and in addition throwing in the weighty Spanish claims to the territory of the Pacific Northwest. Adams would have insisted on Texas as well had he been able to gain support from Monroe and other Cabinet members.

In the meantime, formal recognition of the new Latin American republics presented a problem which Monroe attempted to solve in 1818 by getting England to join in a simultaneous statement of recognition. Four years later, having failed to receive British support, the United States extended recognition on its own. A year later France invaded Spain, and the faint possibility of a Franco-Spanish invasion of Latin America arose. Faced with this threat to the new British markets in Latin America, the British Foreign Minister, George Canning, proposed to the United States government a joint protest against European intervention. Monroe and most of his Cabinet and advisers, flattered by the prospective partnership, were inclined to accept.

Not so Secretary of State Adams. Wishing to avoid becoming "a cock boat in the wake of the British man of war," Adams prevailed upon Monroe to decline the British proposal and instead to make his own declaration unilaterally in a Presidential message. It was Adams's correct assumption that Britain would support the doctrine with its navy out of self-interest, regardless of how the declaration was made. The result was the Monroe Doctrine, declaring on the one hand that the United States would not concern itself with intra-European politics or wars, and on the other that the United States considered the Americas to be no longer subject to further colonization by European powers.

The Monroe Doctrine stated a policy which the United States had been formulating from the first days of the federal government—in Washington's Farewell Address, in John Adams's termination of the French military alliance, in Jefferson's first inaugural address, and in the statement of Congress opposing foreign occupation of the Floridas at the time of the American occupation of West Florida. Universally popular in the United States, the Monroe Doctrine remained the basis of American foreign policy throughout the nineteenth century, despite the entire lack, except during the Civil War, of any American military and naval force capable of enforcing it. No European nation recognized its validity, and one or another of them on occasion violated it with impunity. Nevertheless, while Britain wished to maintain open markets in Latin America and remained queen of the seas in an age of sailing vessels, it was almost all the long-range foreign policy the United States needed to have.

WESTERN STATE-MAKING

The Monroe Doctrine was the diplomacy of a nation which had turned its back on Europe and was busily moving westward. From the War of 1812 to the Civil War, westward expansion and Western state-making provided an endlessly unsettling factor in the national political life. This proved most shockingly so in the case of Missouri. In the course of the congressional debates over the admission of Missouri as a state, Rep. James Tallmadge of New York proposed an amendment to the enabling act prohibiting the introduction of any more slaves into the new state. The Tallmadge amendment brought slavery to the floor of Congress as a critical issue for the first time in the nation's history, and the fury that it aroused on both sides came, as Jefferson said, like a fire bell in the night, rousing both Northerners and Southerners to their first realization of the national danger inherent in the slavery issue.

With the House of Representatives containing a decisive majority of free-state representatives, Southerners came now to regard the Senate, divided in 1820 equally between free and slave states, as the special guardian of their peculiar institution. In a compromise handled by Henry Clay their anxieties were somewhat allayed by the admission of Missouri as a slave state, while Northern feelings were quieted by the simultaneous admission of Maine as a free state and by the prohibition of slavery thereafter in all the rest of Louisiana Territory lying north of 36° 30'. That settled the issue in Congress for a generation, but the slavery question remained in men's minds on both sides of the Mason and Dixon line and lurked behind all the other sectional controversies that divided the nation.

Westward expansion and Western state-making in the postwar period had ceased to inspire the awful forebodings among conservative Easterners that had followed the purchase of Louisiana. By 1824 even that most perfectly correct Bostonian Edward Everett had arrived at the conclusion that "by the wise and happy partition of powers between the national and state governments . . . all bounds seem removed from the possible extension of our country, but the geographical limits of the continent." Still, Everett and his friends were less than happy with the perceptible democratization of the nation which accompanied the westward movement.

DEMOCRATIZATION

The six new states were Indiana, Mississippi, Illinois, Alabama, Maine, and Missouri, Louisiana had entered the Union as a state in 1812, and all these provided for white manhood suffrage except Louisiana and Mississippi. In addition, by the eve of the War of 1812 universal white manhood or taxpayer's suffrage was the rule in New Hampshire, Pennsylvania, New Jersey, Maryland, North Carolina, and Georgia. It existed in South Carolina also, but under conditions that rendered it innocuous to the ruling group. Thus the adding of the new states would in itself have created a preponderance of democratic governments among the states of the Union, but on top of that, radicals called conventions in three of the populous older states, Connecticut, New York, and Massachusetts, and won them to the side of popular rule. The result was that after 1821 the few states which retained property qualifications were anachronistic deviations from the accepted rule.

Connecticut conservatism was the victim of the unhappily timed Hartford Convention, which undermined the authority of established church and state and led to the democratic victory in the state constitutional convention of 1818. Nor were the Federalists in Connecticut's neighboring states spared. Advocates of the new democracy succeeded in calling constitutional conventions in New York and Massachusetts that broadened the suffrage and eliminated some of the more antidemocratic provisions of the older documents in those states. If the ruling groups in those states could have withstood the force of triumphant nationalism, they were unable to withstand the outraged popular sentiment aroused by the panic of 1819.

The panic of 1819 was the severest depression the Western farmers had ever experienced. Most of them were still in the process of making payments on their land, and the panic faced them with the prospect of mass eviction and the likelihood of debtors' prison. In Tennessee they found their spokesman in Felix Grundy, who pushed through the legislature various relief measures, including a bill establishing a state loan office to tide the debtors through the depression. In state after state the debtors grasped control of the government as they had not done since the depression days of the Confederation. For instance, when the Bank of Kentucky suspended payments, the legislature passed a stay law and established a new bank authorized to issue bank notes to the amount of 3 million dollars. At the same time the legislature voted a mere $7,000 toward establishing the bank, a sum sufficient to pay for the printing of the notes.

Most of the state legislation proved ineffectual, and the only significant national law the panic produced was the Land Act of 1820. A series of enactments in 1796, 1800, and 1804 had reduced the minimum size of federal lands being sold from 640 to 160 acres and had reduced the minimum price per acre from $2 to $1.64. The minimum down payment had been lowered from 50 percent, and the time for further payments had been extended from one to four years. The Land Act of 1820 made possible the purchase of 80 acres of government land for $100. A Relief Act also was passed to assist those who had been unable to meet the earlier requirements.

ELECTION OF 1824

The panic had no effect whatever on the unopposed reelection of President Monroe in 1820, and Monroe, for his part, all but ignored the panic in his second inaugural address. In the course of his second administration prosperous times returned to the nation. In this apparently placid atmosphere a few gentlemen from Virginia and a few machine politicians from New York got together in 1824, as they had regularly done since 1800, to select the next President and Vice President. Beginning with the Jefferson-Burr collaboration, this tight little Virginia–New York alliance had controlled every presidential election. The Virginia group was made up of a small knot of newspapermen, bankers, judges, and planters who had been organized during Jefferson's first administration into the secret Richmond Junto. In New York, where politics were bitterly factional, control had changed hands over the period from Burr to DeWitt Clinton to Sen. Martin Van Buren, who in 1824 controlled New York politics through an exclusive combination known as the Albany Regency. The South and West had consistently followed where New York and Virginia led, and so had Pennsylvania, the most democratic state in the Union, which had consistently been too riven by internal political battles to produce a favorite son of its own.

As part of the extraconstitutional development of the party system, it had become the practice to delegate the formal task of nominating presidential candidates to a caucus of the congressmen of each party. Since the Republican party was unopposed in 1824, it seemed evident that the caucus candidate would be the next President. And so he might have been, had not the chosen candidate, Secretary of the Treasury William H. Crawford, been stricken by paralysis. But Crawford's apparently hopeless condition created a vacuum which sucked in favorite sons from around the nation, including Henry Clay, John C. Calhoun, DeWitt Clinton, and John Quincy Adams. With no clear political differences to divide them and with no hope of receiving the caucus nomination, they all campaigned against the caucus as a usurpation of the rights of the people. So hot did the issue become that when Congress met to nominate Crawford, only 66 members attended out of a total of 261 congress-men, and the system was never again used. It was replaced by the nominating convention, originated at the state level in 1824.

It was the first Pennsylvania nominating convention which brought Andrew Jackson abruptly to political prominence, but it was the supporters of Clay and Calhoun, not those of Jackson, who called for the convention in the first place. Indeed, until the convention Jackson was not taken seriously as a candidate by experienced politicians, and not a single one of them in Pennsylvania supported his candidacy. He was looked upon as a backwoods figure who did not fit the aristocratic Washingtonian mold of the Presidency. It was true that he stirred the common people, but as a leading Pennsylvania politician put it, this was but "an effervescence that can accomplish nothing," for the common people did not have a hand in the selection. This line of reasoning changed overnight when the convention met and nominated Jackson by a landslide.

In 1824 the presidential electors, who originally had been appointed by the state legislatures, were chosen by popular vote in all but six of the twenty-four states. In the election of 1824 Jackson won a plurality, but he fell short of a clear majority, and in the electoral college he received only 99 of the 261 votes. As the Constitution directed, therefore, the names of the first three candidates, Jackson, Adams, and Crawford, were presented to the House of Representa-tives for a vote, Calhoun having bowed out of the contest to win the Vice Presidency and Clay having finished fourth. Adams received the support of Clay in Congress and won on the first ballot. Then Adams appointed Clay Secretary of State, and was hardly in office before the next presidential cam-paign was under way, waged chiefly on the issue of an alleged "corrupt bar-gain" between Adams and Clay by which the people had been robbed of their first choice for President.

THE JOHN QUINCY ADAMS ADMINISTRATION

John Quincy Adams's main historical function as President was to facilitate the transition to democracy by a stern abstention from the vulgar mechanics of politics. The author, shortly before his election as President, of a brief history of political parties in America, Adams apparently was quite unaware of the nature of party politics as they developed during his time in office. As had Washington and John Adams before him, he saw himself as a patriot President, above party, ruling with the advice and assistance of the best and wisest in the nation. His chief political advisers Clay and Webster urged him to use the patronage to strengthen the National Republican party that had supported his candidacy, but Adams refused to cooperate. He even permitted his political enemy John McLean to remain in charge of the richest source of patronage as Postmaster

General on the grounds that McLean was a competent administrator. "Mr. Adams," the political boss Thurlow Weed later wrote, "during his administration, failed to cherish, strengthen, or even recognize the party to which he owed his election; nor as far as I am informed, with the great power he possessed did he make a single influential friend."

The opposition, meanwhile, moved aggressively to organize for victory behind the new leader Andrew Jackson. Among the "eleventh hour men" who had leaped aboard the Jackson bandwagon following the Pennsylvania nominating convention, the leading figure, and the chief organizer of the Democratic party, was Senator Van Buren of New York. Van Buren toured the South to bring rather reluctant Southern gentlemen to the side of the upstart Western aristocrat Jackson. He faced the equally difficult task of uniting the Clinton and Tammany factions in New York, though in this he was assisted by the timely death of DeWitt Clinton, who had nursed trouble-making vice-presidential ambitions. And finally Van Buren devoted his energies as United States senator to the task of creating an effective anti-Adams alliance.

Adams brought to the Presidency a vision, fully shared by no other prominent figure in public life, of a strong national government providing for the general welfare through a coordinated program of national development. He favored a moderate protective tariff and extensive internal improvements financed out of federal funds. The government would promote the improvement of agriculture, commerce, and manufactures. Beyond that it would establish a national university, finance scientific expeditions, and patronize "the elegant arts, the advancement of literature, and the progress of the sciences, ornamental and profound." It was a program which held attractive features for some groups in the country, such as manufacturers who would receive tariff protection, but it was presented in such an elevated and disinterested manner as to appeal to almost nobody. No other President in American history was ever more out of tune with his times than Adams, with the possible exception of Hoover during the Depression years. For the "Little Magician" Van Buren he was an easy mark.

The Senate, which would have almost nothing to do with Adams's program, made history during his administration by its acrimonious and largely meaningless debate on whether to send representatives to a Pan-American congress in 1826. The heat of the arguments appeared in retrospect to have been quite artificially created. The debate ranged to such subjects as the institution of slavery and the frightful character of slave insurrections. It produced sharp exchanges between senators and the President, and it confirmed the Calhoun faction in its opposition to the administration and joined it to the Van Buren group in support of Jackson, who under any circumstances was plainly going to win the coming election. And indeed Jackson won the election by the most overwhelming popular mandate of any President in the nineteenth century.

With his defeat Adams was dropped by the National Republicans and so was his ambitious program. "My own system of administration," he confided to his diary, ". . . had been undisguisedly abandoned by H. Clay, ingloriously deserted by J. C. Calhoun, and silently given up by D. Webster." Thus defeated by enemies and disowned by friends, the indomitable Adams entered alone upon the most remarkable period of his career. He entered Congress as the representative of Quincy, Massachusetts, against the wishes of his family, who thought it a demeaning office for a former President to hold. And there, until struck down on the floor of the House by an apoplectic stroke in 1848, he fought a single-handed battle for civil rights and against the extension of slavery. Refusing to join the abolitionists and with no political organization behind him, he nevertheless became the most effective opponent of slavery in the political world of his time.

BIBLIOGRAPHY FOR CHAPTER 8

George Dangerfield, The Awakening of American Nationalism, 1815–1828 (1965)

F. J. Turner, The Rise of the New West, 1819–1829 (1906)

Raymond Walters, Jr., The Virginia Dynasty (1965)

R. C. Wade, The Urban Frontier, 1790–1830 (1959)

P. W. Gates, The Farmer's Age (1960)

S. F. Bemis, John Quincy Adams and the Foundations of American Diplomacy (1949) and John Quincy Adams and the Union (1956)

Dexter Perkins, The Monroe Doctrine, 1823–1826 (1927)

Shaw Livermore, Jr., The Twilight of Federalism, 1815–1830 (1962)

E. S. Corwin, John Marshall and the Constitution (1919)

CHAPTER 9

JACKSONIAN DEMOCRACY

JACKSON'S PRESIDENCY

Jackson in office was the visible sign of the people's triumph. His inauguration is remembered, not for what he said, which was very little and to no clear point, but for the motley crowd of farmers and mechanics who obtruded themselves upon a ceremony which formerly had been reserved for gentlefolk. Traveling by horse and by foot over roads made all but impassable by the spring rains, these common people converged on Washington by the thousands, some of them coming 500 miles for the occasion. Muddy and unmannerly, they crowded their way uninvited into the postinauguration reception, and they were threatening to reduce the White House to a shambles until they were diverted by tubs of punch hastily carried to the White House lawn. They announced their sovereignty to the world.

There were hostile observers who found this inauguration of democracy disgraceful, and not surprisingly: as the French observer Alexis de Tocqueville noted, many Americans of wealth, position, and education privately despised democracy. Publicly, however, they were compelled to accept the prevailing democratic shibboleths. Privately they might be guided by sensible and decorous religious conventions; publicly they were obliged to conduct themselves so as to give no offense to the prevailing mores of the evangelical religions. They might profess to despise a society that made money the naked measure of social position, but new rich were coming constantly on the scene, and there seemed to be no way to keep them out. And however much certain rich men might despise the democratic process, the age of Jackson taught them the hard lesson that if they desired the political power they felt their position entitled them to, they would have to go to the people to get it. As a class the aristocracy had become separated from the national character, which was democratic.

What followed Jackson's White House reception was anticlimax. It turned out that Thomas Jefferson had disturbed himself unnecessarily over the possibility of a Jacksonian coup d'etat against the republic. The new President and his chief lieutenants thought of themselves, not as political innovators, but as good, safe Jeffersonians whose duty it was to safeguard the people against dangerous centralizing tendencies in the national government. Where Jackson departed from the Jeffersonian tradition, the difference was often largely a matter of style. Jefferson believed that a good government was one which operated so quietly as to go almost unnoticed; Jackson acted on the principle that a good democratic government ought to trumpet forth in the name of the people now and then.

Where Jefferson, fearing the city mobs, placed his reliance upon those "who labor in the earth," Jackson presented himself as the champion of the workingman as well as the farmer. In practice, however, the two men followed very similar policies toward those who labored in the shops and mills. The Jeffersonians had eagerly made common cause with both the urban radicalism of the Democratic Societies and the urban political machinery of the Tammany Society, and Jackson drew political strength from these same elements. Yet he showed no marked interest in the problems which were peculiarly those of the city worker. Most Americans were still farmers in Jackson's day, and most of the laborers in whose name he spoke were those who labored in the earth.

The most startling novelty of Jackson's first year in office was his defense of the spoils system, when he argued that rotation in office freed the nation from the threat of an entrenched bureaucracy and that "the duties of all public offices are, or at least admit of being made, so plain and simple that men of intelligence may readily qualify themselves for their performance." Certainly this conception was a world apart from Jefferson's natural aristocracy. But it was also true that Jackson proved reluctant to follow his own advice and that the turnover in personnel under him was roughly comparable to that under Jefferson. It was not until the 1840s that the spoils system came into its own.

There remained more basic differences between Jeffersonian republicanism and Jacksonian democracy. Jackson departed from the Jeffersonian idea that government was a necessary evil and by its very nature an abridgment of liberty. "There are no necessary evils in government," he declared. "Its evils exist only in its abuses. If it would confine itself to equal protection, and, as Heaven does its rains, shower its favors alike on the high and the low, the rich and the poor, it would be an unqualified blessing." Jefferson, with his generation, feared the tyranny of the majority. Jackson supposed that the nation was secure against tyranny so long as it was under majority rule. As the first President literally to represent the popular will, Jackson conceived of himself as the embodiment of the majority and in its name the special guardian of the Constitution. It was in this emphasis upon the sovereign will of the majority that the Jacksonians departed farthest from the Jeffersonians.

Jackson led a party without a political program of its own, and no doubt his political lieutenants deeply desired that he avoid ever arriving at a program. He had been elected by high-tariff and low-tariff men, by broad nationalists and states-rights men, by inflationists and hard-money men, and by friends and foes of extensive federal internal improvements. Under such circumstances the interests of the party seemed best served by doing as little as possible about anything. Jackson himself seemed to think that he possessed a political program and, furthermore, that he had presented it to the public in his first annual message to Congress. The message contained no specific recommendations for domestic legislation, however, and it led to the passage of no bill.

The Peggy Eaton episode may well have been the most important event, so far as the Presidency was concerned, of Jackson's first three years in office. The chivalrous President used the full weight of his office to defend the wife of his friend Secretary of War John Eaton against the snobbery and aspersions of Washington society, and the event was important, because it contributed to the political break between Jackson and Vice President Calhoun, the husband of Washington's leading socialite. Until the Eaton affair Calhoun had reason to suppose himself the heir apparent to Jackson; afterwards the widower Van Buren, partly by the kindly attentions he paid Mrs. Eaton, won the gratitude of Jackson which later helped him to the Presidency. As the most important event to follow the democratic revolution of 1828, however, the Eaton episode was significantly lacking in ideological import.

Jackson's most vigorous executive action in those first years was the Maysville Road Bill veto, which placed him in opposition to federally financed intrastate internal improvements on grounds of both economy and constitutionality. Jackson broke no new ground with the veto, but merely reaffirmed a principle established by several of his predecessors. Nor did the veto commit him to any very clear policy in the field of internal improvements, for subsequently he signed other similar measures on the grounds that they were national rather than local in scope, and the federal internal improvements program was continued during his administration. Jackson's treatment of the tariff question was similarly vague, cautious, and middle-of-the-road. He signed both the tariff of 1832 and the compromise tariff of 1833, but neither of them was passed as an administration measure. They were associated rather with his presidential rival Clay and so hardly could serve to separate the Jacksonians from their political opponents.

THE NULLIFICATION CRISIS

Until the last months of Jackson's first administration the most fiercely contested controversy was one that divided the Jacksonian coalition itself: the controversy over the doctrine of nullification, arising out of the opposition of Vice President Calhoun and other South Carolinians to the so-called "tariff of abominations," the tariff of 1828. Though Calhoun had earlier favored the protective tariff believing that it would serve to foster a cotton textile industry in

South Carolina, it had not done so, the textile industry was concentrated in New England, and South Carolina's cotton economy was suffering from soil depletion and from increasing competition in cotton production from the newly opened region of the lower Mississippi Valley. In 1828, then, Calhoun and South Carolina favored free trade, and Calhoun anonymously prepared his *South Carolina Exposition,* denouncing the "tariff of abominations," which particularly favored the economic interests of the middle states. Furthermore, Calhoun went on to argue the nullification doctrine, the doctrine that the several states had the constitutional authority to set aside such federal laws as the tariff of 1828.

The argument that the states were ultimately sovereign, and not the federal government, had been put forward in 1798 by Madison and Jefferson in the Virginia and Kentucky Resolutions directed against the Alien and Sedition Acts, and in 1815, when the Jeffersonians were in power, the antiwar Federalists of New England had somewhat more tentatively developed a states-rights argument in the Hartford Convention. It was left to Calhoun, however, to develop the argument that the federal government was no more than a marriage of convenience among the sovereign states and that the Union could be legally dissolved by reversing the process of its formation. Just as the Constitution had been ratified by state conventions, so the states could summon conventions to nullify national laws. It would take three-fourths of the states to nullify such a law, but each state retained the right to withdraw from the Union as a final resort. This line of constitutional argument became the accepted Southern belief and the one that the South acted upon in 1860 and 1861.

Until the last months of Jackson's first administration the initiative in political affairs continued to be assumed, not by the President, but by the Congress, as had been the case since 1809 when Jefferson went home to Monticello, and the Senate remained the main center of activity, as it had been during the Adams administration. Here, during the winter of 1829–1830, the debates rose in an awesome crescendo of magniloquence from a somewhat peevish discussion of how to sell federal land to the grand debate between Sen. Daniel Webster of Massachusetts and Sen. Robert Y. Hayne of South Carolina on the fundamental nature of the Union.

In a 2½-hour oration Hayne discussed New England's treason during the War of 1812 and other controversial subjects. He made his main impact, however, by defending the doctrine that sovereignty rested with the states, not with the federal Union, and that therefore the states possessed the authority to nullify within their boundaries unconstitutional federal laws, such as the tariff of 1828. Webster of Massachusetts, declaring that "I will grind him fine as a pinch of snuff," held the floor for four hours several days later to deliver what came to be one of the most admired of American orations, on the loyalty of New England, the treasonableness of the nullification doctrine, the horrors of civil feuds, the glory of the flag, and "Liberty *and* Union, now and for ever, one and inseparable!"

Jackson, from whom the nullificationists hoped to receive support, made known his disapproval in a famous Jefferson Day dinner toast, "Our Union, it must be preserved," to which Calhoun made the equally famous reply, "The Union—next to our liberty, the most dear." The break between Calhoun and Jackson on the personal level meanwhile was precipitated by the Peggy Eaton episode and then made irrevocable by the revelation that in 1818 Calhoun as Secretary of War had recommended Jackson's punishment for his invasion of Spanish Florida. With these developments Van Buren replaced Calhoun as the man Jackson would name his successor, and Calhoun, with nothing now to lose by it, came forth as the main leader of nullification. Congress responded in 1832 to the general dislike of the tariff of 1828 with a tariff reform which, while adjusting rates downward, did so in response less to Southern complaints than to objections of Northern industry.

South Carolina moved at once. A newly elected legislature called for a special convention, which in turn voted overwhelmingly to nullify the tariff and secede from the Union if the federal government tried to enforce it. Jackson, returned to office by another landslide vote, issued a Nullification Proclamation promising to meet treason with force, and the Senate passed a Force Bill empowering him to use the armed forces for the purpose. Henry Clay at the same time introduced a compromise tariff calling for major reductions in duties over a nine-year period. Jackson signed the new tariff bill simultaneously with the Force Bill. South Carolina thereupon withdrew its nullification ordinances and passed a further one against the Force Act.

Victory was claimed by all sides. In truth, however, the Charleston fire-eaters had suffered a humiliating defeat from which some of them did not recover. The anticipated support from other Southern states had not been forthcoming, and strong Unionist sentiment in western South Carolina would probably have ignited civil war in the state had the nullification ordinances been carried out. From that time until the Civil War a group of men in Charleston remained, as the state's leading historian has said, like a foetus in a bottle, unchanged by passing events, waiting for the opportunity that finally came to them to lead the South out of the Union.

THE BANK WAR

Had Jackson not been presented by Congress with a bill rechartering the United States Bank in 1832, he would have entered the campaign for reelection as little involved in any real political issues as he had been four years earlier; for the leaders of the opposition, Clay and Webster, had supported and had even led the fight against nullification. As it happened, Nicholas Biddle of Philadelphia, president of the bank, upon the advice of Webster and others, called for a new charter four years before the expiration of the existing one. Knowing Jackson's hostility to the bank, Biddle and congressional leaders reasoned that political considerations would force him to sign the bill if it were presented to him before the election. Jackson instead returned the bill to Congress with what has remained the most famous veto in American history, and he launched an attack on the bank that continued throughout his second term, serving, more than any other circumstance, to crystallize national political forces at last into two separate organized political parties of Whig and Democrat.

The early history of the second United States Bank had been in sorry contrast to the brilliant beginnings of the first bank in Hamilton's time. Greedy for high profits, its directors had extended credit incautiously and then on second thought had called in bank notes so suddenly they helped precipitate the panic of 1819. This sudden contraction of credit had been followed by a run of failures among flimsy state banks, and then, amid farm foreclosures and business failures, the branches of the Bank of the United States had gathered in large amounts of property from the bankruptcies it had helped to create. In Cincinnati, for instance, the bank actually acquired a large part of the city in house lots, hotels, business firms, warehouses, and iron foundries.

For the time being the bank survived the depression-born hostility and reformed its ways under more responsible management, but the sentiment that supported Jackson a decade later in his fight against the bank had been created. In 1823 Biddle, a Jeffersonian Republican who voted for Jackson in 1828, became president of the bank and administered it in a manner which has since won him high praise from financial historians. He continued, however, to incur the wrath and suspicion of many in the country, both among those who wanted credit on easier terms than the bank permitted and those who accused it of dishonest profits through the manipulation of credit. On the one hand there remained the state banking interests whose lending activities were curbed, and on the other there were the hard-money men of the old Republican school who would have liked to abolish all banks and restrict financial transactions to payments in gold and silver.

Jackson, it turned out, was of the old school, distrustful of all banks and in favor, not of a nationally chartered bank, but simply of a bank of deposit attached to the Treasury and deprived of the lending function. Upon taking office, he let Biddle know that, while he appreciated the services the bank had performed for the government, he distrusted all banks and beyond that was convinced, despite *McCulloch v. Maryland,* that a federally chartered bank was unconstitutional outside the confines of the District of Columbia. His vaguely threatening remarks concerning the bank in his first message to Congress inspired congressional investigations of it. These came to nothing, but supporters of the bank were thereby given good warning and so were led to the tactical error of demanding the rechartering of the bank four years early.

Jackson's veto was vigorously forthright in style and electric with ideology.

It is to be regretted that the rich and powerful too often bend the acts of government to their selfish purposes. Distinctions in society will always exist under every just government. Equality of talents, of education, or of wealth can not be produced by human institutions . . . but when the laws undertake to add to these natural and just advantages artificial distinctions, to grant titles, gratuities, and exclusive privileges, to make the rich richer and the potent more powerful, the humble members of society—the farmers, mechanics and laborers— who have neither the time or the means of securing like favors to themselves, have a right to complain of the injustice of their government.

This line of argument, although it represented the dominant economic radicalism of democratic America, was by no means new, nor was it peculiar to American democratic thought, except in its aversion to titles and its pointed concern for the farmers, mechanics, and laborers. With those exceptions Jackson's statement might well have been presented more than two centuries earlier amid loud cheers to that Elizabethan House of Commons which in 1601 successfully forced the Queen to rescind certain chartered monopolies. The Bible of economic liberalism, Adam Smith's *The Wealth of Nations,* was published in the same year that Jefferson wrote the Declaration of Independence. *The Wealth of Nations* was the economic declaration of independence for the British businessmen, against state regulation of business and state favoritism, including the favoritism of protective tariffs. They went on to win England to free trade over the opposition of the landed interests during the second quarter of the nineteenth century. Jacksonian America, meanwhile, experienced a somewhat similar struggle with the sides roughly reversed. The landed interests of the cotton kingdom won a partial victory for free trade over the opposition of the tariff-minded business community. Economic liberalism was not accepted by the American businessman, and if it was accepted privately by Jackson, he did not advocate it as President.

Jackson did place himself at the forefront of the antimonopoly fight with his bank-bill veto, but he did so in a highly qualified manner. The veto lashed out at the principle of monopoly itself, but specifically it attacked a national, as opposed to a state, monopoly. Indeed, one of Jackson's arguments against the bank was that it infringed upon the rights of the less powerful banks which had been chartered by the states. The monopolistic state banking interests fully appreciated this argument, as their strong support of Jackson in 1832 indicated. On the other hand his veto message brought him also the strong support of the radical hard-money antimonopoly Democrats—the Locofocos, as they were called—who until then had been rather indifferent to the old hero of the Battle of New Orleans. This Locofoco movement, while attacking monopolies in general and the Bank of the United States in particular, was not proposing laissez faire. The Locofocos accepted government control, and they did not oppose government support for private enterprise. They simply wished, as Jackson said, to live under a government which would "shower its favors alike on the high and the low, the rich and the poor."

THE SECOND JACKSON ADMINISTRATION

Against this collection of mutually antagonistic but uniformly enthusiastic Jackson supporters, the former Adams men, known as the National Republicans, held a national convention, nominated Henry Clay, denounced Jackson for his bank-bill veto, and went down to resounding defeat. Meanwhile, several of the most promising younger politicians in the anti-Jackson camp, notably Thurlow Weed and William H. Seward of New York and Thaddeus Stevens of Pennsylvania, disgusted with the National Republican party under Adams, had broken away to join an odd little party which apparently seemed promising at the moment.

The Anti-Masonic party had its origins in 1826 in the disappearance and suspected murder of a Mason named William Morgan who was planning an exposé of the Masonic order. Suspicion that he had been murdered by fellow Masons aroused the old American hostility to secret societies, and on this issue alone a new party was created which placed its candidate, William Wirt, in the election of 1832. Wirt won a few thousand votes and the party disintegrated. Its historical importance is in the training in grass-roots politics it gave to the future leaders of the Whig party, who were determined to out-Jackson Jackson in popular-election techniques and who finally succeeded in doing so in the election of 1840.

The bank-bill veto could not deprive the bank of its four more years of life, and Jackson's second administration was dominated by the continuing fight with the institution and administration efforts to find some practical alternative to it. Jackson removed government funds from the bank and distributed them in "pet" state banks, although he had to replace his Secretary of the Treasury to do it. The withdrawals were necessarily gradual, for they would in turn require the bank to call in those loans to private banks which had been made on the basis of the government deposits. Biddle, for his part, called in loans more rapidly than was necessary in order to create an economic crisis for which the administration would be blamed. Pressure from the business community forced him to stop the practice, and the nation moved swiftly from depression to an inflationary boom encouraged by the added capital provided by government deposits in state banks and by release of state banks from the restraint of the Bank of the United States.

The government further encouraged the boom by permitting public land to be purchased with paper money issued by the state banks and then permitting the land to be used as collateral for the purchase of further land. In response to the appeals of hard-money men within his party, notably Senator Benton of Missouri, Jackson in 1836 issued the Specie Circular, requiring gold or silver for the purchase of public land. Then he retired and left the ensuing depression in the hands of his successor.

THE ELECTION OF VAN BUREN

Times had never been better, though, than they were during the presidential campaign of 1836, and the anti-Jackson forces, in the opinion of their younger leaders, were doing nothing constructive to meet the problem of Jackson's popularity. "Our party as at present organized," wrote Thurlow Weed in 1834, "is doomed to fight merely to be beaten. . . . The longer we fight Jacksonianism with our present weapons, *the more it won't die!* . . . With Clay, Webster, or Calhoun, or indeed any man identified with the war against Jackson and in favor of the Bank, or the Bank's shadow, the game is up." The new Whig party of which he spoke, created out of the bank war and the nullification crisis, was essentially a coalition of the National Republicans who had gone down to defeat with Clay and the broadcloth party of Southern gentlemen.

From the point of view of economic self-interest, the Southern cotton planters probably had less reason to oppose Jackson than they had to oppose the Northern and dominant wing of the new Whig party. They were offended, however, by the vulgar equalitarianism of Jacksonian democracy and by the spirit of assertiveness it engendered in the leathershirt class in the South. And however much Southern planters outside South Carolina might disapprove of the attempted unilateral nullification of the tariff, they were nevertheless sensitive to any attack on the principle of state sovereignty, and ever more so as the slave states assumed a smaller and smaller minority position in the nation. Taking the name Whig as the opponents of "King Andrew I," the coalition of Northern high-tariff nationalists and Southern free-trade states righters did what it could to combat the party of popularity.

Clearly the unpopular party and unable to agree on a campaign platform, the Whigs in 1836 attempted to win the Presidency by conducting the election in the manner originally intended by the founding fathers, who, never anticipating the rise of political parties, had supposed that the presidential electors would split their votes among favorite sons and that the House of Representatives would choose among these. The Whigs ran Webster in New England, William Henry Harrison in the middle states and the West, Hugh L. White in Tennessee, and Willie P. Mangum in South Carolina (where electors were still chosen by the legislature).

The stratagem failed, for Van Buren received a clear majority of the electoral votes, but it did produce one hopeful omen for the Whigs. Wherever Harrison had run, he had stirred excitement among the people. Long out of the political limelight, Harrison was best remembered for his part in the Battle of Tippecanoe, twenty-five years earlier, where he had managed to avoid defeat at the hands of the wily Indian warriors. With no more than this to recommend him, he had won more than a half million votes. Harrison and some of the younger Whig politicians kept this in mind as the panic of 1837 broke upon the nation.

ELECTION OF 1840

Retaining leading Jacksonian politicians in his cabinet, Van Buren attempted to apply Jacksonian solutions to the severe depression that came upon the nation shortly after he entered office. He proposed to reduce the price of lands that the federal government had placed on the market and that had not been purchased. He proposed legislation protecting squatters in their equity so far as the improvements they had made on their lands were concerned. Sharing Jackson's suspicion of the national banking system, he proposed an "Independent Treasury," where federal funds would be retained out of the hands of the nation's bankers. Democrats joined Whigs to prevent passage of the Independent Treasury Act until 1840, however, and the Whigs repealed it a year later. Meanwhile, depression conditions continued into the election campaign of 1840.

Hopefully, at a time of rising unemployment and business failures, the younger Whigs gathered their strength behind Harrison in the 1840 convention. Amid extravagant praises of the unhappy presidential aspirant Clay, the nomination went to Harrison, while the vice-presidential nomination went to the Virginia aristocrat John Tyler as a sop to the Southern wing of the party. In the campaign that followed, Thurlow Weed was the leading figure. Under him the Whigs developed grass-roots organizations and centralized direction. They levied campaign contributions so vigorously as to arouse in Horace Greeley the fear that they would "drive our rich men out of politics." All that was needed was a campaign issue, and this was provided by a campaign slur against Harrison in a letter to a Baltimore newspaper: "Give him a barrel of Hard Cider, and settle a pension of $2,000 a year on him, and my word for it, he will set the remainder of his days in his Log Cabin, by the side of a 'sea coal' fire and study moral philosophy."

Omitting the damaging charge that their candidate was a student of moral philosophy, the Whig politicians grasped the rest of the statement as an issue entirely sufficient to their purposes. They launched a nationwide circus performance working endless variations on the theme that their candidate was a man of the people, born and living in a log cabin and content to drink hard cider. As for Harrison himself, that dignified country gentleman whom the professionals would have preferred to see stay home moved about the country giving long speeches in which he referred from time to time to his log-cabin background. In vain did the Democrats protest that Harrison had been to the manner born, while

Van Buren was a poor boy who had made good. The Whigs got their point across, and they got out the vote in unprecedented volume. On the basis of a vote more than half again as large as in 1836, the Whigs won handily, even though Van Buren received 400,000 more votes than in his victorious 1836 campaign.

Following his election, Harrison was brought forward by the Whig politicians to deliver an inaugural address which he had written by himself despite Daniel Webster's protests. It appeared from his inaugural that Harrison wished, as John Adams and John Quincy Adams had before him, to become a patriot President after the model of George Washington. He would select his aides from among the most capable members of society regardless of party, and he hoped that his administrations would be such as to bring an end to party conflict. A month later, exhausted by the furious onslaught of office seekers, President Harrison died of pneumonia, and his place was taken by Vice President Tyler, states-rights advocate, opponent of the tariff, and enemy to any Whig scheme for the reconstitution of a national bank. After a fruitless struggle to force the Northern Whig program through Congress over Tyler's vetoes, the Whigs in Congress caucused and wrote their President out of the party. The Northern Whigs had been poorly rewarded for their exertions, but they had learned at last how to make Presidents in democratic America.

BIBLIOGRAPHY FOR CHAPTER 9

G. G. Van Deusen, The Jacksonian Era, 1828–1848 (1959)
A. A. Cave, Jacksonian Democracy and the Historians (1964)
H. C. Syrett, Andrew Jackson (1953)
A. M. Schlesinger, Jr., The Age of Jackson (1946)
Marvin Meyers, The Jacksonian Persuasion (1957)
D. T. Miller, Jacksonian Aristocracy: Class and Democracy in New York, 1830–1860 (1967)
Edward Pessen, Jacksonian America: Society, Personality and Politics (1969)
Robert Remini, The Election of Andrew Jackson (1964) and Martin Van Buren and the Making of the Democratic Party (1959)
G. R. Taylor, The Transportation Revolution (1951)
Bray Hammond, Banks and Politics in America from the Revolution to the Civil War (1957)
W. W. Freehling, Prelude to the Civil War: The Nullification Controversy in South Carolina, 1816–1836 (1966)
C. S. Sydnor, The Development of Southern Sectionalism (1948)
R. G. Gunderson, The Log Cabin Campaign (1957)

CHAPTER 10

EXPANSION AND CONFLICT

EXPLORATION AND EXPANSION

Considering the overriding influence of the westward movement in the nation's history, the federal government tended to take a rather casual attitude toward its Western possessions during the early nineteenth century, but it did carry out a number of major exploratory ventures. President Jefferson, an enthusiastic westward expansionist, planned a scientific expedition overland to the Pacific in 1803, remarkably enough while Louisiana Territory was still a French possession. Under the direction of two army officers, Meriwether Lewis and William Clark, the expedition set forth from St. Louis in May 1804 and during the next six months ascended the Missouri River into North Dakota. After a winter among the Mandan Indians the party continued on during the next year to the mouth of the Columbia. The return trip to St. Louis was made by September 1806. Hugely successful, returning with rich geographic and scientific information, the expedition was followed by others during Jefferson's second administration, but nothing approaching systematic and comprehensive exploration was undertaken. Then in 1819, the year of the Transcontinental Treaty, an expedition was sent out which reported the Great Plains to be a great American desert, unfit for human habitation. Thereafter for another generation the government mainly left Western settlement to the free enterprise of trappers, farmers, and missionaries.

In the opening years of the century the idea of gradual expansion of the nation to transcontinental proportions seemed almost too fantastic for consideration. Many had had doubts about the feasibility of maintaining a republic on the scale of the original thirteen states, not to speak of extending it to the Pacific. Even Jefferson, while envisioning the gradual movement of farmers into the vast West, did not see this in terms of an eventual transcontinental nation, but rather in terms of "free and independent Americans, unconnected with us but by the ties of blood and interest, and employing like us the rights of self-

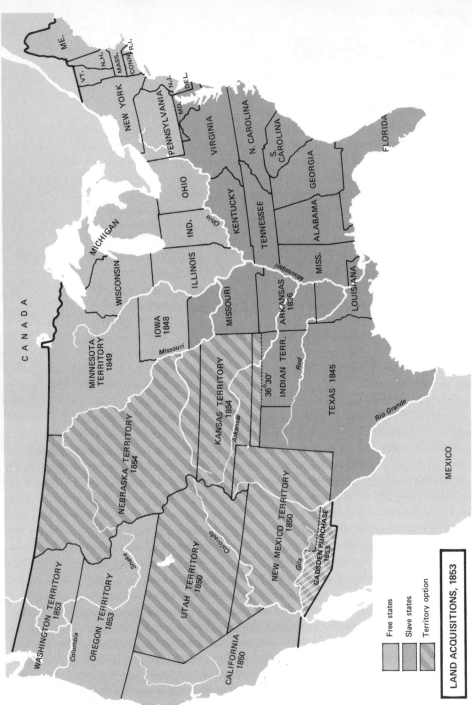

LAND ACQUISITIONS, 1853

Free states

Slave states

Territory option

CANADA

ME.

VT.

N.H.

MASS.

CONN.

R.I.

NEW YORK

PENNSYLVANIA

N.J.

DEL.

MD.

VIRGINIA

N. CAROLINA

S. CAROLINA

GEORGIA

FLORIDA

OHIO

IND.

KENTUCKY

TENNESSEE

ALABAMA

MISS.

LOUISIANA

MICHIGAN

WISCONSIN

ILLINOIS

Ohio

MISSOURI

ARKANSAS 1836

Mississippi

IOWA 1848

Missouri

MINNESOTA TERRITORY 1849

KANSAS TERRITORY 1854

36°30'

INDIAN TERR.

Red

TEXAS 1845

Arkansas

Rio Grande

MEXICO

NEBRASKA TERRITORY 1854

UTAH TERRITORY 1850

Colorado

NEW MEXICO TERRITORY 1850

Gila

GADSDEN PURCHASE 1853

WASHINGTON TERRITORY 1853

Columbia

OREGON TERRITORY 1853

Snake

CALIFORNIA 1850

government." That a nation which took months to traverse could be governed on representative principles seemed unimaginable. Even so ardent an expansionist as Sen. Thomas Hart Benton of Missouri looked upon the Rockies as marking the farthest feasible westward limits of the nation until the coming of the railroad changed his ideas.

The Mexican government, completing its long struggle for independence from Spain, had less reason than the United States to suppose that it could assert its authority effectively over the even more extensive territory extending from Upper California to Central America. The Spanish missions in much of this area were secularized following Mexican independence, and the garrisons were withdrawn. Lacking an expansive population of its own, the Mexican government very incautiously decided to grant concessions to foreigners who would nominally pledge their allegiance to the new nation. It bestowed on Moses Austin of Connecticut, Pennsylvania, Virginia, and Missouri a large territorial concession in Texas, which was confirmed by the Mexican Congress in 1823 and settled by Moses' son Stephen the same year. Within a decade the American colony, under the strict proprietary rule of Stephen Austin, had increased to 20,000 population. Austin appears to have taken his Mexican citizenship seriously, but in the thirties the American settlement swelled beyond his ability to control it, and the antislavery policy of the Mexican government threatened the slave property of the immigrants.

In 1835 President Santa Anna of Mexico abolished the federal form of government, prohibited further American immigration, and made large grants in Texas to Mexican supporters. The Americans thereupon formed a provisional government of their own, against which Santa Anna promptly rode at the head of the Mexican Army. At the Alamo in 1836 he wiped out the entire garrison of 200 men and moved on to complete the destruction of the new Lone Star Republic. A Texan army under Sam Houston was waiting for him at the San Jacinto River, however, and the resulting American victory brought the war to a conclusion. Santa Anna himself was captured, and he never again attempted to regain the Texan province. Houston was elected president of the republic, which then requested admission to the United States.

During the negotiation of the Transcontinental Treaty John Quincy Adams had been the nation's most forceful advocate of the acquisition of Texas from Spain. In 1836, however, Adams, now in the House of Representatives, was a leading opponent of the extension of slavery. By that time the new Northern sentiment to which Adams appealed naturally opposed the acquisition of new slave territory. Under the circumstances President Jackson remained cautiously correct in his dealings with Texas, extending it American recognition following congressional approval on his last day in office. President Van Buren opposed annexation out of deference to antislavery sensibilities, and the Texan government thereupon began to approach France and England for the political support it had been denied by the United States. Under these new circumstances and with Tyler of Virginia as President and Calhoun of South Carolina as Secretary of State, Congress was persuaded to annex Texas in 1845 by a joint resolution.

The nation, which in the election of 1844 confronted the issue of Texan annexation, faced also the much-longer-standing issue of whether to annex Oregon Country and, if so, how much of it to annex. During more than two generations of Canadian border controversies with England, American governments had taken an almost indifferent attitude toward the question of the Pacific Northwest. Despite the good American claims to it, it had seemed so far away as to be impossible to absorb into the American republic. Little was known about it, but on the basis of the scanty available reports it was not thought to be an especially inviting country. More serious, meanwhile, were the Eastern border disputes, marked by violence and threats of war along the northern frontiers of New York, Vermont, and Maine.

From 1798 to 1842 British and American commissions worked to reach agreements on the American-Canadian boundary lines which had been so ambiguously described in the treaty of 1783 and based upon such inexact geographic knowledge. After the War of 1812 newly appointed commissions continued discussions leading to an arbitration by the King of the Netherlands which the United States refused to accept. Border relations continued uneasily, threatening to disrupt into war in 1837. In that year Canadian troops sank the American steamship *Caroline* on the American side of the Niagara River, and over British protests the state of New York tried, but acquitted, one Alexander McLeod. This was followed in 1839 by the informal Aroostook War between American and Canadian lumberjacks, and again war sentiment rose. The British and American governments were both peaceably disposed, however, and Lord Ashburton arrived from England determined to reach a final settlement.

The resulting Webster-Ashburton Treaty of 1842 split the difference between the British and American claims concerning the Canadian-American boundary so far as the area west to the Great Lakes was concerned. The solution was facilitated by the fact that each side secretly possessed a map that favored the claims of the opposing nation. In 1933 a further map was discovered, indicating that the American claims regarding the Maine boundary had in fact been correct.

Settlement of the Oregon question, meanwhile, hinged from the English point of view largely on the business policy of the Hudson's Bay Company, which in 1821 had received a monopoly of trading rights in the Northwest. Interested primarily in the fur trade, the Hudson's Bay Company was anxious to discourage the settlement of farm communities, whether British or American, in the fur-bearing regions of the Northwest. Although the English were in the area earlier than the Americans, the Americans had the better claim to the territory south of the Columbia River, on the basis of Capt. Robert Gray's discovery of the Columbia in 1792 (a claim that was weakened, however, by the lack of evidence that he claimed it officially in the name of the United States) and the Lewis and Clark expedition, which had explored the area in the next decade. These good American claims were strengthened in 1819 by acquisition of the Spanish claims, extending back to the papal bull of 1493 that awarded Spain all of North and most of South America and buttressed by subsequent Spanish explorations.

The main early American effort to occupy the region was John Jacob Astor's establishment of the trading post of Astoria. When the war of 1812 broke out, however, Astor had to sell out to the more powerful British interests in the area. Several unsuccessful American attempts at settlement in the 1830s served to publicize the area as potentially rich in agriculture, abounding in fish and game, and providing the forest environment to which American settlers had been accustomed during two centuries of farming. Of special influence was the missionary Jason Lee, who settled in the Willamette Valley in 1834.

Until 1843 the Hudson's Bay Company provided government in Oregon under the direction of Dr. John McLoughlin at Fort Vancouver. McLoughlin followed a friendly policy toward American settlers but at the same time used his influence to direct them to areas south of the Columbia River, the vague British-American agreement concerning the territory being at that time the temporary one of "joint occupation." In 1842 the first sizable group of American emigrants moved along the Oregon Trail through Laramie and South Pass in Wyoming, settled in the Willamette Valley, and established their own provisional government. By 1844 their numbers had increased to about 2,500. The area having been ruined for the fur trade by farmers, the Hudson's Bay Company withdrew its headquarters to Vancouver Island, taking away the main British motive for delaying final settlement. Until this point the American government, its attention focused on Texas, had largely ignored the fact of American settlement of Oregon, although Webster and Ashburton had discussed the question informally in 1842. Then the rising volume of migration along the Oregon Trail thrust the question abruptly into politics and joined it to the controversy concerning admission of Texas in the election campaign of 1844.

POLK'S EXPANSIONIST OBJECTIVES

In the election of 1844 the seasoned politicians Henry Clay and Martin Van Buren were still fighting the old bank war, and they were caught unaware by the enthusiasm for expansion. Consequently they were done out of the Presidency by a comparatively little-known congressman from Tennessee, James K. Polk, who ran on the program of extending the national borders north, south, and west. A former governor of Tennessee and later Speaker of the House of Representatives, Polk was far from being entirely a political unknown, it is true, but he was still the first dark horse in American election history, winning the

Democratic nomination with the support of Jackson after the failure of Van Buren to receive the required two-thirds vote of the convention. Polk won the election in a close contest which would have gone the other way had not Clay lost sufficient votes in New York to an abolitionist candidate, James G. Birney of the Liberty party, to throw that state, and with it the nation, to Polk.

Although Polk was a Southern slaveholder, he was, like the slaveholder Jackson, a thoroughgoing nationalist who refused to be influenced by the slavery controversy in his expansionist aims. During the campaign the annexation of the free territory of Oregon had been rather secondary as a political issue to the question of whether to admit slaveholding Texas as a state. Robbed of the credit for acquiring Texas, Polk moved single-mindedly and with complete effect toward his other expansionist objectives in areas where slavery was highly unlikely to penetrate. His first act was to reach agreement with England on the Oregon question in order to free himself for his more grandiose designs against Mexico.

Despite extravagant claims made on both sides during the half century that the Pacific Northwest was under discussion, the area really at issue had been the area from the Columbia River north to the 49th parallel, including the southern tip of Vancouver Island. The Americans had at one point agreed to draw the boundary at the 49th parallel, and when the British Foreign Minister suggested this line except for the British retention of all of Vancouver Island, Polk was happy to accept. Amid a certain amount of aggressive talk about "54° 40' or fight," the treaty was ratified by Congress in 1846, the same year that the Mormons set forth from Nauvoo for the promised land of the Great Salt Lake.

Although little had been said about it during the campaign, it was the rich and mysterious land of California more than anything else that fired Polk's ambitions for America's larger future. Of California little was definitely known at the time Polk became President. In 1840 Richard Henry Dana, Jr.'s *Two Years Before the Mast* had appeared and given a detailed account of southern California life and glimpses of the San Francisco Bay region. In 1844 John C. Frémont gained a reputation as a modern Marco Polo by his account of his California travels, and the American consul in Monterey, California, Thomas O. Larkin, was doing his best to acquaint the government with its Far Western opportunities. To the vision of the apparent richness and variety of California was joined the old dream of the Western route to Cathay. That San Francisco Bay provided excellent harbor facilities was universally attested to, and by 1846 the practicality of a transcontinental railroad was past doubt. With the acquisition of California and whatever intervening territory existed, the quest of Columbus would be brought to a most successful conclusion by President James K. Polk.

There had been attempts to purchase California from Mexico during the administrations of Jackson and Tyler, but what was now known was that Mexico was hardly even in possession of the land. The Catholic missions, through which the Spanish had extended their control, had lost their authority, and power was exerted locally by individual land barons such as the Swiss-American John A. Sutter in the Sacramento Valley. The fear that either France or England was prepared to capture California, fully justified in the case of England, gave urgency to Polk's aims. In 1845 he sent John Slidell to Mexico with the authority to buy Upper California and points east. When the Mexican government would not receive Slidell, the Polk administration suggested a California revolution. This was arranged by American and pro-American settlers under the leadership of Larkin, only to miscarry through the intervention of the exuberantly incompetent Frémont. Frémont later joined in a second effort which established California as the Bear Flag Republic, but by that time Mexico and the United States were already at war.

THE MEXICAN WAR

Following the Mexican refusal to deal with Slidell, Polk ordered Gen. Zachary Taylor into territory disputed with Mexico between the Nueces River and the Rio Grande. In April Mexican troops attacked some of Taylor's men. In May Polk sent a war message to Congress declaring that the Mexicans had shed American blood on American soil. Congress responded overwhelmingly with a declaration that war existed between the two countries. So little was known about the vast territory of Utah, New Mexico, and California which Polk proposed to acquire that his strongest support came from the slave states and his strongest opposition from Northern antislavery opinion, although as it turned out the whole region was geographically destined to be free territory.

California was quickly placed under American control through the naval action of Commodore John Sloat at Monterey and the taking of San Diego and Los Angeles by Col. Stephen Kearny, who marched overland from Independence, Missouri. The main line of attack against Mexico under the command of General Taylor, meanwhile, was south from the Rio Grande to Mexico City. A brilliant victory by Taylor at Monterrey made him a possible Whig presidential candidate, and Polk altered the main strategy to an attack on Mexico City west from Veracruz under the direction of Gen. Winfield Scott. While Taylor was beating Santa Anna in the north at Buena Vista, Scott captured Veracruz in March 1847, won a major victory in the Battle of Churubusco in front of Mexico City in August, and a month later stormed the hill of Chapultepec and occupied the Mexican capital.

Following the victories at Buena Vista and Veracruz Polk sent the chief clerk of the State Department, Nicholas Trist, with Scott's army to negotiate the peace. Polk's terms were the Rio Grande boundary, cession of New Mexico and California, and right of transit across the Isthmus of Tehuantepec. Scott arranged an armistice for negotiations, invading Mexico City afterwards when Santa Anna decided, on the basis of the terms, to return to the fight. Trist, recalled by Polk following the breaking of the armistice, remained against instructions to negotiate the Treaty of Guadalupe Hidalgo in February 1848, by which the Mexicans capitulated to Polk's terms. Polk in turn, against a rising demand to retain all of Mexico, rammed the treaty through the Senate. Then this absolutely successful President—he also succeeded, where his predecessors had failed, in settling the banking and tariff questions according to hardmoney, proplanter principles—declared that his task was completed. Refusing to run for a second term, he stepped out of office to bequeath to his successor the task of attaching this ungainly new territory peaceably to a Union already perilously balanced between the slave states and the free.

THE SLAVERY ISSUE AND
THE COMPROMISE OF 1850

The Mexican War was hardly declared before the slavery issue was raised in Congress in the Wilmot Proviso to a bill to purchase additional land from Mexico. David Wilmot, a Pennsylvania congressman, moved that slavery be excluded from all territory to be purchased from Mexico. This would have prohibited slavery south of $36° 30'$ latitude, where it was permitted in Louisiana Territory under the terms of the Missouri Compromise. As a practical matter, geographic conditions would probably have been sufficient to exclude slavery in the Southwest, but the Wilmot Proviso made the matter a moral issue. The proviso failed of passage and failed again the next year, but it introduced the issue which both drove the nation to the verge of disunion in the next few years and dominated the sectional controversy down to the Civil War.

Pending the election of 1848 leading politicians in both parties did what they could to ignore the issue, for it was disrupting to both parties and especially the Democratic party, divided between antislavery "Barnburners" and conservative "Hunkers." The Democrats, nominating the antiproviso Lewis Cass of Michigan, ignored the question in their platform. In order to win the election, the Whigs, with whom the main antislavery strength lay, passed over the party regulars to nominate the war hero Taylor, who was incidentally a slaveholding Southern planter. With nothing to choose between these parties, antislavery Northerners organized the Free Soil party and nominated Van Buren, who polled 10 percent of the popular vote, most of it in New York and New England.

Taylor, who seems to have accepted the Presidency ceremonially as an honor bestowed upon him for his military services by a grateful country, was hurried toward his death in the next two years by one of the stormiest controversies in the history of the federal government. Taylor, like Polk both a Southerner and a Nationalist, wanted to see the new territory organized without worrying about the slavery issue. By the time he assumed the Presidency the gold rush was on in California, within months it attracted a population of about 100,000 from around the world, and when this happened, the President invited California to draw up a state constitution, which it did. He then requested

Congress to vote it into the Union. His commands were drowned out, however, by howls of Southern anguish and threats of Southern secession.

South Carolina's ruling group was ready to leave the Union, and the only issue it thought worth discussing was whether to go it alone or wait for the forming of a Southern confederation. Calhoun, favoring a Southern nationalist movement, was unobtrusively instrumental in calling a state convention in Mississippi, which in turn called for a convention of the Southern states at Nashville. The Nashville Convention of 1850 met while debates were raging in Congress and, to the accompaniment of rebel yells from the fire-eaters, drew up a set of relatively moderate resolutions, chief among which was one insisting upon the extension of the Missouri Compromise line of 36° 30' to the Pacific Coast.

The fire-eaters at Nashville failed twice over, for they failed even to catch the attention of the nation. More momentous discussions were being carried on in the United States Senate, where a debate was proceeding which was in somber contrast to the mainly forensic contest of Daniel Webster and Robert Hayne a generation earlier. Hayne was now long dead, and the reigning titans of the Senate were all of them dying; Webster and Clay would be gone within two years, Calhoun within the month. These three men, each of whom had striven repeatedly for the Presidency, were past all personal ambition except to make a fitting resting place for themselves in the history of the nation. Calhoun made his final testament in the name of Southern nationalism, threatening Southern secession if the North did not submit comprehensively to Southern demands. Against him Clay and Webster appealed for a last compromise which would secure the Southern states in their slaveholding rights while permitting the free westward development of the nation. Webster's stand placed him for the first time in his career under severe condemnation by the most eloquent and literate members of his party in New England, notably Emerson and John Greenleaf Whittier.

It was Clay, the Great Compromiser, who pieced together from various bills thrown up by the controversy a series of measures derisively labeled by President Taylor the "Omnibus Bill," whereby California would be admitted as a free state, the Southwest would be organized as a territory on the basis of "popular sovereignty" without mention of slavery, Texas would be compensated in specie for territory lost to New Mexico (a measure which was attractive to politically influential holders of Texas bonds), the slave trade would be abolished in the District of Columbia, and a·Fugitive Slave Law would be passed which would guarantee to Southerners effective support in the capture of runaway slaves in the free states. Then, exhausted by the struggle, Clay turned his leadership over to the young Stephen A. Douglas of Illinois, who took Clay's main points one by one and steered them through the Senate.

The moderates won, as the nation plainly wished them to, and the nation turned to innumerable other more pleasant ways of achieving its "manifest destiny" than that of fighting an abolitionist war. Yet there remained many in the North who were not abolitionist but refused to accept the Fugitive Slave Law as the law of the land, and Southern fire-eaters continued their agitation for secession. Furthermore the younger generation of senators, joining in the debate, had on the whole demonstrated a distinctly less conciliatory attitude than had the men from whom they were assuming power; Seward of New York, for instance, spoke about a "higher law" which was above the Constitution. And the problem still remained of actually settling the vast expanse of territory under those compromises of 1820 and 1850.

THE ECONOMICS OF SECTIONALISM

During the debates over the Missouri Compromise of 1820 national conditions may have been such as to invite the hope among conciliatory statesmen that a stable, long-range solution to the slavery question could be achieved; this was no longer the case in 1850. Society in the 1850s was in motion in a way that could not have been predicted a generation earlier. This decade saw the greatest relative increase in urban population and immigration of any in the nation's history before or since. It experienced a railroad boom which eclipsed all that had gone before, and, in addition to the settlement of the Far West, it experienced an ever-accelerating westward expansion of the farming frontier across the Mississippi into Iowa, Kansas, Arkansas, and Texas and into the Great Lakes region of Michigan, Wisconsin, and Minnesota. All these states entered the Union during the fifteen years before the Civil War, in addition to Florida, California, and Oregon.

The changes of the fifties intensified the differences between the slave and free states, for they revolutionized the North while leaving the expanding South, by comparison, unchanged. Although many immigrants entered the port of New Orleans, immigration left the South largely untouched. Urbanization altered the South only on its periphery, in New Orleans, St. Louis, Baltimore, Cincinnati, and Charleston. In 1860 five Southern states did not have a single town with a population of 10,000. The beginnings of industrial development were to be seen in Southern cities in the fifties, most notably the iron industry in Richmond, Virginia, and the manufacture of textiles was spreading even into rural areas. Even so, when the war broke out the entire Confederacy did not possess as much machinery for a textile industry as was operating in the one town of Lowell, Massachusetts.

The Old South remained a rural, largely frontier, and westward-moving region producing staple commodities of hemp and tobacco in the upper South, sugar in Louisiana, and rice in pockets along the coastal region from South Carolina to Texas, but mainly it produced cotton. The majority of the 3.5 million slaves in the Confederate states were engaged in the raising of cotton, and it was the expansion of cotton that continually raised the price of slaves in the prewar years. In many areas of the South there were virtually no slaves, and even in the areas of their concentration the large majority of the white population owned none. Of those who did own slaves, about half were more or less well-to-do yeoman farmers working side by side with their bondsmen, hopeful for a turn of fortune which would raise them to gentlemanly station, and anxious lest some piece of ill luck drop them to the status of the poor whites around them. More than half the slaves were owned by the 12 percent of the white population that had twenty or more slaves. From this select squirearchy rose the still more select planter aristocracy, the ten thousand families of the South that were supported by a force of fifty or more slaves.

The squirearchy and the aristocracy absorbed the advantages of slavery; all other major classes in the South suffered from the system, economically as well as socially and politically. Yet slavery established the patterns of aspiration for Southerners generally. The yeoman farmer with no slaves of his own could observe about him no other standard of success than the accumulation of land and slaves. The poorer white could find reason for pride of position only in his whiteness and freedom, since his station in life might otherwise differ little from that of the slave.

Southerners like Cassius M. Clay of Kentucky and Hinton R. Helper of North Carolina, who argued that the average Southerner was damaged by slavery, inspired either indifference or violence among their nonslaveholding audiences. These people had at least a social stake in the system which was isolating and impoverishing them, and their approval of slavery in turn committed them to regard the slaveholders as the special, aristocratic custodians of Southern society, however recently the slaves had been acquired by the upstart "cotton snobs." Cotton, meanwhile, in addition to providing livings for many and fortunes for few, made up two-thirds of the total value of American exports by the eve of the war, leading Southerners to suppose that economically cotton was king in the nation and that "the wealth of the South is permanent and real, that of the North fugitive and fictitious," and fundamentally dependent, taking the world view, on the Southern crop.

In fact, the agricultural wealth of the North was increasing much more rapidly than that of the South, not to speak of the prodigious advances in Northern industrial development. American farmers naturally had been reluctant to move from the forest areas to which they were accustomed, but in the forties and fifties they and the more numerous new immigrants from northern Europe were finding the prairie lands to be wonderfully fertile. Furthermore the novel environment encouraged them to adopt new farming methods. The generation before the Civil War saw a significant conversion to mechanized farming techniques with the application of the McCormick reaper, wheat binders, seed drills, and threshers to the new areas. Those who worked their own land were in a better position to appreciate the value of laborsaving devices than were planters who raised crops by the sweat of the brows of slaves. Consequently Northern farmers had reason to be more receptive to new contraptions than Southern planters.

The transportation revolution also benefited the North disproportionately. The South shared in the railroad boom of the fifties, but it was in the Northwest that the main development took place, and the main result of this development, in conjunction with the Erie Canal, was to free the Northwest from its old reliance on the Mississippi River and the port of New Orleans and to attach it to New York and Philadelphia instead. Southern leaders were aware that they were losing ground to the North in the railroad age, and they worked to regain the loss by seeking congressional authorization to build along a Southern route the first transcontinental railroad to California and the Orient. Spokesmen for the other regions of the nation naturally had other ideas on the subject, and this competition for the first route to the Far West unleashed a series of events leading directly to the Civil War.

MANIFEST DESTINY

Presiding over this onrushing competitive nation was an old-fashioned Jeffersonian Democrat, Franklin Pierce, from, of all places, New Hampshire. A darkhorse candidate whose nomination had been made possible only by factional splits between Douglas of Illinois, Lewis Cass of Michigan, and James Buchanan of Pennsylvania, Pierce had comfortably defeated the better-known but less well-liked Whig candidate, Gen. Winfield Scott of Virginia, in the election of 1852. In domestic politics Pierce pronounced himself a strict constructionist committed to the Compromise of 1850 and to a permanent truce with regard to the slavery question. In this he followed the lead of Secretary of War Jefferson Davis. He intended to compensate for this negative, colorless domestic program, however, by stirring things up somewhat overseas.

Pierce represented the "Young America" element which saw America's "manifest destiny" as but imperfectly fulfilled by Polk's conquests. Canada remained shackled to the British monarchy and Cuba to the Spanish, while farther abroad private Americans were involving themselves in honorable responsibilities which the American government ought, in good conscience, to make its own. American missionaries, shippers, and pineapple planters had for a generation been active in Hawaii, and it appeared that American annexation would now be necessary to prevent the Hawaiians from coming under the dominion of a foreign power. In 1854 Pierce's Secretary of State, William L. Marcy, arranged a treaty of annexation. The Hawaiian insistence on statehood made it impossible so far as the Senate was concerned, however, and the matter was dropped. More successful was the opening of Japan to American trade by the naval force of Commodore Matthew Perry in the same year after more than two centuries of Japanese "seclusion." American ships, following in the wake of the British, had earlier gained trading rights in China and Siam. Despite these gains, however, Americans were disappointed in their exotic dream of capturing the trade of the Orient from their new position on the Pacific Coast.

There appeared to be even better prospects than these closer to home. Canada was not one at the moment, since America was on reasonably good terms with England for the time being, and under any circumstances efforts to acquire Canada would have been fatal to Pierce's Southern-dominated party. To the south, however, there was Mexico, which it was supposed could certainly be induced, one way or another, to relinquish more territory. Better than that, there were heady prospects of a tropical empire extending from Florida to Nicaragua, which was briefly occupied by the American filibusterer William Walker. As these possibilities received thoughtful attention from the administration, his fellow Northerners could hardly have missed the point that Pierce was being drawn consistently toward the equator in his expansionist aims.

The most dramatic incident in foreign affairs, and the one which marked the effective end to serious manifest-destiny activity for two generations, was that of the Ostend Manifesto, delivered in 1854 by the Minister to Spain, the Southern expansionist Pierre Soulé of Louisiana, who was joined in its framing by the Minister to Great Britain, Buchanan, and the Minister to France, John Y. Mason. The manifesto asked Spain to sell slave-ridden Cuba to the United States and added that if Spain did not do so, and if in the American view Spanish possession of the island constituted a threat to American peace and union, "then, by every law, human and divine, we shall be justified in wresting it from Spain if we possess the power." Intended as a confidential dispatch, the manifesto was made public. Amid hue and cry Soulé was recalled, and his views were disavowed by Secretary of State Marcy.

Damage had nevertheless been done to the administration, and it was already suffering at home from a reopening of the slavery issue in connection with the fateful Kansas-Nebraska Act of 1854. Pierce's successor to the Presidency, James Buchanan of Ostend Manifesto fame, would have preferred to busy himself with the expansion of democracy abroad, but he was obliged instead to preside over its disruption at home.

BIBLIOGRAPHY FOR
CHAPTER 10

D. E. Fehrenbacher, The Era of Expansion, 1800-1848 (1968)
G. R. Taylor, The Transportation Revolution, 1815-1860 (1951)
Stuart Bruchey, Roots of American Growth (1965)
Bernard De Voto, Across the Wide Missouri (1947) and The Year of Decision, 1846 (1943)
A. K. Weinberg, Manifest Destiny (1935)
Frederick Merk, The Monroe Doctrine and American Expansionism, 1843-1849 (1966)
S. E. Morison, The Maritime History of Massachusetts, 1783-1860 (1923)
F. R. Dulles, America in the Pacific (1932)
Holman Hamilton, Prologue to Conflict (1964)—the Compromise of 1850
N. A. Graebner, Empire on the Pacific (1955)
Ray Billington, The Far Western Frontier, 1830-1860 (1956)
G. W. Price, Origins of the War with Mexico (1967)
C. A. Singletary, The Mexican War (1960)

CHAPTER 11

THE DIVIDING NATION

THE QUESTION OF SLAVERY

Many objections had been raised against slavery in colonial times, but until the mid-eighteenth century these had been on social and economic grounds. Colonists complained of an oversupply, or they disliked or feared an increasing population of blacks in their midst. Objections to slavery on moral grounds first developed as an organized movement within the Quaker Meetings, and the first antislavery society in America, and perhaps in the world, was founded in Quaker Philadelphia in 1775, within a few weeks of the Battle of Lexington and Concord.

It was in the libertarian atmosphere of the Revolutionary era that antislavery sentiment became an accepted tenet of enlightened opinion in America. During the Age of Enlightenment Southern as well as Northern gentlemen shared a vision of a humane and happy society that would not tolerate the barbaric, degrading institution of slavery. Slaveholders such as Washington, Jefferson, Madison, and George Mason addressed themselves earnestly to the problem of how to correct this evil, but they were never able to advance beyond the hopelessly impractical and equally inhumane solution of wholesale expulsion to Africa or elsewhere. The American Colonization Society, organized to send freed blacks to Liberia, received the support of Southern humanitarians while at the same time demonstrating the absolute futility of this most advanced Southern solution to the problem.

Southern disapproval of slavery in the late eighteenth century was fortified by unfavorable economic conditions. In the worn-out tobacco lands of the Chesapeake region the institution had become unprofitable—in fact a terrible burden—to slaveholders, who were obliged to maintain their slaves even when profitable employment could not be found for them. In the nineteenth century, however, this economic problem vanished in the face of the expanding cotton

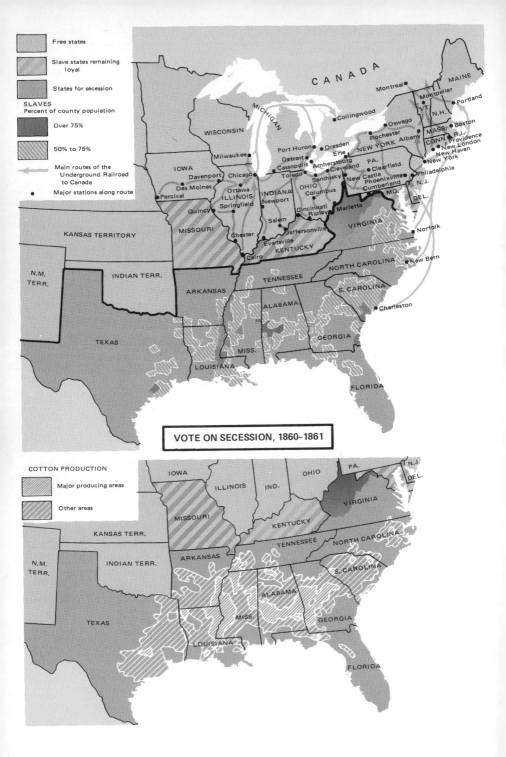

Free states

Slave states remaining loyal

States for secession

SLAVES
Percent of county population

Over 75%

50% to 75%

Main routes of the Underground Railroad to Canada

• Major stations along route

CANADA

Montreal
Montpelier
MAINE
Portland
N.H.
VT.
Collingwood
Oswego
MICHIGAN
MASS.
Boston
WISCONSIN
Rochester
Albany
CONN.
R.I.
Providence
New London
New Haven
Dresden
NEW YORK
New York
Port Huron
Erie
Detroit
Milwaukee
Cleveland
PA.
Clearfield
Cassopolis
Amherstburg
IOWA
Toledo
Sandusky
New Castle
Philadelphia
Davenport
Chicago
Phoenixville
N.J.
Des Moines
Ottawa
INDIANA
OHIO
Cumberland
DEL.
Percival
ILLINOIS
Newport
Columbus
MD.
Springfield
Quincy
Cincinnati
Marietta
MISSOURI
Ripley
Salem
VIRGINIA
Norfolk
Chester
Jeffersonville
KANSAS TERRITORY
Evansville
KENTUCKY
Cairo
New Bern
NORTH CAROLINA
N.M.
TERR.
INDIAN TERR.
TENNESSEE
S. CAROLINA
ARKANSAS
ALABAMA
Charleston
TEXAS
GEORGIA
MISS.
LOUISIANA
FLORIDA

VOTE ON SECESSION, 1860–1861

COTTON PRODUCTION

Major producing areas

Other areas

IOWA
OHIO
PA.
N.J.
ILLINOIS
IND.
DEL.
MISSOURI
VIRGINIA
KANSAS TERR.
KENTUCKY
TENNESSEE
NORTH CAROLINA
N.M.
TERR.
INDIAN TERR.
ARKANSAS
S. CAROLINA
ALABAMA
TEXAS
MISS.
GEORGIA
LOUISIANA
FLORIDA

economy and, to a lesser extent, the acquisition of sugar plantations with the Louisiana Purchase. The invention of the cotton gin and the introduction of a new strain of cotton at the close of the eighteenth century opened up a cotton bonanza which increased prodigiously in the sixty years preceding the Civil War. The cotton plantation, extending itself rapidly through the Southern wilderness, once again provided profitable employment for the multiplying slave force, which reached nearly 4 million by the Civil War period, out of a total Confederate population of 9 million. In the fifties the price of slaves was on the rise, and demands were being made for a reopening of the African slave trade, legally closed in 1808 in accordance with the ruling originally written into the Constitution.

From the end of the eighteenth century on, increasingly strict laws governed the conduct of free Negroes as well as slaves, especially in the lower South. The slave system made impossible any general uprising of Southern blacks, but there were frequent local revolts or plans for revolts, notably those associated with Gabriel Prosser in 1800, Denmark Vesey in 1822, and Nat Turner in 1831. Turner, a slave preacher of Southampton County, Virginia, who was impelled by visions, led an uprising that took the lives of sixty whites before he was captured. Frightened by this insurrection, the Virginia House of Burgesses in 1832 conducted one final discussion concerning the possibility of abolishing slavery altogether. The legislature sought a way out of the slave system and then gave the effort up altogether as, indeed, the Deep South had done from the first.

In an influential report to the legislature on the question, Thomas R. Dew, a professor at William and Mary College, related slavery to history, the nature of civilization, and religion. He found the institution to be essential to civilization, in complete accord with international law, and supported by biblical authority. During the next generation Southern scholars and ministers devoted their energies to documenting and amplifying Dew's argument. The most important of these later writers, George Fitzhugh, advanced beyond Dew to assert the racial inferiority of the Negro, as Dew had not done.

The South self-consciously reoriented its political and legal institutions accordingly. Southern constitutions no longer declared their governments to be founded on the self-evident truth that all men were created equal and endowed with inalienable rights. Rather, the new Southern constitutions declared that all freemen, when they formed a social compact, were equal in rights. Those outside the compact had the right to life and to virtually nothing else. The states proceeded to legislate new systems of laws rigidly defining the place of the slave in society and narrowing the degree of freedom he might be allowed by his master. Though the "peculiar institution" of slavery varied greatly according to region and master on the eve of the Civil War, the tendency was toward an ever stricter control.

THE ABOLITIONIST
MOVEMENT

On January 1, 1831, in Boston, William Lloyd Garrison printed the first issue of *The Liberator,* declaring, "I shall strenuously contend for the immediate enfranchisement of our slave population. . . . I am in earnest—I will not equivocate—I will not excuse—I will not retreat an inch—AND I WILL BE HEARD." Garrison was an agitator, out to stir up hatred of slavery in the complaisant North. With no practical program and for a long time no organization of his own, he demanded immediate and unconditional emancipation. He was heard, and more widely in the South than in the North. His writings, reprinted in Southern newspapers, did much to convince the South of what it was ready to believe, that all Northerners were abolitionists and that all abolitionists were violent fanatics. In New England Garrison won the support of a rather small but highly valuable following, including literary figures such as Emerson who, refusing to join abolitionist organizations, nevertheless lent their talents to the cause.

A second equally dedicated but more moderate abolitionist movement began in the early thirties under the leadership of Theodore Weld, a follower of the lawyer and evangelist Charles G. Finney. With two wealthy New York philanthropists, the Tappan brothers, Weld founded the American Anti-Slavery Society in 1833. Moving west, he for a time attended Lane Seminary in Cincinnati, which expelled him for his abolitionist leanings. He removed to Oberlin with like-minded students, and transformed that college, soon to receive Finney as president, into the most important ministerial training ground in the nation for abolitionist leaders. Closely associated with the Quakers, Weld and his followers advocated a program of gradual, compensated emancipation which would achieve abolition without singling out the slaveholders to make the sacrifice for a cause which was the responsibility of the whole nation. Southerners, however, refused to make distinctions among varieties of abolitionists.

The abolitionists recruited some of their most effective supporters from the South, notably the Quaker Grimke sisters from South Carolina and James G. Birney from Kentucky and Alabama. These left the South necessarily, for by the thirties the slightest hint of antislavery sentiment had ceased to be tolerated there, and this was true of both the upper and the lower South. There were few Southern abolitionists—if indeed there were any others—like big Cassius Marcellus Clay of Kentucky, who fortified his newspaper office with cannon, kept his bowie knife handy and occasionally used it, and stayed put. Even in the North, to be an avowed abolitionist was to be in constant danger of mob violence. Down to the outbreak of the Civil War Northern opinion expressed itself repeatedly in mob actions against antislavery meetings and known abolitionists.

Until the Kansas-Nebraska Bill of 1854, when extension of slavery into the free West once again became the big issue, the most widespread opposition to the system in the North was based, not upon the institution itself, but upon limitations on Northern rights demanded by Southerners for the purpose of defending it. When Southern congressmen passed a "gag rule" in the House prohibiting the presentation of antislavery petitions, Rep. John Quincy Adams fought it year in and year out until he aroused Northern sentiment to force its repeal in 1844.

And when Southern slave-catchers pursuing runaway slaves used the broad terms of the Fugitive Slave Act of 1793 to return South with Northern free Negroes instead, the Northern states, some of which had passed laws prohibiting the immigration of free Negroes in the first place, passed "personal liberty" laws which made the identity of a runaway slave virtually impossible to establish legally. The invalidation of such laws by the Southern-dominated Supreme Court aroused the indignation of Northerners who were little concerned about the plight of the distant and racially unacceptable slaves. The abolitionists appealed to the rights of Northern whites in the case of the gag rule and the personal liberty laws, and they did so again in the cases of the new Fugitive Slave Law of 1850 and the Kansas-Nebraska Act of 1854. By these tactics they finally succeeded in broadening one important part of the antislavery cause into a popular movement.

Black Americans, individually and through organizations such as the Free African Society of Philadelphia, had worked for abolition from the time of the Revolution; when Garrison entered the fight, there were at least fifty black antislavery societies, of which the most active were in Boston, New York, and Philadelphia. The first black newspaper, *Freedom's Journal,* appeared in 1827, and David Walker's pamphlet against slavery, the *Appeal,* appeared two years later. Most influential among the black newspapers was Frederick Douglass's *North Star.* Himself a runaway slave, Douglass entered the abolitionist movement as a public speaker who told the story of his escape to freedom under the sponsorship of the Garrisonian abolitionists. He published his *Autobiography* in 1845 and launched his newspaper two years later. Among other black abolitionists, William Wells Brown and Henry Highland Garnet were notably influential.

The Underground Railway had been spiriting slaves out of the South into free states and sometimes on into Canada since the early national period. Organized initially by Quakers, it became a major responsibility of Douglass and other black abolitionists. Among these perhaps the most active was Harriet Tubman; after escaping herself, she made repeated trips into the South to rescue other slaves. The governor of Mississippi estimated that between 1810 and 1850 there had been 100,000 escapes from the South, representing a loss of 30 million dollars. But from the Southern point of view the economic loss was but a small matter compared to the basic threat to Southern slave society of this ever more successful conspiracy of blacks and whites together that was operating widely in the South as well as the North.

THE KANSAS-NEBRASKA ACT

Although the Compromise of 1850 had produced solutions of the big issues directly related to slavery, including a Fugitive Slave Law to combat the Underground Railway, all Southerners who identified their interests with the institution were bound to view all major domestic issues in the light of the slavery question. One such issue developed from the acquisition of California: that of the route to be authorized for the first transcontinental railroad. Proponents of a Southern route had a powerful advocate in Jefferson Davis, who as Secretary of War directed the Corps of Army Engineers, which was responsible for surveying the possible routes and recommending the best alternatives. From an engineering point of view the extreme Southern route probably was the most favorable, and it won the support of the army engineers. It was the possibility of this route that in 1853 persuaded Congress to approve the Gadsden Purchase, a barren stretch of Mexican desert, thus rounding out, as things happened, the permanent continental boundaries of the United States.

The Middle West had its own resourceful advocate in Senator Douglas of Illinois. Douglas faced the difficulty that his route would cross through areas as yet unorganized territorially. But he was chairman of the Senate Committee on Territories, and he was among the most nation-minded politicians in that time of sectional politics. Douglas was impatient to see the continental nation take form and believed the opening up of the great "Platte River country" to settlement was overdue under any circumstances. In 1854, therefore, he presented a congressional bill to organize the territories of Kansas and Nebraska. To line up Southern votes necessary for passage of the measure, Douglas in his bill opened up the possibility of slavery in the territory in an ambiguously worded provision that at least partially invalidated the supposedly perpetual Missouri Compromise of 1820. The ambiguity did not remain to create its own difficulties, however, for Southern pressure obliged Douglas explicitly to set aside the compromise.

The Pierce administration supported the resulting measure and it was passed into law after months of acrimonious debate. Douglas defended it as following the principle of popular sovereignty laid down by the Compromise of 1850. He further reasoned that under any circumstances slavery would be excluded from the territories when they became states, since the environment was not suited to a slave economy. Repeal of the Missouri Compromise would therefore be but a nominal concession which, he must have supposed, would seriously disturb none but the doctrinaires and fanatics among antislavery Northerners. The event proved this line of reasoning to be the cataclysmic miscalculation that overwhelmed the nation in sectional controversy and rushed it into civil war.

THE DIVIDING NATION

The Kansas-Nebraska Act presented antislavery men with the issue that brought the Northern majority to their side: the issue, not of slavery itself, but of its extension into territories where it did not yet exist, in violation of the Missouri Compromise. Throughout the North anti-Nebraska parties organized themselves immediately on this issue and joined together to form the Republican party, dedicated to preventing the extension of slavery. Created largely out of the disintegrating Whig party and representing a blending of Northern and also border-state opinion, the Republican party was ready for action in the congressional elections of 1854, and the fact that Kansas Territory was opened for settlement at once provided it with a bloody dramatization of the issue.

There would have been troubles enough in Kansas without the slavery issue, since the government opened the territory before extinguishing Indian titles or making surveys, but the Kansas-Nebraska Bill ensured that the troubles would be bloody. A month before the territory was opened, the Massachusetts Emigrant Aid Company—later the New England Emigrant Aid Company—was formed to rush free-state settlers into the area and arm them with Sharp's rifles. Meanwhile, "border ruffians" poured in from Missouri, and some came from the Deep South. By the time the first governor arrived, the Missourians had the upper hand, and they formed a government which limited office holding to proslavery men. The antislavery men later retaliated by establishing their own rival government.

Remarkably enough under a succession of ineffectual governors, hardly anybody was killed for two years. Then John Brown, after a lifetime of unfulfillment in various dubious and unsuccessful business enterprises, achieved a measure of national notoriety by leading a small band to Pottawatomie, Kansas, removing five proslavery men from their beds, and murdering and mutilating them. After a subsequent brush with proslavery men, Brown went east, where the Republican press had suppressed information concerning the "Pottawatomie Massacre." There he was warmly welcomed, Emerson and Thoreau hailing him as the true transcendental hero come at last. In the Senate, meanwhile, a congressman from South Carolina, Preston Brooks, had caned Sen. Charles Sumner of Massachusetts on the floor of the Senate in retaliation for a speech in which Sumner had denounced Senator Butler of South Carolina. Noisy adulation was accorded Sumner and even Brown in New England and Brooks in the South, the whole sectional dispute underwent an emotional transformation, and a good many men on both sides became eager for war.

The Democrats did in this situation in 1856 as they had done in the previous campaign: they nominated a "doughface" candidate—a Northerner who could be counted on to follow the dictation of the Southern wing of the party—James Buchanan of Pennsylvania. The Whig party had already destroyed itself by attempting to ignore the slavery question, and two rival parties were trying to succeed it: the American, or Know-Nothing, party, opposing itself to Catholicism and immigration, and the Republican party, opposing itself to the extension of slavery into the territories. The one nominated former President Fillmore, and the other nominated John C. Frémont. Frémont, "the pathfinder," was famous for his book, largely written for him by his wife, about his California explorations, led by Kit Carson and other experienced mountain men. His lack of a political record made him an available candidate for a new Republican party seeking a new political following in a confused situation. In the election, with the American party running a poor third, Buchanan won 45.34 percent of the votes and was elected, the first candidate since John Quincy Adams to become President against the wishes of the majority of the voters.

Two days after Buchanan took office the Supreme Court rendered a momentous decision in the Dred Scott case. Scott was a slave whose master had taken him to a free state, later to federal territory where slavery was forbidden by the Missouri Compromise, and then back to Missouri. Scott sued for his freedom in the Missouri courts on the grounds of his residence in a free state and in free federal territory. In the course of the suit a New Yorker gained ownership of Scott. The case thereupon entered the federal jurisdiction and went to the Supreme Court.

The Court might have decided the case against Scott on various narrow legal grounds which would have avoided major constitutional issues. Urged by the extremely doughface Buchanan to rule on the question of congressional authority over slavery in the territories, however, the Court took the occasion to declare a federal law, the Missouri Compromise, unconstitutional for the second time in the nation's history. In nine separate decisions the majority of the Court upheld the ruling of Chief Justice Roger Taney that the descendant of a slave could not become an American citizen, even though he might become the citizen of a state, and that Congress could not prohibit slavery in federal territory.

In Illinois in 1858 Abraham Lincoln and Stephen A. Douglas, contending for a seat in the United States Senate, took part in a series of public debates turning mainly on the issue of the extension of slavery into the territories. Without challenging the authority of the Supreme Court, Lincoln contended that the government had the right to exclude slavery from the territories. Douglas associated himself with the argument that the matter of slavery in the territories should be left to the popular sovereignty of the white settlers in the immediate region. He argued that this was the democratic way to dispose of the question, and to his Northern audience he pointed out that as a practical matter this would.exclude slavery from virtually all the lands in question.

In a debate at Freeport, Illinois, Lincoln challenged Douglas to defend his doctrine of popular sovereignty in the light of the Dred Scott decision. Douglas replied that slavery could not exist for a day without local police regulations to support it, and that a territorial legislature could therefore prohibit slavery simply by failing to pass such laws. This commonsense "Freeport doctrine" alienated Southern Democrats, widened the breach in the Democratic party, and did much to keep Douglas from becoming President in 1860.

In October 1859 John Brown led an attack on the Federal arsenal at Harpers Ferry, Virginia, for the purpose of arming Southern Negroes and organizing them into a force which would terrorize the South into emancipating the slaves. Captured by United States Marines, Brown was tried and executed for treason against the state of Virginia. Brown's raid struck a raw nerve: obsessive Southern fear of slave insurrection such as had made a holocaust of Santo Domingan slaveholders. Meanwhile, Southerners could hear all the way from quiet Concord, Massachusetts, Ralph Waldo Emerson's remark that Brown's execution would make the gallows glorious like the cross. Actually, few words in defense of Brown came out of the North at the time, even William Lloyd Garrison hesitating to support him. Democratic politicians were quick to implicate the entire Republican party, however, and Southerners were quick to implicate the entire North. Brown had drawn the first blood in the oncoming war.

Faced with the candidacy of Douglas for President in 1860, the radical Southern Democrats bolted the convention to nominate John C. Breckinridge of Kentucky; also, a Constitutional Union party appeared for the occasion, founded for prosperous and contented old Whigs on the proposition that the crisis should be ignored by both sides and thereby avoided. The Republican party, meanwhile, passed over its leading politicians for the less prominent and therefore less vulnerable Abraham Lincoln of Illinois, who had made a national reputation in his debates with Douglas and had won Eastern support with a moderate speech at Cooper Union in New York. In the election Lincoln won every free state except New Jersey, where the vote was split, and lost every slave state, receiving not a single vote in ten of them. Receiving 40 percent of the total vote, he won an absolute majority in the electoral college by virtue of the concentration of his votes in the populous states.

Upon hearing of Lincoln's election, South Carolina called a convention which voted it out of the Union, and this time South Carolina's lead was followed by the six other states of the lower South, and the Confederate States of America was formed—all before Lincoln had taken office. Refusing to relinquish federal claims to sovereignty over the Southern states, Lincoln moved carefully to avoid alienating either the upper South or indecisive Northern opinion. Determined to retain at least some token of sovereignty, he finally decided to hold the federal Fort Sumter in Charleston harbor, sending supply ships with food to maintain the garrison. South Carolina countered by shelling Fort Sumter and, by firing the first shot, rallied most Northerners enthusiastically to the federal cause. The upper South, however, viewed Lincoln's decision to retain Fort Sumter as a constitutional violation of states' rights, and when Lincoln issued a call for Northern troops, the upper South united with the Confederacy, except for the border states of Delaware, Maryland, Kentucky, and Missouri. In July 1861 the Civil War was launched, with high confidence on both sides, in the First Battle of Bull Run.

The cannon at Fort Sumter blasted through the entanglements of legal and constitutional argument and opened the way for a rush of Northern idealism. Ralph Waldo Emerson, for instance, crammed his journal with thoughts on war, heroism, morality, and freedom. "If the abundance of heaven only sends us a fair share of light and conscience," he wrote a friend, "we shall redeem America for all its sinful years since the century began." His literary colleague Nathaniel Hawthorne, who believed in original sin as Emerson did not, took a more pessimistic and, as it proved, more realistic view of the struggle. No human effort on the grand scale, he wrote of the war, "has ever yet resulted according to the purposes of its projectors. The advantages are always incidental. Man's accidents are God's purposes. We miss the good we sought and do the good we little cared for." The war preserved the Union and rid the nation of slavery, but in a manner and at a cost which could hardly have been conceived of. It proved to be a brutal four-year bloodletting, and it ushered in sinful years such as had never been dreamed of in Emerson's philosophy.

BIBLIOGRAPHY FOR CHAPTER 11

D. L. Dumond, Anti-slavery, 2 vols. (1961)
Louis Filler, Crusade against Slavery, 1830–1860 (1960)
R. B. Nye, Fettered Freedom: Civil Liberties and the Slavery Controversy, 1830–1860 (1949)
W. S. Jenkins, Pro-slavery Thought in the Old South (1935)
Stanley Elkins, Slavery: A Problem in American Institutional and Intellectual Life (1959)
A. O. Craven, The Growth of Southern Nationalism, 1848–1861 (1953) and Civil War in the Making, 1815–1860 (1959)
Allan Nevins, Ordeal of the Union, 2 vols. (1947)
J. H. Sibley, The Transformation of American Politics, 1840–1860 (1961)
David Donald, Lincoln Reconsidered: Essays on the Civil War Era (1956)
K. M. Stampp, And the War Came: The North and the Secession Crisis, 1860–1861 (1950)

CHAPTER 12

CIVIL WAR

MILITARY STRENGTHS
AND WEAKNESSES

Confederate whites were outnumbered 4 to 1 by Northerners, and in material strength their disadvantage was even greater. The South contained but one major ironworks, at Richmond, and in all other important respects as well it was industrially a world apart from the enterprising North. Its comparatively backward railroad system compounded this disadvantage, confronting Confederate generals with tactical problems which Union generals did not face. The primitive state of Southern commerce was reflected in the lack of either a merchant marine or a potential navy. The North was in a position to move almost at will to close Southern ports against the enemy.

For the South, however, the fight for Confederate independence was a defensive war fought from interior lines. Against the defensive strength of the Southern position, overwhelming numerical superiority was indeed necessary, and the far-flung, motley North—much of its population strongly pro-Southern—could not command its manpower as effectively as could the beleaguered South. Nor, during the first three years of the war, was the North able to utilize as skillfully the manpower it did muster. A strong military tradition had drawn some of the most capable Southerners to military service. Competently staffed from the first, the Southern armies faced opponents commanded by men of inferior ability and often quite untrained for their military duties. A more aggressive and able leadership might have brought Northern victory out of the Battle of Antietam in 1862 or at Gettysburg a year later, but the Union commanders in both cases failed to press their advantages. As for the industrial advantages of the North, the Civil War was essentially a small-arms war fought out between foot soldiers and cavalry, and the Confederacy was fairly amply equipped to fight such a war as this from start to conclusion.

Politically the North had the advantage of an established government, in

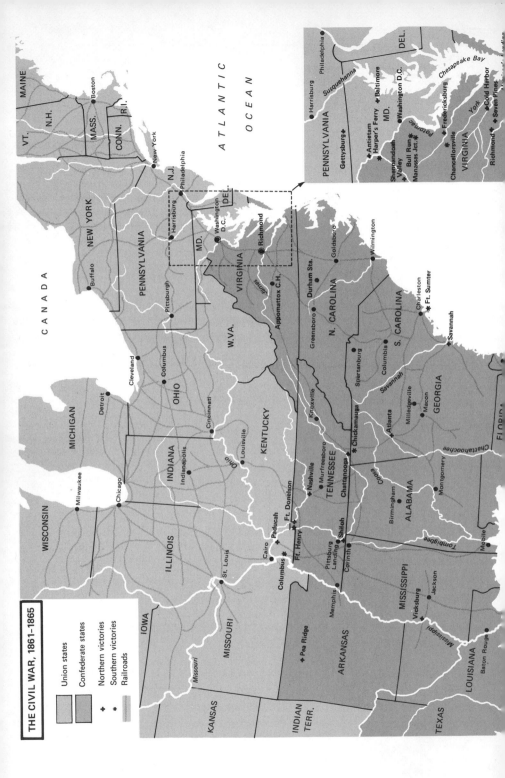

THE CIVIL WAR, 1861–1865

Union states
Confederate states
Northern victories
Southern victories
Railroads

CANADA

MAINE
VT.
N.H.
MASS.
R.I.
CONN.
N.Y.
NEW YORK
Boston
New York
Buffalo

PENNSYLVANIA
Harrisburg
Pittsburgh
N.J.
Philadelphia
DEL.
MD.
Washington D.C.
Richmond

OHIO
Columbus
Cleveland
Cincinnati

INDIANA
Indianapolis

ILLINOIS

MICHIGAN
Detroit

WISCONSIN
Milwaukee
Chicago

IOWA

MISSOURI
St. Louis

KANSAS

INDIAN TERR.

ARKANSAS
Pea Ridge

TEXAS

LOUISIANA
Baton Rouge

MISSISSIPPI
Jackson
Vicksburg

ALABAMA
Montgomery
Birmingham
Mobile

GEORGIA
Atlanta
Milledgeville
Macon
Savannah

FLORIDA

TENNESSEE
Nashville
Murfreesboro
Chattanooga
Chickamauga
Shiloh
Corinth
Memphis
Knoxville

KENTUCKY
Louisville
Paducah
Ft. Donelson
Ft. Henry
Pittsburg Landing
Cairo
Columbus

W.VA.

VIRGINIA
Appomattox C.H.

N. CAROLINA
Greensboro
Durham Sta.
Goldsboro
Wilmington

S. CAROLINA
Columbia
Spartanburg
Charleston
Ft. Sumter
Savannah

ATLANTIC OCEAN

Chesapeake Bay

Ohio
Missouri
Mississippi
Tombigbee
Chattahoochee
Coosa
James

PENNSYLVANIA
Harrisburg
Gettysburg
Philadelphia
DEL.
MD.
Antietam
Harper's Ferry
Baltimore
Washington D.C.
Shenandoah Valley
Bull Run
Manassas Jct.
Fredericksburg
Chancellorsville
VIRGINIA
Richmond
Cold Harbor
Seven Pines
Susquehanna
Potomac
York

contrast to the ramshackle Confederacy, first organized at Montgomery, Alabama, and then reorganized at Richmond, Virginia, after the secession of the upper South in 1861. On the other hand, however divided the Confederacy was on many political matters, it was fighting aggressively for the simple, clear-cut purpose of winning its independence. The North, on the other hand, was engaged in a war to preserve the Union: to return the nation to the condition that had existed before secession. However idealistic a conception of the Union Lincoln and others might hold, the preservation of it did not present the simple, militant objective that independence from it presented to Confederates.

WAR AIMS

When the Southern states seceded, much Northern opinion favored letting them depart in peace, but Lincoln did not waver in his determination to preserve the Union. When the war came, many Northerners were eager to conduct it as a righteous crusade to free the slaves. Horace Greeley, with many others, successively adopted both of these positions. It was to Greeley, the advocate of an abolitionist war, that Lincoln addressed his famous declaration of policy, "If I could save the Union without freeing any slaves, I would do it; and if I could save it by freeing all the slaves, I would do it. . . . What I do about slavery and the colored race, I do because I believe it helps to save the Union; and what I forbear, I forbear because I do not believe it would help to save the Union," to which he added his personal wish "that all men, everywhere, could be free."

Lincoln directed a war that was fought in order "that this nation, under God, shall have a new birth of freedom; and that government of the people, by the people, for the people, shall not perish from the earth." Like Bismarck and other European national leaders, as Bertrand Russell wrote, "he stood for national unity, and like most nationalists he found his justification in the association of his nation with a moral idea. But unlike most others he was justified in making this association. America had been 'dedicated to the proposition that all men were created equal.' "

The President of the Confederate States of America, Jefferson Davis, was a West Point graduate who would rather have been general than President. He presided over a shifting cabinet of indifferently able men who varied in views from extreme states-rights to downright Unionist. He was faced with a discordant Congress which grew increasingly violent during the course of the war, with members going around heavily armed against possible attack from each other.

Davis directed a nation that was caught in the painful cross-purposes of waging an effectively unified war to preserve the divided sovereignties of the individual states. Sensitivity to violation of states rights was especially strong in the older states. North and South Carolina and Georgia resisted the claims of the Confederate government to sovereignty to the bloody end, although they had agreed initially to a Confederate constitution that departed from the federal Constitution in minor states-rights details only.

The Confederate Congress passed the first conscription act in American history, to the principled fury of the states righters and the personal fury of those who could not qualify for one of the clutch of exemptions given to slaveholders, ministers, civil servants, professors, all who could afford to purchase a substitute, and other privileged people. Desperately short of specie and international credit, the Confederacy resorted to issuing currency which fell to one-fifteenth of its face value before the close of the war. It went on to levy one-tenth of the annual produce of the nation. So far did the war strain the South from its original principles that the Confederate government in the desperate last days was contemplating the emancipation of the slaves, in the hope that this would move England and perhaps France to intervene on the Confederate side.

Lincoln suffered the same abuse from his Congress and from the public that the unhappily stiff-necked Davis did, but he absorbed it better, and while he also suffered a good deal of disloyalty from his Cabinet, he appointed more capable men and got better service out of them. His Secretary of State, William H. Seward—until Lincoln's nomination the leading figure in the Republican party—had thought he would become a de facto premier during the incumbency of this unprepossessing, informally educated, provincial politician, but Seward came to learn, as did others, that "the President is the best of us." Unless they were wholly self-deceived, as in the case of Secretary of the Treasury Salmon P. Chase, those associated with Lincoln discovered that he combined a lofty purpose and almost infinite forbearance with a most crafty dexterity in the smaller arts of politics.

Lincoln needed all his political skill to direct a four-year war that Northerners had expected to win in three months' time or less. This expectation had been shockingly disappointed in July 1861 in the First Battle of Manassas, 20 miles from the nation's capital, where the Confederate troops might well have captured Washington had they pressed their advantage. As all prospects for a quick end to the conflict vanished, Lincoln came under attack from Congress and in the national press, which criticized his conduct of the war with increasing ferocity as the war lengthened.

Secession had put the Republicans in the majority in Congress, but congressional Republicans were themselves divided between the moderates, who were inclined to support Lincoln, and the Radicals, who were determined from the outset to convert the war to preserve the Union into a crusade against slavery. In July 1861 Congress passed a resolution in which John J. Crittenden of the loyal slave state of Kentucky declared that the war was not being waged "for any purpose of overthrowing . . . established institutions of those States," but before the year was out the House failed to reenact the Crittenden Resolution by a narrow vote.

In 1864 the Radical Republicans nominated their own candidate, John C. Frémont, to run against Lincoln, while the Democrats nominated the popular general George McClellan, whose lack of aggressiveness had caused Lincoln to relieve him of command. Frémont withdrew from the contest too late in the campaign to be replaced by a new Radical candidate; even so, Lincoln, now running on the "Union party" ticket, won against McClellan by a very narrow margin. Military victory was in sight by the time Lincoln entered his second term in 1865, but the Radicals were continuing to increase their power against him within the party.

DIPLOMACY AND WAR

Following Sumter, Lincoln moved aggressively to save the border states of Delaware, Maryland, Kentucky, and Missouri, which remained doubtful. He called up additional troops, appropriated money on doubtful constitutional authority, and invaded Maryland to place it under martial law. Following a more cautious policy toward Kentucky, he waited until Confederate troops had first invaded that state and then won it to the Union side. In Missouri, the government of which was Confederate in sympathy, the local Union forces, with strong support from the local German-American population, defeated the state forces in the first sizable fight of the war, and Missouri was largely saved for the Union. Northwestern Virginia was detached from its parent state and admitted to the Union as West Virginia in 1863.

To the problems of financing, supplying, and manning the war effort the Union brought incomparably greater resources than the Confederacy, and this brought correspondingly better results. A highly successful bond drive under the leading financier Jay Cooke raised 400 million dollars in 1862, and in the last year of the war bonds began to sell well again. In addition 432 million dollars worth of paper "greenbacks" were issued, and, while they declined to less than half their face value at one time, they always remained usable currency. The supplying of the war was marked by ubiquitous corruption, but the materials were available, and the government was in a position to get them. In 1863 the government instituted a draft, a year after the Confederacy had resorted to it. Draft riots and widespread violations followed, especially in New York City and in the upper Mississippi Valley, where there was much pro-Southern "copperhead" sentiment. Desertions may have been on a larger scale in the Union than in the Confederate army, but so were enlistments, whether voluntary or enforced.

At the outset Confederate confidence had been strengthened by the belief that England and France would inevitably intervene should the war come to deprive their textile industries of American cotton. The leadership of both these nations was sympathetic to the aristocratic Confederacy, as opposed to the democratic Union. Both nations had hopefully recognized the Confederacy as a belligerent and had opened their ports to rebel ships. However, cotton happened to be in long supply in Europe, and pro-Union sentiment was strong among the English people generally, especially after Lincoln's Emancipation Proclamation of January 1863. Shortly after that proclamation the Confederate diplomatic representative in England was recalled and the British consuls in Richmond were ordered home. The British in the meantime had permitted the construction of large ships, built for the purpose of breaking the Union blockade, a matter which troubled Anglo-American relations in the postwar period.

From the Union point of view military strategy was determined by naval supremacy, which invited not only the blockading of the Confederacy but also the dividing of it through control of the Mississippi. Strategy was determined also by the Appalachian Mountains, which divided the conflict into two main theaters. The close proximity of Washington, D.C., to the Confederate capital at Richmond was a controlling factor also, for the defense of each capital was viewed as a matter of high importance to politicians on both sides, irrespective of military considerations. This point was clearly made in July 1861 at the first major engagement, the battle at Manassas, when Washington was so nearly taken. Thereafter all was quiet on the Potomac for almost a year and only a little less so in the Western theater, as the main Union effort was restricted to naval operations which captured key points along the coast and in the spring of 1862 took New Orleans.

The year 1862 saw victories by Gen. Ulysses S. Grant in the West at Fort Henry and Fort Donelson, which were balanced against McClellan's failure to exploit his numerical advantage against Gen. Robert E. Lee in the East. For his lack of enterprise McClellan was replaced by Gen. John Pope, who promptly suffered defeat in the Second Battle of Manassas. McClellan was returned to lead the Army of the Potomac to a disheartening draw at the Battle of Antietam against Confederate troops which his forces outnumbered 2 to 1. Lincoln replaced him with Gen. Ambrose E. Burnside, who, following his fiasco at Fredericksburg, was replaced in turn by Gen. Joseph Hooker. Hooker, following a shattering defeat at Chancellorsville in May 1863, turned over his command to Gen. George Meade. Chancellorsville, where Lee's most brilliant general, Stonewall Jackson, was killed, proved the high point of Confederate success in a war where numbers were counting increasingly on the Union side and where in Ulysses S. Grant a general had been discovered who could make use of this advantage.

The turning point in the war came in July 1863, with major Union victories in both the Eastern and Western theaters of action. In the West Gen. Ulysses S. Grant completed the conquest of the Mississippi with the capture of Vicksburg, which was followed up by the taking of the other remaining Confederate strongpoint on the Mississippi, Port Hudson, Louisiana. Thus Texas, Louisiana, and Arkansas were severed from the rest of the Confederacy. In the East, meanwhile, Lee launched his most aggressive attack on Union soil at Gettysburg,

Pennsylvania, and was repulsed. Lee was able to retire in good order, but the South was never again able to mount a major offensive. Five months later in the West the Battle of Chattanooga cleared the way for the invasion of Georgia, and Gen. William T. Sherman undertook his march to Atlanta, from Atlanta to the sea, and then from Savannah northward, the march which more than anything else broke the Southern will to resist.

Transferred east and appointed supreme commander, Grant launched the Battle of the Wilderness against Lee in northern Virginia in May 1864 and, despite the indecisiveness of the battle, pressed ahead along Lee's right flank, clashing again at Spotsylvania Court House and again at Cold Harbor and then slipping south of Richmond to Petersburg.

In April 1865, with Sherman moving against the army of Gen. Joe Johnston, Grant forced Lee to evacuate Richmond, and the war came to an end after four years of fighting. It cost the lives of more than 250,000 Confederate and more than 350,000 Union soldiers, among them their Commander in Chief, shot to death in Ford's Theater eleven days after the conclusion of hostilities.

THE SLAVERY ISSUE

The immediate issue that had precipitated the Civil War had not been the legitimacy of slavery, but the legitimacy of secession. Lincoln had emphatically upheld the constitutional right of the states to authorize or prohibit slavery within their borders. He would only prohibit its extension into the territories, which he had consistently urged the federal government to do, despite the Dred Scott decision against prohibited slavery in the territories. Lincoln had declared slavery to be a wrong, but he had opposed its extension on behalf of the white man rather than the black. He hoped that the territories would provide "an outlet for *free white people everywhere.*" He believed that blacks and whites could never live together as equals, and he was "in favor of having the superior position assigned to the white race."

The Southern states had a right to maintain slavery, Lincoln declared, but they had no right to dissolve the Union, which was perpetual. Fort Sumter in Federal hands was the symbol of the sanctity of the Union, and when it was fired upon, Northern sentiment rallied to the Union regardless of conflicting opinions on slavery. Lincoln's attitude toward slavery and Negroes was undoubtedly representative of the dominant Northern opinion in 1861, but the war immediately created a new situation involving many concrete problems that the Lincoln formulation did not clearly cover. In this new situation only the abolitionists were arguing a principle regarding slavery that consistently made good sense in a war against a slave society.

In addition to being an evil, slavery was the means by which the Confederacy was carrying out its insurrection against the Union. To free the slaves was to destroy the slaveholder's power. Generals in the field who had antislavery views naturally tended to make this principle a matter of policy, with increasing congressional support. In 1862 Congress passed a Confiscation Act providing that the slaves of all persons supporting the "rebellion" would be "forever free of their servitude, and not again held as slaves." Several months previously it had instituted a program of compensated emancipation for the District of Columbia. Lincoln was caught between the rising strength of the abolitionist Radical Republicans in Congress and the wavering loyalty to the Union of the border slave states. Critically important also was British opinion, for the British government was known to be giving full recognition of the Confederacy serious consideration through most of 1862.

EMANCIPATION

It was under these circumstances that Lincoln in September 1862 issued a statement that on January 1, 1863, slaves in the rebellious areas of the Union should be "then, thenceforward, and forever free." The definitive Emancipation Proclamation, accordingly issued on January 1, declared all slaves in Confederate territory to be free, but at the same time it enjoined them "to abstain from all violence, unless in necessary self-defense." Dryly presented as a military order, the Emancipation Proclamation extended its provisions to no area where the federal government at the moment had the power to free slaves.

Diplomatically, the Emancipation Proclamation produced a favorable reaction in England, which ended the threat of British recognition of the Confederate States; politically, it asserted Presidential authority in an area the Radical Republicans in Congress had sought to preempt through the passage of confiscation acts and other measures. The Radicals had gained strength in the 1862 congressional elections, however, and they were determined to maintain the initiative in striking down slavery and, more than that, in determining the process by which the "Reconstruction" of Confederate states into loyal Union states would be carried out.

In an effort to forestall the Radicals, Lincoln announced his plan of Reconstruction in a proclamation issued in December 1863. With some exceptions, he offered a pardon to supporters of the Confederacy who would take an oath of loyalty to the Union. When 10 percent of the voters of the state, measured by the total votes cast in 1860, should take this loyalty oath and then should establish a state government, Lincoln would extend executive recognition to the government. The Radicals in Congress replied in July 1864 with the Wade-Davis Bill, requiring loyalty oaths from a majority of the voters in the state, rather than 10 percent, and excluding Confederate soldiers and officials from voting and holding office in the loyal government.

Lincoln responded to the Wade-Davis Bill by withholding his signature and continuing his own policy, under which Louisiana, Arkansas, Tennessee, and Virginia created loyal governments with Presidential approval. Each of these loyal state governments was still being created at the time of Lincoln's assassination, however, and the fundamental question of Reconstruction remained to be worked out between Congress and Lincoln's successor, Vice President Andrew Johnson.

Northern Negroes, for their part, had greeted the Civil War as an abolitionist crusade at the outset, and thousands throughout the North had volunteered for duty, only to be rejected on grounds of inadequate citizenship. A meeting of blacks in Boston resolved that "our feelings urge us to say to our countrymen that we are ready to stand by and defend our Government as the equals of its white defenders . . . that full scope may be given to the patriotic feelings burning in the colored man's breast." But out of concern for the effect on border-state opinion, the War Department refused to accept black enlistments until forced to do so by pressure from officers in the field in 1862. Then, following the Emancipation Proclamation, which Lincoln justified as a "fit and necessary war measure," recruitment of Negroes was put systematically into operation, and by the end of the war more than 186,000 blacks had enlisted in the Union army.

Organized as the "United States Colored Troops," black soldiers served in segregated units of heavy artillery, cavalry, infantry, and engineers. They served chiefly under white officers, although two regiments of Gen. B. F. Butler's Corps d'Afrique were entirely staffed by black officers. Initially given menial duties for the most part, at roughly half the pay of white soldiers, black troops increasingly engaged in combat, and they had successfully agitated for a raise in pay to that of white troops by war's end. Black troops suffered a far higher rate of casualties than white troops as a whole; more than 38,000 lost their lives in the Civil War. In the opinion of Lincoln and other contemporaries, as well as modern historians, black troops provided the margin of victory for the North.

ECONOMIC LIFE

When eleven planting states withdrew from the Union, Northern industry tumbled into power. Congress in 1861 passed the Morrill Tariff, revising rates upward, and no later session of Congress met during the Civil War without adding further upward revisions. Excise taxes were levied also, which business did not like, but at the close of the war these were removed while the tariffs remained.

In 1862, with the South no longer present to contest the route, Congress passed acts providing for the construction of a railroad from Omaha to Sacramento. It authorized the Union Pacific to build the eastern section and the Central Pacific to build the western one. It made enormous grants of land to the railroads, to which it added loans ranging from $16,000 to $48,000 per mile. Even then the companies, formed for the purpose by men of moderate means, found it impossible to raise the capital. Consequently the land granted was doubled, and government loans were converted to second mortgages, permitting the companies to acquire private loans on the basis of first mortgages. No provision was made for a government-chartered construction company to build the roads. The controllers of the railroad companies were therefore able to create their own construction companies and, with no government supervision or legislative limitations, to make what profit they liked.

In 1864 the Northern Pacific Railroad was chartered to run from Lake Superior to Puget Sound and was given even more generous grants of land than those accorded the Central Pacific and Union Pacific together. Similar charters and land grants were given to the Atlantic and Pacific in 1866 and to the Texas and Pacific in 1871 for Southern transcontinental routes to San Diego and Los Angeles. The latter two charters were almost immediately acquired by the operators of the Central Pacific along with the land grants, and the roads never reached the West Coast. By that time more than 130 million acres of federal land had been distributed to railroad companies since 1862, although one-third of it was eventually forfeited by companies for not meeting federal terms. On a smaller scale private interests gained vast tracts of timber and mineral lands from government largess during this period. Then the panic of 1873 and revelations of national political scandals brought the period of gargantuan government handouts to a close.

Free land was given to the small farmer also in the Homestead Act of 1862, granting settlers farms free of charge in lots of 160 acres after five years of occupation. This represented the final acceptance by the federal government of the farmers' argument, older than the republic, that the vacant land of the nation belonged to those who settled it and improved it. By the time the act was passed, however, the lands best suited to the one-family farm, which the supporters of the act had had in mind, had been largely taken up. Homesteading the plains regions proved too expensive for most, who found they were better served by purchasing lands which the government had given to the railroads. A further act which was popular with the farmers, the Morrill Land Grant Act of 1862, distributed public lands among the states according to congressional representation—30,000 acres for each senator and representative—for the purpose of financing agricultural and mechanical colleges. The main result of this act was the large-scale advancement of public higher education, especially in the Midwest and Far West, where the best advantage was taken of the law. It served also, however, as another means whereby large areas of public lands were eventually placed at the disposal of politically influential private interests.

The National Banking Act was passed in 1863 and largely revised the next year. In part this was enacted to bring order to a formerly chaotic system in which banks operated under the miscellaneous regulations of the various state charters. In part it was a device to market government bonds issued to help finance the war. The act provided for the establishment of banking associations under national charters. One-third of the capital of these associations was to be invested in government bonds on which the government would pay interest; in addition, it would issue to the banks federal notes worth 90 percent of the cost of the bonds. The banks were to maintain reserves against both deposits and bank notes, and these were to be held in certain reserve cities. Then in 1865 Congress placed a tax on state bank-note issues which drove them out of existence.

Originally the banking legislation was not designed to favor any special group or region, but the reserve requirement enabled New York to establish itself as the main center for bankers' funds, and as the National Banking Act was administered it discriminated heavily in favor of the Northeast. All the New England and middle Atlantic states received bank notes in excess of their quotas at the expense of the rest of the nation. Another important means by which the war was financed was through the issue of 432 million dollars in greenbacks, paper money which was not redeemable in coin. Reluctantly resorted to at the time, the greenbacks remained in circulation after the war to create political as well as economic problems.

The war turned the federal government into a buyer of goods and services on a scale for which the government had neither the experience nor the administrative organization, and war profiteers took every possible advantage of its vulnerability. A "shoddy aristocracy" sprang up in the North on profits made from the necessities of the nation, the phrase deriving from the practice of selling shoddy material for army uniforms, material which disintegrated under its first heavy use. The greatest scandal and the greatest profit were to be enjoyed in the illicit cotton trade. Southern cotton could be sold in New England at almost 1,000 percent profit, and the cotton trade, while bringing the Confederacy valuable specie, made many fortunes in the North.

Nor was it necessary to wallow in corruption in order to do well financially during wartime. To a remarkable extent the vast industrial enterprises of the late nineteenth century had their origins in Civil War opportunities, when young men like Andrew Carnegie and John D. Rockefeller emerged from the war with the capital accumulation that enabled them to rise swiftly to economic power. During the Civil War the number of millionaires in America increased many times over.

The Civil War came at the critical period in American history when the nation was making the transition from an agrarian to an industrial society. None of the other large nations that passed through the experience of the industrial revolution in the nineteenth century was as ill equipped to cope with it politically as the American federal republic. By contrast, England, France, Germany, and Japan all were administered by more effectively centralized governments at the time the industrial revolution centralized their economies. During the crucial period of its transition the American nation was torn by the slavery crisis, civil war, and Reconstruction, with the result that many basic problems of the industrial age did not receive serious concentrated nationwide attention until the twentieth century.

That the United States was undergoing revolutionary economic and social changes was evident, but these changes were widely believed to be beyond effective political control, and they were widely accepted as constituting the march of progress. At war's end, the nation was more immediately concerned with a political Reconstruction that would reunite a chastened South to the nation while somehow absorbing more than 4 million freedmen into its system of democracy.

BIBLIOGRAPHY FOR CHAPTER 12

J. G. Randall and **David Donald,** The Civil War and Reconstruction (rev. ed., 1961)

Thomas Pressley, Americans Interpret Their Civil War (1954)

Clement Eaton, History of the Southern Confederacy (1954)

Bruce Catton, Mr. Lincoln's Army (1951), Glory Road (1952), and A Stillness at Appomattox (1954)

T. H. Williams, Lincoln and His Generals (1952) and Lincoln and the Radicals (1941)

J. H. Franklin, The Emancipation Proclamation (1963)

Benjamin Quarles, The Negro in the Civil War (1953)

F. L. Klement, The Copperheads in the Middle West (1960)

Benjamin Thomas, Abraham Lincoln (1952)

Margaret Leech, Reveille in Washington, 1860–1865 (1941)

David Donald, ed., Why the North Won the Civil War (1968)

RECONSTRUCTION

JOHNSON AND THE RADICALS

The Constitution makes no provision for dealing with conquered states, and at the time of Lincoln's death no agreement had been reached between Congress and the President as to what would be done about the South or who would be in charge of it. Lincoln's pocket veto of the Wade-Davis Bill had set the stage for a contest between the legislative and administrative branches over the issue, but it was a contest in which the Chief Executive appeared to be at a strong advantage against the Radicals in Congress.

The Democrats in Congress were in a weak, somewhat demoralized position: the Republicans dominated both houses. But the Republicans were divided between Radicals and moderates, with the moderates representing the broadest group in both houses. The moderates had developed no Reconstruction program of their own, and it appeared likely that the President could win their support for a program that obliged the South to acknowledge its defeat and accept the abolition of slavery in good faith. The Radicals were not united on a clear-cut program, but they doubted that the South would do justice to the freedmen without being coerced into doing so, and they did not believe that Lincoln would apply the necessary coercion if Congress did not force him to.

Included among the Radicals were abolitionists, whose primary concern was for the freedman, and spokesmen for the economic interests that wished to protect the Civil War economic legislation. There was considerable feeling in Congress that the South should not go unpunished for engaging in four years of rebellion and even greater concern that the South not return at once to the predominant political position it had held before secession. Lincoln's policy of readmitting a state to the Union when but 10 percent of its voters proclaimed their loyalty, and without specific provisions for the freedmen, struck many in Congress as being a capitulation to the ruling classes of the Confederacy.

The assassination of Lincoln brought to the Presidency a man the Radicals believed would follow a course toward the South that they could heartily endorse. Andrew Johnson was a War Democrat from Tennessee who had been placed on the ticket as Lincoln's running mate in 1864, when the Republican party changed its name to Union party, in an effort to win bipartisan support for Lincoln. Johnson, a fiery Jacksonian Democrat, had represented the yeoman farmer in politics against the slaveholding Southern gentry. A roaring frontier stump speaker, Johnson had so roundly denounced Confederate treason and so vigorously advocated confiscations and executions that some Republicans feared he might, indeed, overdo Reconstruction of the South.

Actually, Johnson the stump speaker assumed an oratorical license to say a good deal more than he ever intended to do about punishing the men of the Confederacy, and as President he pursued from the outset substantially the moderate course that Lincoln had initiated. Furthermore, he was no more vigilant on behalf of the freedman than Lincoln had been, and he was at least as determined to fight congressional efforts to determine Reconstruction policy. And where Lincoln had been a Republican who had signed all the Civil War economic legislation into law, Johnson was a populistic Democrat who opposed the business interests that the Republican party represented.

Johnson disavowed Lincoln's 10 percent plan for reconstituting Confederate states, but he recognized the governments established under Lincoln's plan in Arkansas, Louisiana, Tennessee, and Virginia, and he proceeded to recognize other state governments although they failed to comply with various of his demands, such as that they repudiate Confederate debts and declare their ordinances of secession invalid in origin. None gave any blacks the right to vote, and all passed "black codes" which were designed to consign the Negroes to a permanently subordinate position in Southern society.

BLACK CIVIL RIGHTS

Southern whites viewed the black codes as the matter-of-fact recognition of the free status of the former slaves, for they were essentially the same special black codes that had applied to the free Negroes of the South in the prewar period. The free Negro had been legally maintained in a subordinate position before the war, and after the war Southern whites extended this dispensation to all blacks. These codes included vagrancy laws which in their practical operation might have returned a large part of the black population to virtual slavery.

Throughout most of the North as well as the South blacks were disfranchised and discriminated against; and they were more segregated from white society in the North than they had ever been in the South. Indeed, several Midwestern states had prohibited blacks from becoming residents at all. Popular opinion in the North evidently favored a policy of discrimination toward the black race. At the same time, after four years of civil war, there was much hostility toward the

South and much determination that the war should not have been fought in vain. To many the black codes appeared to demonstrate a Southern determination to remain unreconstructed by retaining the slave system in all but name.

Strengthened by Northern reaction to the black codes, the Radicals passed the Freedman's Bureau Bill, extending indefinitely the life of an earlier-created emergency agency and authorizing it to use military force throughout the South to defend the rights of Negroes. Johnson successfully vetoed the bill. It was the last such success he enjoyed, however. There followed the Civil Rights Act, vetoed by Johnson but passed over his veto, which transferred the duty of protecting the Southern Negro from the Bureau to the federal courts and armed the courts with authority to call on military force. It declared all persons born in the United States, except untaxed Indians, to be citizens entitled to equal protection of the law, regardless of local statutes.

The Thirteenth Amendment to the Constitution, forever ending slavery or involuntary servitude in America, was adopted by the states in December 1865, and in 1866 Congress sent them a Fourteenth Amendment embodying the provisions of the Civil Rights Act, as well as denying office to former Confederate officeholders until pardoned by Congress, denying compensation to former slaveholders for loss of their slaves, and repudiating the Confederate war debt. Moderate Republicans had been influential in eliminating harsh provisions that Radicals had wished to include in the Fourteenth Amendment, and in its final form it enjoyed moderate support. Nevertheless, President Johnson advised the reconstructed states to vote against its ratification. All but Tennessee accordingly did, and the way was opened for Radical control of Reconstruction.

RADICAL RECONSTRUCTION

In the campaign for the congressional elections of 1866 Johnson took to the stump, making the "swing around the circle" to deliver speeches against the Radicals and in favor of friendly candidates throughout the North. The campaign was marked by wild and vicious slander on both sides, the Radicals charging Johnson with being a drunkard, among other bad things, and Johnson lambasting the Radicals with charges of treason much like those he had formerly directed against Confederate leaders. The voters evidently were persuaded that Johnson was letting an unreconstructed, impenitent South back into the Union without safeguards for the blacks or for the Union, and they elected the opposition, placing the Radicals in full control of both houses of Congress.

Leader of the Radicals in the House of Representatives was Thaddeus Stevens, misshapen and formidable in appearance and terror-provoking in action. "His conversation," reported his fellow Radical Carl Schurz, "carried on with a hollow voice devoid of music, easily disclosed a well-informed mind, but also a certain absolutism of opinion with contemptuous scorn for adverse argument. . . . What he himself seemed to enjoy most in his talk was his sardonic humor, which he made play upon men and things like lurid freaks of lightning." In the Senate, the Radical leadership was divided among a number of eloquent and forceful men, including Charles Sumner of Massachusetts, Benjamin F. Wade of Ohio, George W. Julian of Indiana, and Zachariah Chandler of Michigan.

In March 1867 the new Congress passed a comprehensive Reconstruction Bill, which it quickly passed again over Johnson's veto, abolishing the reconstructed Southern state governments and dividing the South into five military districts. The bill created, under the supervision of the military, new Reconstruction governments based upon black and limited white suffrage and composed of freedmen and "carpetbaggers" from the North, who cooperated with Southern "scalawags" willing to join the new dispensation. In 1868 three additional acts were passed by Congress amplifying Radical Reconstruction and providing for its administration.

Under Radical authority a majority of the states were again reconstructed and readmitted to the Union in 1868, and the last four—Virginia, Georgia, Mississippi, and Texas—were readmitted in 1871. There followed a tumultuous era of corruption and reform, ending with the reassertion of Southern white authority in one state after another until the final withdrawal of Federal troops from South Carolina, Louisiana, and Florida in 1877.

The idea that the emancipated blacks should receive voting rights had not been widely advocated, even by Radicals, until after their Reconstruction program had been put into operation. In 1869, however, Congress submitted the Fifteenth Amendment to the states, declaring that the right of citizens to vote "shall not be denied or abridged by the United States or by any State on account of race, color, or previous condition of servitude," and giving Congress the power to enact enforcement measures. The amendment was ratified in 1870.

The Fifteenth Amendment did not advance the position of the Negro in the North measurably, and even in the South under Radical Reconstruction Negroes were not elected to public office in proportion to their numbers in the population. Mississippi sent two Negroes to the United States Senate, Hiram R. Revels and Blanche K. Bruce, both of whom had previously been schoolteachers, but they were the only blacks to become members of the Senate until the election of Edward W. Brooke from Massachusetts in 1966. None was elected governor of a reconstructed state, although P. B. S. Pinchback served briefly as acting governor of Louisiana, and only fifteen were elected to the House of Representatives. Blacks were elected in considerable numbers to the state legislatures, and they were in the majority in the South Carolina Legislature. They served as justices of the peace and in other local offices. In general the better-educated blacks were encouraged to seek office, and the qualifications of black officeholders were, on the whole, comparable to those of white officeholders in local positions.

The Northern carpetbaggers ranged from dedicated idealists to greedy adventurers, while the Southern scalawags ranged from leading members of the old order, who had once been Whigs and now thought it appropriate to join the Republicans, to yeoman farmers, who had always been hostile to the old class of aristocratic slaveholders. Whether the legislatures formed of these conflicting elements were more corrupt than the contemporary "gilded age" legislatures of the Northern states is doubtful, and it is clear they were responsible for some very creditable accomplishments, especially in the areas of education and internal improvements. Nevertheless there was much corruption, incompetence, and incurring of heavy state indebtedness.

Whatever its virtues or its defects, Reconstruction was a system that was being forced upon the South by a federal government which was unwilling to finance its thoroughgoing enforcement. Under these circumstances, Southern white resistance developed in the form of secret terrorist societies, such as the Knights of the White Camelia and the Ku Klux Klan. These societies developed grotesque rituals and costumes, distributed warnings to blacks, carpetbaggers, and scalawags, and engaged extensively in midnight raids, torture, and murder. Congress responded with the Force Act of 1870, followed by another a year later, imposing severe penalties against the various Klan practices and allowing the President to suspend habeas corpus in dealing with the secret societies. The Force Acts strengthened Radical control temporarily, at the cost of intensifying and broadening Southern white opposition to Reconstruction.

IMPEACHMENT OF JOHNSON

Although the Radicals had gained control of both houses of Congress in the elections of 1866, they were still obliged to contend with Johnson as President. They were easily able to override his vetoes, but responsibility for executing the congressional program of Reconstruction remained in the hands of the hostile Chief Executive. Since Johnson could not be expected to carry out the program in the spirit intended by Congress, Congress passed a series of laws, with little regard for their constitutional validity, seeking to remove executive control of Reconstruction from the President's hands. And finally, in March 1867, it passed the Tenure of Office Act, declaring it a high misdemeanor for the President unilaterally to remove an officeholder appointed with the Senate's advice and consent. Then, when Johnson suspended Secretary of War Edwin M. Stanton, the House of Representatives reacted by voting 126 to 47 to impeach the President.

The House presented eleven articles of impeachment to the Senate, where the trial of the President on the charge of high misdemeanor took place. The articles were composed of the flimsiest of allegations, for the Radicals were unable to discover any actual legal misconduct on the part of the President.

Even Johnson's suspension of Stanton turned out technically not to be in violation of the Tenure of Office Act. Still, the Senate voted 35 to 19 in favor of conviction, the Radicals failing by one vote to win the necessary two-thirds majority. Johnson remained as President; but with less than a year of his administration left and with no chance of his being nominated for reelection, the Radicals were able to run Reconstruction substantially on their own.

The impeachment and near conviction of Johnson was a tremendous show of power on the part of the congressional Radicals, but it was a costly effort. Some who voted with them for impeachment or conviction came to doubt the wisdom as well as the fairness of the proceeding; the Radicals expended political resources on the trial which, for the sake of their cause, they might better have husbanded. Once congressional Reconstruction had been imposed on the South, Northern support for Radical Republicanism began to wane and the Radical control of Congress to loosen. Thaddeus Stevens died in 1868, and no one could be found to take his place. Charles Sumner began to slip from power, and in 1871 he was deposed as chairman of the Foreign Relations Committee. By that time congressional leadership had been assumed by practical politicians, such as Roscoe Conkling of New York and James G. Blaine of Maine, who at election time engaged in "bloody shirt" charges against the Democratic party as the party of rebellion and who viewed Reconstruction first of all as a practical party matter.

END OF RECONSTRUCTION

The partnership of well-to-do Northern businessmen and impoverished Southern freedmen was an uncomfortable, illogical alliance which aroused no real enthusiasm among Northern Republicans on its own merits, except for the minority of dedicated pro-Negro advocates such as Sumner and Stevens. Both Northern Republicans and Southern conservatives remembered the Whig alliance of former years, and there was strong sentiment in both groups in favor of a Republican party that Southern conservatives could join. Northern industry and capital moved into the South as soon as Southern territory was occupied by Federal troops, and almost at once a rapprochement between Northern business interests and enterprising Southern whites was indicated, from the business point of view.

The cause of the Southern Negro did not stir the North to stop the successful overturn of the carpetbag government in Tennessee in 1869, and during the next two years North Carolina, Virginia, and Georgia returned to white rule as well. Arkansas, Alabama, and Texas followed in 1874 and Mississippi in 1876. Federal troops were finally withdrawn from the South altogether in 1877, when the last Reconstruction governments collapsed in Florida, South Carolina, and Louisiana. Thereafter the South received tacit Northern consent to deal with the black problem as it saw fit.

In retrospect it appeared that the Southern Negro had been poorly served by his Northern supporters. This was in part due to the strong otherworldly religious character of the abolitionist movement. The worst sin of slavery, from the point of view of the most dedicated abolitionists, had been the sin of denying the slave the freedom to work out his own salvation and so prepare himself for an everlasting future life. The physical freeing of the slave from bondage had technically answered this objection, and in the minds of many abolitionists it had accomplished their mission. From this point of view, there remained only the establishment of educational and religious facilities among the Southern blacks to bring them within range of salvation, and impressive and important Northern missionary work was indeed carried out in both these areas.

The Freedman's Bureau had been extremely active and successful in developing education at all levels, working in cooperation with various Northern humanitarian individuals and agencies. At the college level the Bureau had assisted in establishing Howard University, Hampton Institute, Atlanta University, and Fisk University, in addition to a number of others. In religion, Southern Negroes were freed from black codes curbing black preachers and proscribing separate black congregations. The African Methodist Episcopal Church increased its membership from 20,000 to 200,000 between 1865 and 1876; the Negro Baptists grew from 150,000 in 1850 to 500,000 in 1870. Black ministers became community leaders to an extent that had not been the case in Anglo-America since colonial New England, and this process accelerated after the political suppression of blacks in the late nineteenth century.

But in helping the freedman secure his independence, many Radicals had placed unrealistically heavy reliance upon purely political and legal rights. The Thirteenth Amendment abolished slavery, the Fourteenth enacted guarantees of civil rights for blacks, and the Fifteenth extended the vote to them. It was widely assumed that these political rights would place the blacks in a position of political equality with the whites despite the continuing economic dependence of the freedmen on their former masters, who still owned the land the farmers would have to farm for a living. A number of Radicals, including Sumner and Stevens, had fought for legislation to acquire land through purchase or confiscation in order to distribute it among the freedmen at perhaps 40 acres for a family, to give them an economic basis for independence. Rumors of such a program continually circulated in the Reconstruction South, but it never had a chance of passing in Congress.

The Radical Republicans had revoked those Southern black codes that limited Southern Negroes to farming and menial labor, but the postwar South provided little opportunity for blacks to do anything else. Cotton culture remained the basic means of livelihood in the defeated cotton kingdom, and it was the only livelihood that most Southern blacks were trained for. Although an industrialized "New South" developed, notably in the textile industry and the Birmingham steel mills, these industries limited themselves mainly to white labor, and they absorbed but a fraction even of the Southern white labor available. Most Southerners, white as well as black, were restricted to farming, especially cotton farming, for the lack of any alternative.

Working the lands of impoverished property owners, Southern farmers remained substantially outside the money economy. Black and white farmers alike became tenant farmers under a sharecrop system, whereby the tenant was allowed to farm the land in exchange for a share of the crop he raised. Under this system the farmers tended to remain perennially in debt to the owner of the crossroads store, who supplied farm equipment and basic necessities and took a lien on the future crop in exchange. Blacks and whites together lived in a condition of freedom from slavery, but with little choice as to how that freedom would be used.

Northern blacks were segregated into ghettoes and generally kept to the lowest levels of economic life, along with the least advantaged of the newest immigrants, but many of them enjoyed a far wider range of economic opportunity than Southern blacks did. All the cities of the North, and especially Boston, New York, and Philadelphia, supported black communities of educated and well-to-do business and professional people, whose standards tended to be white middle-class standards intensified by the difficulty of attaining and securing a middle-class foothold in white America. As generation followed generation, this black middle class made progress very slowly against odds that diminished little, if at all, down to World War II.

INDIAN RECONSTRUCTION

While Reconstruction in the South was creating what turned out to be no more than a halfway house on the way to freedom for the blacks, a reconstruction of the trans-Mississippi Indian nations was transforming them from free-ranging buffalo hunters to guarded residents of reservations. During the administrations of John Quincy Adams and Andrew Jackson the Five Civilized Tribes of Creek, Cherokee, Choctaw, Chickasaw, and Seminole had been removed from their rich farming lands in Florida, Georgia, and Alabama and settled on arid land in what was to become Oklahoma where they remained by themselves until the opening of Oklahoma Territory to white settlers in 1889. Meanwhile there remained out in the Great Plains and the Southwest more than 200,000 Plains Indians, notably the Sioux, Blackfeet, and Crow in the North, the Cheyenne and Arapahoe in the central region, and the Comanche, Apache, and Navaho in the Southwest.

During the Civil War lead miners and wheat farmers began the encroachment on the hunting grounds of the Plains Indians that inexorably continued throughout the next generation. From 1861, when the Sioux went on the warpath against frontier farmers in Minnesota, there were successions of Indian massacres of white men, women, and children followed by white massacres of Indian men, women, and children. In 1875 gold was discovered in the Black Hills of Dakota Territory, and in 1876 the Sioux, under Sitting Bull and Crazy Horse, struck back at the invading whites. In June they annihilated Gen. George Custer and his 264 troops. They were in turn pursued and many of them destroyed by army forces. A similar fate met the Nez Percé Indians, driven from their lands in Idaho a year later after their resistance under Chief Joseph, and the remainder of the Nez Percés settled in Oklahoma.

In Colorado the Ute reservations were confiscated and opened to white settlement, and in the Southwest only the Apache warriors under Geronimo remained at large, until defeated in 1886. Throughout the Reconstruction era and after, the same abolitionists who were working to secure the freedman in his liberty were working to defend the Indian against the white invader's depradations and the successive breaking of treaties by the federal government. President Rutherford Hayes and his Secretary of the Interior, Carl Schurz, worked to protect the Indians against both governmental and private incursions upon their rights. Their efforts availed the Indians little, however. Most basically, the slaughter of buffalo by the millions deprived the Plains Indians of their main basis for subsistence and made it impossible for them to subsist independent of government assistance.

In 1887 Congress passed the Dawes Act, designed to force the Indians to live like white farmers on private lands to be allocated to the heads of Indian families. In 1890 the report of the Superintendent of the Census declared that "at present the unsettled area has been so broken into by isolated bodies of settlement" that the country could no longer be said to have "a frontier of settlement." That meant, among other things, that the reconstruction of the Indian had been completed, at least until the era of racial rights which began in the late 1950s and continues today.

THE RISE OF JIM CROW

In the South, the blacks remained substantially in possession of the racial rights Reconstruction had given them for a decade after the end of Reconstruction. Until then, the black voter proved no threat to the essential white supremacy of the "Bourbon restoration," the conservative rule of Southern whites acting in harmony with Northern business interests. These Bourbon leaders proclaimed a "New South" that through industrialization would bring progress to their region. But most Southerners, white and black, kept on farming, and in the agricultural depression that settled in during the late 1880s the Southern Alliance of white farmers joined with the Colored Alliance to threaten the Bourbon establishment with a rising and militantly radical Populist party. When that happened, the black voter was seen to hold the balance of power, at least in theory. The Populist movement was broken after William Jennings Bryan's defeat as the Populist-Democratic presidential candidate in 1896, and Southerners, both Populist and Bourbon, moved to strip the Negro of his voting rights and then of his civil rights generally.

Various forms of segregation, notably in the schools, had been sanctioned during Reconstruction, and these naturally continued after it was over. White terrorism and violence against blacks, which Reconstruction had not altogether succeeded in suppressing, also continued. Incidents of violence against blacks increased during the 1880s, and then, during the 1890s, in an atmosphere of rising racism nationally, one Southern state after another passed Jim Crow legislation disfranchising the Negro and segregating him to separate residential areas, railroad cars, waiting rooms, parks, theaters, restaurants, and water fountains. Jim Crow became a part of the Southern way of life as though it had always been the Southern practice.

The outstanding leader of black America in this crisis was Booker T. Washington, the creator of Tuskegee Institute, chartered by the Alabama Legislature in 1881. Washington argued that the primary need of the Southern black was economic self-reliance and that as a practical matter this was mainly to be achieved in agricultural and industrial employment. Blacks should not strive for political power and social equality with the whites in a struggle they were bound to lose. They should strengthen themselves economically and win white support by demonstrating their ability to stand on their own feet and to contribute positively to the welfare of the community at large.

Pragmatically, Washington was urging the only course that was open to the Southern Negroes; where a more aggressive course was open to them, as in the development of Harlem as a black community, Washington demonstrated that he could act aggressively. In the South the black was necessarily on the defensive, however, and not even Washington's conciliatory course could win the black community protection from racist repression and violence. The lynching of blacks in the South, and elsewhere in the nation to a lesser extent, increased from year to year, reaching a climax at the turn of the century.

By then the Supreme Court had rendered decisions that in effect had declared the Fourteenth Amendment legally incapable of ensuring the civil rights of Negroes, but it had rendered other decisions finding that the Fourteenth Amendment did protect business corporations, as legal "persons," against unfavorable state legislation. The Fourteenth Amendment, as its legal meaning changed, reflected the most fundamental reconstruction that had occurred after the Civil War, the economic reconstruction of the nation as a whole. There were vigorous dissenting opinions against these decisions in the Supreme Court, but white America as a whole went along with the idea that the problem of black America was primarily a Southern problem and one which Southern whites should be left to deal with in their own way.

BIBLIOGRAPHY FOR
CHAPTER 13

J. G. Randall and **David Donald,** The Civil War and Reconstruction (rev. ed., 1961)

J. H. Franklin, Reconstruction after the Civil War (1961)

K. M. Stampp, The Era of Reconstruction (1965)

R. W. Patrick, The Reconstruction of the Nation (1967)

Eric McKitrick, Andrew Johnson and Reconstruction (1960)

H. L. Hyman, ed., New Frontiers of the American Reconstruction (1966)

W. R. Brock, An American Crisis: Congress and Reconstruction (1963)

J. M. McPherson, The Struggle for Equality: Abolitionists and the Negro in the Civil War and Reconstruction (1964)

C. V. Woodward, Reunion and Reaction: The Compromise of 1877 and the End of Reconstruction (rev. ed., 1956) and The Strange Career of Jim Crow (2d ed., 1957)

Henry Fritz, The Movement for Indian Assimilation, 1860–1890 (1963)

R. W. Logan, The Negro in America, Life and Thought: The Nadir, 1877–1901 (1954)

P. H. Buck, The Road to Reunion, 1865–1900 (1937)

CHAPTER 14

POLITICS, 1868-1892

THE GRANT ADMINISTRATION

By the time of Grant's election in 1868 the Republican party leadership had already moved over from the abolitionist idealists like Sumner and Stevens to men like Simon Cameron of Pennsylvania and Roscoe Conkling of New York whose chief interest was to secure the wartime tariff, banking, and railroad legislation against an agrarian counterattack and, more than that, to secure Republican political control against a reunited Democratic party. The Republican party had always been a minority party, and there was no reason to suppose it could win an election in 1868 on the basis of those economic interests that its program attracted. In order to win the election, therefore, the Republicans nominated the war's leading hero, Gen. Ulysses S. Grant, and campaigned on the "bloody shirt" argument that a vote for the Democratic party was a vote for the party of rebellion.

Grant himself had always been associated with the Democratic party, so far as he had interested himself in politics at all. He had broken with the Democratic President Johnson, however, and he submitted, unenthusiastically, to the Republican nomination, placing himself in the hands of the party managers. The Democrats in their convention nominated the governor of New York, Horatio Seymour, and went down to defeat by a margin of 310,000 votes. Crucial to the Republican victory was the activity in the South of the Union League clubs; they organized the black vote, which provided the narrow margin of victory. To strengthen this support, Congress, when it met in 1869, initiated the Fifteenth Amendment, declared ratified a year later. It provided that "the right of citizens of the United States to vote shall not be denied or abridged by the United States or by any State on account of race, color, or previous condition of servitude."

Hailed as the savior of the nation and a second George Washington, Grant proved sadly incompetent to cope with the problems confronting him. He failed to familiarize himself with the duties of his office, placing responsibility instead in the hands of friends who over and over again betrayed his confidence. An unsuccessful businessman during much of his prewar career, Grant held successful businessmen in unbounded admiration, a confidence which was betrayed frequently during his administrations and again in later life when he was financially ruined by embezzling business associates. During his eight years in office he made an unusually large number of Cabinet appointments, and many of those who received them were incompetent and corrupt. Of the few who were neither, only one, Secretary of State Hamilton Fish, survived to the end. Before he came to the Presidency, Grant had indicated by his acts a policy of moderation toward the defeated Confederacy, but as President he accepted the program of the Radicals without question.

The Grant administration inherited from the war a maze of administrative confusion and corruption, which in the Lincoln and Johnson administrations had been obscured by war and Reconstruction. During the Grant administrations corruption reached its full-bellied climax, and even before the election of 1872 the nation knew about a good deal of the swindling that was going on. Most spectacularly, in 1869 Jay Gould and Jim Fisk had attempted, through connivance with government officials, to corner the national gold market and so to force those who needed gold for business transactions to pay the monopoly price for it. The scheme went awry on "Black Friday," when the Treasury threw gold on the market, ruining many innocent dealers. Fisk and Gould escaped loss by repudiating their contracts.

The President was more directly implicated the next year in a scheme to annex Santo Domingo in the interest of his private secretary Orville Babcock and others who hoped to acquire a large portion of the island's wealth. Bypassing the State Department, Grant arranged a treaty of annexation which, despite Grant's strong support, failed to pass the Senate. Senator Sumner, who led the fight against the treaty, lost his place as chairman of the Foreign Relations Committee shortly thereafter.

OPPOSITION TO GRANT

The full extent of government corruption was not known during the presidential campaign of 1872, but it was suspected by many, including a number of disenchanted Republicans. In Missouri Grant's trusted political boss was the leader of the "Whiskey Ring," which was systematically defrauding the government of millions of dollars in excise taxes and retaining its political power through the continued disfranchisement of former Missouri Confederates. In 1868 Carl Schurz, Civil War general and idealistic refugee from the German Revolution of '48, was elected to the Senate from Missouri. In the election of 1870 Schurz and other Republicans in Missouri joined the Democrats and defeated the machine, capturing both the legislature and the governorship In the Senate Schurz became the leader of a Liberal Republican movement to remove Grant by the same means, and he was joined in this revolt by influential Republicans such as the editor of the New York *Tribune,* Horace Greeley; the editor of the *Nation,* E. L. Godkin; and former Minister to England Charles Francis Adams.

An alliance with the Democrats in itself seemed certain to assure victory, but there were additional discontented groups that might well be drawn in. There was discontent among the farmers, and an organization known as the Grange had developed through which they increasingly expressed their discontent. Formed in 1867 as a social organization, the Grange was beginning by 1872 to become a vehicle for political reform. The farmers, however, were less concerned about tariff reform and clean government than they were about railroad regulation and managed currency, both of which represented communistic departures from true Americanism, from the point of view of the Britisher Godkin and the German Schurz and other Liberal Republicans. Apparently more promising was the new National Labor Reform party. This party was an outgrowth of the National Labor Union, which had been formed in 1866 under the leadership of William H. Sylvis, president of the Iron Molders Union, out of a heterogeneous collection of craft unions and general reform associations.

The National Labor Reform party disappointed the Liberal Republicans by nominating for President a not especially liberal Supreme Court justice, David Davis, but this was nothing compared to the disappointment the Liberals experienced in the candidate their own convention nominated. The most promising candidate had seemed to be Charles Francis Adams, whose father and grandfather had both won the office. However, Adams did nothing for his own candidacy, the convention got out of hand, and the nomination went to Horace Greeley, eccentric faddist, former abolitionist, and a past vituperative foe of the Democratic party. The Democrats met, swallowed Greeley in order to win Liberal Republican support, and went down with him to defeat; Grant won by more than twice his previous plurality.

The Liberal Republicans survived this debacle because they commanded the wealth and prestige of upper-middle-class America and did not depend on the spoils of office. They believed in government by the wise and good, preferably from their own class. They were liberal in the Adam Smith free-trade sense. They held to the "moral philosophy" that society would function properly if the laws of God—including those relating to supply and demand—were not interfered with. They thought of themselves as reformers, and they thought of reform as consisting of tariff reduction, civil service in place of the spoils system, and the gold standard.

By the eve of the election the scandal of the Grant administration was all seeping into the open. Construction of the Union Pacific Railroad had been carried out by a company, Crédit Mobilier, which had siphoned off huge profits above the actual cost of the road, leaving the Union Pacific to languish for more than a generation with a crippling debt and a faulty roadbed. The management of the Central Pacific Railroad had been guilty of an identical swindle, and both companies had bribed congressmen generously (prior to Grant's coming to office) in order to win government approval for their projects. As the head of Crédit Mobilier Rep. Oakes Ames of Massachusetts had, as he himself explained, handed out stock to congressmen "where they will do the most good to us." Important members of the administration, including Cabinet members, were found to be busy with a multitude of dishonest schemes, selling franchises to collect taxes for profit, selling rights in Indian trading posts, and defrauding the government of excise taxes on whiskey.

The act which aroused public indignation most of all perhaps was the legally honest but unbecomingly greedy "salary grab," by which congressmen voted themselves large retroactive pay raises. These they later rescinded in the face of public indignation. There was from this time forward a general concurrence with Ambrose Bierce's definition of a congressman, in his *Devil's Dictionary,* as a member of the lower house in this world with little hope for promotion in the next.

STATE AND LOCAL CORRUPTION

But corruption in federal places paled beside state and local corruption. The votes of state legislatures and state judges were busily bought and sold. Gould and Fisk, in company with Daniel Drew, had gained notoriety before their gold-conspiracy exploit by perpetrating the most outrageous and swashbuckling example of this practice. The struggles of these men with Cornelius Vanderbilt to control the Erie Railroad between 1866 and 1868 involved state judiciaries and legislatures of New York and New Jersey in an orgy of corruption and favoritism. The blatant speculations which marked the Reconstruction governments in the South received more publicity than Northern statewide corruption, but these robberies in the South were on a much smaller scale than those in the North, mainly because there was less to rob.

The richest loot of all was to be found in the cities, where corruption was practiced most openly and systematically and where such political machines as the Gas ring in Philadelphia and the Tweed ring in New York raked in millions of dollars from bribery, shakedowns, inflated building contracts, and control of franchises. Every large city in the nation was under the control of a similarly corrupt political machine operating with apparently absolute immunity. It was one of the remarkable events of the age when Samuel J. Tilden managed to send Boss Tweed of Tammany Hall to the penitentiary, and it won Tilden the fame which helped to bring him the Democratic presidential nomination in 1876. Nationally the corruption of the "gilded age" was associated with the Republican party, because the administration was of that party, but in fact it was completely bipartisan: the Democrats rooted and hogged right along with Republicans.

PARTY POLITICS

The Republicans by hook and by crook remained in the Presidency from 1869 until 1885, and throughout that period a dominant theme of American political life was the three-cornered struggle within the Republican party between the Liberals, the "Half-Breeds," and the "Stalwarts." The major issue dividing these factions was political corruption. The Liberals, led by Senator Schurz, disapproved of it on moral and ideological grounds; the Half-Breeds, led by Sen. James G. Blaine of Maine, held to the view that rampant robbery was bad for the party; and the Stalwarts, to the extent that they were spoken for by their leader, Sen. Roscoe Conkling of New York, were convinced that the party could survive such scandals if the party machinery stayed in good operating order and the party kept on renominating Grant. The intraparty differences turned to a considerable extent on a personal enmity which existed between Conkling and Blaine, national politics during this period being controlled by the principles of personal loyalty and party regularity, with little regard for political issues.

Blaine would probably have received the Republican nomination in 1876 had it not been discovered at the last minute that he had been involved in an indiscretion, minor by the standards of the day, in connection with the Union Pacific Railroad. His Republican rival Conkling was able to defeat Blaine's candidacy by throwing his support to Gov. Rutherford B. Hayes of Ohio. Hayes brought a momentary unity to the party, for he was an honest man whom the Liberals were willing to support, while the Half-Breeds had no alternative. Thus the thieves fell out and still won the election, but not without a subsequent series of ingenious dodges unparalleled in the history of presidential elections.

In the popular vote Tilden won by a plurality of 250,000 over Hayes. The count of the electoral vote was complicated, however, by the fact that three Southern states, South Carolina, Florida, and Louisiana, were still under Reconstruction governments, and these states each returned two sets of electoral votes, one for each candidate. Even without these contested votes Tilden would have won exactly the necessary 185 had a Democratic elector in Oregon not been disqualified by a technicality and arbitrarily replaced by a Republican. Congress, after several months of violent indecision, appointed a commission of five senators, five representatives, and five Supreme Court justices to judge between the disputed returns. By party affiliation the commission stood 8 to 7 Republican, and by that margin it voted to uphold the Republican returns of each of the three Southern states, thereby electing Hayes by a margin of 1 electoral vote.

THE COMPROMISE OF 1877

Throughout the four months between the election and the inauguration the threat of a new civil war was never absent. On the other hand, the dominant economic interests in both the North and the South were opposed to war no matter who got the Presidency. These groups carried on negotiations outside political channels before and after the decision of the commission, successfully arriving at the compromise which resulted in the peaceful inauguration of Hayes. On the one hand Southern conservatives, who found their forced connection with the Democrats distasteful, had many of them argued for joining the Republican party on the grounds that it represented their interests. Furthermore they wanted federal support for internal improvements, which had been so lavishly handed out in the North and West while the South was out of the Union, and which the Northern Democrats had come to oppose following the revelations of the Grant administration scandals. Northern business, on the other hand, had opposed radical Reconstruction as being bad for business and had looked favorably upon a restoration of the Whig alliance of pre-Civil War years.

Between these groups an informal bargain was arranged. Southern acquiescence in Hayes's election was exchanged for Hayes's removal of Federal troops from the South and his appointment of a Southerner to a Cabinet post. The compromise called also for Republican votes for federally financed Southern river and harbor improvements and for passage of the Texas Pacific Railroad Bill, to give the South its own transcontinental line. The Southerners, in addition to accepting Hayes, were to help the Republicans organize the Democratic-dominated House and so enable them to nominate the Republican James A. Garfield as Speaker. These were not signed agreements, and none were carried out except the removal of troops from the Southern states and the Southern Cabinet appointment, both of which might have taken place under any circumstances. The compromise nevertheless marked a fundamental political realignment, ending Reconstruction on terms which renewed the prewar Whig alliance of Southern planters and Northern business, an alliance that has continued, with occasional interruptions, to dominate Congress down to the present.

HAYES, GARFIELD, ARTHUR

To the disgust of the Stalwarts, Hayes proved throughout his administration to be a Liberal Republican with a vengeance. Indeed, his major Cabinet appointments represented veritable personified repudiations of leading tenets that had guided his party over the previous decade. He named a former Confederate, David M. Key of Tennessee, as Postmaster General, as had been agreed to in the compromise that secured his peaceable inauguration. Beyond that, however, he appointed as Secretary of State W. M. Evarts, the lawyer who had served successfully as President Johnson's chief counsel at the impeachment trial before the Radical Republican-dominated Senate, and for Secretary of the Interior he chose the civil service reformer and idol of the Liberals, Carl Schurz.

Viciously harried by Democrats disputing the legitimacy of his election, Hayes invited the wrath of the Stalwarts in his party immediately on taking office by pressing for civil service reform and by attacking Conkling directly through the New York Customs House, which, under Conkling's direction, was the very model of smoothly operating political corruption. Momentarily defeated, Conkling managed to rally the faithful and put his customs house substantially back in order, but Hayes in turn was successful, with Democratic support, in winning Senate approval for his customs house appointments. The struggle marked the beginning of Conkling's fall from power. More importantly, it checked the tendency of the ruling group in the Senate to assume positive executive authority in patent disregard of the Constitution. From the time of President Johnson this tendency had seemed to be altering drastically and perhaps permanently the nation's form of government.

Hayes had explicitly disqualified himself for renomination at the outset and had furthermore failed to create organizational strength for Liberal Republicanism. The Stalwarts and the Half-Breeds therefore had a free field in the nominating convention of 1880, and with Grant once more available, Conkling apparently possessed the winning candidate. Out of a long deadlock between Grant and Blaine, however, the Half-Breeds emerged victorious with a dark-horse candidate, Congressman James A. Garfield of Ohio. Then, in the interests of party harmony, the vice-presidential nomination was given to a Conkling man, Chester A. Arthur. The Democrats in their turn, in order to remove as far as possible the taint of treason, nominated a Civil War hero named after a Mexican War hero, Winfield Scott Hancock of Pennsylvania, a political novice who has been most famously described as "a good man weighing 250 pounds."

Garfield won with a plurality of 9,464 votes out of 9 million cast and immediately attacked Conkling's empire by appointing an anti-Conkling man to Vice President Arthur's former post, that of Collector of the Port of New York. In the struggle which ensued, the enormously arrogant Conkling sought to strengthen his position by resigning his Senate seat, in company with New York's other senator, Thomas Platt, and applying to the state legislature for reappointment. It proved to be an ill-judged move, for the legislature declined to reelect the two men, and Conkling abruptly and permanently dropped out of political life. It would be too much to say that Conkling's defeat marked the end of an era. To some extent, however, it did mark a transition in American politics from the era of robber politicians, who acquired wealth through politics, to the era of the robber barons, who gained political power through wealth. In the years to come the Senate was to be known as a "Millionaires' Club" where independent spirits such as Conkling no longer dominated.

Five months after taking office, Garfield was shot in the back by a disappointed office seeker who shouted as he fired, "I am a Stalwart and Arthur is President now." Arthur certainly had been one of the spoilsmen, as Collector of the Port of New York, but now he was President. He did not say to his former Stalwart comrades, "I know you not, old men"; in fact, a number of them joined him in his Cabinet. But he vetoed a major pork-barrel bill and cleaned up the mess in the Post Office Department, and in 1883 he signed the Pendleton Civil Service Bill.

Civil service reform had been the main panacea of the Liberal Republicans since the end of the Civil War; they truly believed that it would lead American politics out of a gilded age into a golden one. Grant had put these men off by appointing a Civil Service Commission with no authority, and the reform had advanced little since then despite Hayes's efforts. Then Garfield's death created a martyr for the cause, and Congress passed the Pendleton Act, which provided for a system of civil service based on merit and protected from political reprisal. The act put more than 10 percent of government workers under its provisions immediately, and the percentage increased rapidly thereafter, chiefly because politicians, when turned out of office, wanted to give incoming rival administrations the use of as little patronage as possible. Within a generation more than half of all government employees were classified, with the unforeseen consequence that party coffers no longer could be filled by the postman's mite or anyone else's small contributions; and so the two major political parties became dependent as never before upon men of great wealth.

LABOR CONFLICT

During the administration of President Hayes violent industrial warfare broke out across the nation, and agrarian radicalism for a time presented a real threat to the political balance of the nation. Within a few months of coming to office Hayes faced the Great Strike of '77, which began on the B. & O. Railroad, following hard on the heels of the second of two 10 percent wage cuts for trainmen. The strike spread to the four main Eastern trunk lines and then swiftly throughout the nation, paralyzing transportation and erupting in mob violence in every major railroad city from Baltimore to San Francisco. There had never been anything like it before in American history, and thoughtful Americans could only suppose it was the work of foreign agitators, "anarchists," who from that time until the rise of the American Communist party generally got the blame for each economic discontent that produced violence.

In response to desperate calls from state governors, President Hayes sent out federal troops to suppress the rioting, reluctantly establishing a federal precedent in labor disputes that was immediately and self-righteously followed by each of his successors to the end of the nineteenth century. The violence of the Great Strike resulted from the desperate condition of the railroad workers and the absence of any effective labor organization to assert discipline. The National Labor Union had been so hopeful as to organize a labor party as to field a presidential candidate in 1872, but it had been destroyed in the depression of '73, and few of its component craft unions had survived in any strength.

THE GRANGER MOVEMENT

So far as it came within the purview of President Hayes, the problem of agrarian radicalism—the Granger movement—was the money problem. Involved was the question of whether precious metals provide the only reliable national monetary basis or whether a society can manage its currency according to the economic needs of the nation. Specifically, the monetary radicals wished to print paper money without gold or silver backing. Hayes, a hard-money man, faced during his administration the familiar greenback issue and in addition the entirely new silver issue, which was to divide the nation fiercely fifteen years later.

Since the Civil War, when the government had guiltily issued those 423 million dollars in inflationary greenbacks unsupported by specie, the question of what to do with them had repeatedly vexed the nation. To bankers, to proprietors of old established businesses—especially in New England—and to merchants dealing in international trade, they were the means by which debtors defrauded creditors and a nation defaulted on its obligations to its bondholders and its foreign customers. To farmers, on the other hand, they were a means of receiving more dollars for wheat, and for rapidly developing industries such as steel they were a means of making money available for capital investment. Congress passed various acts with regard to the greenbacks, and the Supreme Court handed down two decisions, one declaring legal tender unbacked by specie to be illegal and the other reversing the first decision. The Resumption Act, passed in 1875, provided that the Treasury, beginning in 1879, would redeem greenbacks in coin. Hayes's Secretary of the Treasury John Sherman, the original author of the Resumption Act, built up a gold reserve to pay for the greenbacks, with such success that nobody bothered to redeem them when the time came.

The period from the panic of '73 to the Spanish-American War was one of generally declining prices in America, as it was in Europe, and in American society the farmer, who still made up the largest element of the population, was hard hit by this tendency. The price of his mortgage and the debts owed on his farm machinery stayed up, while the returns from his produce, with which he had to repay the debts and mortgage, went down. Beyond that, railroad rates tended to stay up where the railroad enjoyed a monopolistic position, and the price of farm machinery and other manufactured goods tended to stay up also, protected by tariffs. Tariffs had been placed on farm products also, but they were of no use to farmers selling on the world market.

Working through the Granges, the farm states met the problem of the railroads by passing the Granger laws establishing state railroad commissions and empowering them to set rates and regulate operating conditions. The railroads refused to cooperate and, further, took the matter to the Supreme Court. In 1877 the Court upheld the Granger laws in the case of *Munn v. Illinois,* on the ground that "when private property is devoted to public use, it is subject to public regulation." Thereafter the Supreme Court became more considerate of the rights of property, and it did not again decide so comprehensively in the public interest for more than sixty years, and even by the time the Munn decision had been handed down, the Granger regulatory laws had been found disappointingly unenforceable.

The transcontinental railroads, which in many cases were worth more than the total wealth of the entire state through which they passed, bought out commissioners and confused the ones they could not bribe. Against the railroad lawyers, the state commissioners were in no position to command the information necessary to fix fair rates or determine minimum safety conditions. The Granger laws served only to prove that railroads had clearly passed the bounds of state regulation. The farmers' cooperatives which had been formed to supplant those thieving middlemen, meanwhile, were going out of business. The one permanent such business to emerge from the movement was a private enterprise, the mail-order house of Montgomery War, established in 1872 in response to the needs of the farmers as expressed by the Grangers.

There remained the possibility of dealing with falling farm prices through controlled inflation. Out of the failure of the Granger experiments emerged the Greenback party, which nominated the New York industrialist Peter Cooper for President in 1876 on the main plank of withdrawing the specie backing for greenbacks. The party polled only 81,000 votes, but in worsening conditions two years later it elected fourteen congressmen by casting more than 1 million votes. Then good times returned to the American farm temporarily and ruined the party, which secured only 308,000 votes for the highly respected Gen. James B. Weaver of Iowa in the presidential election of 1880.

Bad times were presently to return to the farms, bringing with them the same agrarian radicalism. By the time that had happened, however, silver had supplanted greenbacks as the central solution to submerged farm prices, a development which was already getting under way as the Greenback party was reaching its peak of success. Originally the nation had been on the bimetallic standard with the ratio of silver to gold set legally at 16 to 1. Following the California gold rush, however, gold had driven silver from the market, and in 1853 Congress placed the nation on what was essentially the gold standard. By 1873 silver was no longer available for minting because its value on the open market was more than sixteen times that of gold, and Congress, in adopting a new coinage law, failed to provide for the minting of silver even to be used as subsidiary coins, as had been provided for in the 1853 law. In 1873 the "big bonanza" was discovered on the Comstock lode in Nevada, yielding millions of dollars worth of silver at a time when, to the distress of the silver producers, other nations of the world were also ceasing to mint silver and thereby depressing the world market price.

"Silver Dick" Bland of Missouri introduced a bill into Congress calling for the unlimited minting of silver once again at the ratio of 16 to 1. In the Senate, William Allison of Iowa substituted "limited" for "unlimited," and the resulting Blank-Allison Act, passed over Hayes's veto in 1878, called for the minting of between 2 and 4 million dollars worth of silver each month, to be purchased at no fixed ratio to gold but at the current world price. The bill was passed at the behest of politically powerful silver miners, and it had no observable inflationary effect. When hard times came again to the farms of the nation, however, the free-silver issue served to rally a following that was able to capture the Democratic party in 1896 and, from that platform, raise issues that were to bedevil American politics for most of the next generation.

THE CLEVELAND ADMINISTRATION

The Democratic party of "rum, Romanism, and rebellion" met the high standards of Liberal Republicanism five out of seven times during the post-Civil War generation in its selection of presidential candidates. The Republican party during that period nominated only one man, Hayes, who was entirely acceptable by Liberal Republican criteria. On coming to the Presidency, the Republicans Garfield and Arthur tried to be good, but they had both been recruited from the ranks of the spoilsmen. Then in 1884 James G. Blaine—"the continental liar from Maine" as he was called because of untruths he told in connection with certain of his under-the-counter dealings—won the Republican nomination. By contrast Grover Cleveland, the stoutly upright reform governor of New York, won the Democratic one. Under those circumstances the Liberal Republicans—or Mugwumps as they came to be called—decided to "follow a noble impulse," in the words of the comfortably righteous Carl Schurz, and go for Cleveland. Cleveland won with a plurality of 23,000 votes, and the Democratic party returned to power for the first time in twenty-four years.

Cleveland represented the conservative Eastern wing of the Democratic party, as had the Democratic candidates Seymour and Tilden before him, and his views coincided with those of the responsible conservative element on Wall Street. He had been in politics for only four years when he entered the White House, and his mind was not yet made up on all matters. Where it was made up, however, it was pure Liberal Republicanism, and where he was in doubt, Cleveland went to Schurz and his colleagues for the answers. In common with them Cleveland conceived of the President as the impartial umpire of a society that was basically governed by the immutable, God-given, self-operating law of supply and demand. Governments were instituted for the purpose of protecting life, liberty, and property, and beyond this responsibility it was immoral for them to go. A man of exceptionally strong character, Cleveland won the fight with the Senate which Hayes had begun and firmly reestablished the President's appointive power which the Senate had wrested from Johnson. Furthermore, he made his force felt negatively through the use of the veto against veterans' pensions and pork-barrel bills. During his term he vetoed or pocket-vetoed 413 bills.

Cleveland had not given the tariff question any systematic consideration at the time he assumed office, but he soon came to the Liberal Republican view that tariff reduction and extension of the merit system were the two basic reforms which would cure the ills of the nation. These nineteenth-century liberals were shocked, both by the spread of poverty beneath them and by the accumulations of great fortunes above them. The typical spokesman for this brand of liberalism was a member of the well-to-do part of the community who was able to live graciously on his own moderate wealth and therefore had reason to think that that was about as high as a fortune ought to go. Society was operating in a faulty manner when it resulted in such a grossly unequal distribution of the national wealth as had come about. In the view of the liberals, monopoly and plutocracy were the results of governmental interference with the natural order in erecting tariff barriers and bestowing government subsidies. Under conditions of free trade, liberals were sure, monopoly would be broken by international competition, and the bloated fortunes of the new rich would be punctured.

Cleveland devoted his third annual message to Congress entirely to the tariff question, and the second half of his administration was devoted to lowering duties. The House of Representatives responded in December 1887, with the Mills Bill, providing for those moderate beginnings of tariff reduction which Cleveland had in mind. Faced with the congressional elections of 1888, the Democratic-controlled House passed the bill secure in the certainty that it would never pass the Republican-controlled Senate, which kept debating it until the elections were over and then dropped it.

RAILROAD REGULATION

The one significant measure that did pass during the first Cleveland administration, the Interstate Commerce Act, was a congressional response to popular antirailroad feeling which Cleveland signed with considerable reluctance. The inability of the state regulatory commissions to exert any effective control over the interstate railroads in the seventies had been followed by increasing demands for federal regulation. The House and the Senate had each passed such bills, and they were ironing out their differences in 1886 when the Supreme Court rendered a decision in the case of *Wabash, St. Louis, and Pacific Railroad v. Illinois* denying to the states altogether the authority of regulating railroads which crossed interstate lines. The Wabash decision hurried Congress into passing the Interstate Commerce Act, which prohibited all discriminatory practices, including rebates, pools, and charging less for a long haul between major cities, where competition existed, than for a shorter intermediate haul, where monopolistic practices prevailed. It provided that all charges should be "reasonable and just," and it established the Interstate Commerce Commission, the first federal agency of its kind, to administer the law, which would be enforced by the courts.

The act was greeted with popular approval, and it was also supported by the railroads, which realized that some regulatory law was inevitable and liked the loopholes they saw in this one. The law insisted on "reasonable and just rates" without defining what the phrase meant. Though it prohibited long-haul–short-haul discrimination, it did so only under "similar circumstances and conditions," which sounded promisingly vague. The provision for judicial review generally gave the railroads a four-year period of grace while the case was traveling to the Supreme Court. And as things turned out, the railroads received favorable decisions from the archly conservative court in almost every instance.

THE HARRISON ADMINISTRATION

In 1888 the Democratic convention nominated Cleveland without thought of anybody else. The Republicans got Blaine out of the way, and then they were faced with the fact that they could decide on no other candidate who was well known and was at the same time presidential timber. In the absence of an available candidate, the convention nominated the ghost of a former President, Benjamin Harrison, the grandson of William Henry Harrison, who had fought that Battle of Tippecanoe in 1811 with Tecumseh's Indians. Then the Republicans set out in dead earnest to secure the election of the right candidate by buying votes and using money effectively in other ways. They were helped, free of charge, by the British Minister to America, who advised an English-born American to vote for Cleveland in a subsequently much-published letter. The result of it all was that while Cleveland quadrupled his plurality of 1884, he nevertheless lost the election to "young Tippecanoe" by 65 electoral votes, a handful of votes in New York State deciding the issue in this as in so many nineteenth-century elections.

Harrison did not know much about politics and did not really attempt to learn how to be President. Everything was arranged for him, including a Cabinet with Blaine as Secretary of State and John Wanamaker, the rich department-store owner, as Postmaster General. There was the usual furious rotation in office (which had also occurred when the politically pristine Cleveland entered the executive mansion), and then the administration settled down to the main business of distributing favors among special interests. The liveliest figure in the Harrison administration was the amputee Civil War veteran "Corporal" James Tanner, Commissioner of Pensions, who promised to raise all veterans' pensions and contributed to history the one memorable statement of the Harrison administration,"God help the surplus," as he cheerfully distributed all the money he could find.

The year 1890 was a red-letter year for legislation: the Sherman Antitrust Act, the Sherman Silver Purchase Act and the McKinley Tariff all were passed. The antitrust act in its final version was intended by many who voted for it simply as something to appease the popular feeling against monopoly without doing anything to imperil the interests of the monopolists. It passed the Senate 51 to 1. The law prohibited all combinations in restraint of trade but used words such as "conspiracy," "monopoly," and "trust" without defining them. It thus shifted to the courts the responsibility of deciding what was meant, and from the point of view of big business, the Supreme Court in 1890 was in good hands.

Neither the Harrison nor the Cleveland administration was enthusiastic in its prosecution of the new law, but within five years several antitrust suits had been brought to the Supreme Court and had been lost by the government. In 1895, in *United States v. E. C. Knight and Company,* the government tried to dissolve the sugar trust, which controlled 98 percent of the sugar refined in the nation. The Court held that this control did not constitute a combination in restraint of trade, since the sugar trust was a manufacturing monopoly to which the monopoly of trade was incidental. The decision met with the complete satisfaction of Cleveland's Attorney General, who wrote a friend that he had never believed in the law anyway. Until the twentieth century, the law was applied in earnest mainly against labor unions, a purpose for which it had not been designed at all. Commenting on the Sherman Antitrust Act the political humorist Peter Finley Dunne observed that "what looks like a stone wall to a layman, is a triumphal arch to a corporation lawyer."

The Sherman Silver Purchase Act and the McKinley Tariff were companion measures, Eastern Republicans reluctantly supplying votes for the one in exchange for Western support for the other. The Silver Purchase Act provided for the monthly purchase by the government of $4\frac{1}{2}$ million ounces of silver bullion, against which the government would issue silver certificates redeemable in gold as well as silver. The value of silver was not fixed at a ratio of 16 to 1 with gold as the inflationists demanded, and the measure failed to check the deflationary trend. In the view of many conservatives, however, it was a wicked bill, fraught with potential dangers to the financial system. On the other hand, many spokesmen for this point of view found much to please them in the McKinley Tariff, which once again raised rates on imports all along the line. The purposes of the tariff, according to the author, Rep. William McKinley of Ohio, were to secure "the great comforts to the masses" and to assure "the safety and purity and permanency of our political system."

In the election of 1892 the Democrats, who had captured the House two years earlier, renominated Cleveland, and the Republicans renominated Harrison. There followed a quiet campaign, disturbed only by the farmers, who organized their own indignant Populist party. Cleveland won by almost 400,000 votes, the largest plurality since Grant ran against poor Greeley. With what apparently amounted to a mandate, Cleveland returned triumphantly to office. He was plunged almost at once into the depression of 1893, the worst depression in the history of the nation up to that time. Faced with problems which were terribly unfamiliar to him, Cleveland was soon rendering dogmatic decisions that split the party he led and were to cripple it for more than a generation.

BIBLIOGRAPHY FOR CHAPTER 14

Matthew Josephson, The Politicos (1938)

H. W. Morgan, ed., The Gilded Age: A Reappraisal (1963)

H. S. Merrill, Bourbon Democracy of the Middle West, 1865-1896 (1953)

D. J. Rothman, Politics and Power (1966)—about the United States Senate

Irwin Unger, The Greenback Era (1964)

C. V. Woodward, Reunion and Reaction (rev. ed., 1954)

Ari Hoogenboom, Outlawing the Spoils: A History of the Civil Service Reform Movement, 1865-1883 (1961)

R. H. Wiebe, The Search for Order, 1877-1920 (1967)

W. E. Binkley, American Political Parties (1958)

G. H. Mayer, The Republican Party, 1854-1964 (1964)

CHAPTER 15

PLUTOCRACY AND POPULISM

Temporarily diverted from normal development by the Civil War, American industry expanded uncontrollably from war's end to the depression of 1873, checked itself, reorganized into larger units, and expanded again at a redoubled rate to the depression of 1893. Deeper than the earlier depression, that of '93 was the occasion for correspondingly more thoroughgoing consolidation and for the rapid conquest of the economy by finance capitalism. Politically triumphant over the agrarians after the Civil War, the businessmen prowled fearfully through the jungle of free enterprise destroying one another and being destroyed, until the titans of Wall Street at the turn of the twentieth century managed to bring a semblance of order to the economy and a semblance of security to the business community. And out of this violent process of boom, bust, bankruptcy, receivership, and consolidation, the United States emerged at century's beginning the undisputed industrial leader of the world.

RAILROAD DEVELOPMENT

Basic to this industrial growth and consolidation was the railroad industry, huge beyond comparison to that of any other nation in the world and the main basis for the rise of heavy industry in the United States. When the panic of '73 hit, there were about 70,000 miles of railroad in the nation; by the time of the panic of '93 there were about 170,000. The climax was reached in 1914, at the dawn of the gasoline age, with 256,000 miles of railroad. By 1860 the American railroads were consuming more than half the iron produced in the nation, despite their heavy importations from Great Britain. Still in its infancy at the time of the war, the American iron and steel industry remained concentrated along the eastern seaboard and relatively small-scale. When high tariffs were placed on iron and steel following the war, this condition rapidly changed. With the

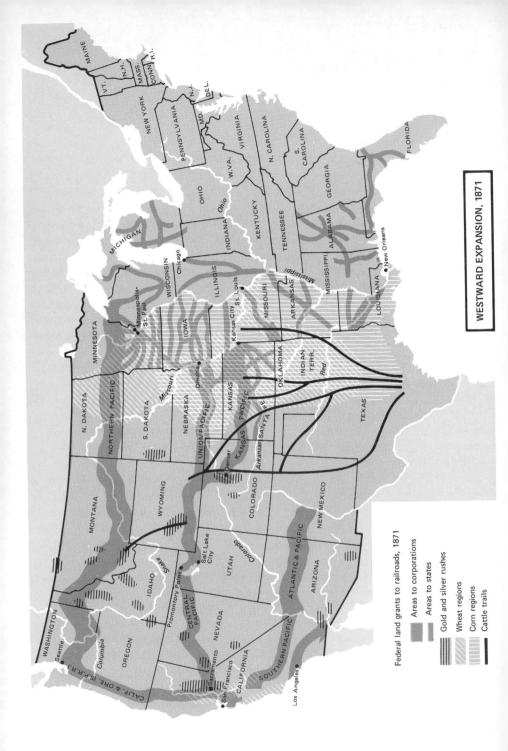

WESTWARD EXPANSION, 1871

Federal land grants to railroads, 1871

Areas to corporations

Areas to states

Gold and silver rushes

Wheat regions

Corn regions

Cattle trails

MAINE

N.H.

VT.

MASS.

CONN. R.I.

NEW YORK

N.J.

PENNSYLVANIA

MD.

DEL.

W.VA.

VIRGINIA

OHIO

Ohio

INDIANA

KENTUCKY

N. CAROLINA

S. CAROLINA

GEORGIA

TENNESSEE

ALABAMA

FLORIDA

MICHIGAN

WISCONSIN

Chicago

ILLINOIS

Mississippi

MISSISSIPPI

LOUISIANA

New Orleans

Minneapolis–
St. Paul

IOWA

St. Louis

Kansas City

MISSOURI

ARKANSAS

MINNESOTA

Missouri

Omaha

OKLAHOMA

INDIAN
TERR.

Red

N. DAKOTA

NORTHERN PACIFIC

S. DAKOTA

NEBRASKA

KANSAS

UNION PACIFIC

KANSAS PACIFIC

SANTA FE

Arkansas

TEXAS

MONTANA

WYOMING

Denver

COLORADO

NEW MEXICO

Colorado

IDAHO

Snake

Salt Lake
City

UTAH

ATLANTIC & PACIFIC

ARIZONA

Promontory Point

CENTRAL
PACIFIC

NEVADA

Sacramento

San Francisco

CALIFORNIA

SOUTHERN PACIFIC

Los Angeles

WASHINGTON

Seattle

Columbia

OREGON

CALIF. & ORE. (S.P.R.R.)

large-scale development of the iron ranges of Minnesota and the coalfields of the Appalachians came America's rise to industrial world leadership in the next generation.

Out of the commotion of civil war, Reconstruction, and westward expansion emerged a railroad barony that wallowed in violence and corruption. Union Pacific had been gutted by Crédit Mobilier, and except for speculative purposes it remained a losing venture for more than a generation. Central Pacific, however, similarly gutted by its operators, remained in the hands of the "big four"— Leland Stanford, Collis P. Huntington, Charles Crocker, and Mark Hopkins— who had been unable to unload it at a good price following the exposure of Crédit Mobilier Making the best of a bad thing, these men absorbed the Central Pacific into Southern Pacific and became the political as well as economic rulers of a half dozen Western states. Cornelius Vanderbilt, an old man by the eve of the Civil War, capped one of the most successful business careers of his day by entering the railroad industry and gaining control of the New York Central. These men, and others like them, became rich almost beyond belief and apparently powerful beyond control.

Yet to be the master of one of the nation's great trunk lines was to be astride a monster which was never entirely submissive to control and never out of danger from its fellow monsters. Railroad managers ceaselessly sought escape from the struggle for survival. They organized together in railroad pools, attempting to stabilize prices, to divide the traffic equitably among themselves, and to operate in safety from one another. Public hostility and federal laws attacked such agreements, however, and mutual suspicion and company violations of the pooling agreements even more effectively destroyed them. The managers were captives of their own companies, and their companies were caught up in the powerful centralizing tendencies of the day.

Terrified of one another, the railroads were still forced to submit to the dictates of their major customers on pain of being destroyed by the loss of trade to a rival. Rebates from published traffic rates were demanded by heavy users of the railroads, rebates that in turn helped the favored users to destroy competitors in their own field. The leading example of this practice, and the classic case study of an American monopoly, was the Standard Oil Company.

OIL AND IRON

The first commercial oil well in American history was drilled in western Pennsylvania in 1859, and into this fiercely competitive field, less than a decade later, stepped the greatest of the captains of industry, John D. Rockefeller. Concentrating on one phase of the oil industry, oil refining, Rockefeller successfully organized a local pooling arrangement which placed his company in control of a major portion of the industry in Cleveland. On the basis of its large volume of trade the Standard Oil Company demanded and received rebates from railroads competing with each other for the Cleveland traffic. For a time the company received not only rebates but equal "rebates" for all the oil shipped by a competitor.

In the following years Rockefeller bought out or drove out all his important competitors and extended his monopoly of the refining industry to control of the oil fields, rails, pipelines, and distributing agencies. The depression of 1873 ruined many competitors, some of whom had overextended themselves in the attempt to compete with Standard Oil. By 1879 Rockefeller controlled 95 percent of the American refining capacity and virtually the entire world market. Reorganized in 1879, Standard Oil was ordered to dissolve thirteen years later by the Ohio State Supreme Court. In 1899 the company reappeared as the Standard Oil Company of New Jersey, availing itself of that state's lax corporation laws to remain a legal monopoly until dissolved by the United States Supreme Court in 1911. And where Rockefeller had shown the way, other industries—steel, copper, sugar, tobacco, rubber, leather, and so forth—soon followed.

The American iron industry, although it had a history as long as that of the nation, enjoyed a spectacular development rivaling that of the newborn oil industry in the postwar years, a development associated with Andrew Carnegie much as that of the oil industry was associated with Rockefeller. Carnegie concentrated his resources in the iron industry in 1873, behind the newly raised iron and steel tariffs, relied for markets on his close associations with leading railroad men and ignored the depression to build the largest steel mill in the world. Without attempting to monopolize the field, he developed efficient methods which gave him the advantage of his competition, as had indeed been the main basis of Rockefeller's original success. He then proceeded to make himself as independent as possible of all outside sources. He bought vast holdings in the Mesabi iron ranges and in the Pennsylvania coalfields; he also acquired his own railroads and ore boats. At the close of the century, despite rising competition, Carnegie remained independent and the most important figure in the industry.

PLUTOCRATIC POLITICS

With the emergence of these captains of industry a transition occurred in national politics: control passed from the spoilsmen of the era of Blaine and Conkling to the business spokesmen of the era of Nelson Aldrich and William McKinley. By the late nineteenth century senators frankly identified themselves with special interests; a senator might be recognized as the New York Central man or the Standard Oil man. And they were joined in the Senate by captains of industry themselves, such as George Hearst and Leland Stanford. By 1900 at least twenty-five multimillionaires held seats in the "Millionaires' Club."

These leaders of big business were thoroughly plutocratic in outlook. They believed that they owned the country and that those who owned the country should rule it. They personally took the credit for the tremendous material progress the nation was experiencing, and they tended to believe that material productivity was the proper index for judging the success of a society, with little or even no reference to how the products were distributed through society. "The consumption of iron," wrote the iron manufacturer and politician Abram S. Hewitt, "is the social barometer by which to estimate the relative height of civilization among nations." By that barometer civilization in America was improving at a great rate; by the social barometers of the laborers and the farmers, however, it seemed, if anything, to be loosing ground.

ORGANIZED LABOR

Manpower for America's industrial development during the second half of the nineteenth century was provided by a ceaseless and increasing immigration of laborers. The Germans and the Irish continued to stream into the country down to the twentieth century, and beginning in the 1880s, they were joined by the "new immigration" from central and southern Europe, Italians being the most numerous. Few members of the new immigration understood English, and few, aside from the Jews, knew anything of life in urban and industrial society. For American employers, they were sources of cheap labor who were also effective as strikebreakers. To native Americans who entered the labor market from rural America, they were threats to job security and the means by which wages could be beaten down.

Yet the idea of America as the land of opportunity for all men of ambition remained strong among American workers, foreign-born and native alike, and the strength of this idea remained a persistent obstacle to the cause of organized labor. In the labor movement it stood in the way of socialists and other political radicals, who largely failed in their efforts to bring labor into opposition to the capitalist system. The Industrial Workers of the World, organized in 1905 in the Western mining and farming regions, was the first revolutionary labor organization to achieve any degree of success in America, and the I.W.W. remained noteworthy chiefly for its revolutionary zeal and not for the size of its membership.

Following the collapse of the National Labor Union in the 1870s, the Noble Order of the Knights of Labor emerged in the 1880s as a major attempt to unite American labor in a single union. Under the leadership of a Philadelphia tailor, Uriah S. Stephens, and later more effectively under Terence V. Powderly, it opened its ranks to unskilled as well as skilled labor—in fact to everybody except, specifically, professional gamblers, bankers, liquor dealers, and lawyers. There had been fifteen years of slow beginnings; then the Knights of

Labor won a major railroad strike against Jay Gould, its membership leaped abruptly to 700,000, and it became a powerful pressure group, successfully agitating in 1885 for a law prohibiting the importation of contract labor.

Then in 1886, during a campaign by the Knights and others for an eight-hour day, a labor meeting at Haymarket Square in Chicago was broken up by police. Someone threw a murderous bomb, and a riot followed. In the absence of any good suspects to charge with the bombing, eight anarchists were accused of murder on the grounds that they had used incendiary language which incited the deed. Four were executed, one committed suicide, and the other three were pardoned six years later, when Gov. John P. Altgeld came to office in Illinois. In the meantime, a nationwide wave of antilabor sentiment followed the Haymarket riot, the Knights of Labor gradually declined, and as it disappeared, its place as the leading labor organization was taken by the American Federation of Labor.

Formed in the 1880s of skilled craft unions under the leadership of Samuel Gompers, the AFL set itself against both the utopianism and the indiscriminate admissions policy of the Knights of Labor. It sought membership primarily among the craft unions, which could command a degree of bargaining power, and it limited itself to the short-range nonpolitical objectives of shorter hours, better pay, better working conditions, and the closed shop. With the capitalist system it had no quarrel. "The way out of the wage system," Gompers declared, "is through higher wages." It organized as a federation of national unions, each of which enjoyed autonomy within the federation.

The AFL won its first major victory in 1890, when it secured a labor contract with the Carnegie Steel Company, and it suffered its first main setback two years later, when it lost its first main strike at Carnegie's Homestead plant in Pennsylvania. Victorious against a small army of Pinkerton private detectives, the strikers were beaten by the state militia and the courts. At first they had the support of some public sympathy, but an anarchist's attempt to assassinate the president of Carnegie Steel, Henry C. Frick, made the public associate striking with foreign radicalism again and weakened the strength of organized labor as the depression set in in 1893.

In that first year of the depression Eugene V. Debs organized the American Railway Union, which, unlike the older Railroad Brotherhoods, was open to all railroad workers and not just to the skilled elite. In 1894 the Pullman Company near Chicago discharged a third of its workers and cut the wages of the rest by as much as 40 percent. Debs's Railway Union joined the resulting strike, providing money and cutting the Pullman cars off trains. The railroads naturally wanted government intervention but were not inclined to go to the prolabor Governor Altgeld for it. Constitutionally the federal government had no authority to intervene with troops except at the governor's request, but Cleveland intervened on the pretext of ensuring that the federal postal system would continue to function. In the process the strike was put down and Debs was jailed. And the courts played a new suppressive role, issuing an injunction against the strike on the grounds that it involved a conspiracy in restraint of trade under the terms of the Sherman Antitrust Act.

Under depression conditions and under continuing government hostility, the unions did well to retain their organizations and survive until better times after the turn of the century. That the major national unions survived the depression intact was of far greater significance than were their temporary bloody defeats.

MINING AND CATTLE FRONTIERS

Settlement and exploitation of the Far West had gone on apace throughout the period of civil war and Reconstruction. Completion of the first continental railroad—the combined Union Pacific and Central Pacific systems—was delayed by the war until 1869, but in response to the news of gold out west, horses, mules, and oxen were kept in a lather as settlements appeared throughout the region extending from the Rocky Mountains to the Pacific. Discovery of gold in California converted that quiet Mexican outpost in two years into a state of the Union supporting a population of more than 90,000, or seven times the population of agrarian Oregon, where settlement had gone on for a decade. Unlike most of the Western mining areas, California's was set in potentially rich farming land. The gold rush was virtually over by 1852, but the population of California quadrupled during the fifties on the basis of California agriculture and the port facilities of San Francisco Bay.

Gold and silver were discovered at Pikes Peak in the territory of Colorado in 1858 and again the next year on the Comstock lode in what became Nevada. During the Civil War further mining discoveries opened up areas in what became Washington, Idaho, and Montana, and in the seventies the final major strike occurred in the Black Hills of Dakota Territory. These mining areas, unlike those of California, required large-scale operations involving heavy capitalization, with the result that almost from the beginning the areas came under the control of a relatively few companies, generally financed by Eastern or San Francisco interests. In the wake of the gold rushes remained forsaken ghost towns and remnants of the original population staying on to farm, work the declining yields from the consolidated mines, or work on the railroad. Within a generation, in most of these areas, the railroads had become the dominant economic interest and the controlling political agent.

The age of the open-range cattle kingdom came into existence almost as suddenly as that of the mining frontier, and it dropped even more abruptly into the past. Cattle, which had ranged Texas in Spanish times, were first demonstrated to be marketable on a large scale in 1866, when the first "long drive" was made to the railroad town of Sedalia, Missouri. During the next twenty years cattle by the million were driven annually to the new railroad towns, Dodge City and Wichita in Kansas and Cheyenne and Laramie in Wyoming.

Cattle soon came to dominate the economy of Wyoming as much as mining had dominated that of Nevada. This was the era of the cattlemen's wars with the "nesters," single-family farmers breaking up the open range, and with the sheep ranchers. Then from 1885 to 1887 two bitter winters and a scorching summer destroyed hundreds of thousands of cattle and drove the cattle ranchers to more modest and methodical cattle enterprises.

This was the era also of the wars with the Plains Indians—the Arapahoe, the Cheyenne, the Apache, and above all the Sioux—an era climaxed by the destruction of George A. Custer and his troops at the Battle of the Little Bighorn in 1876 and mainly concluded with the capture of the Apache leader Geronimo in 1886. Thus there came to a close the age which produced such colorful figures as Wild Bill Hickok, Wyatt Earp, Calamity Jane, and Billy the Kid, and with them produced an American tradition which apparently remains an inexhaustible source of fascination to all the world.

By the time of the Civil War the farmer's frontier had extended to the first tier of states west of the Mississippi and, with the main exception of Mormon Utah, leaped across the "Great American Desert" to the inland valley of California and the Willamette Valley of Oregon. Americans had naturally been reluctant to move out of the forest areas into the grassy plains region. There they faced the problems of inadequate water supply, lack of building materials, and lack of protection against ranging cattle. These were to some extent remedied by the invention of barbed wire, the use of windmills, and the development of extensive, as opposed to intensive, farming techniques, supported by the use of farm machinery.

Huge, heavily capitalized "bonanza farms" paid rich returns on the investment in many cases. For the average single-family farmer, however, life on the high plains was hard, dreary, and often unsuccessful. Settlement in this area was encouraged during the Civil War by high wartime farm prices, a decade of exceptionally heavy rainfall, and the advertising campaigns of the railroads. Later, drought conditions on the "sod house frontier" kindled white-hot leadership for the farm protest movement beginning in the late 1880s.

THE POPULIST REVOLT

The farmers suffered a longer depression than any other major segment of the population—for them, the "panic of '93" had begun five years earlier—and they held disproportionately heavy voting power under the American representative system, especially in the Senate. They were also able to look upon themselves in a way the workingmen were not, as representing the traditional American values. As a result of all these factors, they developed power steadily during the depression, a time when the unions did well to remain on the defensive.

The new wave of farm discontent arose this time not so much in the Middle West, where the Granger movement had been strongest, but in the cotton country of the South and the wheat region of the Great Plains. The Middle West, with a more stabilized railroad system, increasingly diversified agriculture, and growing urban markets close at hand, tended to stay Republican through the whole period of agitation. In the South and in the plains region farm protest organizations emerged in the 1880s and joined together in the Southern Alliance on the one hand and the National (Northern) Alliance on the other, plus a smaller Colored Alliance. Various differences of opinion enforced by old Civil War animosities kept these alliances separate, but they drew up similar reform programs and worked in cooperation with each other. In 1890 they entered politics, and in 1892 they joined together at Omaha to found the People's, or Populist, party.

The Populists launched their program with a fiery preamble, written by Ignatius Donnelly of Minnesota, condemning the ubiquitous corruption of the two major parties. It went on to denounce the system by which "the fruits of the toil of millions are boldly stolen to build up colossal fortunes for the few," breeding from "the same prolific wombs of governmental injustice" the "two great classes—tramps and millionaires." It asserted that "a vast conspiracy against mankind has been organized on two continents," by which silver was systematically being demonetized around the world in order to enrich the international bankers at the expense of the rest of society.

The Populist platform called for government ownership of the railroads, immediate increase in the national currency, and the unlimited coinage of silver at the ratio of 16 to 1 with gold. Additional planks included political reforms: the secret ballot, direct election of senators, and the initiative and referendum, by which voters could petition for special legislation. In an effort to attract labor votes, the platform endorsed the eight-hour day for government workers, immigration restriction, and enforcement of the law against imported contract labor. The party nominated Gen. James B. Weaver of Iowa for President, supported him with more than a million popular and 22 electoral votes in the election, and raised up a lively group of leaders including "Sockless Jerry" Simpson and "Bloody Bridles" Waite.

Although it started out along so many broad avenues of reform, the Populist attack for various reasons tended to concentrate its force on the one overriding objective of currency reform for the next four years. One reason for this was that the one important source of wealth for the party was the silver-mining interests, which were enthusiastic contributors in proportion to the importance the party placed on the silver issue. Repeal of the Silver Purchase Act in 1893 served also to focus attention on the money issue, and in 1894 there appeared the immensely influential William H. Harvey's *Coin's Financial School* exposing the "Crime of '73," by which, he charged, silver had been demonetized at the direction of the international bankers in order to increase the value of their capital at the expense of the value of everybody else's property and product. To those who argued that silver would drive out gold and leave the United States without the necessary medium for international trade Harvey replied that America could force the world to accept its system. If England refused to cooperate, he continued, the United States would be justified in going to war for the cause of humanity.

The depression of '93 was already five years old for the farmers by the time it struck the business community in the year Grover Cleveland returned to the Presidency. The depression had been brought on mainly by overly rapid railroad construction, the decline in the purchasing power of the farmer, and depression conditions abroad, which, in addition to affecting foreign markets, had forced foreign business interests to sell their American investments. There was a run of bank failures through the South and West, and in the summer of 1893 the Erie, Union Pacific, Northern Pacific, and Santa Fe railroads all went into bankruptcy. Within a year the number of unemployed had risen to 4 million, and workers who held their jobs were subjected to sharp and often repeated wage cuts.

THE SILVER ISSUE

The whole nation agreed that the money system was at the root of the trouble, but there was a diametric difference of opinion as to how. For the farmers, struggling under depressed prices for farm products, the problem lay in the insufficiency of currency, which could be remedied by the unlimited coinage of silver at 16 to 1. For Cleveland and the other "gold bugs," the fault lay with the Silver Purchase Act of 1890, which had caused the hoarding of gold and had weakened business confidence.

To check the run on the gold supply that was accompanying the depression, Cleveland called an emergency session of Congress and pushed through the repeal of the Silver Purchase Act. When the run on the federal gold reserve continued, he arranged through a banking syndicate directed by J. P. Morgan for a loan of 65 million dollars, half of it from abroad. This helped to end the crisis, at great political cost to Cleveland, who was charged with being the lackey of Wall Street, most loudly, of course, by the silverites. Cleveland sustained a further defeat in 1894; in response to his call for a lowering of the tariff, the Wilson-Gorman Tariff, providing for no significant reductions in duties, was passed without his signature.

The Populists found villains aplenty, but with the repeal of the Silver Purchase Act President Cleveland became the central one. "Cleveland might be honest," supposed William Jennings Bryan, "but so were the mothers who threw their children in the Ganges." The attack spread within the Democratic party, dividing its Southern and Western wings from their party's Eastern leader. Therefore the Republican party, when it held its nominating convention in 1896, had good reason to be optimistic about the forthcoming election. The Republican party, it is true, had its own silverite faction, which bolted the convention after that gathering accepted a "sound-money" plank, but it was not so severely damaged by the issue as the Democratic party.

In the Democratic convention the radicals gained control and made of the platform a blanket repudiation of Cleveland's administration. The debate over the money plank produced the most famous speech in convention history, when the young William Jennings Bryan spoke "in the defense of our homes, our families, and posterity" against the gold standard, concluding with his famous injunction, "You shall not press down upon the brow of labor this crown of thorns, you shall not crucify mankind upon a cross of gold." The young Nebraska politician won the nomination and thereafter received the endorsement of the Populist convention, and this "Cross of Gold" speech set the keynote for the first campaign since before the Civil War to revolve around major national issues.

In 1896 the Republican party was in the hands of a politically astute, candidly honest, and engagingly reasonable new national political boss, the Ohio industrialist Mark Hanna. Rather looked down upon by the genteel as a "diamond in the rough," Hanna was a kindly realist who saw beyond the simple certitudes of Liberal Republicanism to an industrial America where the rich would rule, in part by their great power and in part by giving to the people an increasing share of the increasing wealth their labor was creating. Hanna was not altogether successful in persuading his friends in the Union League Club that everybody ought to have a fair share; he had greater success in organizing his colleagues for the purpose of seeing to it that the rich should rule. In the nominating convention, he secured the candidacy of his protégé William McKinley, and then he directed a campaign that was remarkable for its organization and its unprecedented expensiveness.

For the impoverished Democratic party, the campaign was by contrast the personal effort of Bryan, who traveled continually through the nation to deliver more than six hundred speeches. The result was that though he carried the Solid South, the plains states, and the silver states, Bryan lost every state in the Northwest and Northeast, as well as California, and went down to defeat by a margin of 600,000 votes. It was the worst defeat of a major presidential candidate since 1872. The defeat and the divisions it created damaged the Democratic party for years to come. The Populist party, meanwhile, was destroyed by its support of the Democratic Bryan, the return of farm prosperity, and discoveries of gold in South Africa, Australia, and Alaska, which brought to the farmers the inflation they had wished to achieve through silver. By the time the nation went officially on the gold standard, with the Currency Act of 1900, the farmers had lost their interest in the money question, and for a generation, until hard times came again in the 1920s, they remained correspondingly less concerned about reform politics.

FINANCE CAPITALISM

The election of McKinley was a victory for a Republican party in which control had been won from the spoilsmen by the big business interests, organized by Hanna. It was therefore appropriate that under McKinley's Presidency industrial consolidation should proceed at a faster pace than at any other time in American history. And the depression of 1893 had prepared the way for finance capitalism. As in previous depressions, bankruptcies facilitated consolidation, and this was most evidently true in the case of the railroads. The novelty of the new consolidations was the centering of control, not finally in the hands of the railroad men themselves, but beyond them in the hands of the Wall Street financial giants. Railroad men remained to operate the roads, but control was centralized over major areas, and competition was eliminated so far as possible. The same process took place in all major areas of American industry.

There were two main centers of financial control on Wall Street: J. P. Morgan and Company and the rival firm of the Rockefeller interests, Kuhn, Loeb, and Company. These were the only two American financial houses with extensive European connections. The Morgan group, working through the National Bank of Commerce and the First National Bank of New York, controlled the operations of banks throughout the nation and influenced the policies of major corporations. Among these U.S. Steel—created by Morgan out of Carnegie's former holdings, combined with other steel companies and subsidiary businesses, and accounting for the greater part of the nation's steel-producing capacity—was famous as the nation's first "billion dollar corporation." The Rockefeller group, working through the National City Bank, the Hanover City Bank, and the Farmers Loan and Trust Company and driven by the pressure of finding outlets for the ever-increasing volume of profits from Standard Oil, similarly created its network of railroads under the control of Edward H. Harriman and similarly arranged combinations in other industries. Aside from U.S. Steel and Standard Oil, the industrial combinations that emerged included the American Tobacco Company, Amalgamated Copper, the American Sugar Refining Company, International Harvester, and General Electric.

To big business the McKinley administration contributed the Dingley Tariff, which once again raised duties to the highest point in history. The main service of the administration, however, was in appointing sympathetic men to the Interstate Commerce Commission and the Attorney General's Office and then permitting the masters of capital to do as they wished. In 1904 John Moody, in his *The Truth about the Trusts,* found that two-fifths of the manufacturing capital of the nation was concentrated in 318 companies and that these in turn were largely controlled by the Morgan and Rockefeller groups. The study concluded that "these two mammouth groups jointly . . . constitute the heart of the business and commercial life of the nation."

The conquests of the finance capitalists did much to create the atmosphere that made the Progressive movement possible. The climax of consolidation was the occasion for a brief labor-management honeymoon, which saw Hanna and Morgan cooperating cordially with Gompers in various enterprises and also saw a rapid increase in AFL membership. During the United Mine Workers strike of 1902 Mark Hanna and J. P. Morgan were instrumental in helping Theodore Roosevelt settle the strike favorably for the workers. The newfound sense of security on Wall Street was demonstrated in the presidential campaign of 1904 by the willingness of Rockefeller and Morgan to support Roosevelt despite his reputation as a trustbuster. The Republican party was their party, and they had reason not to be greatly disturbed by Roosevelt's denunciations of "bad" trusts. Progressivism bloomed in the quieter time of the early twentieth century, when the struggling, recalcitrant robber baron had been supplanted (except in the newly developing areas of the economy, such as the automobile industry) by consolidated and comparatively cooperative management.

BIBLIOGRAPHY FOR CHAPTER 15

E. C. Kirkland, Industry Comes of Age: Business, Labor and Public Policy, 1860-1897 (1961)

T. C. Cochran and **William Miller,** The Age of Enterprise: A Social History of Industrial America (1942)

R. W. and **M. E. Hidy,** Pioneering in Big Business, 1882-1911: History of the Standard Oil Company (1955)

N. J. Ware, The Labor Movement in the United States, 1860-1895 (1929)

Blake McKelvey, The Urbanization of America, 1860-1915 (1963)

W. P. Webb, The Great Plains (1931)

J. F. Doble, The Longhorns (1941)

Fred Shannon, The Farmer's Last Frontier: Agriculture, 1860-1897 (1945)

C. G. Fite, The Farmer's Frontier, 1865-1900 (1966)

S. J. Buck, The Agrarian Crusade (1919)

J. D. Hicks, The Populist Revolt (1931)

P. W. Glad, McKinley, Bryan and the People (1964)

CHAPTER 16

IMPERIAL AMERICA

POST-CIVIL WAR ISOLATION

The United States was more densely isolationist during the thirty years following the Civil War than in any other period in its history. During the 1880s Africa was divided among the frantically scrambling European nations at a time when they were gaining additional protectorates, colonies, and concessions in Asia, but the United States was comparatively immune to the fevers of imperialism. The slavery controversy had checked manifest-destiny tendencies in the fifties, and the Civil War apparently had supplied the generation that passed through it with as much martial adventure as it cared to experience. Then, during the Reconstruction era, economic development of the South and West had provided American capital with the chance for colonial exploitation within the national boundaries. Northern bankers found more profitable and safer outlets in Southern railroads and textile mills and the iron industry of Birmingham, Alabama, than would have been available to them outside the continental United States, and the mining and cattle frontiers of the West and the bonanza ranches of the Great Plains provided colonial opportunities for which American capital competed vigorously with that of Britain and continental Europe. It was only after the cattle lands had been fenced in and the mining regions had settled down to methodical, consolidated enterprises of declining productivity that Americans began to look beyond the nation's boundaries in the spirit of the "new imperialism" of the age.

THE MONROE DOCTRINE

The fixed principles of American foreign policy before the Civil War had consisted of the Monroe Doctrine and freedom of the seas, but the war had presented European nations with opportunities for large-scale violations of the Monroe Doctrine, which Spain took advantage of in Santo Domingo and France

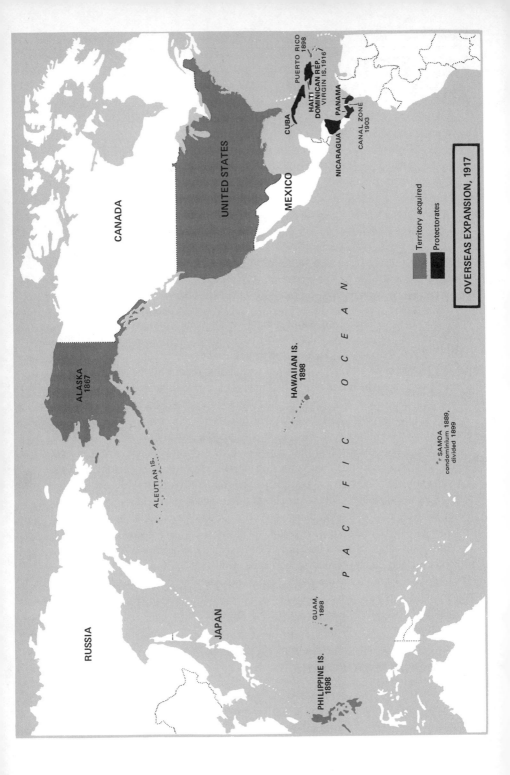

RUSSIA

JAPAN

PHILIPPINE IS.
1898

GUAM,
1898

PACIFIC OCEAN

SAMOA
condominium 1889,
divided 1899

ALEUTIAN IS.

ALASKA
1867

HAWAIIAN IS.
1898

CANADA

UNITED STATES

MEXICO

CUBA

PUERTO RICO
1898

HAITI
DOMINICAN REP.
VIRGIN IS. 1916

PANAMA

CANAL ZONE
1903

NICARAGUA

Territory acquired

Protectorates

OVERSEAS EXPANSION, 1917

in Mexico. Chaotic conditions in Mexico in the late fifties, which had moved Buchanan to think of the fruitful possibilities of another Mexican war, had given an opening to European nations. Having originally joined with Spain and England in protest against Mexico's suspension of its international obligations, the French invaded Mexico unilaterally, occupied Mexico City, and, in 1863, invited Archduke Maximilian of Austria to form a monarchy under French protection.

Maximilian's Mexican empire received general European recognition, and he was filling his mind with thoughts of extending his conquests into South America when the American Civil War came to an end. With it ended Maximilian's bright prospects. Departing from the wartime policy of neutrality toward Maximilian's Mexico, President Johnson's Secretary of State William Seward assumed an increasingly aggressive attitude toward the Mexican empire, demanding that the French set a time limit for evacuation. Since Seward's demands were backed up by 50,000 troops in Texas, Napoleon III of France withdrew his troops, and Maximilian met his fate before a Mexican firing squad, in February 1867.

Spanish attempts to reannex Santo Domingo, meanwhile, had collapsed before the Civil War was over. At war's end Seward was ambitious to use the nation's great war-created military and naval power to resume the expansion that the slavery controversy had interrupted. He hoped to acquire Caribbean possessions, the Hawaiian Islands, and, in time, Canada. Unsupported by public sentiment, he was successful in the purchase of Alaska from Russia and the occupation of the Midway Islands in 1867, but unsuccessful in other promising schemes extending from Santo Domingo to Pago Pago.

ANGLO-AMERICAN RELATIONS

More popular for the moment among the American people was the project of wresting Canada from England in retaliation for British hostility during the war and for the damages done by Confederate blockade runners, including the *Alabama,* which the British government had permitted to be constructed in Scottish shipyards. As chairman of the Senate Foreign Relations Committee Senator Sumner was the leading spokesman for the view that Britain should be charged with half the cost of the war, a view expressed in the so-called "*Alabama* claims." These huge claims against England were used by expansionists to justify the United States in annexing Canada at a time when it had the military force to accomplish the feat.

The Grant administration, including Secretary of State Hamilton Fish, at first accepted Sumner's estimate of claims against Britain, but Grant became offended with Sumner for other reasons, and Fish came to look upon such exorbitant claims as unreasonable and futile. On its part, the British government came to regret having permitted the construction of blockade runners, partly because in so doing, it had established a precedent which other neutral nations might in the future use against it in time of war. In 1871 the Washington Treaty was arranged between England and the United States, providing for submission to international arbitration of the *Alabama* claims and also certain fishing disputes. The treaty contained a British expression of regret for having permitted the "escape" of the blockade runners from Scotland. This expression of regret ensured that the American claims for direct damages would be met, since they implied British admission of culpability. The treaty, which contained settlement of a number of additional smaller disputes, passed the Senate overwhelmingly, with even Senator Sumner voting for it.

The treaty quieted Anglo-American relations for a generation, but the British ruling classes had not come to like the American democracy any better, and Americans, especially Irish-Americans, continued to look upon England with varying shades of hostility. And as the century drew to a close, developments in Latin America placed the two nations once again in conflict. As the United States industrialized, its interest in Latin American markets and raw materials naturally increased. The American government, especially under Secretary of State James G. Blaine in 1881 and from 1889 to 1892, responded to this growing interest by trying to achieve closer economic ties with the nations of South America. Blaine failed in attempts to create a Pan-American customs union, but he did win advantageous individual commercial treaties. European interests, especially English, were no less attracted than the Americans by the Latin American possibilities. In 1893 British and German business interests endorsed a rebellion in Brazil, which for a time threatened America's favored economic position in that nation. In 1895 Britain blockaded the Nicaraguan port of Corinto and occupied the island of Trinidad off the coast of Brazil. France meanwhile made threatening advances against Santo Domingo and attempted to occupy an area in Brazil which it had previously claimed but never governed. Against the background of these events the Cleveland administration precipitated the Venezuela crisis in 1895.

THE VENEZUELA CRISIS

At issue was a long-standing boundary dispute between Venezuela and British Guiana, which had been made critical during Cleveland's first administration by the discovery of gold in the disputed territory. Britain had maintained its position against Venezuelan protests, and the Cleveland administration, its offer to arbitrate having been declined by Britain, had done nothing more in the matter. The situation remained much the same when Cleveland returned to office, but the President on that occasion made up his mind to do something different. In the only widely popular act of his distressing second administration, Cleveland directed his Secretary of State, Richard Olney, to deliver a message to the British government announcing that the United States intended to intervene in the dispute and make final settlement. That it had the power as well as the right to do so was apparently not to be doubted. "The United States," the note declared, "is practically sovereign on this continent and its fiat is law upon the subjects to which it confines its interposition. Why? It is not because of the pure friendship or good-will felt for it. . . . It is because in addition to all other grounds its infinite resources combined with its isolated position render it master of the situation and practically invulnerable against any and all other nations."

At the time of that note, the entire American Army stood at about 28,000 men. Dispersed in small numbers for Indian patrols, this force was without either the training or the organization to fight a coordinated major battle. In addition to the army, there was a National Guard of about 100,000 men, divided under the commands of the state governors and largely untrained except for some close-order drill. The guard officers, elected by the guardsmen, had no special military training. The navy, neglected since the Civil War, was without a single modern battleship, although plans for naval expansion were in the designing stage and construction was in progress. Britain, by contrast, maintained a large, well-trained army and possessed the most powerful navy in the world. For the United States to have intervened by force in the Venezuela dispute would have been out of the question. In a showdown with England the United States might have invaded Canada, but the circumstances were hardly more favorable for such a venture in 1895 than they had been for the ill-starred venture of 1812.

It is impossible to know how Cleveland and the United States would have worked their way out of their difficulties had England remained firm in its rejection of arbitration, which it undoubtedly intended to do originally. As it happened, England found itself suddenly in serious trouble in Europe and South Africa and, wishing American friendship, bowed to the demands for arbitration. The United States was therefore able to continue unchallenged in its easy assumption that an isolated and lightly armed nation really could stand guard over one of the world's two hemispheres. The results of World War I only confirmed the nation in this view. On the eve of World War II, therefore, the American attitude toward military affairs had in important respects not yet emerged from the eighteenth century.

THE NEW IMPERIALISM

The immense American enthusiasm for Cleveland's assertive attitude toward the Venezuela dispute heralded the arrival of that new spirit of imperialism which reached its climax three years later, in 1898, in the Spanish-American War. A new generation of Americans had arisen which had taken no part in the Civil War, and some of its more red-blooded members were spoiling for some kind of fight of their own, so long as it was in a good cause. These men were imbued with the spirit of the new imperialism that still raged abroad, and, for a brief span of years at least, Americans generally joined in with the spirit of the times. The new imperialism differed from the old of the seventeenth and eighteenth centuries in the great power the industrial revolution had given the colonizing nations to dominate the "lesser breeds," as the colonized peoples came to be known. The emphasis was no longer on strategic trading posts, but on control of the whole territory in order that it might be well exploited by Western methods.

Lacking in the old imperialism, chauvinism was a driving force in the new, supported by the growing conviction, alien to eighteenth-century America even in slave areas, that inferior races existed whom the superior race had the duty to rule. The fiercely competitive European powers that divided Africa in the 1880s in large measure did not do so for economic gain, which seemed unlikely to result, but rather to enhance the glory of the conquering nation. Missionary zeal, important in the old imperialism, was important in the new one too, and was an especially strong motive so far as America was concerned.

In 1885 Josiah Strong, a Congregational minister, published an influential book, *Our Country,* in which he called America to its duty to "dispossess many weaker races, assimilate others, and mold the remainder, until, in a very true and important sense, it has Anglo-Saxonized mankind" and established a "Christian stewardship" throughout the world. In 1895 the national enthusiasm aroused by Cleveland's threatened intervention on behalf of the Venezuelans was an indication that a great many American people were tending toward the point of view of the Reverend Mr. Strong.

THE SPANISH-AMERICAN WAR

Several months before the Venezuela note, the second Cuban insurrection within a generation broke out against the feeble, inefficient, and corrupt Spanish colonial regime. The regime had used harsh methods to suppress the earlier insurrection, from 1868 to 1878, and in the course of it the American ship *Virginius* had been captured by the Spanish and fifty-three of its crew summarily executed. Nevertheless, despite the natural burst of outrage in the United States, it had not severed relations with Spain as a consequence. In 1895, however, the new insurrection, which the Spanish were trying to put down as harshly as before, was taken up by the newspapers and eagerly followed by the public as a dramatic distraction from the wretched domestic conditions of the depression. The two leading New York rivals, Joseph Pulitzer's *World* and William Randolph Hearst's *Journal,* gave it most enterprising coverage, and their accounts were avidly copied by other newspapers throughout the country. The press presented lurid and dramatic accounts of the guerrila warfare, the Spanish concentration camps, methods of Spanish torture, the cruelty of Gen. Valeriano "Butcher" Weyler, and, best of all, the Black Spaniards' incarceration of the heroine Evagelina Cisneros.

A Cuban junta established itself in New York at the outset to work for "Cuba Libre," and American investors, who had increased their properties in Cuba since the previous insurrection, were soon calling for American intervention. When a Spanish gunboat fired on the American ship *Alliance,* talk about going in and taking over became quite widespread, but it had no effect whatever on President Cleveland, who declared American neutrality and stood pat. Cleveland's successor McKinley at first was similarly disinclined to meddle. America's Cuban investments were not very large, and American business interests generally opposed engaging in any international adventures that might unsettle business conditions at a time when they were improving rapidly and the delicate and all-important process of business consolidation was under way.

A war party did exist in the Republican party, however, and events played into its hands. The New York *Journal* obtained a letter the Spanish Minister to America, Enrique de Lôme, had sent to a friend, commenting disparagingly upon McKinley. Thus dishonored, the American nation had not yet recovered from the insult when the new American battleship the *Maine,* at anchor in Havana harbor on a mission of "friendly courtesy," exploded and sank, on February 15, 1898, with the loss of more than 250 lives. The cause of the disaster was never discovered. A naval inquiry could find no shred of evidence connecting the Spanish with the explosion, but the investigators, naturally not wishing to put the blame on the navy itself, allowed themselves some lame speculations about the possibility of Spanish mines. The "yellow press" reported that the Spanish undoubtedly did it and demanded war. Driven by popular pressure and by influential men within his party, McKinley made stern demands on the Spanish government, which, being in enough trouble already, substantially capitulated to them. Himself a man of peace, McKinley faced a bellicose Congress that now demanded war no matter what the Spanish government did. Unwilling to disrupt his party, McKinley responded to the Spanish capitulation with a previously written war message to Congress, adding the postscript that the Spanish government already had agreed to the American demands.

What followed was a sorry little struggle in Cuba to which the incompetent Cuban governor general with six weeks warning could muster but 1,700 men at Santiago. Incompetence and confusion on the American side were also scandalous, but 17,000 American troops were nevertheless landed in Cuba, unopposed. The brief battle at Santiago, featuring Theodore Roosevelt's celebrated charge up San Juan Hill as the leader of the "rough riders," sufficed to bring to an end four centuries of Spanish rule. Two days later the defective Spanish fleet, which American ships had bottled up in Santiago harbor, received an order to destroy itself rather than surrender, and in broad daylight Adm. Pascual Cervera sent his wooden ships against the American blockade. They were destroyed at a cost in dead and wounded of 474 Spaniards. The entire war cost the United States less than 400 fatalities in combat and more than 5,000 through disease and food poisoning.

CONQUEST OF THE PHILIPPINES

To most Americans, including apparently the President, the war at the outset had been purely one to free Cuba. There were some, however, who from the first had had larger ideas, and among these was Assistant Secretary of the Navy Roosevelt. Roosevelt shared with others of his generation, such as Sen. Henry Cabot Lodge and Adm. Alfred T. Mahan, a Darwinistic view of the power struggle among nations which was rather more European than it was American. In this view, nations became great through the fitness of their people, the willingness of their people to express themselves in war, and the spiritually strengthening experience of war itself. "When great nations fear to expand, shrink from expansion," Roosevelt declared, "it is because their greatness is coming to an end." He further believed that "no triumph of peace is quite so great as the supreme triumphs of war."

To this doctrine Admiral Mahan had contributed an internationally important theory concerning the relationship of sea power to national power. Historically, Mahan found, naval power had been the key to national power. Naval power in turn required far-flung naval bases. American national power, Mahan argued, depended upon a powerful navy with naval bases in the Caribbean and the Pacific. Mahan's arguments influenced British and German naval construction more than American, but they had their effect on the expanding American Navy also, and in 1898 Roosevelt was in a position to do something about Mahan's demand for those naval bases. With the war in Cuba in prospect, Assistant Secretary of the Navy Roosevelt took advantage of the absence of his superior to send orders to Commodore George Dewey, in charge of America's Pacific squadron at Hong Kong, that he must keep in readiness for offensive operations in the Philippine Islands. This was substantially the plan of operations that the navy had worked out on its own. Accordingly Dewey, upon receiving word of war, sailed into Manila Bay and sank the small, helpless Spanish fleet. He was without troops to occupy Manila, but within three months he was rescued from this anomalous position by 11,000 American soldiers supported by the Philippine patriot leader Emilio Aguinaldo.

Taking Manila proved an easy matter, but thereafter for more than three years the Americans fought a much longer and bloodier struggle than the Spanish-American episode, now against Aguinaldo and his guerrilla fighters. In the course of that struggle, furthermore, the Americans found themselves resorting to the concentration-camp horrors and methods of torture which in the beginning had aroused American sentiment against the Spanish in Cuba. The

Americans were not yet in full possession of their new empire before they had reason to regret its acquisition.

THE AMERICAN EMPIRE

The war had been launched in a chivalrous spirit with no thought of conquest, and Congress had written that spirit into law with an amendment to the declaration of war, put forward by Sen. H. M. Teller of Colorado, pledging Cuban independence. Once in the war, however, America was swept by imperial ambitions, to which Congress gave vent during the week of Roosevelt's charge up San Juan Hill with a joint resolution annexing Hawaii. Two weeks later McKinley had so far freed himself from his earlier anti-imperialist inhibitions as to demand Puerto Rico and Guam as the price of an armistice.

Then people began to think about taking the Philippines—first Manila, then Luzon, and then all of them. By the time of the treaty negotiations McKinley had become convinced that "there was nothing left for us to do but to take them all, and to educate the Filipinos and to uplift and civilize and Christianize them, and by God's grace do the very best we could by them as our fellow men for whom Christ also died." The United States dictated the terms accordingly. Cuba was to become independent, Guam and Puerto Rico were to be taken outright, and the Philippine Islands were to be purchased for 20 million dollars. In February 1899, after a sharp debate, the treaty passed the Senate by the necessary two-thirds majority, with but two votes to spare, and the government faced the unprecedented problem of absorbing into the American democratic system subject peoples in noncontiguous territories extending halfway around the world.

The organizers of the empire were embarrassed by rising bipartisan opposition to the conquests, expressing itself through the Anti-Imperialist League and pointing out all the difficulties and inconsistencies and apparent unconstitutionalities involved in the maintenance of an imperial government by a federal democracy. In the face of this opposition, the government moved diffidently; it established no "Secretary of the Empire" to administer the new acquisitions, but instead took them one at a time and tucked them under other departments, such as Navy and Interior. Cuba, to the surprise of the rest of the world (and to the regret of the people of the United States sixty years later), did receive its independence, but only under the restrictions of the Platt amendment to an army appropriations bill of 1901. By these terms, the United States asserted its authority over Cuban diplomatic and financial affairs as well as various other internal Cuban matters, reserving the right to occupy Cuba militarily and also the right to buy or lease Cuban land for the purpose of establishing naval stations. Cuba received its limited independence only after incorporating the terms of the Platt amendment into its constitution.

Annexation of the Philippines and Puerto Rico raised constitutional problems, since it was not the American intention, as it was in Hawaii and Alaska, eventually to admit these territories to statehood. The Supreme Court wafted away these perplexities, however, in a series of "Insular Cases," in which it found that Congress had the right to keep a territory "like a disembodied shade, in an intermediate state of ambiguous existence for an indefinite period," which was to say, among other things, that it could simultaneously retain the territory as American soil and raise up tariff barriers against it. As to the natives' rights in these "unincorporated" territories of Puerto Rico and the Philippines, the Court found that they had "fundamental" rights to life, liberty, and property but not "procedural" rights, which the Court never defined comprehensively.

Nevertheless, it must be said for the American masters that they did not by any means avail themselves of all these sovereign advantages. Representative institutions were established at the outset, and in 1917 American citizenship was extended to the Puerto Ricans, being denied the Filipinos because eventual independence was contemplated for them. American governments encouraged economic imperialism unselfconsciously, but with political imperialism they had as little to do as possible.

"BIG STICK" DIPLOMACY

The Caribbean conquests caused no major diplomatic complications, for the United States was in a position to assert itself effectively against any potential foreign enemy's challenge, and Roosevelt after he became President in 1901 was able to apply an unrestrained "big stick" diplomacy to this area. Faced with the fact that Caribbean nations were repudiating European debts and the possibility that European powers would make this a pretext for conquest, he in 1904 enunciated the Roosevelt corollary to the Monroe Doctrine: since the United States would not tolerate European intervention in America, the United States must assume the responsibility for upholding legitimate European interests by occupying the defaulting nations and administering the repayment of their honest debts. Beginning with the occupation of the Dominican Republic in 1905, this policy was followed by Roosevelt and his successors—including Wilson, who had denounced it as immoral before taking office—until the coming of the New Deal.

The new American position in the Caribbean, as well as the two-ocean naval requirements that the war had dramatized, served to revive interest in an isthmian canal in Central America. In 1901 treaty negotiations freed the United States from diplomatic commitments to England regarding canal construction, and Roosevelt moved vigorously to accomplish the task on taking office. Of two alternative routes one through Colombia was chosen, partly because of lobbying by successors to a bankrupt French canal company there who saw their opportunity to snatch profits from disaster by selling out to America. When reluctance of the Colombian government to come to terms threatened this Panamanian enterprise, company officials, with American naval support, staged a little revolution and established the Republic of Panama, which elected a government of canal-company officials and quickly came to terms with the United States. Construction proceeded at once, and the Panama Canal was opened in 1914, leaving disagreeable Latin American feelings toward the United States which Congress in 1921 did something to assuage by a 25-million-dollar grant to Colombia.

ASIAN DIPLOMACY

Acquisition of the Philippines, on the other hand, presented the United States with problems it could not so easily dispose of. There the United States found itself amidst Russian, English, French, German, and Japanese colonial rivals, and in this fast company it was committed to the defense of a gigantic archipelago, for which it had nothing like the requisite naval and military resources. McKinley's Secretary of State, John Hay, exhibited America's fundamental weakness in the Orient by sending an "Open Door" note to imperial rivals in the Far East, inviting them to agree to equal privileges and equal trading rights for all nations in all the "spheres of influence" they had wrested from China. Despite the fact that no nation agreed to his terms unequivocally, Hay remarkably enough announced that they had done so and that the Open Door policy was in effect. There followed the rising of the Chinese nationalist Boxers against the extraterritorial foreign communities in China, which was put down by an international force and made the pretext for further dismemberment of China. Hay met this with a second note, calling for the imperial powers to guarantee "Chinese territorial and administrative entity," with no better success.

Roosevelt, while not overtly repudiating the Open Door idea, developed a policy of his own that depended fundamentally upon maintaining a balance of power between the two leading Asian nations, Japan and Russia. Following his mediation of the Russo-Japanese War in 1905, Roosevelt was faced with Japanese resentment, which was heightened when Japanese were segregated in the San Francisco city schools. Roosevelt persuaded the San Francisco schools to integrate and gained from the Japanese a "Gentleman's Agreement" not to increase the number of Japanese passports to America if the United States would not pass a humiliating Japanese exclusion law. Then he sent the American fleet around the world as a salutary demonstration of American power. Then in 1908, in the Root-Takahira Agreement, Roosevelt recognized Japan's special interest in Manchuria, where he was happy to see Japan and Russia contesting each other, Open Door morality aside.

This balance-of-power diplomacy, however, was reversed by the "dollar diplomacy" of Roosevelt's successor, President Taft, whose policy was to strengthen America's positions in the Caribbean and the Far East through the expansion of private American investments. In the Caribbean this policy worked well enough, at the cost of stirring up more anti-Yankee feeling than Roosevelt's taking of Panama ever had done. In the Far East, however, it was disastrous. When Taft urged American financiers into Manchurian enterprises, Japan and Russia were quick to smooth over their mutual differences in order to unite against the United States. Under any circumstances, however, possession of the Philippines placed the United States in a damagingly weak position. Just as Canada throughout the nineteenth century remained diplomatically a British hostage in American hands, so the Philippine Islands became an American hostage in the hands of Japan, serving to weaken America's bargaining position with Japan from the first Open Door note down to Pearl Harbor.

BIBLIOGRAPHY FOR CHAPTER 16

F. R. Dulles, Prelude to World Power: American Diplomatic History, 1860–1900 (1965) and America's Rise to World Power, 1898–1954 (1955)

H. K. Beale, Theodore Roosevelt and the Rise of America to World Power (1956)

Walter LaFeber, The New Empire: An Interpretation of American Expansion, 1860–1898 (1963)

E. R. May, Imperial Democracy: The Emergence of America as a Great Power (1961)

H. W. Morgan, America's Road to Europe (1965)

Walter Mills, The Martial Spirit (1931)—orgins of the Spanish-American War

R. L. Beisner, Twelve against Empire (1968)—the anti-imperialists of 1898

W. H. Callcott, The Caribbean Policy of the United States, 1890–1920 (1967)

A. W. Griswold, The Far Eastern Policy of the United States (1938)

George Kennan, American Diplomacy, 1900–1950 (1951)

CHAPTER 17

PROGRESSIVE REPUBLICANISM

THE ELECTION OF 1900

Reform was a cloud no larger than a man's hand in 1900, when McKinley was reelected to the Presidency. The contestants in that election were the same as those in the election of 1896, but the contest was wholly different. Good times had come again in the intervening four years, and as a consequence Bryan had been deprived of any good political issue upon which to campaign. He campaigned on the issue of imperialism. He himself had abetted the acquisition of the Philippines, however, and two years after the "splendid little war" too many Americans were still exhilarated by the event and still in a mood to want the sun never to set upon the American empire. Consequently McKinley won by a considerably wider margin than he had in 1896 on the slogan of the "full dinner pail."

Going in with a sure winner, the Republicans gained further political advantage from the election by nominating Theodore Roosevelt as Vice President and thereby removing him from New York politics, where his reforming activities as governor had disturbed the Republican political machine of Boss Platt. Everything seemed to be going right for the Grand Old Party and its business-minded backers when, seven months after his return to office, McKinley was assassinated and, as Mark Hanna bitterly complained to his colleagues on the funeral train, "that damned cowboy" Roosevelt was plucked from the oblivion of the Vice Presidency and put into the White House.

THEODORE ROOSEVELT

Descending on the nation with flashing teeth, blazing pince-nez glasses, and a high shrill voice of righteousness, Teddy Roosevelt dominated the political scene as no President had since Andrew Jackson. Like the Democratic Franklin D. Roosevelt who was to follow him, he combined a vivid impression of stormy radicalism with an ingrained patrician conservatism. He sensed the amorphous will of the people, and he gave voice to it forcefully and amorphously. By no means the radical reformer that many of his fellow Republicans feared him to be, Roosevelt tried to quiet their fears on coming to office, announcing that he would be guided in his acts by the realization that it was McKinley and not he whom the American people had elected as their President. But this irrepressibly rambunctious political leader immediately and dramatically altered the tone of the nation's politics. He rallied the scattered forces of reform, and the country swiftly passed over into the Progressive era.

The Democratic party had already gone Progressive with its capture by Bryan in 1896, and Progressive reformers continued to dominate its councils. That victory, however, had occurred when the Democratic party was reduced to minority status in national politics, where it remained except briefly under Wilson down to the Great Depression. It was the conversion of the majority Republican party to reform, therefore, that marked the arrival of the new era. And this conversion, in times of prosperity, is harder to account for than the Democratic conversion in times of depression, since Roosevelt drew his following in large measure from those who had voted in 1900 for McKinley Republicanism and who four years earlier had voted fearfully against Bryan Democratic Populism.

The immediate reason, certainly, was Roosevelt's forceful personality, for he was able to change people's minds almost overnight. A case in point is William Allen White, the famous and politically influential editor of the Emporia *Gazette* in Kansas. White had first gained national fame in an editorial attack against the Populist reformers in Kansas. Then Roosevelt came along like a shining knight and won White, with millions of others, to the cause of Progressive reform. "I was a young arrogant protagonist of the divine rule of the plutocracy," White later remembered, when Roosevelt "shattered the foundations of my political ideals. As they crumbled then and there, politically, I put his heel on my neck, and I became his man."

ORIGINS OF PROGRESSIVISM

Roosevelt Progressivism had been prepared for in many ways during the preceding generation. Faced with the continuing and increasing problem of poverty in an industrializing nation, the old self-righteous humanitarianism of the pre-Civil War period was giving way to the new scientific philanthropy that viewed poverty less as a moral problem than as a social one for which the community as a whole was directly responsible. The last quarter of the nineteenth century had seen the establishment of various sorts of state commissions which, while they may have achieved little actual reform, had gathered many statistics revealing to the respectable citizenry the horrors of the system they were tolerating.

And muckrakers were beginning to rub the noses of these people into those conditions of corruption, sin, and squalor of which they were already painfully aware. Most effectively of all, the Social Gospel movement, dedicated to closing the gap between the social order and the teachings of Jesus Christ, was exerting itself powerfully to mold the thinking of the new generation. The Social Gospel had by no means made a general conquest of Protestantism, even in the Northern cities where its strength lay, but its influence had been concentrated upon those middle- and upper-middle-class citizens who were to become the heart and soul of the Progressive movement.

Everybody had known all along that the cities were sinfully bad, and good-government groups, or "goo-goos" as they were called, were organizing in the eighties and nineties to do what they could about the situation. It was a discouragingly Augean task, but Tammany Hall was temporarily unseated in 1894, and Chicago was under a reform government by the end of the century. In 1901 the industrialist Tom Johnson, converted to reform by Henry George's *Progress and Poverty*, became mayor of Cleveland, and during the next generation he made Cleveland a model for municipal reform nationally.

Urban reformers tended to find that the trail of corruption led to the statehouse, and sentiment for statewide reform was strong when Roosevelt took office in 1901. In that year Robert M. La Follette became governor of Wisconsin, and he launched the most ambitious program of state reform to be undertaken during the Progressive era. It included tax reforms, railroad controls, conservation measures, factory inspection procedures, a workman's compensation law, and various purely political measures such as the direct primary election for senators, which was expected to take politics out of the hands of the "interests" and place it in the hands of the "people." La Follette was followed, during the next decade, by Hiram Johnson in California, Charles Evans Hughes in New York, Woodrow Wilson in New Jersey, "Alfalfa Bill" Murray in Oklahoma, and additional Progressive reform governors in state after state.

PROGRESSIVE IDEOLOGY

Wisconsin Progressivism, in the extent of the state intervention which it entailed, represented the movement in its most radical form. Progressives actually were by no means united in their programs. They were united rather by a common background, which was mainly urban, middle-class, Protestant, and older-generation American, and by a common mood, which was righteously moral. Governments should be returned to the people, and the most popular devices by which it was hoped this would be achieved were the direct election of senators, in place of their election by state legislatures, and initiative and referendum measures, by which private citizens by petition could place reform measures on the ballot and vote them into law. During the first decade of the century laws such as these were passed in dozens of states, and in 1913 the

Seventeenth Amendment to the Constitution was passed, providing for the direct election of senators in all states.

Some Progressives hoped that these purely political reforms would be sufficient to reform the nation; others saw the need for social reforms to protect the individual against exploitation. Almost half the states had already passed laws limiting child labor by the end of the century, and others rapidly adopted them in the years thereafter. Laws limiting the number of working hours for women were passed by most states during the Progressive era, and fifteen states had passed minimum wage as well as maximum hours laws for women by the time the Supreme Court declared such laws to be unconstitutional in 1923 in the case of *Adkins v. Children's Hospital*. During the Progressive years most states passed accident insurance laws providing protection for workingmen and their families that had been altogether lacking under common law.

Progressives were brought to the support of these social reforms partly out of a sense of Christian duty and partly out of a fear of the alternative consequences of proletarian discontent. The Socialist party under the leadership of Eugene Debs was rising in popularity; it received 6 percent of the national vote in the presidential election of 1912, and Socialists were actually winning municipal elections in various parts of the country. A relatively moderate form of Christian socialism won in these local elections, rather than the class-warfare socialism of the revolutionary Marxians, but it frightened responsible citizens into doing something for the lower classes.

At the other end of the scale, the plutocracy had to be held to its responsibilities by the national government and deprived of the political control it had wrested from the people. Still, the Progressive movement occurred during times of prosperity, and the Progressives themselves wished to do nothing to disturb a system that was in good operating order. That the new order of finance capitalism was here to stay was conceded by many Progressives, including Roosevelt, but the directors of the great combinations must not say, "The public be damned," as William Vanderbilt had done. It was high time for the will of the people to assert itself through the government and place these giant corporations to some extent under public control in the interest of the general welfare.

When Roosevelt gave voice to this indignantly righteous but temperately middle-class point of view, he rallied the nation behind him and behind those Progressive tenets which were rather vaguely understood but most fervently believed in, "the principles of Theodore Roosevelt."

ROOSEVELT PROGRESSIVISM

During his second year in office T. R. made two dramatically original demonstrations of executive power, one in support of organized labor and the other in opposition to those two giants of Wall Street, Morgan and Rockefeller. In May

1902 the United Mine Workers struck for shorter hours and higher wages against the coal-mine owners. Comparatively weak and divided, the coal industry was unhappily spoken for by the president of the Reading Railroad, George F. Baer. Baer brought the scorn of the nation down on all the owners by declaring that the miners, whose working conditions were generally known to be dramatically wretched and lethal, would be protected "not by the labor agitators, but by the Christian men to whom God in His infinite wisdom has given control of the property interests of the country."

Against such a man and with no anarchists blowing anything up for the moment, the sober Bible-quoting president of the U.M.W., John Mitchell, was in a position unprecedented in American labor history: he might win the sympathy of the nation and thereby win the strike. As the strike lengthened toward winter and the mine operators refused to arbitrate, Roosevelt prepared to seize the mines and operate them. With the aid of Morgan and Hanna he then persuaded the operators to submit to a commission of arbitration, which decided in favor of a substantial wage increase and shortening of hours.

It was the first time the American government had intervened on the side of labor, and it was therefore a highly significant event in American history. Roosevelt never again intervened in such a manner, but his handling of that strike and the support of public opinion which he won for his novel prounion stand constituted a major event in the rise to power of organized labor in America.

Roosevelt simultaneously defeated the Wall Street behemoths in the Northern Securities case, successfully carrying through the courts an antitrust suit against a railroad combination arranged by the Morgan and Rockefeller groups. Exultant that "the most powerful men in this country were held to accountability before the law," Roosevelt went on to bring similar suits against other trusts, including Standard Oil and American Tobacco Company, both of which were ordered dissolved during his successor's administration. Although victory in the Northern Securities case won for Roosevelt the title of "trustbuster," it did not seriously alienate the bankers whose trusts he was busting. Morgan was sufficiently worried to make a trip to Washington, to the delight of Teddy and the nation, but he went away apparently satisfied that the President would do nothing seriously to disarrange the establishment.

Roosevelt's attack on Northern Securities has been criticized on the diverse grounds that, on the one hand, in selecting railroad trunk lines for his test case, he chose a form of industrial combination which was most obviously defensible as contributing to a smoothly operating transportation system and, on the other hand, that the victory was nearly meaningless, since the combination was thereafter effectively achieved by other means. And indeed, throughout both his administrations Roosevelt's attitude toward the trusts was thoroughly ambivalent. The political humorist Finley Peter Dunne described this attitude exactly when his Mr. Dooley said of Roosevelt, " 'The' thrusts' says he, 'are heejous monsthers built up by th' inlightened intherprise of th' men that have done so much to advance progress in our beloved counthry,' he says. 'On wan hand I wud stamp them undher fut; on th' other hand, not so fast.' " T. R. was torn between his highly popular public image as a trustbuster and his private conviction that these consolidations, though they should submit to a degree of government control, were inevitable and on the whole beneficial to society.

In 1904 Roosevelt ran for the Presidency against a conservative colorless Democrat, Judge Alton B. Parker, and won by a landslide. Then, having resuscitated the Sherman Antitrust Act in his first administration, he brought the Interstate Commerce Act to life in his second. In 1903 the Elkins Act had been passed, prohibiting the railroads from making rebates to customers and providing punishment for violations—an act which was both in the public interest and in the interest of the railroads themselves. In 1906 the Hepburn Act was passed, empowering the ICC to set maximum rates, and in 1910 the Mann-Elkins Act was passed, placing the burden of proof on the railroads themselves when they appealed the decision to the courts. Some objected that the Hepburn Act failed to place the commission in command of sufficient facts, but thousands of cases were quickly brought before it, and many rate reductions resulted.

In 1906 the Pure Food and Drug Act was passed, providing modest beginnings to a system of federal inspection. More important than any of these acts, probably, were Roosevelt's conservation activities. Acting under a Forest Reserve Act of 1891, he set aside many millions of acres of land as national forest areas and checked the encroachments on public lands which until that time had proceeded against only the most haphazard federal opposition.

In 1908 Roosevelt stood at the very height of his popularity. Mark Sullivan wrote that "the relation Roosevelt had to America at this time, the power he was able to wield, the prestige he enjoyed, the affection he received, the contentment of the people with him—their more than contentment, their zesty pleasure in him—composed the lot of an exceptionally fortunate monarch during a particularly happy period of his reign." Reelection would have been a near certainty, but Roosevelt honored an earlier pledge not to run again and selected his friend Secretary of War William Howard Taft to succeed him.

Taft defeated Bryan, running for the third and last time, and launched his administration as the appointed caretaker of Roosevelt Progressivism. Roosevelt went on extended travels abroad, and for the next few years his encounters with lions in Africa and emperors in Europe remained front-page news throughout the United States, along with the news of the continual troubles that President Taft was finding himself in.

THE TAFT ADMINISTRATION

Things went wrong for Taft from the beginning. Taking upon himself the responsibility for tariff reform, which Roosevelt had been shrewd enough to avoid, he called Congress into special session to reduce tariffs. Lobbyists and

Old Guard Republicans succeeded in blocking any major downward revisions, and when Taft signed the resulting Payne-Aldrich Tariff he broke with congressional Progressives, before he had been in office for six months.

Roosevelt as President had been a past master at appearing to hold more power than he actually held and at avoiding the confrontations that would reveal his vulnerability. According to Mark Sullivan, the basis of T. R.'s popularity had been "that he had, in the plain sight of the common man, presented spectacle after spectacle in which business, capital, corporate power, took off its hat in the presence of the symbol and spokesman of government." Actually Roosevelt had not been in a position to do this, and he had been careful to conciliate the men of Wall Street and to avoid open contests, such as tariff fights, with their representatives in the party and in Congress.

At the time Roosevelt had become President, Mark Hanna had been in firm control of the party, and he retained considerable authority until his death in 1904. Had Hanna lived a few months longer, he might have been in a position to block Roosevelt's renomination had he chosen to do so. After Hanna's death, Roosevelt gathered party power into his hands, but Congress was another matter.

For a generation after the Civil War, while Republicans held the Presidency except for Cleveland's two terms, Congress remained shakily balanced between the two parties. Then the Democrats suffered, first from Cleveland's depression of 1893 and second from the Cleveland-Bryan party split of 1896. Republicans gained a majority in both houses of Congress, and they remained in control of both houses when Taft took office.

In this period of Republican congressional ascendancy the party had created power systems in both houses that enabled it to control legislation against both the congressional Democrats and the Republican executives. In the Senate a group of four men maintained control through their committee chairmanships and their power over appointments. In the House Thomas B. Reed alone, as Speaker, held the power over appointments and determined the rules of procedure of the House. At the time Taft came to office, the Speaker was Joseph G. "Uncle Joe" Cannon, who had earned his reputation as the gruff guardian of the federal Treasury. Both men were very Old Guard.

During his first term Roosevelt received support from Western senators who were particularly attracted by his fight for conservation, reclamation, and irrigation measures. To this group were added by the end of Roosevelt's Presidency a vociferous block of Midwestern Progressives known as the insurgents, including La Follette of Wisconsin, Cummins of Iowa, Nelson of Minnesota, and Bristow of Kansas. By the time Taft arrived in office the insurgents were mobilizing for a contest with the Old Guard for control of the Senate, and in this struggle Taft would either have to be for them or against them.

Taft came to office with a distinguished record as a lawyer and public administrator, but he had never before run for political office, and his lack of political experience was an evident weakness in his dealings with Congress. His position was further weakened by his legalistic and sharply limited conception of the Presidency. Initiative, which had been so vigorously asserted from the White House in Roosevelt's time, returned to Congress, in part because that was where Taft thought it belonged constitutionally.

A friendly 350-pounder, Taft was personally offended by the "yelping and snorting" of the insurgents, and though he did not approve of the objectives of the Old Guard, he found their company more pleasant. Then, as the attack against him mounted, he found their support necessary. He nevertheless demonstrated a Progressivism that angered the Old Guard by supporting the Sixteenth Amendment to the Constitution, the income tax amendment. Passed by Congress during his first year in office and ratified by the states in his last, the income tax amendment proved in time to be one of the most momentous reforms of the entire era. Although he did not go far enough to please the insurgents, Taft further brought the displeasure of the Old Guard upon himself by advocating greater government controls over railroads and by instituting twice as many antitrust suits in one administration as Roosevelt had done in two. This increase in antitrust action made the Old Guard maddest of all, but even this failed to win Taft the insurgents' support, for they complained that the dissolved companies retained their unified control by appointing the same members to the boards of the technically competing companies.

The occasion for the irreconcilable breach between Taft and the insurgents was the Ballinger-Pinchot controversy. Richard A. Ballinger was Taft's Secretary of the Interior; Gifford Pinchot was chief forester in the government and T. R.'s trusted friend. Pinchot objected to the returning of Alaska land to the public domain and the selling of Alaskan coal land to a Morgan-Guggenheim syndicate. When Taft would not support Pinchot against Ballinger, Pinchot publicly denounced Ballinger, for which he was naturally dismissed from his government post.

It appears in retrospect that Taft was an able and conscientious conservationist, but Pinchot, "the Sir Galahad of the woodlands," persuaded the insurgents to the contrary, despite the findings of a joint congressional committee in Ballinger's favor. The Democratic Progressive lawyer Louis D. Brandeis made a brilliant case against the President and his Secretary of the Interior in the congressional hearing, and, more importantly, Roosevelt took Pinchot's side of the case. Roosevelt returned to America in 1910 and launched on a speaking campaign, including a speech at Osawatomie, Kansas, in which he called for a "new nationalism" of broad federal welfare programs, extended federal control over business, and implementation of direct democracy.

Roosevelt had not yet announced his candidacy for Taft's position, but he had announced his political program, and his loyal following had good reason to throw their support behind his candidacy. Robert La Follette of Wisconsin did not count himself among that following, however. In La Follette's opinion Roosevelt was merely "the ablest living interpreter of what I would call the superficial public sentiment of a given time, and he is spontaneous in his reactions to it." La Follette early made himself available as the insurgent candidate, and he received endorsements from many Progressives, a good many of whom, however, took the first opportunity to bolt to Roosevelt when he threw his hat in the ring in February 1912.

In the Republican convention that followed, the contest was between Roosevelt's tremendous popularity and Taft's and the Old Guard's organizational power. The convention was openly rigged, and Taft won on the first ballot. But even before the first ballot Roosevelt supporters were bolting the convention, and in August, at a convention of their own, to the tune of "Onward Christian Soldiers," they created the Progressive party. Roosevelt told them that they stood at Armageddon and battled for the Lord and also that he personally felt strong as a bull moose, and the Bull Moose Progressive party set out to win the election against Taft and whomever the Democrats might offer.

BIBLIOGRAPHY FOR CHAPTER 17

G. E. Mowry, The Era of Theodore Roosevelt, 1900–1912 (1958)
Arthur Link, Woodrow Wilson and the Progressive Era, 1910–1917 (1954)
E. P. Goldman, Rendezvous with Destiny: A History of Modern American Reform (1956)
Richard Hofstadter, The Age of Reform from Bryan to FDR (1955)
H. U. Faulkner, The Quest for Social Justice, 1898–1914 (1931)
R. H. Wiebe, Businessmen and Reform: A Study of the Progressive Movement (1962)
Gabriel Kolko, The Triumph of Conservatism: A Reinterpretation of American History, 1900–1916 (1963)
D. M. Chalmers, The Social and Political Ideas of the Muckrakers (1964)
A. F. Davis, Spearheads for Reform: The Social Settlements and the Progressive Movement, 1899–1914 (1967)
Roy Lubove, The Urban Community: Housing and Planning in the Progressive Era (1967)
August Meier, Negro Thought in America, 1880–1915 (1963)
Marc Karson, American Labor Unions and Politics, 1900–1918 (1958)
S. P. Hays, The Gospel of Efficiency: The Progressive Conservation Movement, 1890–1920 (1959)

CHAPTER 18

BIPARTISAN PROGRESSIVISM

THE ELECTION OF 1912

In choosing Governor Woodrow Wilson of New Jersey as its candidate, after a struggle that went for forty-six ballots, the Democratic party selected a candidate well calculated to unify a divided party. As usual, the Democrats were split between the rural Populist-Progressive wing led by William Jennings Bryan and the urban business-minded wing symbolized by Tammany Hall and Wall Street but drawing substantial support from Bourbon politicos in the Midwest and South.

Since the turn of the century the Democratic nomination had alternated between Bryan in 1900, the conservative New York judge Alton B. Parker in 1904, and Bryan in 1908, and in 1912 Parker was elected temporary chairman of the convention against the determined opposition of the Bryan forces. And in 1912 as in each of the preceding conventions, the memories of Cleveland's depression of '93 and the free-silver fiasco of '96 still burned. Bryan was adamant that the choice now should not be made by the urban East, and when Tammany Hall switched its votes to Speaker of the House Champ Clark from Missouri on the tenth ballot, Bryan switched his support from Clark to Wilson, who won thirty-six ballots later, mainly against Clark and the choice of the Southern wing, Oscar Underwood of Alabama.

Once nominated, Wilson presented himself, with entire justice, as a Southerner (from Virginia) with a Southern regard for states rights and simultaneously as the economically sound Progressive governor of an Eastern and urban-oriented state and also the chosen candidate of the champion of Western Progressivism, Bryan. That was not enough to recommend him to Tammany Hall, after some things he had done to the political bosses in New Jersey, but it was enough to heal the basic party division and give Wilson the victory in the three-cornered election.

A noteworthy fact of the election was that the three major candidates were all scholars as well as politicians, Taft specializing in jurisprudence, Roosevelt in American historical writing, and Wilson, with a Ph.D. from Johns Hopkins, in political science and specifically in American government. The most recent scholar of any distinction to become President prior to Roosevelt had been John Quincy Adams, and from that time on, the politicians seemed to have agreed that the White House was not the place for such persons. Roosevelt had never been intended by the political bosses to come to the Presidency, but in doing so, he set a precedent that changed the range of its character in the twentieth century, much as Jackson had changed it with his defeat of John Quincy Adams.

As befitted scholars in politics, the three contenders presented their arguments in the form of general ideas, and out of a contest chiefly waged between Roosevelt and Wilson two alternate lines of liberal argument developed that were to continue to divide liberal opinion in America down through the New Deal. Roosevelt presented the concept of modern liberalism which he had labeled "the new nationalism," having derived the term from his reading of Herbert Croly's *The Promise of American Life,* published in 1909, to which Wilson opposed a more traditionally American liberal concept that he termed "the new freedom."

Roosevelt's new nationalism was boldly outlined in the Progressive party platform, which endorsed a protective tariff, powerful federal regulatory commissions to control industry and guard the general welfare, and constitutional reforms, such as direct election of senators and initiative, referendum, and recall procedures, to facilitate direct democracy. Measures fulfilling two particular planks in the Progressive platform, one plank calling for a federal income tax and the other for direct election of senators, had already been sent to the states by Congress for ratification and became the Sixteenth and Seventeenth Amendments to the Constitution the next year.

Roosevelt's enthusiasm for Croly's book was an enthusiasm for a thesis regarding big business and big government that Roosevelt himself had long believed to be substantially true. In contrast to his reputation as the great trustbuster, Roosevelt as President had believed that the development of the great corporations, such as U.S. Steel, was a natural and generally beneficent tendency, the means by which material progress was working itself out, and he had long believed that a powerful Federal Bureau of Corporations might guide this evolutionary development in the public interest, whereas trustbusting remained a negative and perhaps destructive and probably largely useless approach to the problem.

Croly argued the fallacy of the American democratic idea of government by and for "the people" and of government dispensing equal justice to all. Practically speaking, society was made up, not of one people, but of numbers of conflicting interests, and it was the responsibility of the government to negotiate among them. Legislation on behalf of one interest group inevitably worked against another. Railroad regulation favored the customers at the expense of the carriers. Antitrust laws favored the small producers at the expense of the large producers. What modern democratic government required were the honest and dispassionate services of a dedicated and informed bureaucracy that would continuously mediate these conflicting interests for the good of the whole. Croly romantically believed that democracy is virtue.

Roosevelt, the squire of Oyster Bay, was not a city-bred politician, but he had served as police commissioner of New York City, and he had cultivated the acquaintance of urban muckrakers and reformers like Lincoln Steffens, Jacob Riis, and Jane Addams. Among these reformers, Addams was probably the most distinguished supporter of the Bull Moose party, and T. R. was in turn influenced by her to argue in favor of cultural pluralism: the freedom of immigrant groups to develop their traditional cultures in American society and the conviction that America would be enriched by this cultural diversity. When war broke out in Europe two years later, however, it was Roosevelt who led the attack against cultural pluralism, and it was he who coined the term "100 per cent Americanism" that the American Legion later adopted as its motto.

Roosevelt's criticism of trustbusting and his support of tariffs were welcome signs for Wall Street, and the Wall Street executive George Perkins was conspicuous among T. R.'s advisers and supporters. Others in the party were highly suspicious of Perkins, and it was later the contention of the young Bull Mooser Harold L. Ickes, who was to become Secretary of the Interior under Franklin D. Roosevelt, that Perkins and what he represented had destroyed the Progressive party. More obviously it was Roosevelt who destroyed it, by returning to the Republican party after losing the election and urging all other Progressive party men to do likewise. A good many of them instead switched to the party of Wilson, who as President became increasingly sympathetic to some of the leading new-nationalist ideas that Roosevelt had supported as presidential candidate.

The new freedom of the Virginian Woodrow Wilson was consciously Jeffersonian, with a Jeffersonian concern for individual liberty, equal opportunity, and local autonomy against the power of the state and the power of what the Jeffersonians had called "the monocrats" and the Progressives called "the interests." Wilson argued that once monopolies were permitted to establish themselves, they were able to put themselves beyond the power of government to control them. Accordingly he argued for "regulated competition" enforced by stringent antitrust laws as the only feasible means by which the government could control the interests on behalf of the people.

The outstanding intellectual in Wilson's camp, who certainly influenced Wilson as Croly never influenced Roosevelt, was Louis D. Brandeis, the corporation lawyer turned Progressive crusader. It was the contention of Brandeis that "a corporation may well be too large to be the most efficient instrument of production and of distribution, and . . . it may be too large to be tolerated among the people who desire to be free." In the era of finance capitalism he was the most sophisticated exponent of the antimonopoly argument that through the nineteenth century had been voiced by Jeffersonians, Jacksonians, Grangers, and Populists, and more conservatively by Liberal Republicans.

In the election Wilson won a large majority of electoral votes but only 41.82 percent of the popular vote, as compared to 27.45 for Roosevelt and 23.17 for Taft. The Democrats gained control of both houses of Congress, however, and Progressive Republicans joined Progressive Democrats to give Wilson a measure of bipartisan liberal support such as Roosevelt had never enjoyed as President. And Wilson, upon taking office, lost no time in making strikingly effective use of that support.

AMERICAN SOCIALISM

The election of 1912 was actually a four-cornered contest, with the Socialist candidate, Eugene V. Debs, receiving nearly 6 percent of the popular vote. That was more than twice his vote in the previous presidential election, and as things turned out, it was the high tide in the fortunes of the American Socialist party. Nobody knew at the time, however, that the party would not continue to grow as it had grown in the previous decade. To Progressives, Debs and the Socialist party represented the threat of a dreadful class conflict that might await the nation if it delayed too long in making social reforms. The paternalistic Progressives preferred to bestow benefits upon the lower classes rather than have the working classes grasp them for themselves, even though they might gain those benefits by entirely constitutional means.

Marxian socialism had been dismissed as disreputable doctrine by respectable Americans in the late nineteenth century. A Socialist Labor party had been organized in the year of the Great Railroad Strike, 1877, but it had represented no more than a small scattering of anarchists, syndicalists, and socialists until the Pullman strike of 1894 radicalized Debs and brought him to the leadership of American socialism. The American Socialist party was founded in 1901 under Debs's leadership, and as a presidential candidate he increased his showing from .67 percent of the popular vote in 1900 to 2.98 in 1904 and 2.83 in 1908 to 5.97 in 1912.

Debs had arrived at his socialist position, not by being persuaded by Marxian argument, but by having in practice experienced an inability to gain justice for the working man under the American capitalist system. He remained a radical reformer, rather than an ideological Marxist, and the Socialist party under his leadership naturally tended to reflect this pragmatic outlook. The party derived much support from reform-minded Protestant churches, and to that extent it took on the character of Christian socialism.

At the same time, the party drew a sizable portion of its following from the new immigration, as was indicated by the growing number of foreign-language units in the party. These recent immigrants tended to be better acquainted with Marxist doctrine than they were with American ways, and there developed an inevitable conflict within the party between the native and the foreign-born elements.

From the outset Debs's Socialist party was too conservative to suit some American radicals, and in 1905 these organized the Industrial Workers of the World under the leadership of William D. "Big Bill" Haywood. The I.W.W. advocated direct action, and it dedicated itself to the struggle which "must go on until the workers of the world organize as a class, take possession of the earth and machinery of production and abolish the wage system." Mainly active in Western mining and farming regions, the I.W.W. in 1912 attempted to organize textile workers in Paterson, New Jersey, and Lawrence, Massachusetts. For these and other reasons the radicals were worrying Progressives and conservatives in 1912. There were groups of anarchists in the major cities, and Emma Goldman, a magnetic personality, barnstormed the nation straining free-speech rights to the limit everywhere she went.

RADICAL INTELLECTUALS

Greenwich Village had long been a haven for artists and agitators, but it was in 1912, with the organization of the Liberal Club and the publication of the *Masses,* that it became a coherent national focal point for youth-oriented radical revolt. The Greenwich Village movement was dominated by upper-middle-class, college-educated, old-stock American youth, such as *Masses* editor Max Eastman and John Reed, the leading American champion after 1918 of Bolshevik communism. These young Americans were in revolt against their own Puritan-capitalist heritage. Joined to their "liberation movement" were Village artists and poets and writers, together with the social-settlement people in the orbit of Columbia University.

The Greenwich Village movement agitated for woman's rights, free love, socialism, anarchism, individual self-realization, Freudianism, cultural pluralism, the increased enjoyment of life and art, and whatever else was new and apparently worthwhile. It thought of itself, as the policy statement of the *Masses* declared, as being "frank, arrogant, impertinent, searching for the true causes . . . directed against rigidity and dogma wherever it is found. . . ." And it continued to gain strength, in cities throughout the nation as well as in New York, until America entered World War I and the lid was clamped on radicalism of all sorts.

The social workers within the Greenwich Village movement or on the fringes of it developed the argument for cultural pluralism, opposing the melting-pot concept of America as a place where the immigrants were expected to reform themselves into the already established old-stock image. And in addition to championing the rights of ethnic groups generally, they concerned themselves with the rights of Negroes in an increasingly racist America.

BLACK AMERICA

Harlem began to make its name as the black cultural capital of the nation as more and more Southern and West Indian blacks migrated to New York after the turn of the century and tended to settle in Harlem rather than to scatter around Manhattan as before. Concurrently, bohemian radicals and radical Progressives directed more and more attention to problems of race discrimination against Negroes. The National Association for the Advancement of Colored People was started in 1909, with W. E. B. Du Bois, Jane Addams, Franz Boas, John Dewey, and Oswald Garrison Villard among the founders, and the National Urban League was organized two years later. The most influential intellectual in this development was the Columbia anthropologist Franz Boas, whose studies of Harlem blacks, as well as other American ethnic groups, were serving to demolish the racial theories that until that time had been generally current among educated Americans.

In this advocacy of the rights of Negroes, the bohemians, the settlement workers, and the university professors were not speaking for the Progressive movement or much influencing it at the moment. They may have influenced Theodore Roosevelt, who had invited Booker T. Washington to the White House for lunch on one occasion. However, the indignant reaction to this from many of Roosevelt's Progressive followers had discouraged him from any further gestures of the kind, and in fact racial segregation in the federal government began while he was President.

The Progressive era was also the Jim Crow era, when blacks were methodically deprived of voting rights in the South and were increasingly forced to submit to segregation in housing, transportation, schools, and so on. The Jim Crow laws had not been passed immediately after the end to Reconstruction, but were rather the product of the national racialistic and imperialistic frame of mind near the turn of the century. Once begun, segregationist laws and practices extended through the North as well as the South. They had received the assent of the Supreme Court, which upheld segregationist practices by individuals in some civil rights cases in 1883 and upheld segregationist laws by states and municipalities in the case of *Plessy v. Ferguson* in 1896, effectively nullifying the legislation and constitutional amendments of the Reconstruction period in this respect.

From the mid-eighties until his death in 1915 Booker T. Washington remained the foremost leader of black America, with his program of separatism, accommodation to the demands of white America, and black economic progress through those agricultural and mechanical opportunities that remained open to blacks in a Jim Crow society. Washington was a Southerner, from Georgia and Alabama, whose program of accommodation had been dictated by the circumstances that confronted him in the Deep South. But in the course of the Progressive era Washington's program and leadership were increasingly challenged by Northern black intellectuals and radicals, of whom the most prominent was W. E. B. Du Bois, a Harvard Ph.D. from Massachusetts. Washington's policy may have been realistic in Georgia and Alabama, but it was hardly advanced enough for Northern black intellectuals, especially those in areas like Boston where the abolitionist tradition lingered on. Du Bois was among the original founders of the NAACP, and he soon became the most active figure in the organization, fighting for black civil rights on a basis of absolute equality with white. The Progressive era was an important period of transition in Negro thought and in the attitudes of radical white intellectuals toward black America and the race question, but white Progressive America was, as a whole, unaware of or influenced by these developments at the time.

WILSONIAN PROGRESSIVISM

Like Taft, Wilson was a learned authority on the Constitution, but unlike Taft, he had reached the conclusion that under the Constitution the President should provide Congress with forceful leadership. Like Taft also, except for his two years as governor of New Jersey, he was without political experience. His career had been that of a professor of political science at Princeton University and later president of Princeton. Temperamentally he was restrained, diffident, dogmatic, and self-righteous. If politics is the art of compromise, Wilson was as little suited to political life as any man who ever entered the Presidency.

It might therefore be supposed that this administration would have been marked by the same weaknesses that had marked those of such similarly touchy men as John Adams, John Quincy Adams, and, in the Confederacy, Jefferson Davis. Wilson, however, was a remarkably effective speaker with a gift for capturing national aspirations in striking phrases. In 1913, furthermore, despite his minority status as President, he had the support of a Democratic-controlled Congress backed by insurgent Republicans, and he launched his administration with a dazzling display of power in the field of tariff reform. Wilson appeared in person before Congress to present his tariff message, the first time since the eighteenth century that a President had done so. Congress responded with the Underwood Bill, which passed the House only to be altered past recognition under the influence of lobbyists in the Senate. Against them Wilson directed an eloquent attack, which Progressive senators supported with an inquiry into lobbying. The result was the Underwood-Simmons Tariff, incorporating the first significant tariff reduction since before the Civil War and a graduated income tax to compensate for the resulting losses in revenue.

The new tariff was followed by the Federal Reserve Act, creating the Federal Reserve Board, appointed by the President, with control over Federal Reserve banks in twelve districts throughout the nation. The Reserve banks were owned by all nationally chartered banks and by any state banks that chose to join by subscribing 6 percent of their capital. The Reserve banks did not themselves engage directly in banking, but operated only as agents of the member banks, to which they issued a new currency, Federal Reserve Bank notes.

A banking reform law had been passed in response to appeals from the banking community following the "bankers' panic" of 1907, when inelasticity of credit had forced major banking institutions to close down. But this Aldrich-Vreeland Act of 1908 had been viewed as only a temporary measure, and both parties had advocated further reforms in their 1912 platforms. The Federal Reserve Act brought heated attacks from bankers, mainly on the grounds that the Federal Reserve Board was placed in government hands instead of private ones. Within a decade, however, more than two-thirds of the banking resources of the nation had placed themselves under the new system.

In 1914 an act was passed establishing the Federal Trade Commission and giving it the authority to investigate industries engaged in interstate commerce for violations of antitrust laws and for "unfair" trade practices. Like the ICC, the FTC could resort to the courts if its orders were not obeyed. This act was followed by the Clayton Antitrust Act, which attempted to make explicit what had been left so vague in the Sherman Act. It prohibited a number of specific business practices, notably the interlocking directorates by which Standard Oil had retained its unity after dissolution by the courts. It prohibited price discrimination leading to monopoly. The Clayton Act further exempted labor unions from its provisions, although in purposely vague terms, and went on to prohibit court injunctions against strikers except where protection of property was involved.

Wilson considered his program to have been largely completed with the creation of the FTC, and he failed to give active support to the Clayton Act. Furthermore, he appointed bankers and businessmen to the Reserve Board and conciliatory men to the FTC. The continued prodding of the insurgents in the Senate led to the La Follette Seamen's Act in 1915, abolishing the crime of desertion in the merchant marine, but Progressivism appeared to be drifting into the past, as signs of a coming depression in 1914 brought Wilson, as they had Roosevelt in 1907, cautiously to closer cooperation with Wall Street.

As the election of 1916 approached, however, Wilson moved noticeably to the left, at the urging of important advisers, notably Bryan and Louis D. Brandeis. In that election year Congress passed the Federal Farm Loan Act authorizing loans to farmers through special farm loan banks which accepted farm property as security. It passed also the Adamson Act establishing an eight-hour day for workers on interstate railroads, the Keating-Owen Child-labor Act, government subsidies for various state programs, and the first major federal highway construction program. All these measures were passed with administration support. Having begun his first term as essentially a nineteenth-century liberal not very far removed from the Grover Cleveland school, Wilson appeared at the time of his campaign for reelection to be moving to the vanguard of radical Progressivism, with its emphasis on federal responsibility for the general welfare. Whether he could have achieved further reforms against growing opposition in both parties and whether he would have wished to do so, however, are both open to question.

END OF AN ERA

With Roosevelt back in the Republican party following his defeat in 1912, the reunited party in 1916 nominated for President the moderately Progressive Supreme Court justice Charles Evans Hughes. Wilson won reelection against Hughes by a large popular plurality, though he barely won in the electoral college. By that time the issues of domestic reform had been overshadowed by those of neutrality and the World War, and the peace vote went heavily to Wilson. Then, a month after his second term began, America entered the war, and the Progressive era came to a close.

The essential purpose of Progressivism had been to reaffirm traditional, preindustrial American assumptions of goodness and evil and to hold the machine age accountable to them. It had engaged in a variety of economic and political reform programs, but its fundamental concern had been with moral reform for the nation. Reviewing the era autobiographically in 1925, the Progressive reformer Frederic C. Howe remarked on how comprehensive and fundamental this force of moral principle had been to his generation.

> Early assumptions as to virtue and vice, goodness and evil remained in my mind long after I had tried to discard them. This is, I think, the most characteristic influence of my generation. It explains the nature of our reforms, the regulatory legislation in morals and economics, our belief in men rather than institutions and our messages to other peoples. Missionaries and battleships, anti-saloon leagues and Ku Klux Klans, Wilson and Santo Domingo are all a part of that evangelistic psychology that makes America what it is.

From the vantage point of the 1920s it could be seen that the Progressive efforts to make big business accountable to the people had substantially failed; for the regulatory agencies themselves had become the compliant servants of the business interests they were intended to control. The Supreme Court emasculated the laws that states had passed to guarantee decent working conditions for the laboring population, especially women and children. The state reforms aimed at placing political control in the hands of the people, such as initiative and referendum procedures and direct election of senators, all failed to carry out the intentions of the reformers.

Where Progressivism succeeded most significantly was in creating a climate of opinion in which the business world became aware that it possessed social responsibilities and in which social justice for people in all walks of life became a national ideal. The Progressive creed of social responsibility and justice was a paternalistic creed and by no means a generous one where black and ethnic America was concerned. Nevertheless, it represented a major reorientation of national values. In the national postwar reaction against Progressivism, the "dollar decade" of the 1920s did not revert to the irresponsibly individualistic social morality of the gilded age, and in the Great Depression this Progressive creed of the social obligation of government, of business, and of right-thinking people was its most important legacy to the New Deal.

BIBLIOGRAPHY FOR CHAPTER 18

See bibliography for Chapter 17.

CHAPTER 19

INTERVENTION, DEMOBILIZATION, ISOLATION

THE MEXICAN REVOLUTION

"**I**t would be the irony of fate," remarked Wilson, the scholarly authority on America's domestic politics, "if my administration had to deal chiefly with foreign affairs." Wilson's first experiences in the unfamiliar areas of diplomacy gave weight to his remark. Having denounced Roosevelt's policy of intervention in Latin America, he found himself soon doing the same. After extended and futile dealings with the Dominican Republic and Haiti, he sent in the Marines as Roosevelt and Taft had done before him. And though he had also denounced Taft's dollar diplomacy, he acquired rights in Nicaragua, through his Secretary of State Bryan, which in the interests of American business virtually reduced that country to an American protectorate. Then, faced with the continual crisis of the Mexican revolution throughout his administrations, Wilson involved himself more embarrassingly in the affairs of a Latin American nation than Roosevelt or Taft ever had done.

The Mexican revolution, beginning in 1910 under the leadership of the constitutional liberal Francisco Madero, succumbed to a counterrevolution and Madero's assassination in 1913 by Gen. Victoriano Huerta. Huerta was opposed by constitutionalists under the leadership of Venustiano Carranza, but his authority appeared established, and the nations of the world therefore extended recognition to his government. Wilson, however, against the demands of American business interests with a billion dollars worth of Mexican investments, withheld recognition on the grounds that the Huerta government did not rest upon law or upon the consent of the governed. In doing so, he established the novel "moral diplomacy," unknown in international law, which has since frequently guided America—during the twenties in the case of Soviet Russia, during the thirties in the case of the Japanese puppet state of Manchoukuo, and, until recently, in the case of Communist China—and which has remained a strange and annoying practice to other nations of the world.

When nonrecognition did not achieve a Mexican government Wilson approved of, he made a minor incident the pretext for the occupation of Veracruz. This bloody reprisal united all factions in Mexico against him, and Wilson was happy to be rescued from his difficulty by the offer of Argentina, Brazil, and Chile to arbitrate the disputes between the United States and Mexico. Subsequent raids on American soil by the Mexican bandit Pancho Villa invoked American retaliation, and a punitive American expedition found itself 300 miles inside Mexico. Formal recognition of the Carranza government in March 1917 came in time to help avert a war that was being demanded by many. Certainly Wilson's conduct toward Mexico had been high-handed. Nevertheless his acceptance of arbitration by the "ABC powers" was the first move toward the Pan-Americanization of the Monroe Doctrine which was the central tenet of the Good Neighbor policy as it developed during the 1930s.

WORLD WAR I
AND AMERICAN NEUTRALITY

After 1914 Wilson was necessarily distracted from his Latin American concerns by the war in Europe, which placed increasing strains on the simplicities of America's isolationist foreign policy and on the complexities of America's ethnic makeup. Americans knew little about the conditions leading up to the war, which broke out that summer, and news of it came as a surprise, but at the time it did not seem seriously likely to involve the United States. Europeans themselves assumed that it would be won by one side or the other within a matter of weeks or months, and Americans accepted that conclusion. As the war continued, however, it aroused increasingly disturbing loyalties and animosities in America and created increasingly perplexing problems concerning America's position as a neutral.

Although Wilson urged Americans to be impartial in thought as well as action, majority opinion in the United States tended to favor the Allies from the first, because of the predominantly Anglo-Saxon origins of the nation and because Germany had launched its main attack through neutral Belgium, in violation of treaty obligations. The British had a large measure of control over the means of communication to America, and they were much more skillful than the Germans in their propaganda activities; their accounts of German atrocities in Belgium later proved largely false, but at the time they were widely believed in America. On the other hand, there remained millions of Americans of German descent and millions more of Irish descent who naturally tended to oppose themselves to the Allied cause.

In the early stages of the war it was the English rather than the Germans who inspired official American protests, through their violations of the American conception of neutral rights. English and French naval power was early successful in laying down a blockade of the Central Powers against contraband, and

Britain then extended the definition of contraband to include virtually all important items of commerce. Beyond that, Britain asserted the right to take American and other neutral ships into Allied ports for examination, in violation of previous concepts of neutral rights under international law. These infringements on the rights of neutrals were met by repeated American protests, but trade with Germany in the meantime was dwindling to nearly nothing, while trade with the Allies was booming and rapidly bringing the United States out of the recession of 1914. Dependent on this growing trade for its continued prosperity, the United States was soon confronted with the fact that continuance of the trade could be made possible only by loans to the Allies, which would give them the capital to purchase from America. Faced with this prospect, the Wilson administration reversed its former policy and permitted the extension of private American loans to the Allies.

In 1915 the German government established a war area around the British Isles where enemy ships were destroyed by submarines without warning. Against the urgent advice of Secretary of State Bryan, Wilson insisted that Americans were within their neutral rights to travel on passenger vessels of belligerent nations. In May 1915 the British *Lusitania* was sunk with a loss of more than a thousand lives, including the lives of more than a hundred Americans. The American government sent notes of protest, one of which Bryan refused to sign on the grounds that it constituted virtually a threat of war. He was replaced by the pro-British Robert Lansing, and thereafter Wilson, to a greater extent than before, became his own Secretary of State.

American protests following further sinkings succeeded in altering the German policy of submarine warfare, and the elections of 1916 were held during a period of relative quiet in America's relations with the warring European nations. In January 1917, however, Germany announced its intention to sink all vessels within a prescribed war area, in the belief that although America would probably enter the war as a consequence, Britain could be starved into submission before American force could save it. Wilson responded by breaking diplomatic relations and authorizing the arming of American merchantmen.

In February British naval intelligence turned over to Wilson an intercepted message from German Foreign Secretary Arthur Zimmermann to the German Minister in Mexico instructing him to offer the Southwestern portion of the United States to Mexico in exchange for a military alliance, in the event that the United States went to war with Germany. In March Americans learned that Czarist Russia had been overthrown by a provisional republican government. As a consequence of this, they began to see the war as a struggle between the democracies, England, France, and Russia, and the autocracies, Germany and Austria-Hungary. On April 2, following the sinking of some American merchant ships by the Germans, Wilson went before Congress and, urging that "the world must be made safe for democracy," asked for a declaration of war, which was voted two days later by an overwhelming majority of both houses.

For two decades after the war disillusioned Americans argued hotly the questions of why America entered the war and who was to blame. The widely held assumption was that entrance had been a disastrous error based on a malign conspiracy. Many blamed the trickery of the British, and then, in the midthirties, a Senate committee headed by Gerald Nye reached the conclusion, widely believed at the time, that the purpose of American entrance had been to save the investments of American bankers and munitions manufacturers.

The weakness of this accusation rested in the lack of evidence that these groups exerted any influence upon Wilson, and upon the fact that Wilson in his foreign policy had consistently resisted the appeals of American businessmen with Mexican investments. Writers since World War II, while granting a general predisposition of the nation, and even more of the administration, in favor of the Allies, have tended to agree that American entrance into the war was decided most basically on the narrow grounds of violation of traditional conceptions of neutral rights, especially where those violations resulted in loss of life.

AMERICAN INTERVENTION

It turned out that the Germans made two errors in their calculated risk of unrestricted submarine warfare in 1917. They destroyed shipping to England on schedule, but England did not starve into submission as soon as the German timetable said it should. And the United States entered the war on schedule, but it armed itself and made its force felt much more rapidly than either the Germans or the Allies had anticipated. The French high command had hoped that, at the most, 500,000 American troops would be raised and sent to Europe; yet 4 million were in uniform at war's end, and 2 million of these were in France. These two errors lost Germany the war at a time when victory seemed almost certainly in its grasp.

Upon declaring war, the Congress of this mainly unarmed, polyglot, federal democracy immediately conferred upon its President wartime powers exceeding those of any of the leaders of its new allies. Wilson in turn delegated much of this new authority to the Council of National Defense, under which a series of boards were created that brought the national economy under dictatorial control. Chief among these agencies was the War Industries Board, directed by Bernard Baruch, which rationed materials, fixed prices and schedules, decided on all governmental purchases, and directed the conversion of peacetime industries to wartime production.

The Railroad Administration under the direction of Secretary of the Treasury William Gibbs McAdoo assumed control of the railroads of the nation and operated them as one unified system. The Emergency Fleet Corporation supervised the expansion and operation of the merchant marine. The Food Administration under Herbert Hoover fixed the price of food and allocated priorities to such good effect that the United States, while continuing to eat well, trebled its exports of foodstuffs and meat.

Thought control was entered upon by the government in a similarly centralized, efficient, and thoroughgoing manner. To some extent the government shared the German assumption that the mongrel character of American society would divide it along old-country lines, and against this possibility the Committee on Public Information launched a massive campaign to make Americans hate the "Hun." Mobilizing an army of sidewalk speakers and commandeering the audio-visual resources of the nation, this committee was immediately successful in converting the Germans in American eyes from a nation of home folks and music lovers to a depraved race of lustful killers. Beethoven and Mozart were banned for the duration. Sauerkraut became "liberty cabbage," wieners became "liberty sausage," and dachshunds became "liberty pups."

Congress passed the Espionage Act in 1917, making it a prison offense to discourage loyalty, and then passed the Sedition Act in 1918, providing imprisonment for people who spoke or wrote in an abusive way on any of a list of subjects, including the flag and the Constitution. About 1,500 persons were arrested under these laws, including the Socialist presidential candidate, Eugene Debs, and the Socialist congressman from Milwaukee, Victor Berger. The American Socialist party, on its side, increasingly dominated as it was by recent immigrants, had invited suppression by being the only major socialist party in the world, with the exception of the Russian Bolsheviks, not to support its own country in the war effort. In addition to these repressive acts on the part of the government, private groups throughout the nation did what they could to keep people with strange names or accents under control and see that they bought their full share of Liberty bonds.

The Wilson administration also appealed to the better nature of the American people. Wilson himself was the incomparable spokesman for libertarian ideals. The Fourteen Points, which he announced in January 1918 as the main goals of the war, made an enormous impression not only upon the American people but upon the entire world, strengthening the Allied sense of purpose while offering Germans and Austrians brilliant glimpses of the brighter side of their impending defeat. Beginning by calling for "open covenants openly arrived at" and ending by espousing the creation of a League of Nations, the Fourteen Points depicted a world lighted by the principles of peace, disarmament, free trade, and the national self-determination of all peoples.

The Allies desperately needed immediate naval and military support. America could do little for them at the moment on the battle line, but the American Navy, due mainly to the writings of Admiral Mahan and the activity of Roosevelt, was in good condition to attack German submarines and open the sea-lanes once again to starving England. The later troop transportations were carried through by the British and American navies so effectively that no American troopship was torpedoed on its way to Europe during the war.

The United States had learned enough from the pratfalls of the Spanish-American War to create a general staff for its army and to increase the army in size. Then the bipartisan demand for "preparedness" during the presidential campaign of 1916 had brought further results. When America entered the war, however, the combined strength of the army and the National Guard was still less than 400,000. A Selective Service Act was passed at once, and it went quietly and effectively into operation, in contrast to the violence and evasion that had met the Civil War draft laws.

It was only after the nation had entered the war that the government became aware of how close the Allies were to defeat, and a year of further preparation was required before substantial assistance could be rendered. In the spring of 1918, Communists having taken power in Russia and withdrawn that country from the war, Germany mounted a massive attack on the West, and "the race for France" began barely in time to turn defeat into victory for the Allies. Initially distributed among English and French armies, the American forces were later united under Gen. John J. Pershing. American troops launched successful counterattacks at the Battle of Belleau Wood in June and the Second Battle of the Marne in July. In September they participated in force in the Meuse-Argonne sector of the final offensive that brought the war to a conclusion, at a cost of more than 100,000 American lives.

THE VERSAILLES TREATY

The victors met at Versailles in January 1919, and among the members of this Paris Peace Conference Wilson was the one dominating figure. He represented the one major nation that was rising in military strength; the will to fight had been all but destroyed among those who had undergone the full four years of war. Wilson's idealistic plans for the postwar world had fired the imagination of people throughout the world, and although the Allies were not committed to these plans, they were necessarily the basis for the discussion of peace terms.

There were weaknesses in Wilson's position, however, which he failed to take properly into account. In the congressional elections of 1918 he had called for a Democratic mandate to carry him through the conclusion of the war and the establishment of the peace. The result had been a sweep of both houses of Congress by the Republicans. Wilson's failure to curry Republican support or even to take any prominent member of the Republican party to Paris with him was, under these circumstances, a disastrous act of political thoughtlessness. He was also misled in supposing that the adulation accorded him in Europe gave him the strength to speak to the peoples of Europe over the heads of their national representatives at the peace table. Elections had been held in England, and they had indicated a popular desire for revenge which the English Prime Minister Lloyd George was obliged to take into account.

The resulting treaty nevertheless was in accord with the Wilsonian proposals in a number of respects. An independent Poland was reconstituted, the Hapsburg monarchy was broken up into independent states created on ethnic grounds, so far as was possible, and boundaries were elsewhere rectified on the same basis. Above all else a League of Nations was created in response to what had been and remains a characteristically American ideal.

In return for these achievements Wilson naturally was forced to make compromises. He rashly upheld the first of his Fourteen Points, concerning open covenants openly arrived at, in the knowledge that secret covenants had already been made which bound the Allies to violate certain of the points. Italy had been promised the non-Italian port of Fiume as part of its price for entering the war. When the Italian Prime Minister Vittorio Orlando insisted upon it, Wilson had the presumption to appeal to the Italian people against him, with adverse results not only in Italy but also among the Italian-American population.

Wilson won on this issue at the conference, but Italy withdrew as a consequence, and at that moment in the proceedings Japan came forward with proposals that similarly violated Wilson's principle of self-determination. Unwilling to see a second major power depart from the peace table, Wilson acquiesced in Japanese designs on Chinese territory. The most blatant violation of the principle of self-determination was the establishment of an independent Austria, against the desire of its German-speaking people to annex themselves to Germany. But it was, after all, unthinkable that the price of defeat for Germany should have been the considerable increase of its size and power in Europe.

Wilson made other concessions to the European desire for revenge, including the huge reparations which Germany was forced to pay France and England into the indefinite future. These reparations were rationalized, furthermore, on the grounds, which German scholars were quick to prove historically untenable, that Germany had been solely responsible for the coming of the war. As he made one concession after another, Wilson came to place greater and greater importance upon the League of Nations, where the United States would be a leading member and where, when passions cooled, the injustices of the Paris Conference would be rectified.

THE LEAGUE OF NATIONS

Sentiment in the United States was apparently in favor of such a League, and more importantly, sentiment in the United States Senate was favorable. There were senators who were bitterly opposed, however, and they represented a growing host of Americans who disapproved of the peace treaty for various reasons. Americans of German, Irish, and Italian descent did not like it, and traditional isolationists, strong in the Midwest especially, wanted no part of the League of Nations.

In the Senate the fight against the treaty was led by the vindictive Henry Cabot Lodge, whose old friend Colonel Roosevelt had been deprived of the war leadership by Professor Wilson and who had himself lost the chance for the Presidency to which he had given much thought. Returning from Europe to fight for the treaty, Wilson was stricken with illness and sequestered in the White House. Isolated from the changing events, he insisted that the treaty be accepted by the Senate without the reservations demanded by Lodge and others. He succeeded in defeating the Lodge reservations, but the Senate, which certainly would have joined the League under some terms, failed to provide him with the two-thirds vote necessary to ratify the peace treaty. By a wide margin it was defeated, and the United States was set upon the isolationist course it doggedly followed for the next two decades.

World War II and the conditions of the world that survived it naturally changed the past in the minds of American scholars, and gave rise to new criticisms of Wilson's foreign policy. It is today generally argued that America's reason for entering the war was too narrow, on the one hand, and that its objectives once it was in the war were too broad, on the other. America entered the war on the grounds that through submarine warfare Germany had violated a conception of neutral rights which, while held by many Americans and other people, had no provable validity in international law. Then, once in the war, the United States made it a war "to make the world safe for democracy."

Critics have argued that American security before, during, and after the war depended upon the maintenance of a balance of power in Europe, and that this, therefore, should have been the reason for entering the war and also the guiding consideration at the peace table. Wilson and other members of his administration were aware that American security depended on the balance of power, but the American people were not, and would not have fought to maintain it. Wilson met this situation first with the legalism which has always touched a responsive chord with the American people and second with the visionary idealism of the Fourteen Points. The treaty itself was not such a harsh one, given the circumstances, but it disappointed millennial expectations in America and invited a national repudiation of Wilson and Wilsonian internationalism.

POSTWAR ISOLATION

Wilson tried to make the election of 1920 a referendum on the question of whether to join the League of Nations, but his efforts were frustrated by both major-party candidates, James Cox and Warren G. Harding, neither of whom committed himself clearly on the issue. Harding's landslide victory did not necessarily indicate a repudiation of the League, but it expressed a popular reaction against Wilsonian idealism. Following his victory, Harding settled the League question to the evident satisfaction of most people in his first message to Congress, by declaring that the United States would have nothing to do with it, and Secretary of State Charles Evans Hughes, a few years later, explained why. "The League of Nations," Hughes said, "by its constitution presupposed that peace could be maintained by economic pressure and military force." This, he said, was a dangerous error. The one true "Pathway of Peace" was through the uniting of the will of the peoples of the world in its favor and the maintaining of it through the process of agreement. Throughout the twenties, there remained dedicated champions of the League in America, but the argument of Hughes was generally acceptable, and the United States, signing a separate peace with Germany, went it alone.

The return with a vengeance to traditional isolation after the brief internationalist interlude was hurried along by America's emotional reaction to the war and to the terms of the Peace of Versailles. The postwar disillusionment, which expressed itself in American politics and literature as well as diplomacy, has remained something of a puzzlement to European observers, because the reaction appears disproportionate to the experience. In terms of actual war, of battle casualties and of spiritual exhaustion, the United States got off comparatively lightly, yet the revulsion against war sometimes seemed more universal and disillusionment with wartime idealism more complete in the United States than in the European nations which were ravaged by it.

Americans were convinced that they had been duped into joining a war which was no affair of theirs and then had been hornswoggled by their erstwhile associates at the peace table. They accepted as martyred prophets that "little band of willful men" who had held out first against entering the war and last against joining the League. Among these, Sen. William E. Borah of Idaho became the most forceful and influential spokesman for the new isolationism. Beyond refusing to meddle with the League, the United States refused also to join the World Court. Rather, it put forward its own peace plans in the Washington Conference of 1921 and the Kellogg-Briand Pact of 1928, both of them undertaken on the insistence of Senator Borah.

The Washington Conference was called to meet the problem of a naval arms race among nations that at the moment could not well afford one. So far as the United States was concerned, the main problem was presented by Japan, emerging more powerful than ever following the war, in the region of America's unarmed Philippine Islands. To the surprise of the delegates, Hughes, instead of opening the meeting with a formal observance of the amenities, launched at once into a detailed plan for the destruction of capital ships already built or in the process of construction by the major naval powers.

Naming the specific ships he had in mind to a total of sixty-six foreign and thirty American, Hughes won a disarmament victory unique in diplomatic history, whereby a ratio of 5 to 5 to 3 would be maintained between the United States, Britain, and Japan, with smaller ratios for Italy and France. Japan and other nations further agreed to abide by the Open Door policy of respecting the administrative and territorial integrity of China, the agreement that Hay had failed to obtain at the opening of the century. A separate treaty between the United States, Britain, Japan, and France provided for consultation in the case of future Far Eastern disputes. It was all a diplomatic success upon which Hughes might well congratulate himself, for the United States gave away nothing it wanted, but events were to prove that it was something less than the permanent solution to Asian affairs that Americans assumed it to be.

The Kellogg-Briand Pact of 1928 was entered into without enthusiasm by the French Premier Aristide Briand, who really wanted binding military commitments from the United States against a resurgent Germany. What developed eventually was a promise that most of the nations of the world signed to renounce war as an instrument of national policy except in self-defense. And that, in the minds of Americans, settled that problem.

More seriously damaging to international relations than the American faith in a "parchment peace" was America's unwillingness to adjust to its new role as the financial center of the world. Through its history down to World War I, American economic development had been financed by foreign investments, which America had paid for by exporting more than it imported. The war reversed this situation by turning the United States into a creditor nation, faced with the necessity of importing more than it exported in order to export the dollars necessary for the repayment of debts owed to it by other nations.

It would have been difficult enough for Americans—especially American farmers—to make the wrenching adjustments necessary to meet this new situation, but the government refused even to acknowledge that the situation existed. Instead of inviting greater imports, it passed the Fordney-McCumber Tariff in 1922, substantially reenacting the Payne-Aldrich Tariff of 1909 with a number of additions; then in 1930 the climax in American tariff history was reached with the Hawley-Smoot Act, passed over the protests of thirty-four nations. In 1924, with the Allies unable to pay their American debts and the Germans unable to pay their reparations to the Allies, the Dawes Plan was instituted, whereby the United States loaned money to Germany with which Germany paid reparations to the Allies with which the Allies paid interest on their American debts. American capital, meanwhile, was colonizing Europe as well as most of the rest of the world, helping to prepare the way for world depression when Americans withdrew their foreign investments following the crash of 1929.

THE GREAT RED SCARE

"Once lead this people into war," Wilson allegedly said on the eve of his war message to Congress, "and they'll forget there ever was such a thing as tolerance." Conformity would be the only virtue, and every man who refused to conform would have to pay the penalty. Wilson then proceeded to carry out his prophecy through the Committee on Public Information and enforcement of the Sedition and Espionage Acts. The administration mobilized public opinion all too effectively for the good of the nation, for when the war came to an end, the reconversion of public opinion to peacetime purposes was not so readily achieved. The Wilson administration, which had begun with the new freedom, ended with the Great Red Scare.

The democratic Russian revolution of the spring of 1917 gave way to the Bolshevik revolution in the fall, and the triumph of communism in Russia was followed by a call for world revolution and the organization of the American Communist party. In 1919 a series of mysterious bombings took place, and postal clerks discovered three dozen bombs addressed to important persons in business and political life. In 1920 a bomb was exploded on Wall Street, killing thirty-eight persons. The persons responsible for most of these bombings were never discovered, and there was no evidence of Communist complicity, but to many Americans it appeared that the proletarian revolution was at hand and that the most stringent measures should be taken to defend Americanism.

The main sufferers from the Great Red Scare were the labor unions, strengthened in membership during the war and awaiting peace to strike for better terms. During the war Samuel Gompers, serving as a member of the Council of National Defense, had pledged labor not to strike if the war were not made the means by which labor was exploited. Collective bargaining was assured labor in return, and various war labor boards were created to settle disputes. The result was that organized labor did make substantial gains in real wages and even greater gains in membership. AFL membership rose from 2 million in 1915 to more than 4 million in 1919. The gains in real wages had lagged behind the gains received by industry and agriculture, however, and in 1919, with the wartime restraints removed, the unions went out on strike. More than thirty-five hundred strikes took place that year, the biggest ones being those called by United Mine Workers and by nonunion U.S. Steel workers. At the time, half of the steelworkers still worked a twelve-hour day and a seven-day week.

The strikes and the bombings occurred during the same period, and businessmen, while genuinely fearing a Red insurrection, saw that the Red scare might well be worked to their own advantage. Their ideal was the "American plan," by which they meant either the open shop or the substitution of management-controlled company unions for independent labor unions. The Wilson administration had been by far the most prolabor administration in the nation's history, but in Wilson's formerly prolabor Attorney General A. Mitchell Palmer the businessmen had a doughty supporter.

Abetted by Palmer, the steel industry was able to associate the steel strike with Red radicalism in the public mind and defeat it absolutely. Management in the coal industry followed, in the U.M.W. strike, with the charge that the conservative John L. Lewis and his United Mine Workers were being directed by Moscow, and Palmer halted the strike by an injunction. The strikers ignored the injunction and eventually received substantial raises in pay. The times were against the unions, however. AFL membership dropped by more than a million during the next three years, and the company unions gained in membership throughout the twenties, aided by open support from government agencies such as the Railroad Labor Board.

Palmer launched a nationwide Red hunt, rounding up thousands of suspects and establishing himself momentarily as a national hero. His hopes for the Democratic presidential nomination were defeated, however, when many of his arrests proved to be on false grounds and when his warnings of a May Day rising were followed by nothing. The Red scare was over by the election of 1920, but the allied hatred and suspicion of foreign-born Americans was not appeased until passage of the National Origins Act of 1924.

IMMIGRATION RESTRICTION

The first Literacy Test Bill, designed to curtail the great new immigration that had started in the 1880s, had passed Congress in 1897 and had been vetoed by President Cleveland, and thereafter similar bills had been vetoed by Taft and Wilson. But in 1917 Congress passed a Literacy Test Bill over Wilson's veto. Wilson had been hardly more anxious than the congressional majority to permit the massive immigration from southern and Eastern Europe to continue, but by the time he became President spokesmen for ethnic voting blocs compelled him to oppose any comprehensive restriction measure. In 1907 the new immigration reached an all-time high of nearly a million, and in that year the German-American Alliance and the Ancient Order of Hibernians signed an agreement to oppose all restriction in order to protect continued German and Irish immigration.

The wartime agitation for "Americanism" and against "hyphenated Americanism"—especially German-American "hyphenism"—moved Congress beyond the new Literacy Test Law to the Quota Law of 1921. This act limited annual immigration from any nation to 3 percent of persons of that national origin residing in America in 1910, restricting total immigration to about 350,000. But this failed to satisfy the restrictionists, and in 1924 they secured the National Origins Act, which reduced the quota to 2 percent and based it on the 1890 census, before the new immigration had established itself in America, instead of the 1910 census.

JAPANESE-AMERICANS

Together with the National Origins Act, Congress passed the Japanese Exclusion Act to eliminate the small quota the Japanese would have been allotted under the general immigration law. The Exclusion Act was an episode in the violent history of West Coast oriental-American relations that began with the arrival of Chinese in the gold-rush era. The mere presence of Chinese had aroused racial animosities among the Americans, and these had increased with the importance of the Chinese as a labor force in the Far West. They had built the railroads, and afterwards they stayed on and engaged in farm work for lower wages than whites would accept. The Chinese were also adept business-men, and the pressure of their competition grew ever more painful to Western proprietors of small businesses.

There were riots and lynchings, and California politics became absorbed with the "yellow peril" in the late 1870s, and in 1882, with the help nationally of the Knights of Labor, the Chinese Exclusion Act passed into law. Thereafter the Chinese-American population declined from 107,000—it was down to 75,000 in 1930—and in the early years of the twentieth century anti-Chinese sentiment had subsided and was making way for anti-Japanese agitation.

About 25,000 Japanese had immigrated to the United States by 1900, and the momentum of this immigration picked up rapidly during the next decade. These Japanese were farmers, and in truck farming and gardening it proved impossible for Americans to compete with them. They were conspicuously neat and clean and honest and polite, and they trained their children to obey the teacher in school and learn to be good Americans. But they were an alien race, clannish and secretive, and like the Chinese they held religious beliefs that, from the American Christian point of view, were heathen. And with the Japa-nese as with the Chinese, the Californians feared that they were on the verge of being overwhelmed by massive waves of immigrants from the immeasurably vast Orient.

The Gentleman's Agreement of 1907 had both ended Japanese children's segregation in the San Francisco school system and restricted passports to America for Japanese laborers. But several years later California passed laws prohibiting Japanese immigrants from owning land. The Japanese government kept to the Gentleman's Agreement, but Japanese-Americans raised large fam-ilies, and the growing Japanese-American population convinced many that heavy immigration was continuing.

This obsession with the Japanese-Americans was a West Coast obsession rather than a national one, except that nationally there was concern over the expansion of the Japanese empire in Asia. American responsibility for the Phil-ippine Islands greatly increased this concern. In this context, Japanese immigra-tion was viewed as Japanese infiltration, and to many Americans the Japa-nese Exclusion Act was justified on this ground. Meanwhile Japanese had settled in the Hawaiian Islands until they far outnumbered the white Americans and became the dominant ethnic group, without arousing the fears that far fewer Japanese immigrants had aroused in California.

BIBLIOGRAPHY FOR
CHAPTER 19

Harley Notter, The Origins of the Foreign Policy of Woodrow Wilson (1937)
Arthur Link, Wilson the Diplomatist (1957)
D. M. Smith, The Great Departure: The United States and World War I, 1914–1920 (1965)
E. R. May, The World War and American Isolation, 1914–1917 (1959)
H. G. Peterson and **G. C. Fite,** Opponents of War, 1917–1918 (1957)
S. W. Livermore, Politics Is Adjourned (1966)—wartime politics
Selig Adler, The Isolationist Impulse (1957)
N. G. Levin, Jr., Woodrow Wilson and World Politics (1968)
R. A. Stone, ed., Wilson and the League of Nations (1967)
L. E. Ellis, Republican Foreign Policy, 1921–1933 (1968)
R. H. Ferrell, American Diplomacy in the Great Depression (1957)

CHAPTER 20

NORMALCY AND ABNORMALCY

WOMAN SUFFRAGE AND THE ELECTION OF 1920

The handsome and affable Warren G. Harding was an enormous relief to the American people after eight years under the Presidency of the Puritan professor. Wilson may have wished to make the League of Nations the main issue in the election of 1920, but the ailing President had lost control of his party, and the American people were concerned about other matters such as prohibition, immigration restriction, and the Chicago White Sox scandals. The Democratic nominee, Gov. James M. Cox of Ohio, though he himself favored the League, was the choice of the machine politicians rather than of Wilson. Cox's running mate was Franklin D. Roosevelt. The Republican party bosses selected the little-known Senator Harding of Ohio and, avoiding all issues, including the issue of the League, carried him to the most resounding victory in the history of popular presidential elections up to that time. For Vice President the Republicans nominated Gov. Calvin Coolidge of Massachusetts.

The election of 1920 was the first one to be held under the Nineteenth Amendment to the Constitution, passed the year before, extending the vote to women. Success had come to the woman-suffrage movement, after three quarters of a century of struggle, largely on the basis of the growing support it received from reform and church groups. These groups had been impressed by the effectiveness of women, especially through the Women's Christian Temperance Union, in the campaign for prohibition, and they had reasoned that if women were given the vote, they would bring virtue to American political life. It was therefore ironic that the first administration to be voted for by the women should have been one of the most corrupt in American history.

Historians, most of whom are men, have generally concluded that the woman-suffrage amendment has had little effect on politics. The presidential election statistics, however, do not bear this out. Down to 1920 the landslide elections of Jackson and Roosevelt were unusual, the vote generally being rather evenly distributed between the two major parties. From 1920 on, however, the landslide election has been normal, and it appears that woman suffrage is mainly responsible for this. Women are apparently less controlled by party loyalty than men and more apt to vote for the individual candidate regardless of party considerations. This was especially evident in the 1950s when the wives of labor-union men defected from the Democratic party to vote for Dwight D. Eisenhower.

THE HARDING ADMINISTRATION

Harding caught the spirit of the times and contributed a new word to the language when he declared that "America's present need is not heroics but healing; not nostrums but normalcy; not revolution but restoration." It was evidently Harding's intention to return the nation politically to the by then golden age of William McKinley in the days before the reformers had taken over. But Harding already had been overtaken by events. The war had gone beyond a nullification of the Progressive reforms to place big business more thoroughly in control of the nation than ever before. It had been the businessmen who had directed the War Industries Board and the other wartime agencies, and the politics of the home front had necessarily been those which served the interests of the most powerful elements in the various industries.

As Wilson himself had predicted, the war had placed the government at the mercy of the business community, and advantage had naturally been taken of this situation. During the four years of the war the number of Americans with annual incomes in excess of $50,000 had more than doubled, and industrial consolidation had been given government assistance for the purpose of creating more effective war machinery. Farmers also had profited greatly from wartime markets, with the bad result in their case that they overextended themselves and prepared the way for depressed farm conditions in the twenties.

Harding made some distinguished appointments to his Cabinet, including Herbert Hoover as Secretary of Commerce, Andrew Mellon as Secretary of the Treasury, Charles Evans Hughes as Secretary of State, and Henry C. Wallace as Secretary of Agriculture. Other appointments, however, were handed out to what came to be known as the "Ohio gang" of boon friends whom Harding liked to bum around with in the White House. From the outset Harding was audibly baffled by his duties, and his friends set out at once to capitalize on his incompetence.

His political manager, Harry Daugherty, was made Attorney General and allegedly set forth to feather his nest by fixing cases involving the Department of Justice. Charles Forbes, a former army deserter, was made head of the Veterans' Bureau, and he cost the government about a quarter of a billion dollars in thefts. In what became known as the Teapot Dome scandal, Secretary of the Interior Albert B. Fall made hundreds of thousands of dollars leasing government oil lands in Wyoming and California on the sly. Increasingly aware of the corruption that surrounded him and borne down by the burdens of office, Harding died in August 1923, before the scandals had become known to the nation, and Vice President Calvin Coolidge became the Chief Executive.

PARTY POLITICS, 1924 AND 1928

An honest, shrewd, thrifty, narrow-minded Yankee, President Coolidge said and did little. He was at his most active in issuing vetoes of legislation passed by Congress. Coolidge retained the able and honest members of the Cabinet to give the administration as much luster as it wanted; the dishonest ones went out, some of them to jail. As a consequence, to the chagrin of the Democrats, the Republican party was standing in a perfect posture of probity by the election year of 1924. Coolidge, who had come to symbolize prosperity and the American Way, won the Republican nomination as a matter of course, and the Democrats, who had depended on the corruption issue, could think of no good alternate issue—at least none upon which the party itself could agree.

The Democratic party, normally the more disheveled of the two parties, was in worse disarray in 1924 than at any time since the silver campaign in 1896. Two issues, prohibition and Catholicism, divided the party, with the rural, old-American Democrats standing behind William Gibbs McAdoo and the urban, recent-immigrant Democrats lined up behind Gov. Al Smith of New York. The struggle between the Protestant dry McAdoo and the Catholic wet Smith went for 103 ballots, and then the party compromised on a J. P. Morgan lawyer, John W. Davis.

There were many in the country who did not like what the Republican administration stood for and who at the same time had the sense to see that the Democrats that year stood for nothing. These malcontents included farmers, who were not sharing well in the prosperity, labor-union men, who did not fit quite anywhere in the American Way, and old-line Progressives yearning for the old campaigns. These people created a new Progressive party, nominated fighting Bob La Follette of Wisconsin, and ran on a platform of farm-labor reform, although labor-union support weakened as the election approached. The result was a landslide for Coolidge over Davis, with La Follette gaining 16.5 percent of the vote.

In 1928 the Democrats returned with the same sorry division in the ranks but also with Smith's followers determined that their Irish-American hero from the sidewalks of New York this time should not be denied. The Protestant-dry faction succumbed rather than repeat the previous performance; with little hope of victory under any circumstances, it permitted the nomination to go to Smith.

The Republicans still had prosperity on their side and, beyond that, Secretary of Commerce Hoover as their tremendously popular candidate.

The result was a foregone conclusion. After a bitter campaign waged over the religious issue, Hoover won by a landslide. He broke the Solid South for the first time since the Civil War. But Smith's candidacy brought the major cities of the North to the side of the Democratic party, also for the first time since the Civil War. In that respect Smith's campaign was an important step in the process whereby the Democratic party emerged once again, after three quarters of a century, as the indisputably dominant party in the nation.

HOOVER REPUBLICANISM

Harding had made the most famous statement of Republican policy in 1920, when he had declared that "what we want in America is less government in business and more business in government." The remark expressed a conviction which was held more fervently by Coolidge than it had been by Harding. During the Coolidge administrations it became a clearly formulated ideology, and Secretary of Commerce Hoover became its chief philosopher.

The post of Secretary of Commerce had been hardly more than an honorary one until Hoover took it over, but during his tenure it became the most active and formative of all the Cabinet positions. Indeed it is probable that Hoover did more to direct the nation's course as Secretary of Commerce than Coolidge did as President. At the center of Hoover's program was the trade-association movement, wherein the firms within an industry would use the Commerce Department as a central clearing office to pool ideas and patents, standardize and simplify production methods and articles of manufacture, and indirectly— although this was not Hoover's intention altogether—reach agreements concerning markets, wages, and prices. Hoover believed that competition was wasteful and that a lot of it ought to be abolished. It was of the utmost importance to him, however, that the trade associations be voluntary and self-directed. Government coercion, in his view, would have meant an end to liberty, whereas "industrial self-government" was the model of free government. The result was a continuation of the process that the war had encouraged of ever-increasing industrial consolidations, benignly assisted by the ICC and FTC that had been created to defend the nation against them. The creation of circumstances that would be favorable to the small businessman was one of Hoover's prime intentions, but one of the most basic results of the trade-association movement was increased authority of big business over its smaller competitors. Harding had appointed as Secretary of the Treasury one of the three or four richest men in the country, Andrew Mellon of the aluminum monopoly, who won the unstinted admiration of Coolidge and Hoover and who devoted his career in office to freeing the rich from the tyranny of taxation. Initially Mellon was checked by insurgents in the Senate, but some reductions were made in

1921 and 1924, and then in 1926 the Revenue Act was passed slashing taxes. In 1928 further tax reductions virtually nullified the tax system of the Wilson administration.

The Supreme Court, meanwhile, worked to obliterate remnants of Progressivism which could not be reached by congressional enactment or Presidential appointment. Against labor unions, the Court in 1915 had upheld the yellow-dog contract, making the promise not to join a union a condition of employment. Then, in a series of decisions, the Court stripped unions of protection they thought they had received in the Clayton Act. In *Hammer v. Dagenhart* in 1918 it declared the Child-labor Law to be an unconstitutional extension of the commerce clause of the Constitution, and in *Adkins v. Children's Hospital* in 1923 it outlawed a minimum wage law for women in Washington, D.C.

THE FARM BLOC

The farmers retained strength in the state legislatures and in Congress, and they did battle throughout the twenties with the business governments. Wilson's farm program had created the conditions out of which emerged the Farm Bureau Federation, which during 1921 helped to organize the "farm bloc" of senators from rural states and congressmen from rural areas. With farm acreage actually declining and the farmers' share of the national income dwindling rapidly, the agrarians came at last to see themselves as a special interest group rather than as the true representatives of the American majority. Organizing on this basis, they were able to achieve much by their congressional strength.

The farmers had gained heavily during the Wilson administration and during the war, but they suffered during the recession of 1921. Corn, wheat, and cotton farming remained in a markedly depressed state throughout the twenties. And the farmers generally did not share in the rapid economic progress of the industrial areas, nor did farm prices rise behind tariff barriers as did prices of the manufactured goods which the farmers, in common with others, wanted. To meet the farmers' problems, the farm bloc in the early twenties pressed successfully for a series of enactments increasing their credit facilities, exempting farm cooperatives from antitrust suits, and placing the middleman with whom the farmer dealt under governmental scrutiny.

The farm bloc failed, however, in its major effort to achieve the McNary-Haugen plan, whereby the government would raise farm prices by purchasing at home and dumping abroad. Coolidge vetoed this measure twice following its passage through Congress. Defective in its failure to provide for production controls, the McNary-Haugen Bill developed some of the ideas and the leadership which finally triumphed with the agricultural program of the New Deal. Two days after Coolidge vetoed the McNary-Haugen Bill, he increased the pig-iron tariff by 50 percent, thereby permitting a price rise of 50 cents per ton. In the view of his administration, government would take care of business alone, and business would take care of the nation.

SCIENTIFIC MANAGEMENT AND MASS PRODUCTION

From the days when the Puritans first established a New Zion in the wilderness Americans have always had a message for the world, and the profane world of postwar America was no exception. Turning from the crusade to create a pure Christian democracy, the twenties preached the gospel of the American Way. Probably most Americans in that decade were convinced that the chief contribution of the United States to civilization lay in its achievements in the field of business enterprise. Nor were Americans by any means alone in this thought. Teams of experts came from the corners of the earth to see how this miracle had been achieved. The Germans coined a word for it, "Fordismus." In Russia, it was said, Henry Ford was honored above all other foreigners. Of all America's messages this is the one which has been most eagerly received by the world.

Mass production was the key to the American Way. Ford said much too much for himself when he claimed to have invented mass production, but certainly he ranks as one of its master creators. The distinct contribution generally credited to Ford is the moving assembly line, with its revolutionary change of factory organization. Beyond that, Ford was a tireless tinkerer searching for improved methods, whether in minor details or on such a scale as would require the scrapping of a factory. And it was Ford who possessed the democratic vision of a nation of car owners and who devoted his life to producing automobiles for the masses.

Scientific management, or Taylorism as it was called after its chief originator, Frederick W. Taylor, established itself in the twenties and worked production miracles for American business. Taylor, a shop foreman during the late nineteenth century, had been struck by the tremendous losses factories sustained because of the settled opposition which existed between labor and management and the tendency of the worker to do as little as possible for his pay. The fault, Taylor argued, rested with management. It was the responsibility of management to know plant operations to the last detail so that it could instruct each worker on the most efficient method of carrying out his task and then could measure his work by exact standards. Beyond that, incentive pay would encourage the worker to increase his productivity. Scientific management might well double the value of a factory, or of the industry of a nation, and all might benefit accordingly.

Like Ford a tireless tinkerer, Taylor put his system into effect at Bethlehem Steel Company with spectacular success, yet he was slow in gaining support from industry as a whole. His tinkering upset routine. Labor was suspicious of Taylorism and rightly so. During the twenties scientific management resulted in great increases in the national income, but the stockholders and executives benefited from the speedup systems much more than the working force. And an important aspect of scientific management, as it was understood in the twenties, was the company union, which was on the verge of overtaking the declining AFL in total membership when the Great Depression struck.

Basic to the new prosperity, which exceeded anything that had ever been known anywhere in the world, were the increasing use of gasoline and electricity in place of steam power and the development of new articles of manufacture based on these sources of energy. The rapid supplanting of the railroad for many purposes by automobiles, trucks, and buses further vastly improved the transportation system, facilitating the distribution of the new mass-produced goods. And protected by high tariffs, American business enjoyed a domestic market that was not remotely rivaled elsewhere in the world. In 1929 the national income of the United States was far greater than that of all the other major industrial nations of the world combined.

Of all the new industries the automobile was most important to the material progress of the twenties. From an annual production of four thousand in 1900, the output of automobiles had increased to more than four million annually by the close of the twenties. At the opening of the century the automobile had been the rich man's plaything, which Wilson thought was doing more than anything else to stir socialistic discontent among the masses. But in 1914 Ford, driven by the vision of the common man's car, was assembling Model T Fords in the space of an hour and a half, at a cost within the reach of the average American skilled workman.

Where Ford led, General Motors followed in the twenties with the Chevrolet, while the more expensive cars came to be similarly mass-produced. The automobile was the symbol of America, and the factory parking lot filled with workingmen's cars was one of the most startling attractions America offered to foreign visitors. The production of oil increased sixteen times and that of iron and steel five times during the first three decades of the century.

As the use of electricity increased, its uses proliferated. The twenties experienced the first popular use of electric appliances: stoves, refrigerators, toasters, vacuum cleaners, irons, and radios. The number of telephones in the nation doubled between 1915 and 1930 to more than twenty million. The American chemical industry, a more recent development, experienced an even more rapid expansion. The war drove the government to producing potash, nitrates, and dyes which formerly had been imported from abroad, the most notable achievement being the construction of the chemical plant at Muscle Shoals in the Tennessee Valley. Synthetics became the basis for major new industries in the twenties, including Bakelite, rayon, and cellophane.

MASS PRODUCTION
AND DEMOCRACY

Socially, the material progress of the twenties was a profoundly democratizing force. Although the rich got richer faster, it was the increased wealth of the working classes that resulted in the much more momentous alterations in the character of society. American workers, whose real wages had remained almost unchanged during the Progressive era, saw their purchasing power rise rapidly in the twenties while their workweek tended to decline. U.S. Steel reduced its working day from twelve to eight hours in 1923, and Ford introduced the five-day week in 1926.

The equalitarianism of mass production and standard brands was also introduced. The graded differences in machine-made clothing did not display differences in wealth so clearly as contrast between the tailor-made and the homespun had. Even though he could not afford the custom-made possessions of the rich man, the average man could have his own car and his own radio. The new inventions and production methods brought to society as a whole inexpensive forms of diversion in the radio, the phonograph, and the movies.

This tendency toward social democratization owed much to the fact that immigration restriction took place at the same time that domestic laborsaving devices became widely available. The very rich might still be able to afford a retinue of servants at higher wages from the declining supply. The middling groups in society, even though they were improving themselves economically, found that they no longer could afford a staff of three or four servants, but they also found that they could very handily supplant all but perhaps one servant by introducing household appliances and by moving to smaller houses or to apartments.

Wars have tended to improve the position of women in American society, and World War I was no exception. Just as the Civil War was the occasion for the entrance of women into teaching on a large scale, so World War I was the occasion for their invasion of secretarial jobs, and the twenties provided ever-widening opportunities for women to work in a variety of fields.

MANNERS AND MORALS

During the two decades between 1910 and 1930 the urban population of the nation rose from 46 percent to 56 percent, and women's skirts rose from the ankle to the knee. The number of inches between the hemline and the ankle was rightly taken as the index of the revolutionary change in morals and manners that accompanied and followed World War I, and responsible elements moved to check the revolution by putting women back into their old clothes. Fashion writers warned that the American woman had ''lifted her skirts beyond any modest limitation" and decreed that she should drop them the next year. The YWCA issued a national "Modesty Appeal" and reported that it was getting good results. Bills were introduced in the Utah Legislature fixing skirts at 3 inches above the ankle and in the Virginia Legislature fixing necklines at within 3 inches of the upper part of the throat.

In April 1920 some Americans were diverted from the Great Red Scare by the publication of F. Scott Fitzgerald's *This Side of Paradise,* which told of "one vast juvenile intrigue" against the old moral order. The thing had apparently been going on even before the war, and year by year it was getting worse. Girls who would not have thought of entering a saloon in the days of legal drinking were bellying up to the bar in the illegal speakeasies with skirts short, stockings rolled below the knees, and lips and cheeks daubed with the lipstick and rouge that formerly had been the trademark of the streetwalker.

By all available evidence, nineteenth-century American society in all but the "degraded" classes had been Victorian through and through. Victorian Englishmen visiting America had had occasion to express their shocked surprise that Americans went beyond the forms of Victorianism to the very substance of it. The lavish parties of the gilded aristocracy had been wholesome, decorous affairs. The chaperones had played an indispensable role in youthful gatherings in upper society. Somewhat lower down on the social scale they had not been present in person perhaps, but they had been present in spirit—at least if one can believe that W. D. Howells really knew what was going on in his day. Then it all changed. The younger generation suddenly rebelled, and the older generation, unable to lick them, joined them. By the mid-twenties the waltz had given way to the Black Bottom and the Charleston, and except for the bluenosed drys and what H. L. Mencken called the "Bible-belters," it could almost be said, in the words of Irving Berlin, that "everybody's doin' it now."

That this most non-Wilsonian new freedom was not simply a postwar phenomenon is evident from an examination of prewar Greenwich Village, where the horn already had been blown brassily for the moral as well as intellectual revolt against traditional America. The Progressive movement, which had achieved the perfect society for its generation, evidently left the younger generation with the uneasy feeling that there must be something better. The Progressive movement had striven for changes which would reestablish the old values amid new circumstances; the younger generation rejected the older values on the grounds that they had no relevance to current circumstances.

The Lost Generation found plenty of intellectual arguments to defend their new emancipation, but the revolution in morals was not primarily a cerebral development. Darwinism convinced many intellectuals that there were no eternal verities in religion or in morals, that Dreiser's Sister Carrie was to be admired as one who adjusted to circumstances and not to be condemned as a fallen woman. For most Americans, however, Darwin and the theory of natural selection probably contributed less to the new social conduct than did Thomas Alva Edison and the electric light. Material and technological progress represented a triumph not only over nature but also over nature's God. Liberal churches responded to this urbane attitude by adding on game rooms and coffee rooms and toning down the otherworldly aspect of religion.

The decline of the family as the basic unit of society can be dimly seen even in earliest colonial times, when a public school system was established to perform a duty which the heads of households were found not to be performing adequately. In the early nineteenth century the further breakdown of the family as an integrated unit took place in New England when farmers' daughters, ceasing to make homespun, bought manufactured cloth with money they had earned at the textile mill.

Then the move to the city converted the large family from an economic asset to an economic liability, and a decline in the birthrate rapidly took place. The father, away at work during the day, necessarily left the upbringing of the children pretty much to the mother, who, if she wanted, could often leave it up to the maid, freeing mother, father, and child from the continuous association which circumstances formerly had forced upon them. The general tendency was to lose old values and gain new freedom, and when the children showed the uses that could be made of the freedom, their elders proved quick to learn from them.

Sexual restraint had given cohesion to the old order, and sexual freedom was the most explosive force in its demolition. Sex became the stock-in-trade of the movies and also of the tabloid newspapers, which made their appearance in the postwar period. The "petting" question became the topic of the day. The American psychiatrist A. A. Brill began translating the work of Sigmund Freud into English in 1913, and Freud himself was agreeably surprised to notice how well his ideas were known "even in prudish America." As popularized in America in the twenties, Freud was understood to prove that life was sex-centered and that human and social ills stemmed from sexual repression. Some came to look upon uninhibited sexual expression as the universal panacea, much as Sylvester Graham had viewed dietary reform in the mid-nineteenth century.

Sexual liberty was especially a declaration of independence for women, for even Howells conceded that the boys he grew up with, although models of deportment with nice girls, nevertheless felt free to stray across the tracks. The flapper was the symbol of the jazz age. The American male could offer no more meaningful symbol for whatever freedom he had won than the arctic raccoon coat combined with the Hawaiian ukulele. It was clearly the women rather than the men who in the twenties increased their freedom, winning political rights, legal rights, broader economic opportunities, and a degree of mechanization of household drudgery, and largely winning, in principle at least, social equality with men.

NATIONAL PROHIBITION

Together with the Nineteenth Amendment extending the vote to women, the Eighteenth Amendment extending prohibition to everybody was a final bequest of the Progressive movement to the roaring twenties. The rise of prohibition and of Progressive reform, beginning in the 1890s, had been parallel developments with much in common, and those who were behind them had cooperated in bringing about various moral reforms, especially at the local and state level.

Progressives tended to be wary of prohibitionists because the temperance men tended to take over the reform groups they joined and commit them to Sunday closing laws or other exclusively prohibitionist aims, and in some areas, notably Wisconsin, the two groups directly opposed each other, but generally the Progressives accepted prohibition as an important objective in their quest for a moral society. They disapproved of the Prohibition party's rigidity, but they cooperated with the more pragmatically political Anti-Saloon League, which had been founded at the close of the nineteenth century as the organization of most of the Protestant churches in the war against the "drink evil." Skillfully manipulated by the nonpartisan Anti-Saloon League, Progressives were led first to support local option laws in the local campaigns against red-light districts, then to support statewide prohibition, when local option dramatized the wetness of surrounding wet areas, and finally to support national prohibition, when statewide prohibition proved impossible to enforce.

The Anti-Saloon League launched its campaign for national prohibition in Congress in 1913 and immediately stepped it up when America entered the war. Wartime prohibition was successfully urged on grounds of the wartime need to conserve grain, although Food Administrator Herbert Hoover denied the validity of the argument. The prohibitionists also successfully identified the liquor interests, especially the brewers, with the German enemy, arguing that the profits from beer were going to Germany to pay for bullets to kill American boys.

Wartime prohibition became law as the war itself was coming to an end, and then the Eighteenth Amendment was ratified by the rural, old-stock–dominated state legislatures and became a part of the Constitution on January 1, 1920. It remained in the Constitution until its repeal in 1933, and during those years it overshadowed everything else in American life as the major subject of public discussion.

Although prohibition had been an important objective of American reformers since the 1830s and though it won the support of most Progressives, it is highly unlikely that it would ever have become law on the basis of a national referendum. It would hardly have been voted for by the German, Irish, Italian, and other non-Anglo-Saxon ethnic groups, for it was directed particularly against their drinking habits. In addition there were many drinking Anglo-Saxons, some of whom theoretically favored prohibition to keep the immigrant groups in line, but who, as it turned out, did not intend to give up their own drinking habits if they could help it.

Wartime prohibition appeared effective at first, but within a year or two moonshining and bootlegging and rum-running were developing new sources of supplies, and speakeasies were springing up in all the sizable cities of the nation. The maintenance of a national law which a major part of the population refused to accept resulted in a climate of opinion that supported the bootlegger in order to get the booze and even hailed the racketeers as upholders of personal liberty. Organized crime had existed in America before the Eighteenth Amendment, but the nationwide crime syndicates of modern times are substantially a product of the era of "Scarface" Al Capone. The attempt on the part of the churches, especially through the Anti-Saloon League, to enforce the law through cafe raids and hip-flask raids and other such niggling forms of repression meanwhile introduced a widespread anticlericalism that remained after prohibition had been repealed.

THE KU KLUX KLAN

The drys, who had confidently predicted that prohibition would usher in the millennium, were driven to fury and frustration by the wholesale breakdown of enforcement, and it is particularly in the context of the fiasco of prohibition that the nationwide reactionary violence of the Ku Klux Klan in the early twenties is to be understood. The Klan had been organized in Georgia in 1915 and was initially promoted as an anti-Negro organization, after the manner of the long defunct post-Civil War KKK. When it failed to attract a large following on this basis, its promoters expanded its activities into the fields of preparedness, nativism, and the Great Red Scare. But it was not until the Great Red Scare was over and the breakdown of prohibition had begun that the Ku Klux Klan swept the nation, enrolling millions in its fight to preserve the moral and ethnic purity of Anglo-Saxon America.

Under the protection of hooded secrecy, Klansmen terrorized blacks, Jews, Catholics, foreigners, and radicals, but the largest number of victims actually were other old-stock Americans who in one way or another were deemed to be violating the moral code of the community, notably the prohibition laws that rural, old-stock America had secured for the nation after three-quarters of a century of struggle. The Klan expressed itself in floggings, mutilations, and the burning of homes and churches. Drawing its membership from the rural Protestant native stock that was rapidly dwindling in national importance, it fought a desperate, blindly self-righteous fight for what it thought was true Americanism.

At the same time the secrecy of the Klan provided opportunities for robbery and for working off personal spite. A rising political power in several states, the Klan collapsed following revelations of corruption and immorality among some of its leaders in 1925. It had proved powerless to enforce prohibition or rescind the jazz age. The passage of the National Origins Act of 1924 left it without any major national political objective, and wherever the Klan had achieved political power, it had been unable to formulate workable policies and stick to them.

The twenties are often presented as a decade of reaction between major periods of reform, which is a perverse way to consider a decade characterized by unprecedented social change. Politically the decade was antireformist, but it was more truly an apolitical decade than a politically reactionary one. The decade is primarily significant, not for the fury of the reactionaries, but for the momentous changes that were making them furious.

BIBLIOGRAPHY FOR CHAPTER 20

William Leuchtenburg, Perils of Prosperity, 1914–1932 (1958)
John Hicks, Republican Ascendency, 1921–1933 (1960)
A. M. Schlesinger, Jr., The Crisis of the Old Order, 1919–1933 (1957)
G. M. Ostrander, American Civilization in the First Machine Age, 1890–1940 (1970)
F. L. Allen, Only Yesterday (1931)—social history of the 1920s
R. S. and **H. M. Lynd,** Middletown (1929)—sociological study of Muncie, Indiana
T. C. Cochran, The American Business System (1957)
George Soule, Prosperity Decade, 1917–1929 (1947)
Irving Bernstein, The Lean Years: A History of the American Workers, 1920–1933 (1960)
R. K. Murray, Red Scare, 1919–1920 (1955)
D. M. Chalmers, Hooded Americanism (1965)

CHAPTER 21

THE GREAT DEPRESSION

ECONOMIC DEPRESSIONS
IN AMERICAN HISTORY

Almost as regular as clockwork the United States has plunged into a severe economic depression once every generation under peacetime conditions. The first one occurred in the Confederation period. Then, out of the unstable economic conditions which accompanied the French Revolutionary and Napoleonic Wars, depression came again in 1819 and thereafter in 1837, in 1857, in 1873, and in 1893. The brief "bankers' panic" of 1907 did not unsettle the economy for long, but in 1914 signs pointed to another severe depression. The nation was rescued on that occasion by World War I, and it recovered quickly from the recession of 1921, except for certain classifications of farmers and some other smaller economic groups. Then in 1929 it suffered a depression deeper and more enduring than any it had yet experienced.

The depressions of the nineteenth century had been preceded by reckless land speculation and heavy expenditures on internal improvements, especially railroads. Irresponsible banking practices followed by bank failures had been part of the pattern. Furthermore America, as a prime field for foreign investment, had been sensitive to economic conditions in Europe, especially Britain. European business panics, followed by an unloading of European investments in America, had periodically weakened the American economy. In 1929, however, the United States was the world's creditor, and it was the withdrawal of American investments from abroad which knocked the economic props from under other national economies and precipitated the worldwide Depression.

Throughout American history these depressions, despite their regularity, have come as shocking surprises to the American business community and American politicians, and in 1929 the element of surprise was especially marked, for the belief was by then quite generally held that America had at last discovered the secret of perpetual prosperity.

The perennial problem of maintaining a national credit that would be both flexible and sound had been solved, it was argued, through the Federal Reserve System. The evils of competition had been eliminated without fundamental damage to the saving principle of free enterprise, for business was working out its own problems without arbitrary governmental interference. The national product was increasing annually, and the nation as a whole was gaining. To be sure, the distribution of the new wealth was far from equal, but this problem was understood and was being solved.

Broad-visioned businessmen were developing profit-sharing programs for their employees and were distributing company stock among them. The day would come when the workers of America would own their own factories, not through the violent process of Communist revolution, but through the peaceful evolution of responsible, civic-minded free enterprise. "We in America," declared Herbert Hoover in 1928, "are nearer to the final triumph over poverty than ever before in the history of any land [and] given a chance to go forward with the policies of the last eight years, we shall soon with the help of God be in sight of the day when poverty will be banished from this nation."

The New York Stock Exchange, by the late twenties the most spectacular barometer of the nation's material progress, soared to new heights after Hoover's election. Enormous quick profits were made possible in stock speculation by buying on the margin, that is, putting up a small percentage of the purchase price with a broker. It was widely observed at the time that anybody could be rich who wished to be. But the Federal Reserve Board was concerned about the sudden expansion of bank loans, and it took steps to check them. The move, however, came too late.

THE WALL STREET CRASH

The crash descended in October, and when the wild confidence turned to wild panic, no means were found to check the rout. Within days the market values of stocks had dropped by one-third, and it was not found possible to check their downward course for the next three years. By the end of 1932 even the "blue chip" stocks had dropped to a quarter of their 1929 values. Millions of investors had been ruined, and that distrust of the business community and of the economic system which was to remain as a stubborn impediment to improved conditions had settled in.

The wild rise and fall of the market, beyond heralding the coming of the Great Depression, did much to initiate it and to lengthen it, but behind the crash was a fatal weakness in the economy which had been largely overlooked but became evident once the Depression had set in. Henry Ford put his finger on the problem when he explained that the Depression had come because the buying power of the people was all used up. Although wages had risen wonderfully during the decade, they had not kept up with the increased value of the national product. That the nation was producing more than it could purchase was disguised for a time by the growing practice of buying on credit; this delayed the Depression but deepened it once it was upon the nation. The trade-association system, furthermore, had facilitated price-fixing arrangements so effectively that prices did not respond to market conditions. As purchasing power declined, businesses resolutely priced themselves out of their markets.

It had never been supposed that it was the duty of the federal government to intervene in economic matters, either to aid the victims of depressions or to return the nation to prosperity. Depressions had been viewed as deviations from the normal condition of prosperity that were created by a temporary malfunctioning of the law of supply and demand. The problem, it was agreed, was essentially one of overproduction, and the solution was to permit nature to take its course. Unsound businesses would inevitably go to the wall, production would decline to the level of consumption, and conditions would thereafter steadily return to normal. Beyond cutting government expenses, reducing taxes, and maintaining the gold reserves, there was nothing the federal government could or should do in the matter.

THE HOOVER ADMINISTRATION

It is true that Herbert Hoover went beyond this negative conception of the government's role. It is also true that in the face of unprecedented economic and human catastrophe, he moved most reluctantly and slowly, and most reluctantly of all where government assistance would benefit directly those people suffering most desperately from the Depression. A self-made millionaire who had experienced no serious depression since his college days, Hoover throughout his administration held to the optimistic view that prosperity was the normal condition and that during depressions, as well as times of prosperity, the balanced budget should be the highest aim of the federal government.

At the same time Hoover was early convinced that the Depression was serious, that its duration would be indefinite, and that the government would have to do something. His earliest major concern was for depressed farm conditions, and in June, before the crash, he supported a program under which the Federal Farm Board received 500 million dollars to grant loans to farm cooperatives which would work out programs to benefit their members. Working through these cooperatives and directly through its own corporations, the Board financed the purchase of wheat and cotton in order to remove surpluses. By the end of the first year of its experiment, however, it was forced to concede the futility of a program that did not enforce limitations upon production.

A second solution to the farm problem, in Hoover's view, was tariff protection, and he supported the Hawley-Smoot Tariff Act of 1930 chiefly on this basis.

The tariff, however, proved no more effective for farmers producing for the world market than had previous ones, and the act was made the occasion for sharp tariff increases on industrial imports as well.

Hoover's most ambitious attack on the Depression, recommended to Congress in December 1931, was the establishment of the Reconstruction Finance Corporation "to make temporary advances upon proper securities to established industries, railways and financial institutions . . . where such advances will protect the credit structure and stimulate employment." Denounced as the rich man's dole, the RFC disbursed 1.5 billion dollars during its first year of existence, mainly to banks and trust companies. Hoover defended the RFC partly on the grounds that its intended beneficiaries were the smaller institutions and partly on the grounds that the benefits were in the form of loans which would be returned to the government. It remained true that he was notably less willing to extend to the indigent individual the government support he extended to the indigent corporation.

In the face of rising unemployment, which eventually drove one-third of the nation's working force onto the streets, Hoover refused to use federal funds to prevent mass misery until his final year in office. Then, while vetoing a more generous congressional relief program in July 1932, he was moved to sign a bill extending to the states federal loans of 300 million dollars, on the condition, which also applied to the activities of the Farm Board and the RFC, that the money should eventually be returned to the federal government.

In these matters Hoover continued to be controlled by his original assumptions: that federal handouts "would have injured the spiritual responses of the American people," presumably to a greater extent than those of private charities, that the end result of increased federal authority would be the creation of an authoritarian state, and that economy remained the chief concern of the government under any circumstances. "The urgent question today," he told Congress in 1932, "is the prompt balancing of the budget. When that is accomplished I propose to support adequate measures for relief of distress and unemployment."

THE ELECTION OF 1932

In June 1932 the Republicans met in convention and without opposition or enthusiasm renominated Hoover as their candidate. In July the resolutely unpolitical Hoover opened his campaign for reelection by calling out the National Guard against the pathetic "bonus marchers," World War I veterans who marched on Washington to demonstrate for immediate bonus benefits. Amid precipitously worsening conditions the Democrats held their convention and nominated the governor of New York, Franklin Delano Roosevelt.

A distant cousin of Teddy's, F. D. R. had indicated his vote-getting powers by winning the governorship in the Republican year of 1928 and then by winning a second term overwhelmingly two years later. His had been one of the most vigorous of the state administrations in combating the Depression, but his record was not widely known nationally, and he did not especially campaign on it. What he said during his campaign was largely noncommittal and by no means consistent, although one fighting speech before the Commonwealth Club in San Francisco gave some indication of the main directions his administration would take. Against the Hoover of that year, however, Roosevelt's brilliant personality and vague promises of reforms were sufficient to reverse the landslide of four years earlier and open the way for what Roosevelt, in his acceptance speech at the convention, had called "a new deal for the American people."

COMING OF THE NEW DEAL

Roosevelt, according to the ancient Supreme Court justice Oliver Wendell Holmes, Jr., was "a second-class intellect, but a first-class temperament." Unlike the intellectual Hoover, F. D. R. brought to his task no clearly formulated economic theory and no fixed idea of the role the government should play in a depression economy. "The country needs," he declared, "and unless I mistake its temper, the country demands bold, persistent experimentation. It is common sense to take a method and try it. If it fails, admit it frankly and try another. But above all, try something." Unburdened by any association in the public mind with the national debacle, Roosevelt suddenly convinced the American people, as Hoover himself had been glumly determined to do, that they had "nothing to fear but fear itself." The administration opened with a dramatic national bank holiday followed by a merry outpouring of legalized 3.2 beer made possible by congressional modification of the Volstead Act. Momentarily, at least, in full command of the nation's confidence, the Roosevelt administration, in an unprecedented hundred days of administrative and legislative activity, dealt out new deals to the clamoring, desperately needy economic interests of the nation.

Consistency was no New Deal criterion. Each major problem was faced separately, with only passing concern for the effect that each program might have on some other area of the economy. Most sharply criticized in this respect was the program to destroy farm produce in a time of starvation. There was, however, more food being produced than the nation could consume even in good times, and New Dealers saw relief for the starving as a distinct problem to be handled by other agencies. If the result of relief work programs was government competition with struggling private enterprise, then business in its turn would benefit from separate programs designed to aid in its recovery.

Once the nation had lost the bright honeymoon happiness of the hundred days, it fell once again into acrimonious dispute. The New Deal, its enemies charged, was a revolutionary overthrow of the democratic, federal, individualistic American system. In important respects, Hoover declared, it was "fascism, pure fascism."

The champions of the New Deal were more divided than its critics. Many among them delighted in accepting the reforms as constituting a revolutionary break with the dead and discredited past. The more politic among them defended these reforms as the heroic means by which an actual bloody revolution was averted, and narrowly averted, in 1933. At the outset New Dealers tended to treat somewhat casually the question of whether desperate emergency measures could be traced to an immaculately American historical tradition. Increasingly, however, partisans of the New Deal tended to defend it as fulfilling the reform tradition of the Progressive era.

NEW DEAL IDEOLOGY

The answers to such questions were to be sought first of all in the character and purposes of the President, for F. D. R. dominated his age in a manner altogether unprecedented in American history. Ruling always in the midst of violently divided councils, he retained a generally flexible and undogmatic approach to the problems of the Depression. In a famous reply to a question concerning his ideological bent, he decided, after a moment's thought, that he was "a Christian and a democrat."

A patrician reformer in the line of Theodore Roosevelt and Samuel J. Tilden, he was, in the view of recent historians, fundamentally conservative, and, in the view of many reformers in his administration, downright old-fashioned. He might well have nationalized the banks and the railroads in 1933 with virtually no opposition if he had been so inclined, but then, as throughout the Depression, he thought in terms of restoration rather than revolution. A strong admirer of both Theodore Roosevelt and Woodrow Wilson, he had entered politics during the Progressive era and was himself basically Progressive in outlook.

Much old-time Progressive support, Republican as well as Democratic, flowed to the New Deal, which was permeated with the ideals of social justice of the earlier reform period. The Progressive movement itself had sharply divided on fundamental economic issues, however, and these divisions continued to split the New Deal. The spirit of the new freedom burned brightly in such New Dealers as Secretary of State Cordell Hull, who thought in terms of trust-busting and free trade. Against them, and in a commanding position at the outset, were old Bull Moosers such as Secretary of the Interior Harold L. Ickes and younger converts to the new nationalism, who argued for extending government controls over the consolidated economy that was an inescapable fact of modern life.

This neo-new nationalism gained support from the widespread belief that the American economy had reached the stage of maturity and an end to fundamental advances. America's Western lands were now settled and its industrial complex essentially completed. Progress henceforth was to be achieved, not through the moving back of new frontiers, but through the wise husbanding and just distribution of the now limited national resources. This Depression-born pessimism was generally shared by both friends and foes of the New Deal until they gained sudden new insights into the economic potentiality of the nation while mobilizing the economy for World War II.

World War I had also altered the nation's conception of its capabilities, and for the New Deal the precedents arising out of World War I proved of greater practical value in the battle for recovery than those inherited from the prosperous Progressive period. The New Deal attacked the Depression much in the manner of a nation at arms attacking an enemy. The National Industrial Recovery Act, initially the basic recovery program, was a vast scheme for government-directed industrial cooperation developed somewhat along the lines of the War Industries Board of World War I. It was headed by Hugh S. Johnson, who had gained experience in the WIB as assistant to Bernard Baruch. Similarly, George Peek's wartime experiences in mobilizing agricultural resources were made use of when he was placed at the head of the Agricultural Adjustment Administration.

The Tennessee Valley Authority had had its origins during the war in the dams constructed at Muscle Shoals, Tennessee, to furnish power for government industry. The Civilian Conservation Corps was operated on a semimilitary basis with assistance from the United States Army. Governmentally supervised labor arbitration had first been instituted during the war. The war had provided the precedent for the tax policy of the New Deal and, more important than that, had indicated the efficacy and practicality of deficit spending. "Where we spent millions before the war," the English economist John Maynard Keynes had declared, "we have now learnt that we can spend hundreds of millions and apparently not suffer for it." Roosevelt never took an entire liking either to Keynes or to Keynesian economics, but deficit financing nevertheless became the main strategy in the war against the Depression.

As a social movement, the New Deal was a far cry from Protestant, middle-class, moralistic Progressivism. When Theodore Roosevelt invited the Negro leader Booker T. Washington to the White House, his "lily white" following, in the North as well as the South, protested so loudly that he was persuaded not to do such a thing again, and Wilson's appointment of the Jew Louis Brandeis to the Supreme Court was accounted a remarkable act of political bravery. By contrast, Jews and Catholics provided the New Deal with leadership as well as rank-and-file support, and Negroes became an object of concern, at least, to the government for the first time since Reconstruction. To this change the immigration restriction laws of the twenties had contributed much by converting the recent immigrants from the vanguard of an invading horde to a part of a polyethnic national community, the character of which was now permanently set by the immigration laws.

The moral certitudes of Progressives were largely discarded by New Dealers, many of whom shared the anticlerical outlook which had been fostered in the twenties by the fight against fundamentalism and even more by the fight against prohibition. In his speeches Roosevelt retained much of the moralistic and even biblical tone of the earlier age, but at the same time he cheerfully and openly accepted such unrespectable supporters as the Kelly-Nash machine in Chicago and the Hague machine in Jersey City where their support advanced the interests of his party and his program.

Intellectuals, meanwhile, were welcomed unashamedly into the administration and given seats of power from which they were able to frustrate again and again the most modest designs of the machine politicians who had engineered the victory. F. D. R. was much less intellectual in his interests than T. R., Taft, Wilson, or Hoover, but much more than even Wilson he provided a leadership that won the loyalty of intellectuals and a government that gave them authority. During his terms as governor of New York he had acquired the services of a "brain trust," recruited heavily from Columbia University, which he brought with him to Washington.

A number of the brain trusters passed from the scene within a few years, to be replaced, to an extent, by a new circle associated with Harvard Law School and with Supreme Court Justice Felix Frankfurter. The remarkably intellectual and apolitical character of the administration remained, however. Despite his enormous political skills the chief party political boss, Postmaster James A. Farley, found himself continually balked in his attempts to strengthen the party machinery through distribution of the patronage.

No President in the nation's history was the superior of F. D. R. in political skill, and it is not to be supposed that he underestimated the need for party machinery or party patronage. In 1932 he had demonstrated something of his political skill in knitting together the badly split Democratic party. But he remained somewhat distrustful of the machine politicians, and beyond that he was aware that as long as the party remained an alliance between Northern city bosses and Southern Democrats, it would remain a minority party. By shifting authority to political independents like Ickes and Henry Wallace, he helped to broaden the appeal of the party, and in this he was assisted by the standpat Republicanism of the opposition. By the election of 1936 the Democratic party had transformed itself once again into the party of the American majority.

FINANCIAL REFORM

F. D. R. took office in the midst of a banking crisis which was paralyzing the economy. Bank holidays had been declared, temporarily closing the banks in almost half the states, and Roosevelt at once closed all the rest of them for a four-day period, and an emergency session of Congress passed the Emergency

Banking Act legalizing the President's action and providing for the process whereby the sound banks would be reopened. Roosevelt delivered the first of his "fireside chats" over the radio, reassuring the nation of the soundness of the banks. Within the next month most of the banks were reopened, and the crisis was over. The Glass-Stegall Banking act was passed, instituting various reforms in banking procedures including the creation of the Federal Deposit Insurance Corporation to insure bank deposits. The influence of the FDIC in restoring public confidence in the banks of the nation was immediate, profound, and enduring. In 1935 the Banking Act gave the Federal Reserve Board power to regulate interest rates. The key to the victory, however, had been that first fireside chat, by which, as Walter Lippmann wrote, "the nation, which had lost confidence in everything and everybody, has regained confidence in the government and in itself."

Currency manipulation accompanied the banking legislation in an effort to achieve the old Greenback and Populist aim of managed inflation. The President was empowered to issue 3 billion dollars worth of greenbacks. He was further authorized to reduce the gold content of the dollar up to 50 percent and to provide for the unlimited coinage of gold and silver at whatever ratio he chose. Then, to win support of the silver bloc, Congress was obliged to add legislation enforcing government purchase of the national silver production at set rates, a monetarily meaningless addition to the existing currency legislation, which thereafter cost the nation about 100 million dollars annually. As it turned out, the currency reforms disappointed the expectations of everybody but silver interests by having no appreciable effect on commodity prices, which, it had been assumed, would be forced up.

Government control over the New York Stock Exchange was extended through the Securities Act and the Securities Exchange Act, creating the Securities and Exchange Commission to regulate securities and ensuring that information was published concerning the nature of the securities and of the corporations they represented. Later acts extended the authority of the commission; notably the Public Utility Holding Company Act of 1935 placed holding companies under its supervision.

RELIEF AND RECOVERY LEGISLATION

With the banking crisis, relief from starvation for the 12 to 14 million unemployed and their dependents was an obviously urgent matter when the new President took office and Congress established the Federal Emergency Relief Administration, whose director, the New York social worker Harry Hopkins, laid down the principles upon which relief would thereafter be administered. Hopkins determined that work would be performed for relief money. The principle was thereafter followed in the various relief programs, including the Civilian Conservation Corps, the Civil Works Administration, the Public Works Administration, and the Works Progress Administration.

The CCC, which provided conservation work for younger men—healthful and obviously useful work which was noncompetitive with private enterprise—escaped much of the criticism directed against other relief programs. The PWA provided big business with profitable contracts for heavy construction of such things as bridges, dams, and public buildings, in addition to providing work for the unemployed, and was therefore not looked upon as an unmixed evil by the business community.

The "make work" projects of the WPA, such as raking leaves and digging unneeded ditches, drew the heaviest fire from administration critics and introduced the word "boondoggling" into the language. The WPA, which also constructed thousands of school buildings, playgrounds, and other public facilities, was probably the most controversial single measure of the whole New Deal. A public opinion poll taken at the close of the Depression asked what had been the best thing and also what had been the worst thing the New Deal had done, and the WPA received the highest number of votes in both categories.

At the outset the main hope for recovery from the Depression centered in the National Recovery Administration. Under the NRA, businesses in each major industry were invited to draw up codes of fair trade, including the fixing of prices and production quotas, codes which, if approved by the government, would be permitted to regulate the industry in violation of the antitrust laws. As part of these codes, business was obliged to accept agreements concerning wages and working conditions which would be acceptable to labor, and it was obliged to guarantee labor the right of collective bargaining. Both management and labor would thereby receive the order and security necessary to advance them together into prosperity.

Initially the NRA probably had wider support in administration circles than any other enactment, but it soon proved to be the most disastrous failure among the New Deal enterprises. Labor, which at first had welcomed the act, soon found that loopholes existed in Section 7a, the provision added to secure labor's collective-bargaining rights. Price-fixing agreements resulted in an abrupt rise in the cost of living without a corresponding increase in the private incomes of consumers, and this naturally met with howls of public outrage. Business was the chief beneficiary, but smaller businesses, if they were to cooperate, were obliged to operate under codes that had been drawn up by the major businesses in the field and naturally tended to favor them against the smaller ones.

At the same time there were leaders of big business, most conspicuously Henry Ford, who simply refused to go along, and when this happened there was nothing to be done. Hoover's trade-assocation movement of the twenties had been the main forerunner of NRA, but to Hoover this new movement, because it involved a degree of government coercion, was un-American and totalitarian. The codes themselves were hastily drawn up and were officially approved by overworked government administrators, who were often in a poor position to judge the codes on their merits.

The successful operation of NRA required strong public support, and when this began to fall away, adherence to the codes could not be enforced. The act had become an albatross around the neck of the administration when, in 1935, it was invalidated by the Supreme Court and swept out of existence. Thereafter Congress passed various acts salvaging aspects of the NRA which had proved beneficial to small business and to labor.

AGRICULTURAL REFORM

Nowhere in the economy was the paradox of poverty amid plenty more dramatically evident than on the commercial farms of the nation, which produced rich surpluses that were left rotting for the lack of a profitable market. Farm foreclosures followed upon the failure of the Agricultural Marketing Act. Foreclosures were in turn resisted by emergency state laws and by mob violence. Rural America was in a revolutionary mood when Roosevelt came to office, and Congress hurried to pass the Agriculture Adjustment Act. The one major novelty of the AAA was its provision for maintaining high prices through the controlled restriction of production. Farmers were to be paid to limit their output, the payments to be financed by excise taxes imposed upon food processors.

The eventual aim of the program was to raise farm prices to parity with those of the five good farm years preceding the outbreak of World War I. Seven commodities were initially placed under this program—cotton, wheat, field corn, hogs, rice, tobacco, and dairy products—to which a number of others were later added. The government also encouraged marketing agreements between farmers, processors, and distributors whereby numbers of other farm commodities had their prices raised and production limited.

The AAA assisted mainly the politically powerful farming minority which specialized in commercial crops. It largely ignored the subsistence farmer and severely injured tenant farmers and sharecroppers, who were moved off the land withdrawn from production. Various additional programs were therefore devised to alleviate the miserable conditions of the 5 million noncommercial farmers. Loan agencies and resettlement programs offered some assistance, as did the various relief agencies. These programs received continued opposition from landlords, however, and were never remotely equal to the problems they faced.

Loftiest in motivation among the programs of rural reforms was the Tennessee Valley Authority, established in 1933 to operate and extend the government power facilities at Muscle Shoals. Under its original chairman, Arthur E. Morgan, it was conceived of, not as simply a public power project, but as an idealistic social experiment. Society in the Tennessee Valley, which included parts of seven states, was to be comprehensively enriched through government aid and government planning.

Morgan faced the opposition of colleagues on TVA, notably David Lilienthal, who distrusted programs involving comprehensive utopian dictation and saw the need to fight vigorously against the private power companies if TVA was to maintain itself. There was a three-way struggle between Morgan, Lilienthal, and Wendell Willkie of the Commonwealth and Southern utilities holding company, and Lilienthal emerged victorious. On the one hand TVA became a more aggressive producer of public power; on the other hand it moderated its social programs, deferring to the interests of the more prosperous farmers of the region.

UNIONIZATION OF LABOR

Organized labor, reduced since World War I from 12 percent to 6 percent of the national work force, moved hopefully in 1933 to take advantage of NRA Section 7a's guarantee of the right to bargain collectively. Against the unions the employer organizations mobilized to defend the American Way which they had fashioned so successfully during the twenties. In Minneapolis a clash between the Teamsters union and the Citizens Alliance paralyzed the city, killing four and wounding many more. In San Francisco the struggle of the International Longshoremen's Association against the Industrial Association resulted in two dead and many wounded before broadening into a general strike. In Toledo national guardsmen killed two and wounded many in the course of strikes.

In each of these cases union demands were generally met. Elsewhere, however, Section 7a, indifferently supported by the government and little implemented by the AFL, proved generally ineffective. In 1934 the National Labor Relations Board was created; it was independent of NRA but had no power to enforce its opinion. F. D. R., while he thought of himself as a friend of labor, did not see the need for a powerful labor movement. His views were those of the Progressive era, which thought the rights of labor should be protected by governmental supervision rather than by independent labor action. The AFL under William Green, meanwhile, took a view that was hardly more militant than F. D. R.'s.

Then there was a dramatic change, both in administration policy and in the fortunes of organized labor. In its beginnings, this was very largely the work of one man, Sen. Robert Wagner of New York. With little support and considerable opposition from administration officials, Wagner in 1935 introduced into Congress a bill to secure the collective bargaining provisions of Section 7a. The resulting National Labor Relations Act gave the bargaining representative of a majority of workers the right to represent all workers. It gave the National Labor

Relations Board the right to supervise labor elections, and it placed limits upon the employer's power to coerce his employees. There remained a bitter struggle to enforce acceptance of the Wagner Act by employers, but it proved to be the greatest single turning point in the whole history of organized labor.

William Green had spoken wistfully of organizing 25 million workers, but since he, in common with most of the AFL leadership, fought any developments that would disturb the old craft relationships, little was accomplished. The AFL convention of 1934 arrived at a compromise with the advocates of industrial unions which actually left the old craft unions in undisturbed authority. In 1935, however, the break came. Led by John L. Lewis of the United Mine Workers, the industrial unionists formed the Committee for Industrial Organization—later the Congress of Industrial Organizations—which, in 1936, began to organize the steel industry in defiance of the AFL.

In 1937 militant tactics such as the "sit-down strike" brought U.S. Steel, General Motors, and the Chrysler Corporation to terms. Bloody fighting continued elsewhere in the steel and automotive industries through the rest of the thirties, and the AFL and the CIO remained bitterly divided. Nevertheless, the new governmental support and labor militancy brought the labor-union movement to a position of power in the nation which labor leaders could hardly have conceived of in former times. By 1941 total union membership had risen to 10.5 million, more than three times the membership at the outset of the New Deal.

BIBLIOGRAPHY FOR CHAPTER 21

A. U. Romansco, The Poverty of Abundance: Hoover, the Nation, the Depression (1965)

J. K. Galbraith, The Great Crash, 1929 (1955)

Broadus Mitchell, Depression Decade, 1929–1941 (1947)

Dixon Wecter, The Age of the Great Depression, 1929–1941 (1948)

W. E. Leuchtenburg, Franklin D. Roosevelt and the New Deal (1963)

J. M. Burns, Roosevelt: The Lion and the Fox (1956)

A. M. Schlesinger, Jr., The Coming of the New Deal (1958) and The Politics of Upheaval (1960)

R. S. and **H. M. Lynd,** Middletown in Transition (1937)

Paul Conkin, FDR and the Origins of the Welfare State (1967)

Murray Kempton, Part of Our Time (1955)—radical thought in the Depression

O. L. Graham, Jr., An Encore for Reform (1967)

CHAPTER 22

FROM NEW DEAL TO WORLD WAR

CHALLENGES FROM LEFT AND RIGHT

The New Deal was endorsed by hugely impressive victories in the 1934 congressional elections, but in 1935, as the administration approached another presidential election, resurgent social discontent threatened to raise up third parties and thereby wreck the Democratic chances for victory. Although business had been perhaps the chief beneficiary of the New Deal, it had already gone into angry opposition to "that man in the White House." Lower-middle-class and mudsill America had failed to receive major consideration, and leaders were rising up to organize this massive discontent. In California the Socialist Upton Sinclair had captured the Democratic nomination for governor in 1934 and had unsuccessfully campaigned on a thoroughly radical EPIC program—End Poverty in California. His fellow Californian, Dr. Francis E. Townsend, advocating old-age pensions of $200 a month, was gaining a fervent following among the old people of the country. In Detroit a Catholic priest, Father Charles E. Coughlin, built up an enormous radio following with his criticisms of capitalism and advocacy of his ambiguous National Union for Social Justice. Increasingly a spokesman for racism and the corporate state, Coughlin, an early Roosevelt supporter, determined in 1936 to pit his own popularity against that of the President.

Most ominous of all was Sen. Huey Long of Louisiana, whose Share Our Wealth program appeared to be winning national support from unnumbered millions of voters. As governor of Louisiana, with the support of the dirt farmers against the corrupt and entrenched vested interests, Long had gained a mastery over the state which he maintained through an extensive—and graft-ridden—public improvements program on the one hand and terrorism and police control on the other. Moving to the United States Senate, Long set out to nationalize his authoritarian system.

Never very explicit as to the details of the Share Our Wealth program, the "Kingfish," as Long liked to call himself, promised a general redistribution of the wealth and a "homestead allowance" of at least $5,000 for every American family. He attracted Townsendites with promises of old-age pensions of an indeterminate amount. Ably assisted by the spellbinder Gerald L. K. Smith, Long moved in 1935 to organize a party of the nation's discontented which he predicted would sweep the country.

The Marxist left, by contrast, offered the New Deal little competition. The Socialist party under the ministerial Norman Thomas had lost much of the appeal it had enjoyed under Eugene V. Debs. Nor was the Communist party under Earl Browder, which had won only ¼ percent of the popular vote in 1932, to be taken seriously as a political threat. Despite its success in acquiring the allegiance of a cluster of intellectuals, in broadening its support through Communist front organizations, and in infiltrating the government and the labor movement, the party was hopelessly incapable of presenting itself as an American political force. The threat to the New Deal was from native political radicalism.

While angry masses were rising up against the New Deal, the Supreme Court was coldly cutting it apart. Early in 1935 the Court declared the Railroad Retirement Act and the Frazier-Lemke Act, for the relief of farm mortgagors, unconstitutional and then, in a unanimous decision, went on to invalidate the entire NRA. In the Schecter Poultry Corporation case the Court found the NRA to entail both an unconstitutional delegation of authority by Congress to the President and an unconstitutional extension of federal authority under the commerce clause of the Constitution. The Court decisions were so broadly and in some respects so vaguely worded, furthermore, as to threaten other major New Deal programs, such as the AAA, which was in fact declared unconstitutional a year later in the case of *United States v. Butler et al.,* and the TVA, which the Court, as it turned out, upheld.

In the face of these defeats Roosevelt seemed, both to the public and to members of his administration, to have lost the power of leadership he had so forcefully asserted until then, and as Roosevelt waited, administration officials argued heatedly among themselves. The main dispute was between those like Hugh S. Johnson of the NRA, who wished to seek new means to establish federal control over the economy, and those like the "brain truster" Rexford G. Tugwell, who wished to strike out on new courses. By late spring of 1935, however, F. D. R. had regained the initiative and the government was launched upon the so-called "second New Deal."

THE SECOND NEW DEAL

This second New Deal made itself the champion of the people and the enemy of privilege in a series of enactments, chief of which were the Wagner National Labor Relations Act, the Social Security Act, the Wealth Tax Act, and the Public

Utility Holding Company Act. Together this legislation broke the attempted New Deal alliance with big business and transformed the New Deal for the first time clearly into the champion of organized labor, of the aged and the unemployed, and generally of what Roosevelt called the "one-third of the nation ill-housed, ill-clad, and ill-nourished." At the same time it shifted the orientation of the New Deal from the new nationalism of government control to the new freedom of enforced competition combined with enforced social justice. This shift was accompanied by a marked shift in government personnel.

With the Wealth Tax Act the income tax was employed for the first time not simply as a revenue-producing measure, but as a social instrument intended to narrow the gap between the extremes of wealth and poverty. The tax on the largest incomes was placed at 75 percent, and corporate taxes reached an unprecedented height. The Public Utility Holding Company Act struck at the corporate device whereby a holding company, by controlling the stock in ostensibly competing businesses, could operate them in a monopolistic manner. Any holding company that could not demonstrate its economic value to the nation was to be dissolved. The Banking Act, in the meantime, increased federal authority over the Federal Reserve System. It was during the 1935 congressional session that the major relief program of the New Deal, WPA, was created.

But it was the Social Security Act, more than any other, that cut the ground out from under the hopeful demagogues. In cooperation with the state governments, it provided for unemployment insurance, pensions, and assistance to widows, dependent children, the blind, and the disabled. More, perhaps, than any other single New Deal enactment it marked a break with past federal policy. On the state level such legislation had been attempted much less comprehensively. In the federal government, however, it had been true, as Eleanor Roosevelt said, that "there was no recognition that the government owed an individual certain things as a right." Henceforth, she added, it would be accepted "that the government has an obligation to guard the rights of an individual so carefully that he never reaches a point at which he needs charity."

THE ELECTION OF 1936

In the presidential campaign of 1936 everything went Roosevelt's way. Men of great wealth organized the Liberty League against him and in a lavishly financed campaign dramatized their own greedy and reactionary aims. The Republican party drew up a platform that attacked the New Deal, and the convention went on to select as its candidate the governor of Kansas, Alfred M. Landon. A former Bull Mooser who, as he himself said, had cooperated with the New Deal to the best of his ability, Landon was by no means a compelling campaigner, and he was obliged to direct his fight against the party which in many respects more nearly expressed his own personal convictions.

There remained the third-party threat. The highly competent James Farley had said a third party with Huey Long as its candidate would poll 6 million votes, despite the legislative enactments of the second New Deal. But in the fall of 1935 Long was assassinated, and his supporters fell to quarreling among themselves over the succession. As it turned out, William Lemke of North Dakota was chosen by the National Union for Social Justice and the Union, Royal Oak, Independent and Third parties. In the election Lemke gathered in less than 2 percent of the vote. The Communists lost ground, and the Socialist votes declined by four-fifths. Roosevelt's was a massive victory; it brought every state but Maine and Vermont into the Democratic column and piled up overwhelming Democratic majorities in both houses of Congress. The second New Deal had received a mandate, it appeared, that gave Roosevelt unprecedented popular authority to press for further reforms.

The event proved that the New Deal had largely played itself out. A few new reforms were enacted, it is true. A new Housing Act was passed authorizing long-term loans for slum clearance. Tenant farmers received protective legislation, and a new Food and Drug Act increased the power of the Food and Drug Administration. In only one area, however, was significant new ground broken: in the Fair Labor Standards Act, instituting minimum wages for many classifications of workers employed by firms engaged in interstate commerce. Passed in 1938, the act initially established a minimum of 25 cents an hour, which has periodically been increased since then. A year later Roosevelt himself announced the end of the New Deal, declaring that "we have now passed the period of internal conflict in the launching of our program of social reform."

END OF THE NEW DEAL

The very magnitude of the 1936 victory apparently had weakened Roosevelt in his control over Congress by giving members a confidence in their political strength that emboldened them to oppose their popular leader. Also, Roosevelt did not have the patronage at his disposal in 1937 that the change in administrations had given him in 1933. The election was followed by the recession of 1937, which served to cast discredit on the recovery and reform programs and to discourage their extension. As had been the case with Presidents in previous depressions Roosevelt was forced to temporize with those who directed the nation's businesses. On the other hand, bad as they were, economic conditions in 1937 were by no means as desperate as they had been four years earlier, and political conditions were incomparably more stable. Most basically, perhaps, many who had been frightened into supporting changes in 1933 were no longer frightened.

In 1937 Roosevelt committed the greatest political error of his career: with his "court-packing" scheme he gave to his miscellaneous opponents a moral issue around which they could unite against him. Faced with the sweeping invalidation of New Deal legislation by the Supreme Court, F. D. R. presented to Congress a measure effectively authorizing him to appoint an additional judge to the bench for each of the existing six judges who were seventy years of age or older. The proposal was met with howls of outraged reverence for the highest court in the land, and a number of former New Deal supporters joined in its defeat and made it the occasion to go over to the opposition. Roosevelt was able to claim a victory in the fight, even though the bill was overwhelmingly defeated, for the Court thereafter consistently upheld New Deal legislation. Beyond that, all but two of the justices retired during Roosevelt's second administration, to be replaced mainly by New Dealers. Meanwhile a conservative coalition in Congress had once again achieved its dominion.

By then a moderate revolution had taken place which permanently altered the character of American society and its government. The protected status under the government that formerly had been reserved largely to business was extended to agriculture, labor, and those in the nation who were not equipped to provide for themselves. The main outlines of capitalism were little disturbed, but the duty of the government to control it in the public interest was for the first time clearly established. Nor, in retrospect, does the cost seem to have been unreasonably great, although to many contemporaries it seemed prohibitive. The national debt doubled, but so also did the national income. In years to come, New Deal spending came to be dwarfed by the wartime and also peacetime spending of subsequent Democratic and Republican administrations.

The most telling criticism of the New Deal has been that it failed in the main task of lifting the nation out of the Depression. On the eve of World War II there remained nearly 9 million unemployed, as compared with perhaps 13 or 14 million at the time of Roosevelt's first election. It was only when the war contracts began to come in that the Depression really lifted. This criticism is the more damaging when America is compared with the other industrial nations of the world, all of which were emerging from the Depression by the mid-thirties (all of them aided earlier than the United States, however, by large military expenditures).

The great achievement of the New Deal, in the view of contemporaries throughout the Western world, was the maintenance and strengthening of the democratic process under the most challenging conditions the nation had suffered since the Civil War. Roosevelt's victory in 1936 was greeted by the democracies of Europe as a victory for themselves. "You have made yourself," John Maynard Keynes had written Roosevelt early in his first administration, "the trustee for those in every country who seek to mend the evils of our condition by reasoned experiment within the framework of the existing social system. If you fail, rational choice will be gravely prejudiced throughout the world, leaving orthodoxy and revolution to fight it out." The success of the New Deal in this was a truly worldwide triumph in what Roosevelt himself spoke of as "a war for the survival of democracy."

THE GOOD NEIGHBOR POLICY

American foreign policy during the early years of the New Deal appeared to most Americans to have achieved no less than the final fulfillment of the century-old Monroe Doctrine. So far as its relations with Europe were concerned, America had never been stronger in its determination to stand apart. For the first time in American history, Congress passed neutrality legislation giving legal force to this isolationist sentiment. Toward Latin America, in the meantime, the United States was fashioning a "Good Neighbor" policy to make the protection of the Western Hemisphere a Pan-American rather than a unilateral responsibility.

The Good Neighbor policy had been faintly prefigured in Wilson's willingness to submit the Mexican-American controversy to arbitration in the hands of Argentina, Brazil, and Chile. Its main development had taken place during the Coolidge and Hoover administrations. In the mid-twenties the United States was administering the finances of ten Latin American nations, fighting a popular uprising in Nicaragua, and quarreling with Mexico over expropriated American oil lands. Then in 1927 Coolidge named Dwight Morrow Ambassador to Mexico; Morrow and the Mexicans became courteous toward each other, and, for the time being at least, the disputes over the oil lands were settled. Hoover made a highly successful goodwill tour of Latin America, and his administration began to take notice of the fact that "the Monroe Doctrine was a declaration of the United States versus Europe—not of the United States versus Latin America."

The Roosevelt administration went beyond this to sign a convention denying to itself the right to intervene in the affairs of other American nations. Accordingly American troops were withdrawn from Haiti, and the Platt amendment, which had given the United States the right to intervene in Cuban affairs, was revoked. The good American intentions were severely tested in 1938 by the Mexican expropriation of American oil lands. After more than three years of dispute the American oil companies were offered but a fraction of the value of their properties, and under pressure from the American government they accepted.

In 1934 the Reciprocal Trade Agreements Act was passed, authorizing the government to negotiate with other nations bilateral agreements reducing tariffs up to 50 percent. These arrangements were not limited to Latin America, but they were concentrated there. In some Latin American countries—notably Argentina, where the economy was thoroughly competitive with that of the United States—nothing was accomplished. Elsewhere inter-American trade increased, and Latin American nations came to look upon the United States as their means for emerging from the Depression. The substantial success of the Good Neighbor policy was demonstrated during World War II, when all American nations declared war on Germany and Japan, including eventually even Argentina.

ECONOMIC ISOLATION

Toward Europe, despite the Reciprocal Trade Agreements Act, the New Deal policy was fundamentally one of economic isolation. It had been the view of Hoover that economic recovery was to be achieved largely through stimulation of world trade and the improvement of conditions abroad. To Roosevelt, on the contrary, the Depression was a domestic condition best treated in isolation from disturbing world conditions. In this he received the strong support of a nation indignant over the failure of its former allies to repay the debts incurred during World War I.

The debtor nations had argued that the American tariff kept out European goods and deprived Europe of the dollars with which to make its American payments. Issues were raised involving the continued payment of reparations by Germany to England and France and the effect of this on American loans to Germany. Faced with these issues, Hoover in 1931 had proposed a one-year moratorium on all intergovernmental debts. He had further agreed to send representatives to the London Economic Conference in 1933 to seek international agreements on a wide variety of economic matters.

To Roosevelt, however, the objective of international stabilization of currency conflicted with the New Deal program of managed currency. He therefore cabled his refusal to cooperate in this and so effectively disabled the conference. His action was met with protests from many American economists but won the general endorsement of the nation.

It was in this isolationist atmosphere that a Senate investigating committee under Gerald P. Nye of North Dakota subjected to hostile scrutiny the vast profits that bankers and munitions makers had made out of World War I. The committee concluded that bankers had exerted powerful, perhaps decisive influence to bring America into the war in order to protect their loans to the Allies. No evidence was produced to indicate that the Wilson administration had been affected by any such pressure. The conviction was nevertheless quite general among the American people that in entering the war America had been duped by its bankers and that in the settlement of the peace it had been swindled by the wily diplomats of Europe.

In 1934 Congress passed a bill prohibiting private loans to defaulting nations, which was to say all of America's wartime associates with the exception of Finland. Then in 1935, to prevent the recurrence of the neutral-rights controversy that had preceded World War I, Congress passed the Neutrality Act, imposing an embargo of arms shipments upon all nations at war and charging American citizens to travel on belligerent vessels only at their own risk. Roosevelt signed the bill, although he would have preferred an embargo limited to aggressors. A year later the neutrality legislation was reenacted in a stronger form.

THE COMING OF
WORLD WAR II

In September 1931, the Japanese invaded Manchuria. In March 1935, Nazi Germany formally denounced the disarmament provisions of the Treaty of Versailles and increased its military forces. That September fascist Italy invaded Ethiopia. In July 1936, civil war broke out in Spain, the insurgents receiving support from Italy and Germany, the loyalists from Communist Russia. In March 1938, Germany annexed Austria. Seven months later, following the Munich agreement among the leaders of Germany, England, France, and Italy, Germany annexed the Sudetenland of Czechoslovakia, opening up that country to subsequent German occupation. In September 1939, Germany invaded Poland.

Mussolini's conquest of Ethiopia in 1935 and Hitler's reoccupation of the Rhineland in 1936 strengthened isolationist convictions in the United States by demonstrating the impotence of the League of Nations. When Francisco Franco's Falangists rose up against the republican government in Spain, the United States joined England and France in denying aid to that constitutional government. On the other hand, when Japan invaded China in 1937, Roosevelt refrained from invoking the Neutrality Act in order that the Chinese might continue to receive American supplies. When in Chicago in 1937 Roosevelt very vaguely called upon the peace-loving nations of the world to "quarantine the aggressors," the hostile reaction in the nation deterred him from anything that would alarm isolationst sentiment further.

Japan and Italy were but lightly regarded in America as international threats. Germany, however, was seen to be a different matter. With the conquest of Austria and the Sudetenland of Czechoslovakia in 1938 the American mood started to change, and when the invasion of Poland brought England and France into war with Germany in September 1939, the edifice of isolationism crumbled. A Gallup poll found 69 percent of the American people favoring all aid to Britain and France short of war. Against bitter opposition in the Senate the neutrality legislation was revised to permit the cash sale of arms to the Allies.

The American mood nevertheless remained relatively complaisant, if partisan, after the swift fall of ramshackle Poland, a catastrophe that had been looked upon as a foregone conclusion. During the months of "phony war" which followed, Americans, confident of an eventual Allied victory, were distracted by the Russian invasion of Finland.

Then in the spring of 1940 the Nazis struck with a lightning speed which few had conceived possible, through Norway and Denmark, Belgium and Holland and France. Within weeks the conquest of France and the defeat of the French and British armies were accomplished. Pinned to the English Channel at Dunkerque, the British and many of the French fighters escaped, with heavy losses, to England, leaving their machinery of war on the beaches behind them. After

Dunkerque a militarily defeated, almost unarmed England remained alone against the apparently unbeatable Nazi war machine, defended from invasion only by the battered Royal Air Force. In June 1941, the German armies invaded Russia, moving swiftly and at will into the Russian heartland. A week later Mussolini breathlessly brought Italy into the war, barely in time to precede the French armistice. These were the events which increasingly borrowed the attention of the American people from the internal war they were waging against the Great Depression.

As the presidential campaign of 1940 approached, the American nation was in the throes of shocked, angry, and confused debate. There remained the hardcore isolationists, declining in number but highly financed and widely supported in the American press, notably the Hearst newspapers. Isolationists organized the America First Committee to convince Americans that they had no stake in the conflict, and that even if they did, they could not possibly win a war against Germany in Europe. Against the America Firsters, others advocating all aid short of war organized the Committee to Defend America by Aiding the Allies. In addition there were some who wished to commit American troops to the conflict, but down to the bombing of Pearl Harbor they represented a small minority of public opinion. American policy continued to be founded on the wishful thought that somehow an Allied victory could be achieved without American intervention.

That the Democratic nomination would go to Roosevelt was a foregone conclusion by the time of the convention, despite widespread and deep-seated sentiment against a third term. Roosevelt attempted to remove foreign policy from the campaign so far as possible by appointing Republicans to his Cabinet, Henry L. Stimson as Secretary of War and Frank Knox as Secretary of the Navy. At the same time he risked his popularity by giving Britain fifty overage American destroyers in exchange for ninety-nine-year leases on British naval bases in America.

It was in the Republican party that isolationist sentiment was strongest, and there the nomination was won by an internationalist, Wendell Willkie, a public utilities businessman who had gained his reputation fighting the TVA. Both Roosevelt and Willkie promised all aid to the Allies short of war, but the isolationist vote went predominantly to Willkie and the internationalist to Roosevelt, who won by a margin of 5 million votes.

AMERICAN INTERVENTION

As the German Air Force pounded Britain and an invasion fleet stood in readiness to cross the channel, Roosevelt moved to bring aid more effectively to the English. In March 1941 the "Lend-Lease" Bill was passed, authorizing the President to "sell, transfer title, exchange, lease, lend, or otherwise dispose of" materials to "any country whose defense the President deems vital to the defense of the United States." An initial 7 billion dollars was appropriated for the purpose. In April 1941 America assumed responsibility for the protection of Greenland and began patrolling the sea-lanes to that point in the name of hemispheric defense. Then, when German submarines sank American vessels, Congress in November authorized trade with belligerent ports and the arming of American merchant vessels.

In June 1941 Hitler attacked Russia, and in November Roosevelt extended lend-lease aid to the Russians. Already directly involved in the conflict, America awaited the outbreak of formal war with Germany and Italy. Then, in December, war came to the country from Asia.

When war had broken out in Europe, Japan had acted at once to gain advantages in the Southeast Asian possessions of foreign powers. The United States answered by giving notice that it was going to suspend its commercial treaty with Japan, vitally necessary to the Japanese in view of their lack of essential raw materials for war. Japan's answer was the Rome-Berlin-Tokyo Pact, pointedly directed against the United States. The United States replied by placing an embargo on shipments to Japan of aviation gasoline, scrap iron, and steel.

In the spring of 1941 protracted negotiations with the Japanese were undertaken, beginning and ending with mutually irreconcilable terms. In July 1941 Japan assumed authority over all of French Indochina. Japanese assets in the United States were thereupon frozen. In November the Japanese made an unacceptable offer which the American government knew, from decoded Japanese messages, was to be their final one. An attack on American territory was not expected, but warnings were nevertheless sent to the Pacific commanders. The event proved that the warnings were not strong enough, and also that such as they were, they were followed out negligently by the military and naval commanders in Hawaii and elsewhere. The result was the disaster of Pearl Harbor on December 7, which left the United States for the moment virtually defenseless in the Pacific, while it at once unified the nation in the war effort. On December 11 Germany and Italy followed Japan into war with the United States as America mobilized to enter the conflict.

BIBLIOGRAPHY FOR
CHAPTER 22

W. E. Leuchtenburg, Franklin D. Roosevelt and the New Deal (1963)

K. D. Roose, The Economics of Recession and Revival (1954)

C. H. Pritchett, The Roosevelt Court (1948)

Gunnar Myrdal, An American Dilemma: The Negro Problem and Modern Democracy (1944)

R. A. Divine, The Illusion of Neutrality (1962) and The Reluctant Belligerent: American Entry into World War II (1965)

J. E. Wiltz, From Isolation to War, 1931–1941 (1968)

Allan Nevins, The New Deal in World Affairs (1950)

Bryce Wood, The Making of the Good Neighbor Policy (1961)

Herbert Feis, The Road to Pearl Harbor (1950)

GLOBAL WAR

THE MILITARY SITUATION

At the time the United States entered World War II, a German invasion fleet was poised against Britain along the English Channel. The German armies, hundreds of miles inside Russia, were fighting at the gates of Leningrad to the north, Moscow at the center, and Stalingrad to the south. The German Wehrmacht continued to inflict prodigious casualties on the Red Army, and few in the West thought that Russia would hold out long. To the south, Germany ruled the Mediterranean, holding Italy and French North Africa in contemptuous control. Everywhere the German blitzkrieg tactics of mechanization and air power quickly annihilated opposition. It seemed to some of the best-informed Americans that Germany was invincible against all possible military combinations.

Britain had withstood invasion through the exertions of the Royal Air Force, and the British Navy dominated the seas—but only on the surface of the seas. German submarines more deadly by far than those of World War I had to be hunted down by fleets of British and American destroyers far less adequate to the task than those of the earlier war. The German U-boats, busy along the American coastline as well as the British, were sinking merchant vessels more rapidly than they could be replaced by combined British and American construction.

In the Far East the disaster at Pearl Harbor had crippled America's Asian fleet and for the time being had reduced it to a strength far inferior to that of the Japanese. But the damage proved less serious than was at first believed, because the navy's aircraft carriers were not at Pearl at the time and because it proved possible to repair many of the vessels quickly. Militarily the American Army was hopeless to make more than a token resistance against the Japanese, who captured Wake Island and Guam immediately. The Philippine Islands were overrun at once, although American forces at Bataan continued to hold

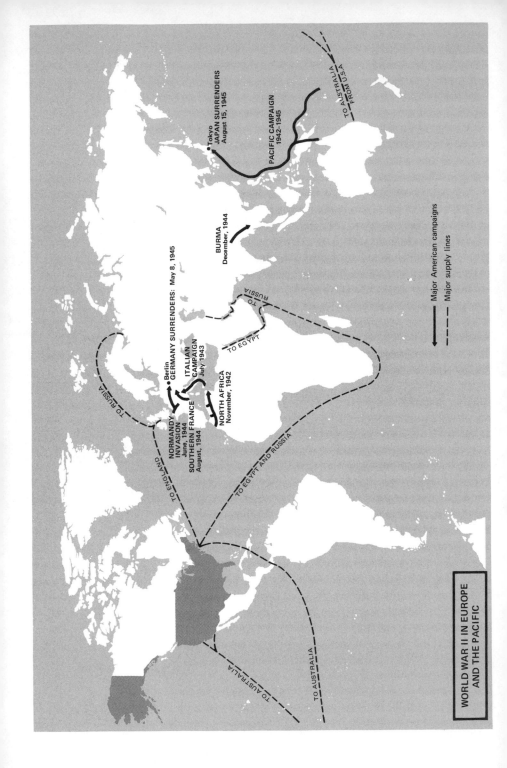

JAPAN SURRENDERS
August 15, 1945

Tokyo

PACIFIC CAMPAIGN
1942-1945

TO AUSTRALIA
FROM U.S.A

BURMA
December, 1944

GERMANY SURRENDERS: May 8, 1945

Berlin

ITALIAN
CAMPAIGN
July 1943

TO RUSSIA

TO EGYPT

NORTH AFRICA
November, 1942

NORMANDY
INVASION
June, 1944

SOUTHERN FRANCE
August, 1944

TO RUSSIA

TO ENGLAND

TO EGYPT AND RUSSIA

TO AUSTRALIA

TO AUSTRALIA

Major American campaigns
Major supply lines

WORLD WAR II IN EUROPE
AND THE PACIFIC

out for five months. In the meantime virtually all of Southeast Asia had fallen to Japanese forces, and the invasion of Australia was expected at any moment.

AMERICAN MOBILIZATION

In relation to its own military potential, the United States came but lightly armed into this global death struggle. Even at that, however, it was far better prepared than it had been at the beginning of any of its previous wars. Naval construction had been pressed by Roosevelt during the Depression partly as a recovery measure, and a massive naval construction program was currently in process, although more than a year would pass before the substantial effects of it would be felt. Japanese knowledge of this impending naval expansion had been a motive in hurrying the Japanese into war with the United States.

Congress in 1940 had passed the Selective Service Act, the first peacetime draft in American history, and at the time of Pearl Harbor a million and a half Americans were in the army. The expansion from a standing army of 200,000 had taken place so rapidly, however, that effective fighting units had not yet been created. Basic military equipment was not yet available, and the leadership was of course inexperienced. Time, it was evident, would be needed to prepare for large-scale land engagements. The navy, supported by a rapidly augmenting air power, was in a position to make its force felt earlier.

And the longer the war lasted, the better were the American prospects; for the United States had never before entered a war in potentially so fit a condition. The national divisions, ethnic and ideological, which had disturbed the home front in 1917 were largely absent in 1941 when Pearl Harbor came. More important than that, World War II was a kind of war that the United States was incomparably well equipped to wage. The blitzkreig war of mobility and firepower had astonished the world when Hitler unleashed it against Britain and France, but compared to the war machine created by America during the next two years, the Wehrmacht was a rather primitive horse-drawn affair. Nothing in the world compared with Detroit as the production center for the new war machinery. Roosevelt's call in 1940 for fifty thousand airplanes a year was dismissed by business leaders as hopelessly unrealistic, but by the close of the war planes were being produced at twice that rate, and war production generally was advancing on a similarly gigantic scale. Nor was this productivity at the expense of quality. American military equipment proved generally superior to that of the enemy. This was markedly true of American airplanes.

Roosevelt brought to the task of mobilization the American experience in both World War I and the Depression. As in both of these, numerous, confusing, and conflicting agencies were created and reorganized and combined and superseded during the war, none of them being permitted by Roosevelt to lessen his authority as Commander in Chief and President. The War Production Board was created and assumed the main task of mobilizing industry, allocating materials, supervising conversion to wartime manufacture, and developing new, government-operated industries such as the synthetic rubber industry. Organized labor signed no-strike pledges and received favored treatment through the War Labor Board, which gave it the power to organize the newly developing wartime industries. A War Manpower Commission worked to redistribute labor to areas where the new industries were developing.

Congress, as in previous wars, chose to finance the war largely through loans, only about 40 percent being raised in taxes. In the meantime enormous profits were made in business, and wages rose rapidly. The Office of Price Administration was created and placed price ceilings upon many consumer goods fairly effectively. Agricultural production rapidly increased despite the wartime decline in farm population. The cost of the war was estimated at 350 billion dollars, or ten times that of World War I. Those who had warned that the doubling of the national debt to 48 billion dollars during the New Deal would be an intolerable burden to the next generation saw the debt increase by an additional 200 billion dollars during the war.

World War I had been marked by widespread violations of civil liberties, and this fact was in the mind of the Roosevelt administration in the course of World War II. Also, there were fewer incitements to the suppression of liberties, since sentiment for the enemy was less widespread. On the score of civil liberties, therefore, the record was better than that of any other American war, with the one glaring exception of the Japanese-Americans in California. Despite the fact that Japanese-Americans in Hawaii, left to themselves, proved loyal to their nation, and despite the fact of heroic contributions to the European war by Japanese-American troops, those on the West Coast were moved from their homes to "relocation centers," most of them for the duration.

ANGLO-AMERICAN
MILITARY STRATEGY

At the outset the British and American forces were united under a single command into the Combined Chiefs of Staff, the Americans dominating its councils by virtue of the greater American military contribution. Those among its members who mainly determined the strategy of the war were the American Chief of Staff, Gen. George C. Marshall, and the American Chief of Naval Operations, Adm. Ernest J. King. Dwight D. Eisenhower was selected by Marshall as Supreme Commander of the European theater of operations; Douglas MacArthur commanded in the southwest Pacific and Adm. Chester Nimitz in the northern and central Pacific. Never before had the United States entered a war under a military leadership as capable as this one. One of the advantages the United States enjoyed over both Germany and Japan was this superiority of its military leadership.

It was agreed that Europe rather than Asia would be the main theater of combat, since Germany was more powerful than Japan and more likely, if given time, to develop rocket missiles and atomic weapons that would give it world mastery. The American Army required another year to ready itself for a major land engagement, however, and in the meantime American force made itself felt mainly through naval actions in Asian waters.

THE WAR IN ASIA AND EUROPE

Two main objectives lay immediately before the Japanese in 1942: the conquest of Australia and the immobilization of the Hawaiian Islands through the capture of Midway. In May the first of these objectives was made impossible by the Battle of the Coral Sea in the area of New Guinea; in June the second was denied the Japanese when they were routed at the Battle of Midway with tremendous losses in pilots, airplanes, and aircraft carriers. These two battles, the first of their kind in the history of warfare, were fought out by airplanes between fleets out of sight of each other. This new form of naval warfare between aircraft carriers had been learned hastily when it was found that the old reliance, the battleship, was all but helpless against air attack.

In August the United States followed up its advantage with an attack on Guadalcanal Island, east of New Guinea, and from that point until the end of the war against Japan it continued to maintain the offensive.

In Europe, the American forces remained primarily in process of preparation during the first year. The Royal Air Force already had gained superiority over the German Luftwaffe, and it hammered at continental industrial areas in massive night raids. In October 1942 the American Air Force launched its first large-scale raid; unlike the British force it flew during daytime, depending for protection on the heavy armor and armaments of its four-engine bombers. Then winter set in, and the heavy raids were not resumed until May of the next year. By then the United States had assumed the major burden, and by the end of the war it had rained a greater volume of destruction on Germany than had England, even from the beginning of the Battle of Britain.

In November 1942 American and British forces landed at Casablanca, Oran, and Algiers to drive the German Afrika Korps eastward against the British forces driving west from Egypt. After inauspicious beginnings the battle surged back and forth across the desert until in May 1943 the German forces were defeated at Bizerte in Tunisia. The attack on Sicily, and then Italy, followed immediately upon the North African victory. Within a month Sicily was cleared of the Germans, and in September Italy surrendered and then proceeded to declare war on Germany. In September 1943 American troops landed at Salerno, and the long, slow, discouraging, and rather unenterprising campaign up the mountainous Italian peninsula began.

THE DEFEAT
OF THE AXIS POWERS

On June 6, 1944, D Day, the Allied forces launched their all-out attack on the German Wehrmacht. The German high command, faced with massive engagements against Russian forces following the holocaustic defeat at Stalingrad, chose to concentrate its Western troops in the coastal cities, leaving the beaches relatively lightly guarded. It was on the beaches of Normandy that the Allies landed, for that reason, constructing their own harbors as they came, despite fearfully adverse weather conditions. Fighting from field to field through French hedgerows, the American Army captured the communications center of St. Lô in July and then unleashed a blitzkrieg the like of which the Germans had never achieved at the peak of their performance. Hitler's refusal to withdraw his armies resulted in heavy losses of men and matériel as the American Army drove northward to connect with the British and create the Falaise pocket.

In August an American army invaded southern France, and within a month France was virtually cleared of the Germans, while Russian armies moved swiftly westward. The war was far from over, however. Retreating behind the fortified Siegfried line, the Germans stalled the Anglo-American advance, and then in December, in a desperate gamble which almost paid off, they launched the first German winter offensive since the times of Frederick the Great. Driving through the Ardennes Forest in the Battle of the Bulge, they appeared for a time to be in a position to capture vast Allied supplies of food and war materials and then to overrun France. Their attack stalled when they failed to capture the communications center of Bastogne, surrounded by them but defended successfully mainly by American paratroopers.

The final rout followed. In March 1945 the Americans had the luck to capture a bridge across the Rhine River at Remagen, and during the following months British and Americans swarmed eastward to make contact with the Russians. Hitler ordered the Germans to raze Germany and fight to the last man, but Hitler's death was announced on May 1, and on May 7 the commander of the German Army signed an unconditional surrender.

In the Asian theater in November 1942, American naval forces engaged the Japanese South Pacific fleet in the area of the Solomon Islands. At stake was the island of Guadalcanal, but the Japanese lost much more than this. In a three-day naval battle their fleet was destroyed as an effective unit. Never again did the Japanese navy willingly oppose the American one. America held the initiative in Asian water and retained it from that time until the end of the war.

The task of undertaking an almost endless series of island engagements was lightened by the strategy of island-hopping toward Japan, capturing key positions and leaving intervening islands to wait out the war, a strategy which had been made possible by the winning of naval and air supremacy. In November 1943 the Marines invaded Bougainville, the northernmost island in the Solomon chain. In February 1944 Kwajalein, in the Marshall Island group, was taken. Saipan in the Marianas fell in June, and Guam was retaken a month later. The conquest of Guam was accompanied by a sea battle which wrecked much of a new Japanese navy, completely rebuilt since the disasters of 1942.

Up until that point in the war the island-hopping had been carried out by the United States Navy and the Marines, the American Army under MacArthur having concentrated on reducing the enemy forces in New Guinea. In October 1944 the army and navy combined in the invasion of the Philippine Islands. The Battle of Leyte Gulf, the greatest naval battle in history, completed the destruction of the Japanese Navy and prepared the way for the army to invade the island of Leyte. In February 1945 the army won control of the main island of Luzon, while the Marines landed on Iwo Jima, on the direct route to Tokyo. Okinawa was invaded in April, and preparations for the invasion of the Japanese homeland were under way.

Then on August 6, the first atomic bomb was exploded over Hiroshima, virtually obliterating the city. A three-day pause followed, and then a second atomic bomb destroyed the city of Nagasaki. Leading military men still resisted surrendering, but at that point Emperor Hirohito asserted his authority, and the Japanese government began to negotiate a surrender. On September 2, 1945, the terms of surrender were signed, and World War II was at an end, at a cost to America of more than 1 million wounded and 325,000 deaths.

MILITARY STRENGTHS
OF THE DEMOCRACIES

Of the world's major nations, the United States suffered by far the least from the war. By contrast, the cost to Russia was about 20 million casualties. By the close of the war there were more than 12½ million Americans in uniform, but proportionately, American men participated in the war on a smaller scale than those of any other major power involved. Where Germany maintained three hundred divisions, the United States created one hundred, despite its much larger population. The reason for placing these limits on the American military force was to leave free a sufficient work force to create in the United States the "arsenal of democracy."

Man for man, however, the American soldiers and sailors undoubtedly counted for more than those of any other nation. The enemy infantryman, both Japanese and German, was far better trained than the American, but in a war that depended upon firepower and mobility, the American was far more effective. Furthermore, although the Germans had devised the new form of warfare, their generals never grasped the full meaning of it as did the American high command. The high commands of both Germany and Japan continued to place their main reliance on the foot soldier in a war which had become first of all a logistical problem.

It was also true that in organization and orderly cooperation the democratic countries demonstrated a great superiority over the dictatorships. In Germany, the Nazi war machine was characterized by confusion, duplication, and often incredible mismanagement, directed overall by an irresponsible paranoid. In Japan, the war machine was rigidly directed by the top admirals and generals down to tactical details. When battles went amiss, the generals on the divisional level had no authority to alter their plans. To make matters worse, the Japanese code of military honor prohibited those in the chain of command from passing along the news of dishonorable defeats. As a consequence, the rigid authoritarians who were directing the war were often systematically misinformed by those serving underneath them.

In a war which depended so much upon scientific enterprise, the democracies had the decisive advantage. They gained enormously from the refugee scientists who had escaped to America and England from Germany, Italy, and Hungary; beyond that, they provided a climate conducive to scientific inquiry. Nazi Germany possessed its own abundance of brilliant scientists, but as events proved, they were fatally mismanaged. At the outset of the war German scientists were at least as advanced as those of any other nation in atomic science. They might well have created an atomic bomb in time to win, but the ultimate decision rested with Hitler, and Hitler diverted the energies of the scientists to rocket warfare, resulting in the murderous but militarily indecisive "buzz bombs."

And finally the greater value that the democracies placed on human life turned out to be an advantage rather than a disadvantage, militarily. The troops were better cared for, generally speaking, and proved to be correspondingly better fighters. This was a major factor especially against the Japanese, who often were defeated by malaria and beriberi before they came in contact with the enemy. In large measure, those democratic qualities that were despised as weaknesses by the overlords of Japan and Germany provided the conditions under which the United States converted itself into incomparably the greatest military power in the history of the world.

WARTIME DIPLOMACY

Determined not to repeat the errors of Wilson, F. D. R. began to work out the terms of the peace even before the United States entered the war. In August 1941 he met with Churchill on an American battleship to draw up an Atlantic Charter outlining the principles which should underlie the postwar world: self-determination, self-government, international economic cooperation, disarmament, and a "permanent system of general security." Thereafter Roosevelt and Churchill, despite their disagreements, cooperated cordially, both in the conduct of the war and in planning for the peace. Russia, on the other hand, declined the offer to unite militarily, and Stalin remained suspicious and often resentful of the leaders of the democracies.

In January 1943 Roosevelt and Churchill met again at Casablanca and worked out the main strategy for the immediate future. In August 1943 they met at Quebec to plan the forthcoming invasion of Europe and the campaign in the Far East. In October 1943 Secretary of State Hull met with the foreign ministers of England and Russia in Moscow to discuss the terms of settlement for Germany. At the Moscow meeting the ministers united in a declaration of intention to create an international organization to keep the peace. In November 1943 Roosevelt and Churchill met with Generalissimo Chiang Kai-shek at Cairo to discuss the war in Asia.

In December 1943, at Teheran, the first of the conferences was held in which Roosevelt and Churchill were joined by Stalin. There the three leaders discussed the coming second front, and Stalin agreed to enter the war against Japan following the defeat of Germany. In the course of those meetings the most basic difference of opinion to develop between Roosevelt and Churchill turned upon the question of the second front, Roosevelt favoring the channel crossing and Churchill favoring an attack on the "soft underbelly" of Europe, the Balkans.

In part this difference of opinion was based upon military considerations. As an Englishman, Churchill tended to think in naval terms, and the Allied naval superiority would have counted for much in such an invasion. Roosevelt, on the other hand, probably appreciated better than Churchill the unparalleled productivity of the American arsenal. The Normandy invasion involved logistical problems which only the United States could have coped with. Churchill remained somewhat dubious about the channel venture, and some leading British military men continued to oppose it actively down to D Day itself. Except for Eisenhower's fixed determination, D Day would probably have been delayed and perhaps abandoned altogether.

Aside from military considerations, Roosevelt's and Churchill's differences were founded upon conflicting views as to the nature of the war and the character of the Russian ally. To Roosevelt and to the American people, the purpose in fighting the war was to win it in as short a time and at as small a cost as possible. Furthermore, F. D. R. felt that he was getting along well with Stalin and that at the conclusion of hostilities the Big Three would be able to work out terms of peace agreeable to all. Churchill did not share Roosevelt's optimism about Stalin, and he wished to pursue a strategy that would strengthen the Anglo-American position against Russia at the war's end. This the attack in the Balkans would obviously do, by leaving central Europe in Anglo-American rather than Russian hands. England was the junior partner in the common war effort, however, and Roosevelt's views, and those of his generals, prevailed.

THE YALTA AGREEMENT

In February 1945, with Germany moving rapidly to defeat, the Big Three met at Yalta and further worked out the terms by which Europe would be reconstructed. Germany was to pay reparations as directed by a reparations commission. The Polish boundaries were fixed, and Stalin agreed to the establishment of a Polish government based on free elections.

Stalin promised "broadly representative governments" throughout central Europe generally. Marshal Tito's government in Yugoslavia was recognized. The structure of the United Nations was agreed upon. Beyond these publicly announced decisions, the Big Three arrived at a secret agreement. Russia would declare war on Japan following the defeat of Germany, and in exchange, the Western Allies would recognize the independence of Communist-dominated Outer Mongolia, and Russia would regain the Asian possessions and rights lost to Japan in the Russo-Japanese War of 1904 and 1905 as well as additional islands.

Later, when the cold war set in, the Yalta Agreement received harsh criticism in America as a betrayal of America's Chinese allies, as well as a betrayal of the peoples of Eastern Europe. Indeed the Eastern settlement did specifically violate promises which Roosevelt and Churchill had made to Chiang Kai-shek at Cairo. Indignation was the greater for the fact that the atomic bomb rendered Russian aid of vastly less importance to the United States. At the time of Yalta, however, the bomb had not yet been tested, and nobody knew whether or not it would ever work. It was further true that Roosevelt's advisers overestimated the Japanese determination to continue the war at all costs. Roosevelt was naturally influenced by the estimates of enormous American casualties which an invasion of Japan would have entailed, when in fact Japan probably would have surrendered without either an invasion or an atomic attack, although not on the same terms.

But the strongest defense of the Yalta Agreement is the argument that Roosevelt and Churchill surrendered nothing to Stalin that Stalin could not have taken just as well without their consent. Russian arms either were or would soon be in possession of the territories involved, and Russian control could be contested only at the cost of a third world war, which would have been politically supportable nowhere in the West. It was also true, however, that the Red Army was permitted to penetrate farther west in the final days of the war than purely military considerations dictated. Had they wished to do so, the Western Powers might have won the race to Berlin.

THE UNITED NATIONS

In April 1945, delegates from fifty nations met in San Francisco to draft the Charter of the United Nations Organization, which had been drawn up mainly during a conference in 1944 at Dumbarton Oaks near Washington, D.C. The

UN was a mainly American conception, just as the League of Nations had been before it, and the final draft was a primarily American document.

Stalin would have preferred to dispense with such a league and manage international affairs through conferences of the great powers. He agreed at Yalta to join such an organization only when it was decided—at least according to the Russian interpretation of the agreement—that each of the great powers, with permanent seats in the Security Council, should be able to veto even the discussion of matters which might require the use of force. At San Francisco the Americans for a time threatened to withdraw from the UN if the veto on procedural questions was retained, as it of course was; yet it is not to be supposed that the American people would have accepted the UN for long had the United States not had the veto power.

The UN Charter established a two-house legislature: the Security Council of eleven members, including five permanent and six temporary members, and the General Assembly, in which all member nations would be represented with one vote, except for Russia, which received three. The General Assembly would discuss questions and make recommendations to the Security Council. The Security Council held the authority to make the actual decisions. To the UN were added a number of additional organizations, including the International Labor Organization and the United Nations Educational, Scientific, and Cultural Organization (UNESCO).

Throughout the long course of these drawn-out negotiations Roosevelt, again remembering Wilson's difficulties, had worked in constant consultation with leaders in the Republican party. He had brought prominent Republicans into his Cabinet as Secretaries of War and Navy. Following his victory over Willkie in 1940, he had sent Willkie to England as his special representative. To the American delegation at San Francisco he had appointed Republican Sen. Arthur H. Vandenberg of Michigan and the former Republican governor of Minnesota, Harold E. Stassen.

When the United Nations Charter came before the Senate, the administration received its reward for this solicitude. Where the Covenant of the League of Nations had been defeated after eight months of acrimonious debate, the Charter of the UN was approved within the week by a vote of 89 to 2. In 1946 the UN took up permanent headquarters in New York City. The United States had taken up its responsibilities as a world leader. It had as yet hardly an inkling of what those responsibilities would entail.

BIBLIOGRAPHY FOR
CHAPTER 23

Fletcher Pratt, War for the World (1950)

L. L. Snyder, The War: A Concise History, 1939–1945 (1960)

K. S. Davis, An Experience of War: The United States in World War II
(1965)

S. E. Morison, The Two-ocean War (1963)

Herbert Feis, Japan Subdued: The Atomic Bomb and the End of the War
(1961)

Eliot Janeway, The Struggle for Survival: A Chronicle of Economic
Mobilization in World War II (1951)

Francis Walton, Miracle of World War II: How American Industry Made
Victory Possible (1956)

Jack Goodman, While You Were Gone: A Report on Wartime Life in the
United States (1946)

M. B. Grodzins, Americans Betrayed: Politics and the Japanese Evacuation
(1949)

L. F. Ellis, The Battle for Normandy (1962)

CHAPTER 24

THE TRUMAN- McCARTHY ERA

WARTIME DOMESTIC POLITICS

I t was not to be supposed that the unified war effort would result in the suspension of what politicians scornfully refer to as "politics." In 1940 the Republicans, officially accepting the New Deal in their party platform, had cut Roosevelt's margin of victory by half, and hope was in sight for victory in 1944; for "that man in the White House" would surely not run for a fourth term. To conservatives the war had presented itself as the opportunity to vanquish the New Deal at last, while to liberals it had presented itself as the opportunity to promote further economic reforms at home, during so vast an enlargement of federal power, and beyond that to carry their missionary work to the world.

From the first the conservatives had the best of it. The war brought the business community back into power at once, and military defeats and highly publicized episodes of military mismanagement gave the Republicans their first good political issue since the coming of the Depression. In the congressional elections of 1942, consequently, the Republican party made gains in both houses of Congress.

Congress had grown conservative even before Pearl Harbor, and throughout the war the congressional coalition of Republicans and Southern Democrats wrung concessions from Roosevelt in domestic matters in exchange for its support of his war measures. Engrossed in the conduct of the war, Roosevelt no longer was able to concentrate on national affairs, which under any circumstances would be bound to be shaped by the exigencies of war.

By the election year of 1944, however, final military victory seemed almost in sight, and "Dr. Win-the-War," as Roosevelt had referred to himself, automatically won the nomination for the fourth term. Having already broken the traditional two-term limitation for the Presidency, Roosevelt was little threatened by the fourth-term issue in his campaign. More serious was the issue of his advancing age and very apparent decline in health. There seemed every likelihood of his failing to survive a fourth term, and one result of this possibility was an unusually vigorous struggle in the convention over the nomination of a vice-presidential candidate.

In 1940, against the wishes of conservative Democrats, Roosevelt had named as his running mate Secretary of Agriculture Henry Wallace. During the war Wallace had spoken for the wing of New Deal missionaries who, their enemies complained, wished to deliver "a quart of milk for every Hottentot." Out of the struggle between the supporters of Wallace and those of James F. Byrnes of South Carolina there emerged a compromise candidate, Sen. Harry S. Truman of Missouri, a relatively little-known figure who, however, had gained some national recognition for his able chairmanship of the Senate war investigating committee.

Against Roosevelt the Republicans nominated Gov. Thomas E. Dewey of New York, who had gained his main national reputation as the nation's leading gangbuster. Dewey's youth and vigor were an added advantage in the campaign against the careworn President. Roosevelt, however, threw himself into the campaign in a remarkable display of vitality that brought him his fourth victory by the margin of 3.6 million votes. Thereafter Roosevelt's physical condition visibly worsened. Awaiting the San Francisco United Nations meeting in April 1945, he was stricken by a cerebral hemorrhage and died immediately.

THE TRUMAN ADMINISTRATION

For the second time in the nation's history the Commander in Chief had been struck down at the moment of victory. When Truman came to office, the American armies pouring into Germany had reached the Elbe, while the Russians were at the gates of Berlin. In Asia the invasion of Okinawa was under way. The San Francisco Conference met two weeks later. Germany capitulated within a month of Truman's taking office, and Japan followed three months after that. Truman came to office with little special knowledge of what the administration was doing; he was not even aware that an atomic bomb was in preparation, the use of which would be up to his discretion. "Boys," he told reporters the next day, "if you ever pray, pray for me now."

Rising in politics in the scandalously corrupt Pendergast machine of Kansas City, Truman had remained scrupulously honest. He had, at the same time, prepared himself thoroughly in the art of politics, however little he was prepared at the time of assuming office to meet the world-shattering problems that abruptly rushed in upon him. As little self-confident on taking office as any President in the nation's history, he grasped his authority forcefully to make some of the most momentous decisions in the nation's history. Humble and cocky by turns, given to off-the-cuff blunders in small matters and masterful achievements in large ones, he was a ward politician who enlarged himself into a major statesman of Western civilization.

For the immediate future, at least, a course of American foreign policy had largely been set when Truman came to office. In domestic affairs nothing had really been planned. The resources of the nation were geared to the task of invading Japan, and production for military purposes continued to increase. Then it all ended. The nation danced in the streets on V-J Day and hurried to get back to what President Harding after World War I had called normalcy.

"Reconversion," as the process came to be called, was a vastly greater operation in 1945 than it had been in 1919. There were more than three times as many Americans in uniform, and there was correspondingly greater government involvement in the economy. For the United States the war had endured three times as long. For millions of Americans it had been by no means an altogether unhappy experience. It had brought full employment, rapid wage increases, and exorbitant profits, despite wage and price controls. It had also, of course, brought severe shortages of consumer goods, and at war's end the American people had accumulated 140 billion dollars in savings. These were the spoils of war which the people had created for themselves, and the people demanded the peacetime conditions that would allow them to enjoy their gains.

The military forces were reduced from 12½ million to 1 million almost immediately, a national disaster as General Marshall said at the time. President Truman fought to no avail against the peace-minded nation for a program of universal military training. Wartime construction had been mostly government-financed, and most of it was convertible to civilian uses. Its transfer to private hands at wonderful bargain prices went on at headlong speed, from the sale of large aluminum factories down to the sale of canteens and leggings at war surplus stores. These pleasant developments proceeded swiftly against the futile opposition of organized labor and liberal groups.

Naturally, not all the fruits of victory were so sweet. Despite price and wage controls, inflation had accompanied the war, and at war's end, with virtually unlimited money and not much to buy, inflation continued apace. With it came also the demand for an end to controls. Organized labor, far more numerous than before, prepared for a trial of strength; businessmen and farmers demanded an end to price ceilings. Old New Dealers called for a new era of reform, while conservatives sought opportunities to sweep away the remaining New Deal restrictions along with the wartime ones. Everyone recalled the parallel postwar period which had begun in 1919, some with horror and some with hope.

Truman, by his voting record in the Senate, was a convinced New Dealer, and during his first year in office he indicated his reformist views in a series of recommendations to Congress. He called for an increase in the minimum wage, a Fair Employment Practices Act to defend against racial discrimination, extension of public works, a federal housing and slum-clearance program, federal aid to education, and a federal health-insurance program. Amid the distractions of reconversion, however, he won little except the increase of the minimum wage from 40 to 75 cents per hour and the Maximum Employment Act establishing the Council of Economic Advisers. In the area of price controls, meanwhile, he followed a wobbly course against determined Republican opposition and under black-market conditions. In the area of labor relations his policy appeared, if anything, even more inconsistent.

As in 1919, organized labor did not intend to submit to the freezing of wages. The United Automobile Workers led with a strike against General Motors for a 30 percent wage increase, and they were quickly followed by the United Steel Workers and by unions in other industries. These demands generally received a good measure of support from the White House until April 1946, when John L. Lewis took his coal miners out on strike in defiance of government recommendations. Then in May the threat of a strike by the Brotherhoods of Locomotive Engineers and of Railway Trainmen inspired an unprecedented counterattack by Truman. To avert the paralysis of a nationwide railroad strike, he went before Congress to ask for a law empowering him to draft railroad strikers. Agreement was immediately reached between unions and management, however, and the proposed legislation was dropped.

TRUMAN AND THE
EIGHTIETH CONGRESS

By the time of the congressional elections of 1946 Truman had alienated conservatives by his New Deal program and alienated liberals by his failure to pursue the program. Reconversion had absorbed 10 million returned members of the armed forces with unlooked-for facility, but unemployment was now increasing, and a postwar depression was widely predicted. International affairs were beginning to have an ominous look, and people were beginning to speak of the coming war with Russia. Inflation was rampant. The honeymoon traditionally accorded an incoming President had been a short one for Truman, who was mercilessly derided in the press. In 1946 the Republicans needed only the slogan "Had enough?" to win control of both houses of Congress for the first time since the coming of the Depression.

The Seventy-ninth Congress had simply ignored Truman's program. The Eightieth came aggressively forward with one of its own. Most of the remaining price controls were lifted, and government appropriations were slashed under the direction of the chairman of the House Appropriations Committee, John Taber, making good his promise to apply a "meat-axe to government frills." Truman vetoed a new tax bill reducing income taxes on the highest incomes by 65 percent and on the lowest by 3 percent. Also vetoed by Truman, but passed again over his veto, was the Taft-Hartley Act, the most contentious enactment of the Eightieth Congress.

Defended as necessary to restore a fair balance between labor and management, which the Wagner Act was accused of destroying, the Taft-Hartley Act outlawed the closed shop—the exclusive hiring of union men—while permitting the union shop—where the employee, once hired, was obligated to join the union. It required a "cooling-off" period following the announcement of intention to strike before the strike could be held. It prohibited various practices such as jurisdictional strikes and secondary boycotts, and it extended certain new legal rights to employers in their dealings with the National Labor Relations Board. The act did not break the labor unions, as was widely predicted at the time, but it did return them solidly to the Democratic ranks. Having thus unequivocally declared themselves, the Republicans renominated the moderately liberal Thomas E. Dewey and moved confidently toward a presidential victory in 1948.

THE ELECTION OF 1948

The postwar trend toward conservatism alone seemed sufficient to secure a Republican victory. It also seemed that President Truman was wrecking the great Democratic coalition his predecessor had created, simultaneously driving away Northern liberals and Southern conservatives. Truman won the nomination against the bitter opposition of many party leaders who were convinced the party could not win with him. Beyond that, he faced the opposition of two new parties which would draw their support mainly from Democratic ranks: the Wallace Progressives and the Dixiecrats. Henry A. Wallace, dismissed from Truman's Cabinet for his loudly spoken soft line toward Russia, headed a party made up of discontented New Dealers and other critics of Truman's hard policy toward the Communists. The Dixiecrats, on the other hand, alienated by Truman's and the Democratic platform's demands for Negro equality, organized behind Gov. J. Strom Thurmond of South Carolina as the States' Rights Democratic party.

Absolutely assured of victory by the public opinion polls, Dewey campaigned mildly on the issue of the need for unity, in order to arouse as few antagonisms as possible against his coming administration. Truman, for his part, largely ignored his opponent, who differed with him little on either foreign or domestic policy. He turned his attack instead on the Republican Eightieth Congress, in a "whistle-stop" campaign covering more than 30,000 miles and entailing more than three hundred speeches.

On this vulnerable Congress Truman successfully focused many of the same postwar discontents that had been directed against his own administration. The result was that with strong support from labor and Northern Negroes and from generally Republican but momentarily unhappy farmers he won by a margin of more than 2 million votes. The Dixiecrats, with somewhat more than a million votes, won in South Carolina, Alabama, Louisiana, and Mississippi. The Wallace Progressives, with an approximately equal popular vote, failed to win in any state. The Democrats regained control of both houses of Congress.

An enormous personal triumph for Truman, the election was a victory also for Franklin Roosevelt and the New Deal. Prior to the election it had been widely assumed that the American people were of a mind to accept a general conservative reform of existing New Deal legislation. Truman's victorious campaign on his "Fair Deal" platform, was generally viewed as a fundamentally significant mandate at least for retaining the existing programs.

Leading from strength for the time, Truman set out vigorously to press for the broad range of legislation that Congress had until then largely ignored. No sooner had he returned to office, however, than international storms broke upon the American political scene, tangling and disfiguring domestic political issues and interfering with the processes of orderly, constitutional government. Fast upon Truman's reelection the nation moved suddenly and violently into the era of Joseph McCarthy; in foreign affairs it moved from the successes of the Marshall Plan to the defeats of the Korean conflict.

COMING OF THE COLD WAR

At the time of Roosevelt's death, as Winston Churchill wrote, "Every question about the future was unsettled. . . . The agreements and understandings at Yalta, such as they were, had already been broken or brushed aside by the triumphant Kremlin. New perils, perhaps as terrible as those we had surmounted, loomed and glared upon the torn and harassed world." The period from Yalta in February 1945 to Potsdam in July was the time of awakening for the American government—though not the American people—to some realization of the bitter meaning of the victory.

General Eisenhower had voiced the almost unanimous American view when, following a trip to Moscow, he had declared that "nothing guides Russian policy so much as a desire for friendship with the United States." Roosevelt was confident that the United States and Russia would get along very well indeed after the war, although his last days were darkened by the beginnings of doubt. Truman, on the contrary, suspected Stalin's intentions from the first, but he could bring himself to do no more than protest angrily against the Russian subjugation of Poland.

On the advice of Eisenhower and over the protests of Churchill, Truman voluntarily relinquished enormous bargaining power to Stalin by withdrawing American troops from the Elbe River back more than 100 miles to the American line agreed upon at Yalta. At Potsdam the Western Allies accepted the accomplished fact of the bloody and dictatorial Russian solution in Poland and arranged for the division of Germany into the four military zones. A Council of Foreign Ministers was created to conclude treaties with Germany's European allies, and Truman returned to America determined to avoid such bleak summit conferences in the future.

In March 1946 Winston Churchill snapped up the offer of the presumptuous president of little Westminster College in Fulton, Missouri, to deliver an address there, and he spoke his mind. "From Stettin in the Baltic to Trieste in the Adriatic, an iron curtain has descended across the Continent. . . . I do not believe that the Soviet Russia desires war. What they desire is the fruits of war and the indefinite expansion of their power and doctrines. . . . I am convinced that there is nothing they admire so much as strength, and there is nothing for which they have less respect than weakness, especially military weakness." He announced the cold war to an American people still far from willing to admit its existence.

In September 1946 Henry Wallace, then Secretary of Commerce, delivered a speech implicitly denouncing the administration's foreign policy for its harshness toward Russia. "I realize," he declared, "that the danger of war is much less from communism than it is from imperialism." Secretary of State James F. Byrnes, negotiating with Russia in Paris at the time, threatened to resign immediately, and Wallace was dismissed from his Cabinet post. Two months after Wallace's speech the Republicans won control of both houses of Congress, and Sen. Robert A. Taft, the nation's most powerful isolationist, became the leader of the Senate.

At this critical moment in world affairs, when America was moving reluctantly into the cold war, Sen. Arthur M. Vandenberg of Michigan emerged as the key figure in American, and therefore world, diplomacy. The leading presidential candidate of the Republican isolationists in 1940, Vandenberg had gradually abandoned the old certitudes under the impact of the war. In 1945 he finally declared his new position in a Senate speech. ". . . I do not believe that any nation hereafter can immunize itself by its own exclusive action. . . . I want maximum American cooperation." It was the notorious Eightieth Congress, dominated by former isolationist diehards, that legislated America into the cold war, and it was preeminently the political skill and reputation of Vandenberg that made this possible.

THE MARSHALL PLAN

In February 1947 the British government sent a note informing the American government that Great Britain was no longer capable of maintaining its support of the Greek government. Unless the United States took Britain's place, the note continued, Greece would no doubt become Communist, Turkey would come under Russian control, and the whole of the Middle East might be swept into the Russian orbit. That the United States must act, despite hostile public opinion, was agreed upon by Truman, Vandenberg, and the new Secretary of State, Gen. George C. Marshall. Truman took Vandenberg's advice "to make a personal appearance before Congress and scare hell out of the country." There he declared what became known as the Truman Doctrine "that it must be the policy of the United States to support free peoples who are resisting attempted subjugation by armed minorities or by outside pressures." He asked for, and received, 400 million dollars to aid Greece and Turkey. A century and a quarter after Monroe stated his isolationist doctrine, the United States finally officially turned its back on the historic policy.

But even worse news was coming from Western Europe, which, in Churchill's words, had become a "rubble-heap, a charnel house, a breeding-ground of pestilence and hate." Communism was fanning out through Western Europe, threatening to capture the governments of France and Italy. With this catastrophe threatening, General Marshall, in June 1947, announced the momentous forthcoming American action in a commencement address at Harvard. The nations of Europe, Communist and non-Communist, were to draw up their own program of recovery. The United States, if it approved the program, would underwrite it to the extent of billions of dollars.

Western Europe went to work at once. Indeed, British Foreign Minister Ernest Bevin leaped out of bed at the news to put his department staff to work. "This is the turning point," he told them. Within the month representatives of the nations of Western Europe were assembled in Paris to draw up the plan. Soviet Russia, meanwhile, had made the whole thing politically possible, so far as the United States was concerned, by prohibiting Communist nations from participating. The resulting Marshall Plan, or Economic Recovery Program, following nominal congressional modifications, received overwhelming endorsement from Congress.

Again Vandenberg was the key figure in the administration victory, and he was aided by the organization of private committees throughout the country to stir up national sentiment in favor of Marshall aid. Most helpful of all was Stalin. In the midst of the congressional debate Soviet Russia overthrew the democratic Czechoslovakian government and placed that country behind the iron curtain. When the roll was called in the Senate, even Taft voted in favor of the program. All told, the program cost 13 billion dollars, much less than had been anticipated. Altogether, however, the United States in the first decade after the war spent 50 billion dollars in foreign aid of all kinds.

In June 1948 the American, British, and French governments announced the unification of their three sectors of occupation in Germany into an independent united West German government with membership in the Economic Recovery Program. Russia retaliated by sealing off access to Berlin for the Western Allies. The United States and Britain countered with the airlift, which for almost a year flew in sufficient supplies to support a population of more than 2 million.

In April 1949 the North Atlantic Treaty Organization was created, joining the United States to the nations of Western Europe in a military alliance and creating a unified international military force under the supreme command of General Eisenhower. Militarily weak by comparison to the Red Army, the forces of NATO possessed the great equalizer, the atomic bomb. Russia shattered this basis for confidence five months later with a successful atomic explosion of its own. In the meantime, the main pressures of communism had shifted dramatically from the West to the Far East.

AMERICA AND CHINA

Americans had traditionally felt a missionary concern for the Far East, which was in contrast to their isolationist rejection of Europe. This sentiment had been especially strong among the Midwestern isolationists, who during the war had opposed the policy of concentrating the main military effort in the European theater. In response to this "China First" sentiment Roosevelt, throughout the war, had insisted on what Churchill called the "absolute farce" of treating Chiang Kai-shek's Nationalist China as a major power. Politically and militarily weak, the Chinese Nationalists at the conclusion of hostilities faced the threat of a growing army of Chinese Communists. American attempts to reconcile the two forces were fruitless, and in 1947 all-out civil war erupted.

The American-supplied Nationalists proved powerless against the more dedicated Communists. Following a year of successive victories the Communists overran all of China by the end of 1949, driving Chiang and the Nationalists to the island of Formosa. Its Far Eastern ally thus overwhelmingly defeated, the United States did what it could to redress the balance of power in Asia, as in Europe, by turning to its former enemy. In 1949 it reversed its policy of breaking up the industrial combinations in Japan, and in 1950 it began to negotiate a peace treaty, which was ratified two years later by the United States Senate. By that time events in the Far East were driving America toward a military alliance with a reluctantly rearming Japan.

THE KOREAN WAR

During the last frantic days of the war, with the Russians hurrying—two days before victory—to win the spoils of victory in Asia, the United States agreed that in Korea the Russians might have the honor of accepting the Japanese surrender in the northern half, as far south as the 38th parallel. Once in control of the richest area of the nation, the Russians created the Communist government of North Korea and thereafter naturally refused to consider unification except on their own terms. Faced with this accomplished fact, the United States, after assisting in the establishment of the government of South Korea, withdrew its forces. One year later, in June 1950, North Korea went on the attack.

The attack found the American military largely dismantled, and it took place in an area strategically most difficult for the United States to defend. The American government had indeed encouraged the attack by explicitly placing Korea outside the American defense perimeter. But a Far Eastern repetition of the unopposed Communist conquest of Czechoslovakia would have been, for the United States, a diplomatic disaster throughout the world, and with this in mind, President Truman summoned a meeting of the UN Security Council to act against North Korea and simultaneously ordered American naval and air forces into the conflict. The Soviet representative's absence from the Security Council, in protest, enabled the United States to achieve UN authorization without threat of Soviet veto and made possible the creation of a United Nations army.

Placed under the command of General MacArthur, the UN forces, including contingents from various nations, were composed mainly of American and South Korean troops. Hopelessly unprepared at the outset, these were necessarily thrown to the slaughter in the opening weeks of the conflict in order to slow the advance and maintain at least a foothold on the peninsula. This objective was successfully achieved in the securing of a fortified bridgehead around the port of Pusan. For five weeks the UN forces held while reinforcements continued to arrive. Then, with a surprise amphibious attack at Inchon, near the 38th parallel, UN forces snatched victory from apparent defeat almost overnight. Within a few days the capital city of Seoul was recaptured, and the harried North Korean Army was fleeing for the border.

Faced with this swift reversal of fortune, the United Nations authorized pursuit into North Korea with the objective of creating a united democratic nation. This authorization was given in the face of Chinese Communist threats to intervene, and MacArthur eagerly implemented it. Moving rapidly northward, the UN army late in November launched the attack that was to bring the conflict to an immediate close. Two days later Communist China attacked with a force of 200,000 troops, overrunning the UN forces and recapturing Seoul. Then the UN forces held and moved slowly on the offensive. By the end of March 1951 Seoul had been retaken once again, the opposing armies faced each other across approximately the original boundaries of North and South Korea, and Truman, with the United Nations, was prepared to negotiate for peace.

Truman was determined to negotiate because for him the main theater of the cold war was Europe and not Asia. Culturally America was part of the European community, and militarily America had much more to hope for from allied, industrial Western Europe than from pro-Soviet, underdeveloped China. On the other hand, MacArthur's long military career had been associated with the Far East. He disagreed, and he went over the head of his Commander in Chief to make his point. In a letter to Joseph Martin, the Republican minority leader of the House of Representatives, he called for a full-scale attack on China, beginning with the bombing of bases within China. His argument that "there is no substitute for victory" struck a powerful chord with an American public baffled and outraged by the bloody and inconclusive struggle. It also struck a powerful chord with President Truman, who relieved MacArthur of his command and ordered him home.

MacArthur received a hero's welcome that made his trip to Washington a triumphal march. His sentimental "old soldiers never die" address to both houses of Congress highlighted the dramatic Korean issue, which remained to enliven the presidential campaign of 1952. As a practical matter, however, Truman's decision had settled the issue. In June 1951 Soviet Russia proposed a truce, and negotiations began shortly thereafter, although they were destined to drag on through the next two years. The result, when all was over, was a return to the original stalemate, at a cost to America of 157,000 casualties, including 53,000 dead. The gains were not as clearly apparent as the losses. They included, however, the return of the American nation to a position of military strength and the beginning of a general realization that in the cold war the finding of substitutes for total victories and unconditional surrenders was to become the continuing and never-ending national purpose in world affairs.

THE ATOMIC BOMB

During the first day of the Potsdam Conference, Secretary of War Stimson passed a note to Churchill: "Babies satisfactorily born." At Alamogordo, New Mexico, the atomic bomb had been successfully exploded. Three weeks later a second bomb destroyed Hiroshima, killing or wounding more than 160,000. The Russians leaped into the war at once before the third bomb destroyed Nagasaki, and the war ended. The bomb had ended the war; the larger question which the explosions at once raised was whether the bomb would end the world. Although Britain and Canada had cooperated in its creation, the bomb was an American monopoly. What Anglo-American know-how made possible, however, would in time be possible for other nations.

The success of the atomic bomb opened the way for the far more devastating hydrogen bomb and ultimately—theoretically—for the cobalt bomb, a single one of which might be sufficient to destroy all life on earth. Impelled by the fear of absolute extinction, the American government in July 1946 presented to the United Nations a plan for the universal control of atomic energy. The United States would relinquish its monopoly to the United Nations. It would destroy all existing bombs, and, in common with all other nations, it would submit to perpetual inspection by United Nations teams to prevent the manufacture of any such weapon in the future. This offer was declined by the Russians, who were hard at work on an atomic bomb of their own and who refused to submit to inspection.

That Russia would succeed eventually in creating an atomic bomb was assumed, but nobody in authority expected such a development in the near future. The United States rested in the confidence that with its monopoly of the bomb it was militarily supreme. It reduced the army to below 600,000 men, which allowed it to cut taxes as well. Then in September 1949 the Truman administration was obliged to inform the American people that an atomic explosion had taken place in Russia. In January 1950 Truman ordered the Atomic Energy Commission to proceed with the development of a hydrogen bomb. In the meantime both nations busied themselves developing other revolutionary new war machinery, both of them aided by compliant former Nazi scientists, who were no longer permitted such employment in their own native country.

SUBVERSIVE ACTIVITY

To those who found the news of the Russian bomb incredible, an explanation was presently forthcoming. In February 1950 the British government announced that Klaus Fuchs, an atomic scientist, had confessed to being a Russian spy. For four years, while engaging in atomic research for the British and American governments, Fuchs had forwarded to Russia all the enormous information at his disposal. The announcement of his confession followed by two weeks the news of the conviction of Alger Hiss on the charge, technically of perjury, but actually of spying for Russia during the days of the New Deal.

Hiss, although never a prominent figure in government, had held various positions of responsibility in the New Deal. At the time he was accused of spying he was serving as head of the august Carnegie Endowment for International Peace. These roles did much to associate him in the minds of Americans with both the idealism of the New Deal and the more conservative idealism of corporate philanthropy. In appearance and in background he was the very model of the patrician Ivy Leaguer; yet he had been charged by Whittaker Chambers, a confessed former Soviet spy, with systematically forwarding secret information from the State Department to the Kremlin during the 1930s.

Chambers identified Hiss as a former Communist before the House Un-American Activities Committee in the fall of 1948 and returned several months later with the charges of spying. Charges were brought by a New York grand jury, and Hiss went on trial in May 1949. Following a split decision by the trial jury, a second jury convicted Hiss in January 1950. By that time it had been, not simply Hiss, but a whole generation that had been on trial. Millions could not believe that events had forced America into those burdensome, dangerous, and crisis-ridden times. A simpler—and for many a more satisfactory—explanation was that there had been a betrayal. Hiss became the personification of this betrayal, and through what he symbolized, many Americans convicted genteel America on the one hand and welfare liberalism on the other of treason to the nation.

McCARTHYISM

To these suspicious Americans this pattern of betrayal was to be seen in ever-darker developments. In August 1949 the State Department issued a white paper announcing the conquest of China by the Communists. Unprepared for this aggrandizement of one-quarter of the earth's people, many Americans could find satisfactory explanation only by postulating some deep-laid plot through which America had "lost" China. Then in 1950 the nation enthusiastically launched a "police action" against North Korea, which developed into the fourth bloodiest—since Vietnam the fifth bloodiest—war in American history.

Into this jittery atmosphere in February 1950 stepped Sen. Joseph McCarthy of Wisconsin, with a talk to the Women's Republican Club of Wheeling, West Virginia. Waving in his hand a letter (which in truth mentioned the names of no Communists), he declared, according to reporters' accounts of the speech, "I have here in my hand a list of 205—a list of names that were known to the Secretary of State as being members of the Communist Party and who nevertheless are still working and shaping the policy in the State Department." And with that—as much to his own surprise, apparently, as to anybody's—McCarthy was off on a four-year career of bullyboy power such as had never before been witnessed in the history of American demagoguery. Denounced by liberals for trampling on civil liberties as a result of its loyalty program in government employment, the Truman administration was denounced by right-wing Republicans for succumbing to Communist influence. "Traitors in high councils of our own government," declared Rep. Richard Nixon of California, "have made sure that the deck is stacked on the Soviet side of the diplomatic tables." There followed the cases of Fuchs and Hiss, then the Russian atomic explosion, then the fall of Nationalist China, then the invasion of South Korea, and then the rise of McCarthy.

Lacking almost altogether the wit and intelligence of Huey Long, McCarthy probably surpassed Long in the art of heavy-breathing intimidation. Inarticulate but doggedly persistent in his accusations, McCarthy discovered in himself a deadly talent for demolishing reputations through innuendo and slander. Politically all else was beyond him. With all his power he developed no effective organization and associated himself with no political program. When he fell from power, he collapsed altogether, leaving nothing behind but a handful of ruined careers and a great deal of bad feeling. For the time being, however, in that atmosphere of bewilderment, resentment, and suspicion, his tactics of relentless accusation were more than sufficient to maintain his reign of terror.

A key to McCarthy's power was his conquest of the United States Senate. When a Senate committee under Millard Tydings of Maryland investigated McCarthy's early charges and declared them false, McCarthy entered Maryland politics during the senatorial campaign of 1950 and dealt the conservative Southerner Tydings a stunning defeat by questioning his loyalty on the basis of outrageously doctored evidence. That display of McCarthy's personal power persuaded most senators not to stake their careers on a contest with McCarthyism. Thereafter both fear and party advantage persuaded Republican leaders to attempt the impossible task of giving measured and discreet support to the spectacular upstart in their ranks. They were encouraged in this course by appreciable Republican gains in the congressional elections which had featured the defeat of Tydings.

THE ELECTION OF 1952

The circumstances were not propitious for Truman's Fair Deal, and Truman, while denouncing McCarthyism out of hand, made the mistake of initially dismissing the Hiss case as a "red herring," a misjudgment which was used against him to good effect. Then evidences of corruption—gifts of a mink coat and a deepfreeze unit in exchange for political influence—served to discredit Truman's administration. The small bribes involved no key figures in the administration, but they added fuel to the growing discontent and the desire to "clean up that mess in Washington." In "Communism, Korea and Corruption" the Republicans found a winning slogan in the presidential election of 1952, and in General Eisenhower they possessed an incomparably popular candidate.

Since the close of the war it had been evident to political leaders in both parties that Dwight D. Eisenhower could no more be beaten as a presidential candidate than Grant could have been beaten in 1868. As with Grant, and Herbert Hoover after World War I, Eisenhower's popularity was the more disturbing to the professionals for the fact that if he chose to run, nobody knew which party he would choose. In 1948 Democratic party leaders, certain in their own minds that Truman could not win, had unsuccessfully urged Eisenhower to accept the Democratic nomination.

In 1952 Republican liberals succeeded where Democratic liberals had failed, and in the Republican convention of that year Eisenhower submitted himself to a bitter struggle against the favorite of the professionals and the conservatives in the party, Senator Taft of Ohio. Supported mainly by the internationalists and the big-business wing of the party, Eisenhower won and launched on a campaign that promised an end to the conflict in Korea and an end to "creeping socialism" at home. His running mate, Richard M. Nixon, had gained his reputation through his role in the conviction of Hiss, and his candidacy served to appease the conservative followers of Taft. The Democrats nominated Gov. Adlai E. Stevenson of Illinois, whose witty and eloquent speeches drew fervent support from liberals and intellectuals without convincing the majority of the voters. Eisenhower won handsomely in a campaign which also narrowly secured Republican majorities in both houses of Congress.

THE FALL OF McCARTHY

It may be doubted that Eisenhower's victory contributed appreciably to the Korean peace settlement, which was by then slowly but almost certainly approaching completion. Nor was the Eisenhower administration able to do much to check the "creeping socialism" of the old New Deal reforms. The main positive results of the victory—and certainly they were momentous results—proved to be bipartisan acceptance of the new American role of global responsibility and an end to that McCarthyism at home which had expressed unwillingness to accept the state that the world was in.

As a member of the party in power, McCarthy continued against the Eisenhower administration the tactics he had employed against the administration of Truman. Centering his attack upon the State Department, he continued his accusations of Communist infiltration, forcing his own personal appointments upon Secretary of State John Foster Dulles and forcing the firing, without evidence, of State Department employees. Successful in this, he moved against the United States Army, accusing a general of coddling Communists. There followed in 1954 a month-long, nationally televised Senate hearing, a vivid exhibition of McCarthy's loathsome technique which rapidly cost him popular support.

The United States Senate thereupon plucked up its courage and condemned McCarthy by a vote of 67 to 22, the fourth such instance in American history. Thereafter ignored by his fellow senators and dropped from the headlines, McCarthy abruptly ceased to exist as a political force. He did not even attend the Republican nominating convention in 1956. He died the year following. By that time Egypt had replaced Korea in the public mind, and the Truman Doctrine of aid to Greece and Turkey had been followed by the Eisenhower Doctrine of aid to the nations of the Middle East. Sputnik and intercontinental ballistic missiles tended to persuade doubters that the betrayal of their world was irrevocable and also that it was not to be satisfactorily explained by any simple theory of conspiracy.

BIBLIOGRAPHY FOR
CHAPTER 24

Eric Goldman, The Crucial Decade—and After: America, 1945–1960 (1961)

H. B. Westerfield, Foreign Policy and Party Politics: Pearl Harbor to Korea (1955)

J. L. Snell, Illusion and Necessity: The Diplomacy of Global War (1963)

Gaddis Smith, American Diplomacy during the Second World War (1965)

John Lukacs, A History of the Cold War (1961)

N. A. Graebner, Cold War Diplomacy, 1945–1960 (1962)

Walter LaFeber, America, Russia, and the Cold War (1967)

H. M. Vinacke, Far Eastern Politics in the Postwar Period (1959)

Robert Leckie, Conflict: The History of the Korean War (1962)

L. W. Koenig, The Truman Administration: Its Principles and Practice (1956)

Cabell Phillips, The Truman Presidency (1966)

Alistair Cook, A Generation on Trial (1950)—the Hiss trial

R. H. Rovere, Senator Joe McCarthy (1959)

CHAPTER 25

THE ERA OF CONSENSUS

THE EISENHOWER ADMINISTRATION

Dwight D. Eisenhower epitomized the ideals of most Americans. He had come out of middle-class middle America to lead his country to triumph over its foreign enemies. Then, like many another American Cincinnatus before him, he had doffed his uniform to aid his country in peaceful enterprises, serving as president of Columbia University. He was an instinctively religious man and a visibly patriotic one. Under him America would be guided by traditional values rather than current and changing theories. Suspicious of the intellectuals the New Deal and Fair Deal had harbored—the "eggheads"— he put his trust in the plain, practical good sense of the business community.

He controlled his righteous anger with difficulty, but he was unaffectedly free with his infectious grin. He had always a great difficulty in expressing what he wanted to say, which was probably an asset in a time when clarity of purpose brought unusually vehement opposition. He inherited a nation more rent by faction than at any time since the Civil War. He bequeathed a nation which had accepted the domestic reforms of F. D. R. and the foreign policy of Truman to such an extent that even the politically ingenious Richard Nixon was at a loss for a political issue in the presidential campaign of 1960.

Himself associated with the Truman foreign policy, Eisenhower chose as his Secretary of State John Foster Dulles, who also had been associated with the postwar diplomatic settlements. As his Secretary of Labor he chose a union official, who was later replaced by a man from management, but on the whole his choice of Cabinet clearly reflected his belief in the Harding dictum that there ought to be less government in business and more business in government.

Eisenhower believed there should be a self-limitation of executive authority, following the aggrandizements of power by Roosevelt and Truman, to the end that the constitutional separation of powers be once again maintained. The nation should return to principles of free enterprise. It was the responsibility of the government to ensure the stable dollar and balance the budget. There should, however, be no reckless return to these true principles. For instance, the farmer should be returned to the world of free competition, but at the same time Eisenhower admonished his Secretary of Agriculture against any dangerously precipitous reductions of price supports.

He appointed a businessman's Cabinet, and it came volubly to the point. His Secretary of Defense, Charles Wilson, the former president of General Motors, wasted no time in unconditionally equating the good of the country with the good of General Motors. His Secretary of the Treasury, George Humphrey, the former president of M. A. Hanna and Co., made it clear at once that the business point of view would inform his Department. His Secretary of Commerce, the industrialist Sinclair Weeks, declared that he had come to Washington to create a "business climate." Secretary of State Dulles, denouncing the policy of containment as cowardice, spoke of liberating peoples in Communist-held countries. He argued for a defense based upon the "massive retaliation" of atomic warfare and a deemphasizing of conventional weapons. He boasted later of having led the nation repeatedly to the brink of war in its diplomatic dealings. And the principles upon which his foreign policy were based, he declared, were those of "openness, simplicity, and righteousness." Like his fellow Presbyterian Woodrow Wilson, he had lost sight of the doctrine of original sin so far as the United States was concerned.

The Eisenhower administration moved at once to effect its counterreforms. A spectacular trip to Korea by the President was followed by—though it probably did little to bring about—the conclusion of hostilities. Price and wage controls, imposed once again during the Korean conflict, were lifted. Control over tidelands oil shifted from the federal government to the states. Federal construction projects diminished, and new checks were placed on government hiring. TVA, as the leading example of creeping socialism, was to be curbed. Natural resources were to be developed by private rather than governmental means, and taxes were to be reordered in such a way as to reduce burdens on business. And all was to be accomplished through a cordial cooperation between the executive and the Congress, unmarred by the Rooseveltian and Trumanesque forms of executive dictation.

Eisenhower never altogether departed in his statements from his original views, but in practice he moved afield from them during his eight years in office, and many like-minded men reluctantly but inexorably moved with him. McCarthy presented him with the earliest severe challenge to his principles. For more than a year Eisenhower meticulously refrained from executive coercion of the legislature, while McCarthy, with the acquiescence of Dulles, ordered hirings and firings in the State Department and dictated the censoring of books in the Overseas Information Service. But when McCarthy denounced an army officer for what amounted to routinely following orders with respect to a suspected

Communist under his command, General Eisenhower retreated from his constitutional position. Slowly and cautiously he brought the government in support of the army and against the senator.

In agriculture, price supports were sharply reduced but then were gradually raised again. In the area of public power, TVA appropriations were severely cut, and TVA was bypassed in a contract with a private Dixon-Yates group to build a power plant on the Mississippi. Public reaction to the revelation of the huge private profits involved, however, resulted in cancellation of the contract. Eisenhower's views in the area of public power were more successfully carried out in the allocating of the power project at Hell's Canyon, Idaho, to private interests. On the other hand, it was during the Eisenhower administration that the American government finally acquiesced in the construction of the St. Lawrence Seaway jointly with Canada.

Eisenhower found his administration to be committing the sin of deficit spending in spite of itself. The budget was balanced in only three out of his eight years, and vast new spending programs were inaugurated. Congress launched also a large public housing program as well as a federal program for school construction. Beyond that, it authorized a highway construction program at a cost of about 32.5 billion dollars, more than all the New Deal relief measures combined. As his second term opened in 1957, Eisenhower found himself battling with a Democratic Congress to defend the largest budget in peacetime history. That year the nation slumped into an economic recession, and Eisenhower returned in 1958 to defend an even larger one.

The administration remained simon-pure on federal health insurance and—aided by labor scandals—on increased legal controls over labor unions. Still, as administration officials worked successfully to increase the minimum wage and to bring 10 million additional citizens under social security, they were forced to admit that when you were the party in control of affairs, things looked different. Thus it was the reluctant Republicans' administrating of the New Deal that won the system final national loyalty.

THE ELECTION OF 1956

The nation reacted against the Republican conduct of affairs by increasing the Democratic majorities in both houses of Congress in 1954, 1956, 1958, and 1960, but nothing that his administration did appreciably lessened the popularity of Eisenhower. Prior to the election of 1956 it appeared for a time that he would be tragically disqualified for reelection by a severe heart attack. He recovered remarkably, however, and running this time against a somewhat less vivacious Stevenson, he was a shoo-in. He doubled his previous margin of victory to win by almost 10 million votes.

There were warnings that Eisenhower's second term would be fatally incapacitated by continuing struggles between a Republican administration and a

Democratic Congress, but nothing of the sort occurred. It is true that presidential vetoes were frequent, but it is also true that the Congress, led by Texans—Speaker of the House Sam Rayburn and Senate Majority Leader Lyndon Johnson—worked in general harmony with Eisenhower's "dynamic conservatism." And the nation, despite rising unemployment and recurrent foreign crises, rested content.

EISENHOWER DIPLOMACY

In foreign policy President Eisenhower placed much reliance on his experienced Secretary of State. Dulles, for his part, despite his active participation in and defense of Truman's foreign policy, now denounced the passive strategy of containment as immoral. Although the conflict in Korea was brought to an end through a compromise with the Chinese Communists, the administration continued to threaten the "unleashing" of the Nationalist Chinese forces on Formosa against the mainland. And while nothing was actually undertaken to remove the Russians from central Europe, much was said about freeing the occupied territories. The stated policy of Dulles was one of constant nudging. "The ability to get to the verge without getting into the war is the necessary art," he declared. "If you cannot master it, you inevitably get into war. If you try to run away from it, if you are scared to go to the brink, you are lost."

In 1954, when communism threatened to envelop Vietnam, American influence prevented a nationwide plebiscite that the Communists would surely have won, but Dulles did not find the necessary support among America's allies or within the American Congress or with Eisenhower, for armed intervention on behalf of South Vietnam. Dulles made this crisis the occasion for the creation of the Southeast Asia Treaty Organization, a military alliance to contain communism in Asia, but he failed to persuade important Asian nations, including India and Indonesia, to join. In 1956, when Hungary revolted against the Communists, it was bloodily subdued by the Red Army. The American government had excellent reason to suppose that armed intervention by the United States would result in thermonuclear war, and it did nothing. The liberation policy actually had already been tacitly abandoned and the containment policy returned to, unknown to most Hungarians.

Probably more important to international relations than the change in the American administration was the change in the Russian leadership. Stalin died in 1953, and after a mysterious struggle for power Nikita Khrushchev emerged as the ruler of Russia. There followed signs of a softening of cold war strategy. The good offices of Russia were used to end the Korean conflict. Russia recognized West Germany and joined the Western Allies not only in signing a peace treaty with Japan, which it was in no position to oppose, but also in signing one with Austria, which it could have wrecked. Both the United States and the Soviet Union had perfected hydrogen bombs and were working on intercontinental ballistic missiles. Under these circumstances Eisenhower, declaring he would "wage a war for peace," agreed to a conference in Geneva with Khrushchev. Nothing resulted but a momentarily friendly "Geneva spirit" that was quickly dissipated by events in the Middle East.

The United States was weakened diplomatically in the Middle East by the support it had given to the new nation of Israel. It nevertheless won most Middle Eastern nations to a Western defense system, but it failed with Gamal Abdel Nasser of Egypt. When Nasser turned to Russia for aid, Dulles withdrew American aid. Nasser responded by seizing the Western-owned Suez Canal, and Britain, France, and Israel thereupon attacked Egypt. Russia threatened to send "volunteers," and the United States denounced the action of its allies, who then gave up the attempt. The result was general bad feeling among the Western Allies and a power vacuum in the Middle East which the American administration tried to fill through what came to be known as the Eisenhower Doctrine. The United States would lend economic and military aid to Middle Eastern nations threatened by communism.

The United States faced the even more threatening rise of Communist influence in the Western Hemisphere as well. Throughout Latin America Communist parties were active and increasing. When a pro-Communist regime came to power in Guatemala, the United States forcibly overthrew it, amid bitter Latin American criticism. Latin America remained impoverished and unstable, and hostile to the United States. Americans suddenly came to realize this hostility existed in 1958, when Vice President Nixon, on a goodwill tour, was mobbed in several Latin American countries.

Then in 1959 Fidel Castro overthrew a pro-American reactionary government in Cuba. Viewed at first as a democratic, patriotic hero, Castro soon revealed himself to be pro-Communist. The Eisenhower administration was still in a condition of indecisive agitation over the Latin American perplexities when it went out of office. The central difficulty, as it had been before, was that as Latin American nations became more democratic, they tended to become more anti-Yankee. Also, as Latin American conditions were improved, with the aid of American money, the populations increased correspondingly, nullifying any possible benefits to the people.

Negotiations with Russia to eliminate atomic weapons continued to founder on the Russian refusal to accept inspection, and they became the more futile as Russia, launching the first intercontinental ballistic missile and the first satellite, grew more confident of its ability to beat the United States in the atomic and stratospheric arms race. Russia had demonstrated its superiority in the development of power for rocketry. Otherwise, the evidence indicated, the United States was militarily superior on the basis of its science, technology, and, above all, ability to produce.

The "Geneva spirit" of Russo-American amity after the summit meeting of 1955 had from the first been an evanescent and wishful thing, and in November

1958 Khrushchev abruptly concluded the cold war truce with the renewed demand for Western evacuation of Berlin. After considerable agitation of the issue the Russian government dropped the subject, and in 1959 Khrushchev paid a goodwill visit to the United States. His reception was generally friendly, and he himself proved a jovial guest, except for his disapproval on moral grounds of the movie *Can-Can,* his annoyance at receiving insults from the mayor of Los Angeles, and his fretfulness at not being permitted to see Disneyland.

Everything was in readiness for a second summit conference in Paris in the springtime of 1960 when an American U-2 aircraft was shot down while flying over Russia. A remarkable example of Yankee ingenuity, the U-2 was a motor-equipped glider which for some time had been flip-flopping back and forth across Russia, too high for Russian antiaircraft and too slow to be maneuvered against by the swift Russian jets, snapping pictures of everything in sight just like any typical American tourist. Khrushchev made this U-2 incident the angry occasion for breaking up the conference, although he had been aware of these activities long before one of the U-2s was successfully brought down. The Eisenhower administration made matters worse by reacting with a series of mutually conflicting untruths that made the administration, with its principle of righteousness in foreign affairs, the butt of international ridicule for the time being.

President Eisenhower had come to office with malice toward none, determined to bind up the nation's wounds and achieve a just and lasting peace. By the time he went out of office his own spirit of goodwill had penetrated the nation to a remarkable extent. That was his greatest achievement. He brought the same spirit, strengthened by a firm sense of what was right, to foreign affairs, with less success. The course that the United States was pursuing in international relations was a good deal less clear in January 1961 than it had been in January 1953. On the other hand, the American people as a whole were now committed to supporting their government in its new world role.

CIVIL RIGHTS
IN THE COLD WAR

The cold war militarized America to an extent which would have been inconceivable at any time in the nation's previous peacetime history. In the name of security, systems of police control and censorship that had been generally alien to American peacetime practice were introduced. At the same time the cold war placed American democracy critically before the bar of world opinion for the first time. From the beginning of its history the United States had self-consciously stood forth before the world as a good example, but the response of the world had never before been of material importance to it. Now, for the first time in its history, the United States was forced to defend its system before the world, against the Communist system.

In this effort it labored under serious disadvantages. To begin with, the United States enjoyed the highest standard of living of any nation in the world, which inevitably made it a stench in the nostrils of the impoverished masses to which it appealed. Equally disadvantageous was the fact that the American people had always been race-conscious, treating as racial inferiors the peoples to whom they were now appealing. The cold war forced Americans to examine their system in the light of world opinion, and in this new light many of them saw grievous faults of which they had formerly been almost unaware. The great sin of American democracy, to which the world situation awakened them, was the old one of its treatment of the black American.

During the New Deal era a reexamination of American racial practices was increasingly suggested to American liberals by the contemporary development of German racist atrocities such as Americans had hardly conceived to be possible. Then, once the nation was at war with Germany, racism was transformed into the ideology of the enemy. In 1941 F. D. R. issued an executive order that "there shall be no discrimination in the employment of workers in defense industries or Government because of race, creed, color, or national origin," and he appointed a Fair Employment Practices Committee to investigate violations of the order.

The war, its scale being so much larger than that of World War I, brought comparably larger numbers of Negroes into the armed forces and into the Northern cities. Between 1940 and 1960 the number of Negroes in the North increased from less than 3 million to more than 7 million. In the South the black population remained almost unchanged, but there was a general exodus to cities such as Atlanta and Birmingham, leaving the countryside dotted with deserted farm shanties. Improved job opportunities presented themselves to Negroes in the Southern as well as Northern cities, and a degree of political participation resulted in addition, but it was the black Northerner who suddenly became a significant political force in the nation. By 1960 there were more blacks in New York than in any other state in the Union, and blacks were concentrated heavily in all Northern cities as major voting blocs.

Under the pressures of the cold war President Truman appointed a Committee on Civil Rights, which reported to him the truth that was becoming obvious to many: "The United States is not so strong, the final triumph of the democratic ideal is not so inevitable that we can ignore what the world thinks of us or our record." Following the recommendations of the committee, Truman pressed Congress for a permanent Fair Employment Practices Commission, the protection of black voting rights, prohibition of segregation in transportation facilities, and a federal antilynching law.

When Southern filibusterers defeated all efforts at civil rights reform, Truman defied the Southern wing of the Democratic party to make civil rights for Negroes a major national issue. Shortly before the election of 1948 he issued an executive order creating a committee which brought about the integration of the armed forces. The pressure of circumstances in Korea brought this into effect there with remarkable results. The black soldiers turned into notably better fighters than they had been while in segregated units, and Southern whites accepted integration as a part of army life and just one more thing to complain about. The surprising success of integration in Korea was followed by a general military integration that constituted a systematic training in racial equality for both black and white draftees under favorable conditions.

As early as 1915 the Supreme Court had commenced to stir itself to uphold the political rights of Negroes. In that year the Court declared unconstitutional the "grandfather" clauses whereby Southern voters were excused from literacy tests if their forebears had been eligible to vote in 1867. The decision was of little consequence, however, since in the one-party South the primary election was all-important and the decision did not apply to primaries because they were not provided for in the Constitution. It was not until 1944 that the Court declared the white primary invalid.

In 1938 the Supreme Court began to reexamine the question of segregation in the schools in the case of *Missouri v. Canada.* In the absence of a state law school for Negroes, it declared that an otherwise qualified black applicant must be admitted to the white law school. In 1950 the Court went beyond this ruling to prohibit the exclusion of Negroes from the University of Texas Law School, on the grounds that the state law school for Negroes was not equal in quality to the white one. Then in 1954 the Supreme Court under Chief Justice Earl Warren issued a unanimous decision in *Brown v. Board of Education of Topeka* declaring all racial segregation in the schools to be unconstitutional.

"Segregation of white and colored children in public schools," the Court declared, "has a detrimental effect upon the colored children. . . . Separate educational facilities are inherently unequal" and therefore deprived Negroes of the equal protection of the laws guaranteed by the Fourteenth Amendment. Accordingly, in a subsequent decision, the Court ordered the Southern states to desegregate their schools "with all deliberate speed."

Throughout the Deep South, the Court's decisions were met with fierce resistance. White Citizens' Councils organized to mobilize private opposition, and state governments passed almost innumerable laws to block any moves toward integration. While the Deep South held firm, there were significant moves toward integration in the upper South. Then in 1957 Gov. Orval Faubus of Arkansas called out the state National Guard to prevent integration in Little Rock. President Eisenhower countered with federal troops, and after a delay of more than two years integration was enforced. Virginia retreated from its program of "massive resistance" and permitted token integration in a few schools chiefly in the northern part of the state, where the population was made up heavily of federal government workers from Northern states.

More than a half dozen years after the original Supreme Court order no integrated school existed in South Carolina, Georgia, Alabama, or Mississippi. Throughout the South, except for completely integrated Washington, D.C., hardly more than 100,000 out of 3 million Negroes attended biracial schools. At the

University of Mississippi in 1962 it required thousands of federal troops to enforce the admission of a single black student, James Meredith, who remained guarded night and day by federal officers as he pursued his studies. Meanwhile, integration proceeded peacefully in most Southern colleges.

White liberals were accustomed to viewing the civil rights question from a paternalistic point of view. They saw it as white America's duty to black America to accomplish civil rights through the established political system of the predominantly white nation and under the direction of biracial organizations, particularly the National Association for the Advancement of Colored People. The landmark Supreme Court decision of 1954 had no sooner been handed down, however, than black Americans began to assume leadership of their own cause.

In 1955 Rosa Parks refused to move to the back of the segregated bus in Montgomery, Alabama. When police were summoned to uphold Jim Crow, the black community of Montgomery responded with the bus boycott from which Martin Luther King emerged as an eloquent spokesman for the cause of black civil rights in the South. The Montgomery bus strike continued to a successful conclusion. Then, in February 1960, four students from the black Agricultural and Technical College in North Carolina sat down at a white lunch counter and ordered coffee, signaling the beginning of the black revolt. During the election campaign of 1960 Kennedy was better informed about what black America was thinking than Nixon was, but events up to that time were not calculated to indicate to either of them the character of the black revolt as it would develop in the sixties.

THE ELECTION OF 1960

The political calm of Eisenhower's final year in office was rippled by a presidential campaign that was devoid of clear-cut political issues but involved a heavy undercurrent of controversy over whether a Catholic should be President. The contest was between two young men, each of whom had risen rapidly to prominence in his party: Vice President Richard M. Nixon of California and Sen. John F. Kennedy of Massachusetts. Nixon was the settled choice of the regulars in his party, but Kennedy had grasped the Democratic nomination in the course of a brilliant presidential primary campaign against Hubert H. Humphrey of Minnesota, a campaign highlighted by Kennedy's primary victory in overwhelmingly Protestant West Virginia.

The religious issue of Kennedy's Catholicism being disavowed by both candidates, the chief subjects for discussion were the economic recession at home and the Castro take-over in Cuba. A political innovation in the 1960 campaign was the series of televised debates between the candidates. No significant differences of opinion emerged from the debates, but Kennedy's performances were generally accounted more attractive than Nixon's, and it was probably this exposure with the better-known Nixon that gave Kennedy the margin of victory.

It appeared from analyses of the election that Kennedy's hairline majority had actually been the result of a large majority of white Protestant votes for Nixon against an even larger majority of the votes of blacks and non-Protestant whites for Kennedy. Having thus narrowly refuted the political axiom that a Catholic could never be President, Kennedy was at pains throughout his Presidency to insist upon the strict observance of the doctrine of separation of church and state, notably in the area of federal aid to parochial schools. Fortunately for Kennedy, he took office during the time of Pope John XXII, whose ecumenical reign brought a mood of harmony to the Christian world unprecedented in modern times. One outstanding accomplishment of Kennedy's administration was his success in winning the evident confidence of millions of Americans who had opposed the idea of a Catholic in the White House.

AMERICAN RELIGION

The election of 1960 occurred at the height of an era of religious resurgence in the United States that had emerged out of World War II. The religious impact of the war itself was partially explained by the saying that "there are no atheists in fox holes," but previous major wars in American history had been destructive influences where religion was concerned. Conditions favorable to religion were evidently present in this postwar period that were absent in previous ones.

One difference was the changed relationship of science and religion. Throughout America's history science had proved itself the enemy of the dominant religious beliefs and practices of the day. Although Puritan ministers had eagerly accepted Newtonian science as providing further revelation of God's works, the main direction of this new science had been away from the original Puritan orthodoxy. In the nineteenth century Darwinian science, with its explicit denial of the Book of Genesis, had been seen at once as the enemy, and those who came to terms with it necessarily compromised their original beliefs in order to do so.

The scientific findings of the twentieth century tended to work in the other direction. The theory of relativity was incomprehensible to all but the specialists, as the theories of gravity and evolution had not been. Under the scrutiny of scientific investigation the universe became more mysterious rather than less so. But more than that, the possibility of an atomic Day of Doom inspired disturbing second thoughts among many who had looked on science and technology as the obedient servants of man and the means to the coming man-made millennium of peace and material well-being for all.

The cold war was waged as a contest against "Godless Communism," and in that context religion became equated with patriotism to a degree that had never previously been true. Eisenhower and other public figures advised all Americans to go to "the church of your choice" as a matter of good citizenship, and reference to God was added to the national Pledge of Allegiance. At the same time America had converted from a Protestant national ideology, spiritually represented in World War I by the Young Men's Christian Association, to a "three-faith" approach to a nation of Protestants, Catholics, and Jews; this three-faith nature of American religion was much stressed in the American armed forces in World War II. The Protestant crusade was over in America, and Catholicism flourished in the suburbs as never before.

Church membership in America rose from about 45 percent in the mid-twenties to about 60 percent in the mid-fifties. Among the nonevangelical Protestant sects, the neo-orthodoxy of Reinhold Niebuhr became increasingly influential, with its return to the doctrine of original sin and of the individual's helplessness to save himself or his society by the force of his own will. But it was the evangelical old orthodoxy preached by Billy Graham and represented by the notably flourishing Baptist churches that made the greatest gains in membership.

The age saw also the rise of new fundamentalist sects, such as the Church of the Nazarene, the Pentecostal Assemblies, and the Jehovah's Witnesses. Many scoffers questioned the spiritual quality of much of this religious manifestation, which was provided with a continual jukebox accompaniment ranging from the wartime musical instruction to "praise the Lord and pass the ammunition" to the peacetime musical injunction to talk to "the Man Upstairs." Without attempting to assay the spiritual value of the religious resurgence, the observation may be made that it was very much in harmony with a patriotic, moderately conservative, and notably consensus-minded era in modern American history.

CONSERVATIVE TENDENCIES

The consensus-mindedness of the era was reflected in main tendencies in American scholarship, including the emergence of what came to be called "consensus history." In 1948, in his *American Political Tradition,* Richard Hofstadter argued "the need for a reinterpretation of our political traditions which emphasizes the common climate of American opinion" and noted that "the existence of such a climate of opinion has been much obscured by the tendency to place political conflict in the foreground of history." Consensus history dominated American historical thought in the fifties and into the sixties. It was isolationist history in that it emphasized the uniqueness as well as the coherence of the American experience, but at the same time it was the product of the new American internationalism; American historians were more immediately aware of the world outside than their predecessors had been, and for this reason they were more conscious of the contrast between American society and other societies of the world.

Another aspect of this consensus-mindedness that sociologists were beginning to discuss in the mid-fifties was what they spoke of as "the end of ideology." The ideologies that had divided opinion, left and right, in America and throughout the world down to World War II seemed to be losing relevance in the fifties. In America the liberal-conservative conflicts of the New Deal era did not clearly fit the circumstances of the affluent, swiftly evolving technological society. The business-minded conservatives of the Eisenhower administration had gone to Washington to put conservative programs into effect. Their objectives had been turned around by the circumstances they found themselves in, and what they accomplished as a result could not be sharply criticized by the liberal opposition on ideological grounds.

There was much discussion in the late fifties about "the new conservatism" that was being advanced by a variety of writers, such as the political scientist Clinton Rossiter, the poet Peter Viereck, and the political columnist Walter Lippmann. Against the contention of Hofstadter and other consensus historians that America had only one political tradition, which was the liberal tradition, the new conservatives traced a conservative tradition back to Edmund Burke and John Adams. By the end of the sixties, the new conservatism was coming to appear so indistinguishable from the liberal tradition of the consensus historians that it was ceasing to provide grounds for fruitful argument.

In the fifties many liberals wistfully recalled the stormy times of the New Deal when they were young, and they would have welcomed a reemergence of radicalism with the oncoming younger generation. Instead they were confronted by what was invidiously referred to as "the silent generation." The generation that grew up during and after the war evidenced a lack of interest in ideological matters. They grew up in the most affluent society the nation had known and also in the most militarized society the nation had known in any peacetime era. Furthermore, this was an era, beginning with the GI Bill of Rights, that extended educational opportunities to a much wider segment of the population than ever before. The silent generation appeared to be satisfied to achieve the material success and security that had evaded the Depression generation of their parents.

Assuming office in January 1961, Kennedy declared in his televised inaugural that "the torch has been passed to a new generation of Americans—born in this century . . . and unwilling to witness or permit the slow undoing of those human rights to which this Nation has always been committed." The nation waited, complacently on the whole, to see how the new generation would handle the nation's affairs.

BIBLIOGRAPHY FOR
CHAPTER 25

E. J. Hughes, The Ordeal of Power (1963)—the Eisenhower administration

R. H. Rovere, Affairs of State (1956)—the Eisenhower administration

Richard Goold-Adams, The Time of Power (1962)—the Eisenhower
administration

H. P. Miller, Rich Man Poor Man (1964)—the economy in the 1950s

J. K. Galbraith, The Affluent Society (1958)—the economy in the 1950s

Samuel Lubell, The Revolt of the Moderates (1965)—politics in the 1950s

Michael Harrington, The Other America (1962)—poverty in America

W. H. Whyte, Jr., The Organization Man (1956)

David Riesman et al., The Lonely Crowd (1950)—the changing American
character

F. L. Allen, The Big Change (1952)—twentieth-century social history

C. W. Mills, The Power Elite (1956)

Will Herberg, Protestant, Catholic, Jew (1955)

Daniel Bell, The End of Ideology (1959)

CHAPTER 26

THE SHATTERED SIXTIES

THE NEW FRONTIER

President Kennedy's "New Frontier" program and President Johnson's "Great Society" program constituted the completion of a "third New Deal" program of reforms that New Deal liberals had unsuccessfully initiated a generation earlier in the years immediately preceding World War II. Only in their emphasis on black civil rights did the New Frontier and the Great Society advance in a fundamental way beyond the aborted aims of the late 1930s. Even there, the Kennedy-Johnson civil rights program had been foreshadowed by the efforts of some New Dealers in the 1930s and by those of President Truman in the late 1940s.

Although Lyndon B. Johnson was nine years older than John F. Kennedy, he too had been born in the twentieth century, and although the political styles of the two men contrasted sharply, both were ideological products of the era of Franklin D. Roosevelt in matters relating to domestic and foreign affairs. This was also true, perhaps even more evidently, of their successor as President, Richard M. Nixon, who had been born in this century and brought up in the political party that learned from Wendell Willkie how to live with the New Deal and then learned from Arthur Vandenberg to abandon isolation in foreign policy for internationalism to the end of containing Russia.

With increasing intensity throughout the 1960s and into the 1970s America underwent a major social conflict in which the opposing sides were drawn substantially along generational lines, with Kennedy as well as Johnson and Nixon turning out to represent the older generation. The silent generation of the fifties was superseded by the rebellious generation of the sixties. The sixties generation was born in the affluent postwar society and tempered in a cold war atmosphere that placed great stress on the democratic virtues of freedom and equality while also stressing the conflicting need to maintain ever-increasing military strength against the potential enemy.

This unprecedentedly affluent generation that grew up in the era of space flight, nuclear armament, computer controls, and television tended to differ in its general outlook from the parental generation that had experienced Wall Street in '29, Munich in '38, and Pearl Harbor in '41. The main storms and stresses of the sixties were related to conflicting generational attitudes toward race and civil rights, material security and progress, moral and religious beliefs, America's world responsibilities, and the nature of true patriotism. Inchoately but pervasively, these storms and stresses were exacerbated by generational contrasts in what came to be referred to in the sixties as "life styles."

The youthful Kennedy administration could hardly have been expected to realize that a generation younger than its own would be violently attacking the assumptions and policies of the New Frontier before the decade was out. The youngest man ever elected to the Presidency, Kennedy gathered around him a group of young, conspicuously Harvard-oriented intellectuals, chief among them his younger brother Robert Kennedy, whom he appointed Attorney General. Highly conscious of themselves as the younger generation in the political world, they were confident that they could open up the New Frontier of mid-twentieth-century opportunities to the American people. But they faced a Congress which was dominated by the same coalition of conservative Republicans and conservative Democrats that had successfully contained the third New Deal in the late thirties and had throttled Truman's Fair Deal in the late forties, and the New Frontier made no more headway in Congress than the Fair Deal had a decade earlier.

Kennedy failed to pass his "Medicare" program, and the fight for federal aid to education became involved in the parochial school question and foundered. Kennedy was more successful in his smaller-scale programs of aid to depressed areas and job rehabilitation for men thrown out of work by automation. In 1962 he won a dramatic victory against the steel industry when he successfully mobilized the government against a scheduled price increase. The industry managed to increase prices later, however, piecemeal and comparatively on the quiet.

Economic conditions improved steadily, if slowly, during Kennedy's Presidency, but the ideal of full employment was far from being reached, and the nonwhite communities of the nation particularly suffered economic hardship. With increasing urgency Negro groups voiced their demands for equality of job opportunities and, even more, for equality in civil rights. Accordingly, the administration fought in 1963 for a tax reduction to stimulate the economy and a civil rights measure to improve the position of the Negro in American society. Both bills remained deadlocked in Congress at year's end.

FOREIGN AFFAIRS
UNDER KENNEDY

As had been the case with Truman, Kennedy won a much greater measure of congressional support in foreign than in domestic affairs. Indeed, his one major victory in domestic affairs, the massive space program, was overwhelmingly endorsed by Congress largely in the context of foreign affairs, to enhance American world power and prestige by beating Russia to the moon. It would be far from true to say that foreign policy had been elevated above party politics; nevertheless, except for a growing congressional disposition to whittle away at foreign-aid measures, whenever Kennedy called for congressional support in the cold war, he got it.

The first major diplomatic development under Kennedy was the disastrous United States–sponsored Bay of Pigs fiasco. Cuban refugees, trained under the direction of the Central Intelligence Agency, were overwhelmingly defeated in their efforts to invade Cuba at the Bay of Pigs and overturn the pro-Communist Castro regime. To some extent this catastrophe was removed from party controversy by the fact that plans for the invasion had initially been made during the Eisenhower administration. The invasion itself, however, had been a Kennedy administration undertaking, and leading Republicans argued that failure to provide the invaders with air support had brought about the defeat. This was to remain a source of political dispute.

The problem of Cuba was later brought home to the American people, as no other problem had been since the Korean conflict, when President Kennedy went before a national television audience to tell it that Russian missile-launching bases were under construction on Cuban soil and that stockpiles of Russian missiles capable of carrying nuclear warheads to American cities were already stored there. Kennedy announced that he had placed the United States armed forces on the alert throughout the world and that he had blockaded Cuba. All Russian vessels sailing to Cuba would be halted and inspected, and those carrying equipment for nuclear warfare would be turned back. The blockade, furthermore, would continue until the Russian missiles and missile sites in Cuba were removed. As a tense world waited for possible nuclear war, Russian ships bound for Cuba turned from their course, and Premier Khrushchev announced that the President's demands would be met.

A lessening of cold war tension followed the Cuba "confrontation," and this relaxation was expressed in 1963 by the signing of an agreement between the United States and Russia, as well as other nations, to ban nuclear-bomb testing except in underground areas. France and Red China, both developing nuclear capabilities of their own, were the notable abstainers from this agreement. A further result of the second Cuban crisis that was favorable to the United States was a reaction against Castro by many Latin Americans who had formerly looked upon him as a nationalistic reformer and who were now more inclined to look upon him as a puppet of the Soviet government. Kennedy's "Alliance for Progress," meanwhile, proceeded at a disappointingly slow pace in its programs for raising Latin American standards of living and encouraging greater cooperation among the several Latin American states, and this situation did not improve in the course of the decade.

In East Asia, despite continuing anti-American demonstrations by Japanese students, no major crisis erupted to unsettle American policy. Economically both Formosa and South Korea made striking advances during the decade, and Japan moved ahead of West Germany to become the third most productive industrial power in the world after the United States and the U.S.S.R. In Japan the pro-American party secured a larger majority in the national Diet than before, while the anti-American Socialist party was sharply reduced in strength at the end of the sixties, thanks in part to the timely return of Okinawa to Japan by the American government prior to the general elections. The renewal of the Japanese-American Mutual Security Treaty was arranged in 1970 with some modifications but without the major disruptions that had been threatened ever since the signing of the treaty ten years earlier.

With the East Asian situation relatively stabilized, the Kennedy administration turned its attention increasingly to Southeast Asia and particularly Vietnam, where conditions had remained highly unstable since the French had been forced out in 1954. Initially intending, apparently, to extend cautiously limited technical and military aid to nations of Southeast Asia, the United States became increasingly involved in the political and military affairs of South Vietnam as the grueling Vietnamese civil war continued indecisively.

The Eisenhower government had extended military aid and had sent military advisers to help the government of Ngo Dinh Diem, but Eisenhower had refused to commit troops to the struggle. By the time Kennedy became President the situation had changed, however, with the formation in 1960 of the National Liberation Front (Viet Cong) in the south, which was openly supported by the North Vietnamese government. In the face of this development the Kennedy administration began to commit troops. Seventeen thousand Americans were stationed in South Vietnam at the time of Kennedy's assassination. Meanwhile, the United States, perhaps unwittingly, encouraged a coup that resulted in the assassination of Diem, and a series of governments had been organized, none of which could attract broad support among the people. How Kennedy would have responded to the worsening situation, had he lived, is a question that has since been firmly answered in almost diametrically contradictory ways by various of Kennedy's close political associates.

During the Kennedy administration and throughout the decade America's never very serious diplomatic difficulties in Europe chiefly concerned America's relations with President Charles de Gaulle of France. De Gaulle made it clear that, for him, the prime purpose of the Common Market was to create a third power in the world to rival the United States and the Soviet Union. He forced the exclusion of Great Britain from the Common Market, and France became the third nation in the world to manufacture the atomic bomb. De Gaulle remained hostile to NATO and to America's leading role in the defense system of Western Europe. He withdrew from politics at the close of the decade, however, after having brilliantly overcome a national uprising led by French students against him and his government, and a relaxation of Franco-American relations followed.

JOHNSON'S DOMESTIC PROGRAM

Midday on November 22, 1963, in the course of a motorcade through Dallas, President Kennedy was assassinated. He was 47. He was the fourth American President to be assassinated, and within the twentieth century alone he was the fourth President upon whose life an attempt had been made.

In selecting Lyndon Johnson as his running mate, Kennedy had chosen a man who had not been and was not intended to become his close political associate. In contrast to the urbane New Englander, Johnson hailed from rural Texas, which had been a most strategic region from the point of view of balancing the ticket, representing as it did the South and the Southwest and to some extent the West and rural America as a whole, in addition, of course, to American Protestantism as a whole. Whether this was Kennedy's main idea in choosing Johnson remains in dispute, but Johnson's regional strength, especially in Texas, did prove essential to the success of the ticket.

Whereas Kennedy's political strength resided chiefly in his charisma—a much-used word in the politics of the sixties—Johnson was strongest in the area of political negotiation. Kennedy and Johnson had served in the United States Senate together, but Kennedy had remained an outsider, while Johnson was early admitted to the inner circle of "the Club." After four years in the Senate Johnson had been elected majority leader by his Democratic colleagues, the youngest man, at 44, ever to hold that position. He brought to his task as President an enormous personal influence in Congress together with the advantage of a tremendous wave of public sentiment favoring the passage of the martyred President Kennedy's legislative program.

From this position of strength, Johnson skillfully directed passage of the Kennedy program. The outstanding achievement was the Civil Rights Act of 1964 prohibiting racial discrimination in public accommodations, including hotels, restaurants, theaters, and housing projects. Congress further implemented Kennedy's "war on poverty" with the Economic Opportunity Act, providing for a number of programs including Volunteers in Service to America (VISTA). In foreign policy, Johnson largely followed the advice of members of the Kennedy administration who chose to continue in his administration, notably Secretary of Defense Robert McNamara and Secretary of State Dean Rusk.

Johnson's administrative feats during his first ten months in office cost him some of his Southern strength; however, the Republicans greatly simplified his political problems by nominating for President Sen. Barry Goldwater of Arizona, an ideological conservative the like of whom had never before received a major-party nomination in all of American history. Campaigning on the slogan "A Choice Not an Echo," Goldwater called for total victory in the cold war and use of a small atomic bomb in Vietnam, and he indicated a quite comprehensive opposition to federal programs as infringements on states rights and individual liberty. Johnson campaigned for peace and prosperity and won by a record landslide.

The next year Congress dwarfed the achievements of the New Frontier of 1963 with Johnson's Great Society program, including the Appalachia poverty program, the School Aid Bill (which ignored the parochial school issue), Medicare, which provided free hospitalization and other medical assistance for elderly people, a major housing program including rent subsidies for low-income groups, and, finally, the Voting Rights Act to outlaw various political means, such as literacy tests and poll taxes, by which blacks had been denied the vote in the South. The 1966 session created a Department of Transportation and added the "model cities" program and a major antipollution program to the Great Society.

After these labors, Congress to some extent rested, waiting to see how all these programs would work out and also waiting to see where all the money to finance them was going to come from. With the costs of the Vietnam War skyrocketing, Congress adopted the policy of passing military appropriations almost without question and then paring appropriations for the domestic programs. The Great Society provided tangible benefits for millions of aged and impoverished people in the nation, and it improved the economic and political condition of much of black America. At the same time, it manufactured added grievances, as programs that were moving forward promisingly were obliged to reduce their operations or discontinue altogether for want of funds. And the expansive rhetoric of President Johnson and Vice President Hubert Humphrey created greater expectations than could be immediately fulfilled.

This "crisis of rising expectations" was intensified by the great affluence of most of American society during a decade when the stock market kept rising along with the gross national product and the federal revenues. Everybody said the nation was rich enough to rid itself of poverty, and almost everybody, including those below the poverty level, was able to possess a television set and to watch the programs and advertisements that dramatized the affluence a majority of the nation shared in. The sixties were a decade of dramatic decline in poverty in America and a decade of dramatic promises to eliminate poverty altogether. As the decade wore on, however, the administration was increasingly obliged to defer these promises until victory had been achieved in Vietnam.

ESCALATION OF
THE VIETNAM WAR

For all the Pentagon's computerized analyses, the possibility that American military force could not prevail in Vietnam was one which did not enter the calculations of the military and civilian policy makers at least until after the Viet Cong's devastating Tet offensive in February 1968. And even then, the Tet offensive was publicly pronounced a Pyrrhic victory that would hurry the day of final victory for South Vietnam and its allies. The Kennedy administration assumed that the United States was virtually omnipotent in a war against a nonnuclear power, so much so that it could practically schedule the time of victory and achieve it by calculating the military power necessary and applying this force on schedule.

When Johnson took office, the initial deployment of 17,000 troops was proving inadequate to support the South Vietnamese Army's efforts against the Viet Cong. In February 1964 Johnson replaced Henry Cabot Lodge with Gen. Maxwell Taylor as Ambassador to Saigon. In August an American destroyer was attacked by a North Vietnamese torpedo boat in the Tonkin Gulf, and the administration ordered retaliatory action. At the President's request, Congress, unaware of earlier American raids against North Vietnam, passed the Tonkin Gulf Resolution, authorizing the President to take such military action as might be necessary to defend against attack or to assist Southeast Asian nations that requested protection. Johnson ran as the peace candidate in the election of 1964, but he plainly never had considered a peace in Vietnam that was not negotiated by America from a position of strength. Indeed, according to the Pentagon history of the war, the Johnson administration had privately reached a "general consensus" in favor of launching the air war that soon followed against North Vietnam.

It was the assumption of the Johnson administration when Johnson took office in his own right in January 1965 that the war could be brought to a close within ten weeks if it were brought home to the North Vietnamese government by concentrated bombing of Hanoi. This was ordered in February 1965. When the bombing missions failed to bring North Vietnam to the peace table, General Westmoreland in an unannounced "change of mission" was authorized to direct in ground action the American troops, who by then had been increased to 50,000. During the next three years American personnel in South Vietnam was increased to more than half a million. The intensity of the bombing raids increased also until in 1968 the bombing tonnage exceeded the total tonnage of all American bombs launched in World War II in both the Asian and European theaters of operation. The "body count" of Viet Cong rose to an enormous and admittedly very unreliable figure, while the known figures on American casualties grew to exceed those of the Korean War.

The cost of the war rose to about 30 billion dollars a year, and the total military budget rose from 51.6 billion in 1964 to 82.5 billion in 1969. American ingenuity applied itself to innumerable devices and adaptations to meet the challenge of the Viet Cong, yet confident predictions of success again and again gave way to rationalizations for the resulting failures, and new predictions of success led to new disappointments. And as the unforeseen and still undeclared Vietnam War came to involve greater American commitment and higher casualties, the alleged importance of the war to the security of Vietnam and then to Southeast Asia and then to Asia and then to world peace was in turn proportionately enlarged, or, to use the term that was coined to describe the American action in Vietnam, "escalated."

BLACK MILITANCY

On the home front, the civil rights crusade was arousing serious conflicts within the black community itself as well as between blacks and whites. Once the Supreme Court had invalidated Jim Crow and the federal government had begun to implement this decision, black Americans, especially those who grew up after 1954, were awakened to possibilities that the civil rights movement previously had not entertained. A semblance of unity was maintained within the black civil rights movement down to the impressive March on Washington in August 1963, the anniversary year of the Emancipation Proclamation. From that point on to the end of the decade, however, black America was increasingly embroiled in dispute over basic black objectives in America.

The NAACP, under the leadership of Roy Wilkins, was the oldest and largest civil rights organization and the one that had been responsible for directing the campaign which led to the 1954 Supreme Court decision. However, the NAACP retained the moderately elitist tradition that its early leader, W. E. B. Du Bois, had represented when he emphasized "the talented tenth" of the black community as the class that should be depended on to advance the cause of the race in America. The approach of the NAACP was primarily a legalistic one that won judicial and legislative victory while avoiding emotional appeals to the black race in America, especially appeals to black pride. The Urban League, which like the NAACP had been launched during the Progressive era, was devoted to solving economic problems of the urban Negro in a practical way. The NAACP and the Urban League were both interracial organizations dedicated to the ideal of an equal and integrated society in America, an ideal that was shared by the politically more radical Negro labor leaders, notably A. Philip Randolph of the Pullman porters' union.

Out of the Montgomery, Alabama, bus strike of 1955 Martin Luther King emerged as the dominating figure in the civil rights movement, but while King and his Southern Christian Leadership Conference sometimes worked at cross-purposes with the NAACP, the two organizations were in accord on ultimate objectives, given the fact that the one organization was directed mainly by Northern lawyers and the other mainly by Southern ministers.

A Southern Baptist minister, King founded his movement on the optimistic Christian faith that man was redeemable, that redemption would come through love, and that black America could achieve its rightful place in American society by nonviolent means and thereby redeem American society as a whole. King continued to place great stress on his belief in the necessity of nonviolence and on his faith that the steady nonviolent pursuit of civil rights objectives would prevail. In his famous address to the Washington civil rights march in 1963, King declared, "I have a dream that one day this nation will rise up and live out the true meaning of its creed: 'We hold these truths to be self-evident; that all men are created equal.' I have a dream that one day on the red hills of Georgia the sons of former slaves and the sons of former slave-owners will be able to sit down together at the table of brotherhood."

The March on Washington involved about 200,000 participants, black and white, and was joined by all the civil rights groups, including two increasingly militant organizations, the Student Nonviolent Coordinating Committee and the Congress of Racial Equality. Both of these organizations had initially accepted King's leadership, and both were on the verge of breaking with King in 1963.

One important black organization that disassociated itself from the Washington march was the Nation of Islam, or Black Muslims. The Muslims comprised a religious order led by Elijah Poole, who renamed himself Elijah Muhammad. Condemning Christianity and American democracy as irretrievably racist, the Nation of Islam preached Muhammadanism and lived as a separated black society under a semimilitaristic and thoroughly puritanical regime that emphasized physical fitness, temperance, plain living, and the virtue of hard work. At the start of the 1960s the Muslims became widely influential chiefly through the activities of their brilliant public speaker, Malcolm X.

The Muslims were not wanted at the March on Washington, and Malcolm X reciprocated this sentiment. Of the march he remarked, "Who ever heard of angry revolutionists . . . tripping and swaying along arm-in-arm with the very people they were supposed to be angrily revolting against?" Malcolm X was expelled from the Muslims, ostensibly for his penchant for making contemptuous public utterances such as this, and in 1965 he was assassinated by Muslim rivals. But the Muslims continued to be a black nationalist influence, and Malcolm X increasingly became the martyr to the cause of black nationalism in America.

Many Negroes of the younger generation made a transition from integrationist civil rights ideals to separatist black nationalism in the course of the grueling, bloody, long, and seemingly fruitless civil rights campaigns in the South in the early sixties. The "sit-in" campaign against Jim Crow that students had initiated in 1960 at the Greensboro, North Carolina, lunch counter had immediately been repeated by other black students throughout much of the South. Then in 1961 the Congress of Racial Equality sent "Freedom Riders" south to violate segregation laws on buses and trains and in depots. The resulting violence forced Attorney General Robert Kennedy to send federal officers to protect Freedom Riders in Alabama. Joined by the Southern Christian Leadership Conference and the newly organized Student Nonviolent Coordinating Committee, the sit-in campaign won a sweeping victory when interstate carriers were ordered desegregated together with their terminal stations.

SNCC and CORE, while acknowledging Martin Luther King's leadership at the outset, tended to be more concerned to rescue Negroes from poverty and oppression than to realize King's vision of a redemption of white America. And as these organizations shifted to voter-registration drives in 1962, and as promised federal support failed to materialize during the following years, a radicalization of the movement occurred, marked by an alienation from white liberals and a distaste for the middle-class objectives of civil rights and integration.

For many black militants the break with the liberal integrationist ideals came following the Freedom Summer of 1964 and the even more bitterly discordant Freedom Summer of the following year, when the regular organization workers in SNCC and CORE and other predominantly black civil rights groups working in the South were temporarily joined by white college-student volunteers. The militants were increasingly disposed to reject white assistance and certainly to reject white leadership. For SNCC the issue was decided in 1966, when Stokely Carmichael won the chairmanship and then issued his call for "black power."

The term "black power" gained currency in the context of a series of riots, beginning with the Watts riot in Los Angeles in 1965, that devastated black ghetto sections of dozens of American cities in the summers of 1965, 1966, and 1967. The Watts riot lasted six days, until 34 persons were dead, more than 1,000 injured, and nearly 4,000 arrested. Similar riots followed during those summers in San Francisco, Chicago, New York, Newark, and Detroit, to name the worst of them. All told, seventy-six cities suffered riots in the black ghettoes, and 140 persons were killed in them. Each summer thereafter, rioting was tensely awaited but did not recur on anything like the same scale.

These "hot summers" were spontaneous outbursts of rage, mainly on the part of the younger generation of ghetto blacks. They were not politically motivated, but they exerted a powerful radicalizing influence on the Negro rights movement, and they gave substance to the term "black power." At the same time, not even the most militant blacks could altogether support an expression of black rage that took the form of destroying black neighborhoods. The black power idea led to the formation of the Black Panthers and other militant separatist groups, but its chief expression in the late sixties was cultural rather than military. The black militants' center of activity had shifted from the Deep South to the Northern cities; it then shifted to the college campuses of the nation.

An important phase of the civil rights crusade beginning in the fifties had been the drive to improve education in the inner cities, and accordingly the colleges and universities of the nation, in their turn, developed recruiting programs to increase their enrollments of Negroes. The purpose was to provide white higher education to larger and larger numbers of blacks in order to give them better opportunities to advance in the white world. Black cultural nationalism emerged out of this college situation in the form of demands of black students for separate living areas and for a curriculum that would particularly relate to them as black Americans.

The demand for Black Studies courses and programs caused turmoil on college campuses, and it also caused turmoil in the black civil rights movement. Civil rights leaders like Bayard Rustin, who had been the leading organizer of the 1963 Washington march, charged that black students were demanding separate courses to avoid having to compete with white students. Rustin argued that Negroes would be obliged to go on living in a predominantly white America and that their problems would continue to be largely economic problems, which a college major in Black Studies would not suit them to overcome.

MEXICAN-AMERICAN MILITANCY

This black cultural nationalism influenced other nonwhite Americans in the late sixties, including Puerto Ricans, Indians, Orientals, and Mexican-Americans. In the San Francisco Bay Area many young nonwhites joined together as the "Third World Force" to give effect to militant nonwhite cultural nationalism at the University of California in Berkeley and more violently at San Francisco State College.

The Mexican-Americans have become, next to the Negroes, the largest significantly disadvantaged ethnic group in America, probably numbering about 5 million. Some of them trace their ancestry in the Southwest to before the Treaty of Guadalupe Hildago that ceded the area to the United States in 1848. The provisions of the treaty guaranteed Mexican-Americans full rights as American citizens, but the territorial and state governments of the Southwest failed to secure them in their rights, including, frequently, their property rights. They had been obliged to accommodate themselves to the system of the conquerors, much as the Negroes in the late nineteenth century were obliged to accept the policy of accommodation that Booker T. Washington spoke for.

Long employed as migrant laborers in the West, Mexican-American laborers were deported in large numbers during the Depression, when "Okies" poured into California to accept fruit-picking jobs. Then, beginning with World War II, a shortage of labor created a situation that attracted hundreds of thousands of legal *braceros* and illegal "wetbacks" to work the fields. Many Mexican-Americans served in the armed forces, and a good many of these afterwards entered college under the GI Bill of Rights and trained themselves for positions that introduced them to still further ethnic discrimination at a higher level.

Some successfully entered politics, including United States Sen. Joseph Montoya from New Mexico and Congressman Edward R. Roybal from California, and the Texan Lyndon B. Johnson was notably sensitive to Mexican-American demands as President. On the whole, however, the Mexican-Americans have remained largely unrepresented in political life.

During the 1960s Mexican-Americans found a leader comparable to Martin Luther King in Cesar Chavez, the organizer of the California fruit pickers' union. Since 1945 the National Farm Workers Association has enjoyed success unprecedented in California history as a labor organization committed to the philosophy of nonviolence, and Chavez, like King, has become a leader of international stature. On the other hand, younger Mexican-Americans—who identify themselves as Chicanos rather than as Mexican-Americans—have turned in the direction of a militant cultural nationalism similar to the black power tendencies in black America. The militant blacks and Chicanos have tended to remain in cordial sympathy with each other, and both have been strongly supported by militant white college groups despite the separatism that increasingly has rejected white assistance.

THE RADICAL
YOUTH CULTURE

Within white America, the transition from the silent generation to the rebellious generation was closely associated throughout the sixties with the black civil rights movement, but in the second half of the sixties it increasingly moved toward an attack on American foreign policy in general and the Vietnam War in particular. White activist college students gained their early training for rebellion in the sit-ins of the early sixties and in the Freedom Rides of 1964 and 1965, and then these same tactics were employed against liberal institutions in the North, beginning with the Berkeley free-speech demonstrations in 1965. The Berkeley sit-ins, protesting the University of California's speaker policy, aroused the same violent response from local public opinion and local police that had marked the sit-ins in the South, and sit-ins and "teach-ins" soon raged widely on university campuses throughout the Midwest and the East. Free speech was a major issue in these, and "Free Universities" were established by students and selected faculty members to teach courses on race and sex and drugs and contemporary revolutionary theory, subjects that were thought to be "relevant"— a key word among black and white radicals—and that were not offered for credit in the curriculum.

The Students for a Democratic Society, organized under the leadership of Tom Hayden of the University of Michigan, condemned America as a racist, imperialist, industrial-military state. The SDS called for the overthrow of the American capitalist system and for the support of such leaders of "people's movements" as Ho Chi Minh, Mao Tse-tung, and Fidel Castro. SDS chapters were formed on campuses throughout the nation. They agitated for black power (despite increasing refusal of black organizations to cooperate with them), student control of university organizations, and separation of the universities from military research and various other federally sponsored programs. The SDS achieved its greatest triumph on the campus of Columbia University in the spring of 1968, when it closed the institution down and forced a change in its administration and many of its policies.

Among the developing radical youth movements, the SDS found itself at odds not only with the black militants but also with the white hippies, who were electing to "drop out" of the American political and social system rather than to overthrow it. The hippie culture traced its origin to the San Francisco Bay Area and the activities of the "beatniks." The beat generation, notably spoken for by the poet Allen Ginsberg and the novelist Jack Kerouac, glorified sex and reck- lessness and the aimless activity of enjoying life at the spur of the moment. Increasingly, from the early sixties on, drugs entered the beat culture, conspicu- ously including the easily manufactured LSD.

Just when the beatniks were appearing in the late fifties, Elvis Presley made his national debut; the Beatles followed shortly, and in the field of popular music the sixties became the era of rock 'n' roll and then folk rock and black "soul music." The unkempt hippie generation that emerged was outwardly remarkable for the sexlessness of long-haired boys and long-haired girls in blue jeans and love beads. Hippies preached the power of love—"flower power"— and "turned on" at pot sessions and engaged in "love-ins." More ambitiously, they formed communes in New Mexico and Arizona, Nepal and Istanbul, and elsewhere in America and around the world.

A climax in hippie history came in 1969 with the staging of a musical happen- ing at Woodstock in upstate New York. More than 400,000 young people attended, and they survived several days of bad weather, drugs, and popular music with remarkably few casualties. Similar performances were soon pro- moted elsewhere with, however, generally more violent and destructive results. A classic rendition of hippie culture, the Broadway musical *Hair* became a spectacular national hit, very successfully road-showing the cities where local authorities did not prohibit its appearance.

This youth culture of the sixties received much legal protection from the Supreme Court, which placed unparalleled stress on guaranteeing civil liberties to both white and black Americans. The Court invalidated censorship laws to the point where the only limitation on literature and art and the performing arts was that a work claim some more serious purpose than a purely pornographic one. Under this dispensation, movies such as *Easy Rider* appeared that ap- pealed broadly to the youth cult, along with an "underground press."

THE ELECTION OF 1968

In 1968, under the pressure of further escalation of the Vietnam War that brought mounting weekly American casualty lists and enemy "body counts," the two traditional political parties, the Grand Old Party and the Democratic party, began to organize themselves for the upcoming presidential elections. With demonstrations against Johnson's escalation of the Vietnam War increasing and criticism among Senate liberals rising, Sen. Eugene McCarthy of Minnesota announced in the fall of 1967 that he was planning to run for the 1968 Democratic presidential nomination. For the next few months McCarthy was comparatively lost sight of. Then, with the aid of devoted student volunteers, he won 42 percent of the vote in New Hampshire primary in February against the Johnson slate, for the first time indicating major grass-roots opposition to the war. Several days later Sen. Robert Kennedy of New York entered his name in various primaries, and for the next few months both candidates attracted large enthusiastic crowds, down to the climactic California primary in June, where Kennedy narrowly defeated McCarthy and then was assassinated during his victory celebration.

At the end of March President Johnson had gone on television to announce the end to the bombing of North Vietnam, except for an area immediately north of the fighting zone, and further to announce that he would not run for reelection, as it had been universally assumed he would. While Richard M. Nixon won the Republican primaries unopposed and received the Republican nomination virtually by acclaim, Vice President Hubert H. Humphrey emerged as the President's choice for the Democratic candidate, as well as the choice of the party organization, the South, and most of the labor movement. Humphrey, who continued to support the administration policy in Vietnam, easily won the nomination, amid anti-Johnson-Humphrey demonstrations of radicals in Chicago who were bloodily suppressed by police in full view of the national television audience.

Humphrey and Nixon were joined in the general election by a third-party candidate, Gov. George Wallace of Alabama, campaigning for all-out victory in Vietnam and law and order against students and blacks at home. In a campaign that relied heavily on prerecorded television broadcasts and commercials, Humphrey regained some ground lost to liberals at the convention, but he narrowly lost both the popular plurality and the electoral vote to Nixon.

THE NIXON ADMINISTRATION

Nixon's victory temporarily relaxed tensions, since no new policy would be forthcoming until Johnson had served out his term. Furthermore the most ardent objectors against the war and in behalf of the blacks and the poverty-stricken had political claims on the Democratic party but none on the Republican party. Nixon took office quietly and colorlessly and appointed to his administration men who were generally conceded to be capable but who, as a group, were remarkable for their failure to represent any major ethnic group in the nation except for the dominant Protestant Anglo-Saxon ethnic minority.

Much was said about Nixon's and Attorney General John Mitchell's "Southern strategy" purportedly compromising on Southern desegregation in exchange for Southern support, but desegregation progressed more rapidly in the early years of Nixon's administration than it previously had. Mitchell more evidently departed from the policy of his predecessor, Johnson's libertarian Attorney General Ramsey Clark, in his emphasis upon increasing police powers in the name of law and order and at the expense of latitudinarian guarantees of civil liberties.

Elsewhere in domestic policy, the Department of Labor under George Shultz won a large measure of confidence from organized labor, while many members of organized labor indicated their proadministration stand on Vietnam in the anti-peace demonstrations of the hard hats in New York and other cities. In the area of antipoverty legislation, Nixon cut the ground out from under the liberals with a major scheme, designed by the liberal intellectual Daniel P. Moynihan, to supplant the welfare system with a federally sponsored guaranteed minimum annual family income. Nixon's worst problem domestically proved to be an economic recession that deepened throughout 1969 and into 1970 and that increasingly was blamed, by Wall Street businessmen as well as college radicals, on the tremendous economic burden of the war in Southeast Asia.

After waiting several months to determine what Nixon's policy regarding Vietnam would be, the antiwar groups started to renew their pressure through demonstrations, culminating in a nationwide "Moratorium" in the fall of 1969. The Moratorium was a major success in terms of numbers of people involved and the general orderliness of the demonstrations. Nixon effectively met the situation, however, by ignoring the Moratorium, so far as that was possible, and by pursuing an announced policy of regular troop withdrawals for the purpose of "winding down" the war and particularly relieving American soldiers from combat assignments.

In April 1970 Nixon reversed his policy of de-escalation by authorizing a limited invasion of Cambodia to destroy Viet Cong bases and supply depots near the Vietnamese border. This decision immediately extended the war to Cambodia as a whole, even though American troops were shortly withdrawn, as Nixon, facing a national uproar, had hastened to promise they would be. The Cambodian invasion aroused antiwar sentiment to an unprecedented degree. Then, on May 4, national guardsmen fired on demonstrators at Kent University, killing four students. Colleges and universities shut down in the midst of nationwide demonstrations lasting from a day to a week or two, and some remained closed for the duration of the academic year.

By that time the undeclared war in Vietnam had lasted longer than any in American history, and "hawks" were increasingly joining "doves" to demand an end to American involvement. At home Congress had enacted the full program of New Deal liberals into existence, and if the Nixon administration continued to curtail many aspects of the Great Society, as the Johnson administration itself had done, the Nixon administration was in its turn offering programs of its own, notably in response to the problem of poverty, that were more sweeping than any attempted by Franklin D. Roosevelt's administrations.

CONTINUITY OF THE DECADES

The public media emphatically greeted the beginning of the year 1970 as the end of the sixties and the beginning of the seventies, which it indisputably was. To be out of the sixties evidently inspired a momentary release of exhilaration such as had not been witnessed when the nation emerged from the forties or from the fifties. The sixties became immediately fixed in people's minds as an era that had ended with the end of the decade, much as the 1920s had been generally recognized in 1930 to be a distinct and unrepeatable era. However, the nation carried most of the problems of the sixties with it into the seventies.

Commenting on the election campaign of 1968, Walter Lippmann had observed that "never before or in any place have 200 million people confronted the consequences of the technological revolution with a heterogeneous population no longer bound by ancestral habits and customs. Nothing on this scale or diversity has ever before been attempted. . . ." These conditions posed problems, he went on to point out, that would not be solved in the next four or eight years providing only that the right man were elected President. These are the fundamental conditions that have confronted America at the opening of every decade since the beginning of the century, and they will continue to pose problems after the Vietnam War has passed into history along with the Korean War and World War II.

BIBLIOGRAPHY FOR CHAPTER 26

T. H. White, The Making of the President, 1960 (1961) and The Making of the President, 1964 (1965)

A. M. Schlesinger, Jr., A Thousand Days (1965)—the Kennedy administration

Tom Wicker, JFK and LBJ (1968)

G. M. Kahin and J. W. Lewis, The United States in Vietnam (1967)

John Brooks, The Great Leap: The Past Twenty-five Years in America (1966)

C. E. Silberman, Crisis in Black and White (1964)

Report of the National Advisory Commission on Civil Disorders (1968)

Reed Sarratt, The Ordeal of Desegregation (1966)

Nathan Glazer and D. P. Moynihan, Beyond the Melting Pot: The Negroes, Puerto Ricans, Jews, Italians, and Irish of New York City (1963)

Paul Jacobs and Saul Landau, The New Radicals (1966)

INDEX